What can possibly go wrong

Mick Macfarlane

Copyright © 2019.
Apart from any fair dealing for the purpose of private study, research, criticism or review, as permitted under the Copyright Act, no part may be reproduced by any process without permission from the author. Every effort to comply with copyright requirements has been made by seeking permission and acknowledging owners of source material used in the text.

Disclaimer:
This book is a collection of memories and reports. Information gathered has come from a wide variety of sources; minutes books, newspapers, library archives, academic reports and other digital and online material, and not limited only to the sources acknowledged here. The personal stories and memories by individuals recorded here are their version of events and have been both provided and reproduced in good faith with no disrespect or defamation intended. Every effort has been made to ensure the researched information is correct. No liability for incorrect information or factual errors will be accepted by the author.

A catalogue record for this book is available from the National Library of Australia

ISBN: 978-0-6484317-0-1 (paperback)

Design cover and interior:
Pickawoowoo Publishing Group

Cover Image: Australian Para Jumper circa 1988 exiting a Dornier 228 wearing 82kg of 'water-jump equipment.

Printed & Channel Distribution
Lightning Source | Ingram (USA/UK/EUROPE/AUS)

Contents

	Introduction	ix
Chapter 1	Royal Navy Clearance Diving (Keel Hauling)	1
Chapter 2	Royal Navy Clearance Diving (Mine Hunting)	12
Chapter 3	Royal Navy Clearance Diving (How Not To Become A Civilian)	37
Chapter 4	Northern Divers (Different to the Navy - Mates off to War)	54
Chapter 5	Yellow Beard (Explaining Some of the Previous Chapters)	96
Chapter 6	Port Emergency Service (Bodies, Rabbits and Chemicals)	102
Chapter 7	NSCA Pararescue (Freddo's Vision)	122
Chapter 8	NSCA Pararescue (Have a Good One)	128
Chapter 9	NSCA Pararescue (Water Jumps and Beret)	162
Chapter 10	NSCA Pararescue (Helitac)	185
Chapter 11	NSCA Pararescue (Lake Eppalock)	202
Chapter 12	NSCA Pararescue (Subsea Expansion – Rookie-7 and Commercial Training)	237
Chapter 13	NSCA Pararescue (Sub Rescue)	252
Chapter 14	NSCA Pararescue (Flamingo Bay)	276
Chapter 15	Melbourne Fire Brigade (Unknown Chemicals)	296
Chapter 16	Helicopter Rescue (Double Stretcher)	319

Chapter 17	Helicopter Rescue (Xanana Gusmao's Been Shot) · 346
Chapter 18	Helicopter Rescue (Walpole) · · · · · · · · · · · · · · · · · 374

Epilogue · 427

Post Script - Memories of Pearce & Loose Cannon · 433

RESPECT FEAR

"To have No Fear will ensure a life of excitement and adventure, but to Respect Fear, will ensure that you live to talk about it."

NSCA PJ 1988

For Mandy, your love and friendship through good times and bad are more important to me than anything.

Introduction

HAVING SPENT TWENTY-NINE YEARS IN operational roles ranging from diving (military and commercial) to professional firefighting (urban, maritime and mountain), marine rescue (surface and subsurface), aviation rescue (rotary and fixed wing), plus another thirteen years teaching emergency response and emergency management in a range of disciplines, I have both seen and been directly involved in some monumental stuff ups!

With retirement on the horizon I have looked back at some of the more memorable of these experiences; drawing on reports, logbooks and personal records to put my recollections to paper. The initial intent of this work was to produce a document for my family, but ultimately it has resulted in analysis of some terrifying, and at times hilarious, events from my past for my peers to evaluate. Although not intended as an academic examination, I have utilised skills acquired later in life from a Master of Emergency Management degree to assess my performance and those I worked with. Don't expect graphs, formulas, in-text citations and references, this is a story intended to make you laugh and on occasion perhaps utter the challenge, 'bullshit, that would never happen!' But I assure you it did.

Occasionally, lack of understanding from those reporting the events I describe merely made us look good. Typically though, the types of stuff ups I've documented didn't always make the evening news or were just buried deep inside a newspaper. Either way, the level of error was regularly diluted (or concealed) with PR spin. For example, how often have you heard news stories with this type of language?

"The extreme nature of the task meant that the search had to be suspended until first light…" or "Weather conditions made the job of responders challenging…"

Although impossible situations occasionally confront responders, these are rare. Therefore, regardless of PR spin, one fact of response will always remain true: as long as humans of any age, race, gender or education level are involved, things will and do go wrong, irrespective of how sophisticated or state-of-the-art equipment may be. Simply put, we are the weak link that causes stuff ups.

Real professionals are acutely aware of such human weakness, and because of this, they develop a 'healthy paranoia' that pushes them to train regularly, and realistically, to maintain appropriate preparedness.

Healthy paranoia is a term an old colleague of mine first coined when briefing a Search and Rescue (SAR) task containing significant challenge. I now use it to describe how a good operator's subconscious regularly challenges the norm. For example, regular evaluation of role responsibilities and procedures, robust debriefs, asking hard questions of your team members, or leaders (early), all help to keep a team sharp – and ultimately this will mitigate the amount of PR spin required. Such healthy paranoia often manifests in daily routine as a simple question.

"What can possibly go wrong?"

The answer is always the same.

"Lots!"

Note 1:

Some names, timings, and locations have been changed to protect those still working in the relevant industries, but for those of you involved at the time I'm sure you'll work out the who, what, when and where.

Note 2:

The news headlines contained in this book are transcribed from memory only. To the best of my recollection they are accurate, but even if they are not, why let accuracy get in the way of a good story... I read that somewhere.

CHAPTER 1

Royal Navy Clearance Diving (Keel Hauling)

As a fourteen-year-old in 1974, I went along to my school pool in Hull, East Yorkshire to take lessons in scuba diving. It was great fun, and after a few weeks of using flippers, snorkel and goggles, I was given my first go on a scuba bottle.

Taking that first breath underwater had me hooked. Simply put, it was the joyful realisation that the tank on my back actually worked, because before taking that breath, I just couldn't fathom the science of it. Yet there I was, wide eyed, breathing, *really* breathing from this magical bit of gear. How cool was that. Furthermore, understanding that I could breathe underwater had firmed up a long-held dream of becoming one of Jacques Cousteau's divers aboard his dive ship, the Calypso - this diving fascination stemmed from around six annual beach holidays in Spain where my brothers (Alex and Ian) and I had learnt to snorkel from around the age of seven. The Cousteau dream had developed further while watching the weekly TV show with mum and dad for the previous couple of years. Seeing his divers in the Pacific, his divers in the Caribbean, doing cool stuff in crystal clear, bathtub-warm water all over the world - well, I knew my future lay with Jacques. Unfortunately, though, I had no real idea how I would become one of his team. Probably just give Jacques a call I guessed, who knew? Obviously still a fourteen-year-old and without any firm plan of action, a logical process for my young mind was to complete some introductory BSAC courses to develop my aquatic skills further. Jacques would surely be impressed. How hard could it be? Calypso here I come.

Over the next two years or so I did just this. Finally, after much bubble blowing in the 25m shallow school pool, undertaken at intervals of every other week or longer if I had lots of homework, I was deemed qualified to venture out of the pool and into a water-filled quarry. But this never happened. You see at the age of sixteen, sub aqua master that I was becoming, Jacques Cousteau was put on hold and I joined the Royal Navy.

I arrived at HMS Raleigh on a cold afternoon in late October 1976 and shortly after that was assigned to Anson Division, class 43, in a blur of an induction process that was somewhat of an eye-opener. I mean, who would be washing my clothes? This, alarmingly, is one early concern I'd had that sticks to mind. However, equally clear in my memory is a state of mind change that had occurred just one week later. Now in uniform, and gaining an appreciation of how mum probably got the skid marks out of my jocks; I thought and acted like I was becoming a fully-fledged, hairy chested, super cool, British sailor.

Buoyed by this newfound assurance, perhaps strengthened by my diving history, I confidently told my Anson 43 classmates that, "I was putting in for CD" - Mine Clearance Diver training.

Not long after this proclamation I and two good mates from Anson 43 (Irish and Steve), with a handful of other CD hopefuls, were to receive a brutal introduction to the difference between a BSAC diver and that of a Royal Navy Clearance Diver; where use of language such as bottles, flippers, and goggles were minor variances lying in the vast chasm between the two.

On the morning of our diver aptitude test the freezing, oil-film covered, zero visibility of Plymouth docks saw to my re-education very quickly. Enhancing this smack-in-the-face reality, plus increasing trepidation, was a man who appeared to be in a constant state of rage. This Chief Petty Officer Clearance Diver put the fear of God into the small group of mainly young boys, who were sadly and literally, just fresh out of school. If we had needed further reinforcement of civilian/military differences, the astonishingly heavy equipment we had to somehow carry on our backs helped. However, it was the claustrophobic nature of the neck-entry dry suits that had to be forcibly stretched apart by candidate 'A' to permit candidate 'B' to squeeze into, in what appeared to be some bizarre reverse birthing ceremony, almost sealed the deal. Ultimately though, when a metal clamp was tightened around the neck and a spanner was used to tighten a waist-fitting to prevent flooding, I suspect most recruits had reached a state of anxiety they had never experienced before. Smiling. Caring perhaps? The Chief also assured us that if we completed any of these sequential 'dressing' tasks incorrectly, hypothermia and drowning was a possibility.

Excluding the bombardment of critical advice that I struggled to absorb, the overriding message from the Chief appeared to be the need for us to pick up the pace.

"Hurry up and get in the water you cunts!"

Although Irish, Steve and I passed this initial aptitude test the collective experience for me, including running out of air while wearing cumbersome lead-inner-soled boots and having to be rescued (more on that later), saw me defer my CD ambitions for the less stressful pursuit of sonar operation.

Sonar, or Sound Orientation Navigation And Ranging, was really cool in training. We hunted simulated submarines, launched simulated depth charges and torpedos, and I loved every minute of it, coming second in my class. Once at sea though, serving on the flagship of the First Flotilla, I realised that sitting in a darkened room listening to ocean static through uncomfortable headphones, deep inside the ship, wasn't for me. Less than a year later having realised my error, I applied for and completed a Ships Divers course. Although a mere four weeks of consolidated anguish designed for the 'paddlers' of the fleet, this relatively simple achievement gave me renewed confidence. Undertaking routine maintenance jobs and practice searches as part of on-board duties, I now, quite frankly, enjoyed putting on all the heavy equipment that had once terrified me; and furthermore, hopping into the typically cold and poor visibility environment that was a constant beneath my ship was a challenge I now welcomed. Cousteau's team? Pack of pussies!

Although this self-assurance was genuine, it was also relative. So it was with a degree of bravado, no doubt bolstered by the many 'dips' proudly recorded in my Royal Navy Divers Log Book, plus travel to the Mediterranean, the USA, and all parts UK, that I re-applied for and was accepted to start CD training.

This 'basic' course was meant to be a simple ten weeks of anguish where fundamental skills were taught and assessed to produce a 'baby' CD. Such an individual would be able to dive to fifty-five meters using mixed gas re-breathing equipment, be confident in zero visibility, be able to identify unexploded ordnance, undertake basic salvage, and a range of other skills that amounted to underwater labouring. Essentially, the job of baby CDs was to get their heads wet when required, day or night, regardless of the sea conditions. Such an individual would not truly be recognised as a CD until a further year of operations had been completed aboard a Ton-Class Mine Hunter. This craft was a notorious pig of a 'boat' that rolled on a millpond, yet it was the necessary evil to progress to a 'Team', but that's another story.

An equally important, yet unofficial component to the baby CD training course involved drinking large quantities of beer after daily instruction was completed. This extracurricular activity was to prove to your Chief that you were suitable material to join the CD branch - I kid you not! An individual was assessed on this capability just as much as his ability to tell the difference between a contact-mine and an acoustic-mine in zero visibility. Indeed, capable divers were removed from training because they wouldn't or couldn't 'cut it on the piss.'

Warning: health and safety Nazi's who insist on filling out a form to tie shoelaces, you have read too much. Close the book now, or you'll have a conniption.

With all that in mind then, visualise the west coast of Scotland in the winter of 1979. Snow on the hills, days of driving rain and piercing wind, icy freezing waters a constant; you know, shitty bloody conditions that only weirdos take pleasure in. Welcome to Oban and deep diving, the last phase of CD training.

On Fridays, while away from Portsmouth and the Royal Navy dive school at Horsea Island, we held pseudo court martials, and after the last dive for the week had been completed 'Psycho' called things to order. As grumpy, uncaring, sadistic bastards go, Chief Petty Officer 'Psycho' Williams was right up there with the best of them. As part of the court martial proceedings, he read out the charges, and I heard my name.

"'Mac said he was 'well,' but apparently… he wasn't." The rest of the boys chuckled at Psycho's remark, "and 'H' didn't call the second connection on the umbilical 'well' for leaks." More chuckles, relief mainly, as Psycho completed 'the list' containing just two names.

We had been using SDDE (Surface Demand Diving Equipment) to 55m. The airline supplying us air, the umbilical, was made up of lengths measuring approximately 15m. Every time one of these entered the water it was the job of the line-tender, 'H' Harrison, to confirm there were no bubbles at the connection by calling clearly, and very loudly, 'well for leaks'. Failure to do this was a breach of safety, hence H's inclusion on the dreaded list.

My inclusion was for another reason, but one I could never admit to officially. The night before diving we had gone past our minimum standard of five pints and were pushing onto the gallon (eight pints), with Psycho along for the night as per usual. Somewhere along the way, we started onto spirits, and everything became a blur. Consequently, this resulted in a sore head and somewhat fragile state at six o'clock the next morning. At this regular hour, we would clamber from our beds allegedly ready for the daily routine of physical training, followed by breakfast and then a jog to the pier for the start of diving operations at 0800hrs.

This beautiful Oban winter morning I was feeling much worse than after a typical evening out. I'm sure you know what I mean? You know, the don't fart or burp because the risk of follow-through or vomiting is too high, often followed by a joyful morning of recovery that lasts well into the afternoon? Well, that was me anyway; as grey skies, twenty-knot winds and occasional hail greeted us for morning sport.

Unfortunately for those of us in this state, or close to it, we had the last of our 55m 'dips' scheduled. These consisted of descending a shot-rope into a dark green world that after about 15m became a very-black-zero-visibility-world. As the light faded with each meter of descent on such dips, ambient pressure slowly began crushing the rubberised fabric of your 'dry-bag' (navy issue dry suit) against prominent folds of skin: armpits, back of knees, ball-bags, etc. The subsequent pain quickly prompting a routine drill before the agony became overpowering.

A short 'squirt' of compressed air from a milk-bottle-size 'suit-inflation' cylinder, located at a diver's waist, directed air into the dry-bag relieving the pressure of the surrounding water. Too much suit-inflation however, and positive buoyancy might be achieved resulting in potentially catastrophic results as the unfortunate individual raced to the surface like a Polaris Missile. Therefore, sensing too much air quickly prompted another drill that required the diver to vent excess air from a latex cuff-seal while both arms were extended upwards. While doing this, with his legs gripping the shot-rope for security, a diver was careful that his numb fingers wouldn't tear the delicate cuff-seal as he hurriedly dumped excess air. A final complication to this naval evolution was the risk of too much venting. In this event, icy cold water would rush in at the wrist creating more joy for the diver already battling hypothermia.

After arriving at 55m, indicated by contact with a large concrete shot-weight, a diver would use the umbilical to signal his position to the evil man at the surface. This would prompt a signal in reply directing the diver to complete the (relatively) simple task of uncoiling a 10m search-line and swimming out into the blackness to complete a circular search around the shot-weight. When finished, the diver would return to the shot, re-tie the line and ascend, all the time being ready to undertake further venting as the air contained within the dry-bag expanded as water pressure decreased thanks to the long-standing gas law published by Robert Boyle in 1662.

In case any of this does appear routine, just for a moment picture yourself with 55m of freezing water above your head. You can't see your hand in front of your face, your fingers are so numb you can't really feel the rope - all 10m of which is doing its best to entwine itself around you, the equipment you wear and your dive-buddy. Oh, I forgot to mention him didn't I. Sorry. You are, in fact, with another diver who is connected by another length of rope attached to each other's biceps, which, like the search-line and umbilical, is trying to lasso the both of you with equal enthusiasm. Finally, both of you have early onset hypothermia and know that the evil man is waiting to punish you, just for the fun of it, if you survive this little adventure.

Simply put, 55m dips required a CD recruit to be fully switched on so as not to stuff up in front of the Chief – a fate far worse than death!

Nevertheless, despite the obvious risks involved with undertaking the scheduled dip, had I advised Psycho of my fragile condition I would be committing a cardinal sin of the CD branch. You never, ever, got yourself into a state that prevented you from diving the next day! Conversely, you could be two-gallons-in at five to eight in the morning, absolutely maggoted, provided that you could, at 0800hrs, don a set and get your head wet. This situation, for good or bad, was the CD branch of the late seventies and early eighties.

Therefore, when Psycho asked my cold and clammy, beer stinking face if I was ready to go on air, in the true tradition of those who had come before me... I lied. The resulting dip wasn't nice. I kept all bodily fluids intact during the descent, but upon leaving bottom, the challenge increased as bubbly gasses expanded throughout my body. Adding to my prolonged joy were a couple of mandatory decompression stops at six and three meters where the minutes, burps and farts ticked by painfully slow. Eventually, I (sorry, my buddy and I) were called to the surface, to climb back up the ladder to then position ourselves in front of Psycho at the dive station.

Upon removing my full-face-mask, I saw that Psycho, six feet away, was grinning. He knew I'd suffered. Bastard! Nevertheless, I reported well (another lie) so that he knew there were no ill effects from the pressure we had been subjected to, and therefore no need to put me in the recompression chamber. Pausing momentarily, his grin fading, Psycho's face returned to steely-eyed Chief Diver.

"Next pair get dressed. I want the reserves of these sets checked and the next pair ready for the water in three minutes."

When he finished speaking, Psycho's eyes scanned the blur of activity he had generated. Satisfied his orders were being carried out he disappeared into the dive tender wheelhouse in search of a brew refill.

Making the most of his temporary absence, I quickly went aft to the stern of the sixty-foot vessel and took up a position away from eyes and ears behind the stern bulkhead of the accommodation. Here, while violently emptying around a gallon of beer into the sea, a familiar voice drifted down from above.

"I thought you said you were well, Mac?"

Psycho, grinning evilly, was leaning on the accommodation deck guardrail two-and-a-half meters above me.

You know that horrible moment when adrenaline is released around your body at the certainty of a painful outcome? Well, this wasn't the first time I had experienced it under Psycho's watch.

Back at the dive station with the rest of the course members assembled for the court-martial, Psycho continued.

"So, what punishment?"

The usual thing was a 'skin-swim' around the dive tender. It was a heart stopper, but I much preferred it to mud-runs, or of late, a nice jog up a Scottish mountain.

"Keel-hauling I think."
What?
"Jock, rig a line."

Keel-hauling is what Nelson did to recalcitrant sailors, and most of them drowned – blokes were dragged the length of the ship, along the keel, while tied to a rope. The last one of these was, well, a long bloody time ago!

A line was dropped over our bow and pulled down both sides of the tender to the dive station – the widest part of the hull. Half of the course took one side and half the other, but Psycho was bluffing... He had to be. Because people could be killed doing this!

"Jock, throw a 'set' on and hop in the water will you."

Jock, a Leading Diver undertaking 'second-dickey' (assistant-instructor) duties, looked as though he had doubts, but he donned a Clearance Divers Breathing Apparatus (CDBA) re-breathing set anyway and stepped over the side.

"Ok Mac" Psycho continued, "You're first. Secure the line to your Sambrown."

I did as I was instructed, taking a bight of the rope and bending it to the webbing eyelet at my shoulder, still sure that Psycho just wanted to make me sweat.

"In you get!"

He'd succeeded. In an attempt to hide my terror I tried to sound blasé.

"Forward or backward summersault to enter Chief?"

Psycho's evil grin softened a touch but came back firm as ever.

"Just get in."

Tied firmly to the keel-haul-line, I back flipped into the water. The boys cheered as I came up and I waved to the crowd, but the laughter stopped when Psycho asked Jock if he was ready.

"You ready too, Mac?"

Shit! I took several deep breaths and then, with cheeks puffed, I nodded up to Psycho with arm extended, thumb up... but he just watched me."

"Are… you… ready?"
Exhaling, I called yes.
"Pull him down!"

The surface and Psycho's face disappeared as the boys on the far side of the tender pulled me under. I had less than half a breath and wasn't at all comfortable. As the rope pulled me further downward, I was bumped and scraped along the steel hull, but when we reached the keel, the line stopped moving. Psycho was a funny bastard!

I could make out through my blurred vision that Jock was close at hand – not that he could offer me any assistance with the CDBA – and that he was watching me closely. I forced a smile, ignoring my lungs pleas for air and did my best to look cool…

'Jokes over Psycho, come on, time to pull me up… Fuck this!'

I pulled on the line hard, desperate for air, and thankfully it moved upward – the surface was still around three to four meters away.

Just as a feeling of dreamy calm was flooding over me, my brain must have recognised a different sensation to water as I splashed to the surface, and as the icy Scottish chill hit me, I snapped awake in one huge gasp. Regaining control and wiping water from my eyes, I sucked in large volumes of air, and up above me I saw Psycho leaning on the rail, he was still grinning.

"How was it, Mac?"

'You prick,' "Piece of piss, Chief!"

"Take him back!"

With barely a breath I was on my way under again, fortunately, without a stop this time. I clambered up the ladder and onto the deck, slumping onto the nearest locker. Psycho didn't speak, but the, not-so-tough-now grin said enough. In a pathetic show of defiance, I grinned in return. He paused, making my blood run cold, but then thankfully he turned away.

"Harrison, you're next."

Poor 'H,' not knowing was hard enough, but seeing it all happen first can't have been nice. A few minutes later he looked and felt like I had as he re-appeared on the surface in a state of near drowning.

News Headline:

The Ministry of Defence has agreed that complaints from some army recruits about being held down as boot polish was applied to their testicles, is a form of bastardisation. Moreover, senior officers investigating these claims believe this is a rare exception, and are confident that bastardisation is no longer practised in the armed forces.

Left: the smartarse author aged 19 wearing CDBA rigged for O2 at Horsea Island. He was Keel Hauled 6-weeks later. Right: 'dressing' in a neck entry dry-bag

Seaman Diver (SD) 28: day one of Clearance Diver training, the author sitting next to Psycho.

CHAPTER 2

Royal Navy Clearance Diving (Mine Hunting)

MINE HUNTERS WERE, AS THE name implies, used to search for subsea ordnance. The type of ordnance we searched for in the seventies and eighties was left over WW2 weaponry designed to sink ships. These mines were either a buoyant type (like the movies) or ground mines.

The buoyant mine was attached to an anchor in the form of a large metal box containing a reel of wire and a mechanism for both releasing and arming the mine. When released, the mine would float up on the wire as the reel unwound to stop at a predetermined depth. Typically, this was below the surface at a depth appropriate to striking a ship's hull, but the buoyant mine didn't need to strike the hull for it to be detonated.

Of the types of buoyant mines available there were two distinctive differences, they were either contact (the large 'switch-horns' seen in movies) or acoustic, smaller horns containing sensors that made the mine go bang when specific sound waves were detected.

Occasionally, over the accumulation of time, corrosion and wave action would cause these mines to be separated from their anchors; but designers had planned for such an eventuality with a device known as a 'mooring lever'.

Attached to the wire at the bottom of the buoyant mine, this angled lever was pulled open on a sprung hinge when the mines travel upwards was halted. This opening action also armed the mine. Consequently, if the wire was cut or broken for any reason the mine was, in theory, rendered safe as the sprung hinge closed the mooring lever. The effectiveness of such a system after 50+ years in the ocean made for interesting discussion aboard Mine Hunters.

The ground mine was much larger and was either acoustic or magnetic (or both), and it destroyed ships by sending a massive pressure wave from the seabed to 'break the back' of its target. Such force also created fire and flooding causing immense grief for the impacted crew.

As Clearance Divers (CD's) it was our job to dive on these weapons after Mine Warfare seamen had located their rough position with sonar. When in the water we had to verify what type the mine was before a decision was made to either destroy it with a counter charge or, leave it in position and mark its location. CD's, renowned for enjoying making things go bang, naturally preferred the former option.

Knowing that all such mines had systems designed to ruin your day, like photosensitive triggers (don't shine a torch) and magnetic triggers (don't dive with metallic equipment), CD's obviously took their jobs very seriously.

HMS Nurton had a crew of about 30. This made for a cramped life on the Ton-Class Mine Hunter where if an individual required privacy he was unlikely to cope with the daily challenges. Seamen were accommodated in two very crowded 'mess-decks', one in the bows and the other just aft of this through a watertight door into a compartment primarily designed for the sonar 'hull-outfit'.

A deck above these tight spaces was the main drag, but in Mine Hunter terms this was a grandiose statement for the very narrow passageway.

Off the main drag was a tiny galley, the Petty Officers mess (small) the Wardroom (miniature), two petite twin berthed officers' cabins and the Captain's cabin, still small, but bigger than the rest. At the forward end of the main drag was three heads for the seamen and one head shared by officers, which doubled as a shower. The seamen's shower was forward of the heads, and you guessed it, it was tiny too.

At the aft end of the main drag, a door opened to the stern deck. This was a cramped space containing a single story superstructure in its centre that lead to the engine room, a dive equipment store and mine warfare equipment store. Behind the superstructure was the 'sweep' deck containing a large reel of 'sweep' wire, 'otter boards', floats and other such gear. This was all towed behind the Mine Hunter and used for cutting the wires of buoyant mines as the Mine Hunter steamed through the ocean – Hunters rarely did this though, leaving that task to their cousins, Mine Sweepers, that had more sweep gear, but no sonar.

Moving forward up ladders positioned on both sides of the 'boat' was the upper deck containing the two-story bridge superstructure. On the lower storey was the sonar room and forward of this the wheelhouse (a backup only). Above the wheelhouse was the small bridge with helmsman's position and tiny navigation room.

From the bridge, you had a view of the bow containing the standard anchor gear and a single Bofors gun – bare-bones weaponry left over from WW2. Looking aft from the bridge wings was a mast and funnel, and you could see the top of the stern deck superstructure too, where a Gemini inflatable boat and its engine and test tank were stored.

The Mine Hunter's hull was made of wood (non-magnetic) and had layers of 'sacrificial planking' that CD's were forever replacing after the boat had been at sea in rough weather. At the keel below the bridge was the opening for the sonar hull outfit. When not mine hunting, this was covered with a relatively flat solid cover (dome), but when mine hunting, CD's removed this by attaching a line from a purposely-positioned winch. With the dome pulled to the deck and secured, a soft-dome was filled with seawater, and the hull-outfit lowered inside it from above, via the aft seaman's mess.

At the stern were twin screws and twin rudders. The rudders had small propellers built into them too. These 'activated rudders' (AR's) were used during mine hunting operations for two reasons, they aided turn capability, and they were very quiet.

So this little boat was to be my home for the next 12 months. I hadn't been looking forward to it, but after less than a day I thought it wouldn't be that bad and was looking forward to good times with the crew.

The dive team was small. Laurie Johnstone was our Petty Officer, and he doubled as the boat's Coxswain (senior NCO), there was Lester McMahan, the Leading Diver and 'TC' a senior Able Seamen (AB) about to do his Leading Divers course and two baby CD's, Craig 'Heff' Heffernan and myself. Our official boss was the First Lieutenant. This bloke was designated a Mine Warfare Clearance Diving Officer (MWCDO), a grand title with a name to match it, Nigel Saint Quinton Belvedere Cuthbertson - more about him later.

Of the other blokes in the seamen's mess, two characters stood out. 'Fish' was a Mine Warfare AB who was openly gay, but in a, 'come here and suck my dick or I'll rip your head off' more macho version of the RN's clichéd 'limp-wrister'. He had been married once, but it didn't last for long. I walked past his bunk one day, he was on the top of the three-tiered racks we had, and he asked if I could help. I looked up, and there was Fish, homemade plaster dildo in hand trying to push it up his bum. I left him to his handiwork.

One day Fish came down into the mess from the heads and showed us his new pet. In a jam-jar, he had a freshly deposited turd. He kept this on the fan-trunking above his bunk and would often have conversations with it, 'hello my little shitty'. Yep, Fish was a character. He planned to remove the lid of the jam jar when he left the ship and put it in the Wardroom ventilation pipe.

Our only 'Gunner' was an AB called Russell. The first week I was on board I would find bits of clothing, a shirt, a beret etc. lying around in proximity to the Bofors gun on the bow and asked whether I should take them back to the mess. The answer was always cautious, 'no, leave it there, that's Russell's.' Russell was on leave, but I was to meet him soon enough.

I headed up to the bow from the dive store to look for Lester and found him in conversation with someone who had his back to me. This individual was wearing regulation navy boots and trousers, but the top was a T-shirt with the sleeves ripped off at the shoulders. This T-shirt contained the torso of a gorilla and sported a closely cropped haircut. It turned toward me.

"Russell, this is Mac Macfarlane, the new diver," Lester advised.

With its knuckles dragging on the deck, the monster completed its slow turn to reveal a hard face that was apparently used to getting its way. On the T-shirt, I saw the words SPURS FUGS and this, combined with the cockney accent that greeted me, suggested that Russell was a Tottenham Hotspurs fan and proudly a 'thug'.

"All right Mac, do you box?"

My crushed hand was discarded as I looked up to keep contact with the gorilla's eyes.

"A little bit Russell, I did the navy novices last year."

The cogs turned slowly and then a grin appeared on its face.

"Ha, we'll see."

Russell's 'uniform' was permitted on a Mine Hunter, the relaxation of the discipline known as 'pirate-rig' was a compensation for the tight living arrangements. It was usually only permitted at sea, but for some reason, nobody ever challenged Russell when we were alongside.

During my first week aboard Nurton the dive team were 'working up' for deep diving. This was a process of undertaking increasingly deeper dives to acclimatise our brains to higher partial pressures of nitrogen. This gas (79% of the air we breathe), when absorbed in a pressurised state could produce the condition of 'narcosis' that affected a divers ability to undertake routine tasks. Commonly described as, 'like being drunk', it was said that divers might try and take off their masks, close cylinders and other such unwise acts while at depth. The only time I ever felt the onset of narcosis while in the water it presented itself as more of an uncertainty, i.e. am I ascending, which way is the shot etc., despite the answer to these questions being readily available.

Our work up consisted of daily trips to the shore-based decompression chamber for 'pot dips' where each day we went deeper until completing a number of 55-meter chamber runs. The First Lieutenant didn't accompany us on any of these dips, and when I enquired why, Laurie said that he was busy with paperwork, and winked.

All navy divers are introduced to decompression chambers as part of their aptitude training, and CD's are exposed to them periodically throughout their careers, but not just for workups.

Before joining Nurton I was working as a second-dickie on a Ships Divers course. In the last week, we were completing their deep dives to 30m, and I was rostered as the standby divers tender. A Petty Officer whom I respected greatly, Bob Oulds, was supervising as two of the students were on the bottom preparing to go out on their search line. When, without warning, the student tending the pair's lifeline called 'divers ascending' and a moment later a rubberised Polaris Missile splashed to the surface 10-feet from the side of our boat. This diver, wearing a dry-suit, had the neck seal extended over the top of his head as his suit expanded like a Michelin-man. As this happened the tender pulled up the end of the lifeline that had apparently been cut; there was a Nano-second of stunned inaction, and then Bob spoke.

"Away standby diver! Get the first one to the ladder and then find the missing one. Mac, give them a hand to get him up."

I passed the standby's lifeline to Bob and assisted the first diver up the ladder. He was standing ok by himself as he removed his mask.

"Diver Hardwick well."

Bob, with hands rapidly paying out the standby's descending lifeline, looked around just as this bloke coughed a spay of blood over the deck. Immediately prioritising tasks, Bob handed the lifeline to one of the students as he gave directives.

"Mac, get him in the pot, and you get in too."

Helping the student out of his gear, I then quickly dumped my cold weather jacket and kicked off my boots before lifting my leg to knee height to enter the circular opening of the 6-man chamber.

As I closed the inner air-lock door Bob's voice was on the intercom.

"I'm going to blow you down fast to thirty meters."

Air rushed into the chamber at a deafening roar pressurising the small compartment and both of us inside it. Instantly I felt pressure on my ears and quickly blocked my nose to blow against pinched nostrils to equalise this, repeating the process again and again as the pressure increased rapidly. In less than 30-seconds Bob reported that we were at, "thirty meters by gauge" and then asked how the student was.

My companion had blood around his mouth and nose. He was breathing ok now, and the bleeding appeared to have stopped. I reported this to Bob, who advised that he would be back in a moment. He still had another diver to recover.

The short version of this story is that while on the bottom in their zero-vis world the other diver, who Bob and the standby had safely recovered, was likely affected by nitrogen narcosis. With him in this state, both the divers had become fouled in the buddy and lifelines, and the 'narc'd' diver thought his buddy was in distress. To save the day, narc'd boy pulled out his knife and cut their lines and then cracked open his buddies suit inflation cylinder (a procedure not taught in any RN dive syllabus) that ensured the disastrous consequences.

The bloke with me inside the chamber, a Royal Marine undertaking the course while he waited for a position with the elite Special

Boats Section (SBS), fortunately lived. Unfortunately, though, he was never going to undertake military diving again due to scarred lung tissue. Reinforcing his plight, he was reminded how close he had come to death by RN hyperbaric medical staff who pointed out that rapidly expanding bubbles had been on their way to his brain after he'd surfaced.

So, you can probably understand my confusion then when our *Royal* Navy, MWCDO, First Lieutenant didn't attend chamber dives designed to prevent narcosis.

Based in Portsmouth on the south coast of the UK, Nurton seemed to spend all its time in Scotland operating out of the RN's Rosyth dockyard near to Edinburgh on the Firth of Forth. A typical operation we undertook while in this freezing and always rainy part of the world was called a 'route-survey'. This consisted of us going backwards and forwards over a chunk of angry sea as the sonar looked for targets for us to investigate. When something of substance was located, we would hear the dreaded words 'away Gemini, away Gemini' broadcast over the boat's tannoy system.

At this announcement, the duty crew consisting of diver, standby and Coxswain would board the Gemini to be lowered into the sea, which was invariably angrier than the previous time. The Gemini contained a large coil of shot-rope to which an anchor was attached, and above this, a sonar reflector called the 'icosahedron' – a multi-surfaced sphere. In addition to this gear were two sets of CDBA and the standard RN boat gear of oars, engine spares and tools.

CDBA, or Clearance Divers Breathing Apparatus, back in the seventies and eighties, was a re-breathing set comprising of mainly black rubberised-fabric with some brass fittings that resembled, to the uninitiated, a pair of unevenly shaped black saddlebags. The diver put the 'saddlebags' over his head through a purposely positioned opening so that one bag, a counter-lung, sat on his chest down to his sternum. The other, much smaller bag, sat on his back just below the shoulders. The bags were held together at the waist by brass buckles. The smaller bag, or 'pouch', the size of half a phone book contained golf-ball-sized lead weights and came together like an envelope with a quick release mechanism at its centre.

In the centre of the counter-lung was an opening about the size of a small side plate where a carbon dioxide absorbent canister was fitted and secured with a non-magnetic metal clamp. Attached to the centre of the CO2 canister was a breathing tube that connected to a full-face mask.

Below the counter-lung was a sleeve where a small twin-cylinder was inserted. For Mine Hunting operations this twin-cylinder was the reserve gas supply and pressurised to 205bar with oxygen (O2). On the back below the weight pouch, brass clips attached two larger horizontal twin-cylinders that contained mixed gas of appropriate proportions for the planned depth, i.e. the average depth of the seabed the route-survey was taking. These cylinders, also charged to 205-bar, were marked with tape around their manifolds that was colour coded for depth. Up to 25m was red, 25-42m was blue, and 42-55m was yellow. Both cylinders were connected to the counter-lung by short hoses, and the mixed-gas-set had a reducer fitted that the diver would pre-set to the required flow-rate before diving.

Understandably, a recruit diver had to be able to assemble the CDBA quickly for operational purposes, but also correctly, because without such skill water may find a way inside the counter-lung to mix with the CO2 absorbent. If this were to happen, a caustic 'soda-lime cocktail' would travel up the breathing tube to ruin the divers day. He also had to be able to use it very effectively if he hoped to pass the course, and this subtle art of buoyancy control and breathing techniques was drilled and drilled again during basic training. Essentially, CDBA was a CD's bread and butter. If he didn't maintain such capability, became blasé perhaps; it was akin to the risk of a soldier not treating weapon drills seriously.

Again, you can imagine my confusion when our *Royal* Navy, MWCDO, First Lieutenant, always tasked me to make up his CDBA. I never saw him undertake this critical task once.

The Gemini was attached to a simple crane system and kept at deck level on the starboard side midships area of the after-deck. When we were on board, a Mine Warfare PO would lower us to a point where the 'leg' of the 40hp Johnson outboard was in the sea. This often meant we were smashed by waves in bigger seas as it was a short leg and the Gemini had a relatively flat hull, but it was pretty normal, and we braced against it. The purpose of holding us above the water was to ensure the engine would start and therefore mitigate the risk of 'broaching'. Johnsons were notoriously hard to start and resulted in endless cursing during the aggressive pull of the starter cord, but this was better than a dreaded broach.

The Mine Hunter maintained headway (about 5kts) during Gemini launching and as such any contact with the water could cause the Gemini, still attached to the crane, to turn side onto the sea and fill with water – a broach. So until the outboard was running the Gemini would not be lowered any further. An additional safety device and essential for day-to-day operations was a boat rope. This line was secured to the Mine Hunter at the bow and connected to the Gemini via a quick release. Its purpose was to hold the Gemini's bow into the sea even if we were to cop a big wave. It was the last line to be disconnected when we were in the water with the engine running and, when returning to the boat, we would connect this first to hold us in position under the crane. The whole process was seamanship 101 and would be seen on any RN vessel when small craft were being operated.

When underway in the Gemini, the Coxswain would position close to the boat and then steer us in the same direction that a large adjustable arrow was pointing to on top of the bridge. The bridge crew manually adjusted the arrow, a bit like a large windvane, so that it lined up with the 'target' the sonar crew had identified.

Once 'on-line' we would lower the shot-rope to the seabed and then pull up 3m of rope and secure this to a small winch called the 'horse' fitted to the Gemini's bow, and then await the Mine Warfare report of sighting our icosahedron on their scope.

In the crowded Gemini, the Coxswain would typically sit on the cover of the Johnson, throttle in one hand, radio in the other; the diver would sit in the middle wearing his CDBA, and the standby would position at the bow working the shot-rope, not wearing his set that was positioned at the Coxswains feet.

"Snoopy, Snoopy, this is Charlie Brown, you are three right, start your conn."

Laurie would acknowledge this initial call and then motor away from the boat correcting his line up the imaginary path to the target. Charlie Brown, Nurton's nickname, would then provide course correction until the icosahedron was next to the identified target.

"Right… straight… straight… right… straight… standby, standby, now!"

On receipt of this call, Lester released the shot-rope from the horse and dropped both anchor and icosahedron to the seabed. We then waited for confirmation that these items were in range of the target before approval to dive was given.

If diving were ordered, I would be directed to, 'get on gas'. With the main-cylinder valve opened there was a constant, yet subtle hiss as the mixed gas passed through the reducer into the counter-lung at 12-litres per minute. This flow rate caused the counter-lung to fill reasonably quickly and so a purpose fitted, manually adjustable, relief valve was opened fully at the top left shoulder. With gas flowing then, a nose clip was put in place, and a five-strap 'spider band' was pulled over my head to hold the full-facemask in place as I bit onto the mouthpiece.

The next step in the 'getting on gas' process involved removing excess nitrogen from my system; although the mixed gas would reduce the amount of nitrogen I absorbed, purging excess would mitigate the risk of narcosis and decompression sickness (the bends) even more. In front of the mask attached to the mouthpiece was a 'spitcock'. This was a two-way valve that I would first twist to align with the counter-lung and then inhale deeply, before twisting to 'atmosphere' (a hole) where I would then exhale. This process was repeated quickly until the counter-lung was flat. Once completed the diver would 'crack' the reserve twin-cylinder to check its function and then breathe for two minutes before repeating the purging process.

The two minutes was used to verify whether a diver could tolerate the different to air gas. If a problem arose, he would just come off gas and breathe fresh air.

As I was completing this drill, Lester, as standby diver, was doing the same, but his set remained on the boat's deck with just the mask in place. Laurie would record times in his supervisor's logbook and when finished would advise,

"Two minutes, clear bag second time."

Purging complete, I would then crack a 'bypass valve' on the reducer to verify I could supply the counter-lung with additional gas from the main supply if required. Operation of this valve sent a 'guff' of gas into the counter-lung, and I would give Laurie a thumb up.

He would then direct me to 'get in the water' where I was held just below the surface to check for leaks. Once cleared, I would move to the shot-rope at the bow with Lester tending to my lifeline, where Laurie would give a final directive.

"Leave surface."

This time was also recorded and was used to calculate the time before I would have to 'leave bottom' to avoid in-water-decompression, not a pleasant process in rough weather.

Once submerged a CD would typically roll forward keeping one hand on the shot and descend as quickly as possible to ensure maximum bottom time. However, with a high-flow-rate of 12lpm filling the counter-lung it sometimes required both hands to pull down the first couple of meters until pressure compressed the counter-lung sufficiently.

On the way down the added pressure would also require the relief-valve to be closed sufficiently, so the CD retained adequate gas in the counter-lung to breathe. But even the simple process of moving gas in and out of your lungs required a conscious effort, but one that had been ingrained during training. Every time a diver inhaled, they drew gas through the granulated particles of CO_2 absorbent contained in the chest-mounted canister, but the critical component of this routine human activity was exhalation.

The CD had to do this with sufficient force to ensure all exhaled gas was pushed through the particles for them to their job. If, for example, a CD were to breathe as though using SCUBA, i.e. relaxed in and out, there was a good chance CO_2 would accumulate in the breathing tube resulting in CO_2 poisoning – not a good thing!

So during a descent in the always poor visibility (5-feet was considered brilliant), a CD would be adjusting the relief valve, adding suit-inflation to the dry-bag, cracking the by-pass if needed and breathing like a weirdo until he reached the bottom.

On the bottom a quick 'one-pull' signal was passed and returned, the diver feeling the tender's attention to his progress through the line. The CD would then uncoil the search-line positioned just above the anchor and, if it was a large target, fin out to the extent of the line and commence a circular search.

While fining around, the CD angled slightly away from the shot-rope to maintain tension on the search-line and, if the Mine Warfare blokes had done their job well, he would soon feel the line snag the target.

When this occurred, the CD would signal 5-bells (2 groups of two and one single) to let those on the boat know that he had found 'something'. He would then follow the search-line in, coiling it as he went.

Inevitably though, when mine hunting the located target turned out to be just another 'FBR'. This was CD code relayed via radio to let the Captain know we had located another 'Fucking Big Rock'. But that was mine hunting.

We spent up to six hours a day or night sitting in the bloody Gemini, never really expecting to locate anything other than FBR's. Despite our pessimistic outlook though, the Mine Hunting fleet was, on average, finding one old WW2 weapon each year.

Lester, Heff, TC and I were talking shit early one evening at the dive equipment store when our *Royal* Navy, MWCDO, First Lieutenant appeared. He was a tall man, probably six-foot-four, had a neatly trimmed beard and a particular way of talking to people that seemed to be reserved to officers of a certain calibre; you know, wankers!

Peering down his nose and without preamble, he asked Lester a question.

"McMahan, see that village over there?"

We were a couple of miles off some isolated Scottish village, and its lights were clearly visible on the dark horizon. Lester acknowledged he could see it and the First Lieutenant continued.

"Good. I want you to deliver a package to the post box there. How long do you think it will take?"

Lester mentally crunched up some numbers and completed the calculations on his fingers.

"About three hours, Sir, allowing for unknown fudge factors."

Not spending much time in small craft himself, the First Lieutenant nonetheless did his own mental calculations and agreed that Lester's maths sounded 'about right'.

"Good, right, I'll get the package and meet you at the Gemini."

Lester stopped him.

"I'll need a bowman Sir."

The First Lieutenant looked down his nose and scanned the sailors before him. His nose stopped at me.

"Take Macfarlane with you."

When he turned and disappeared in search of his package, Lester didn't waist a second.

"Mac, get down the mess and grab some cash and then get a dry-bag on."

Ten minutes later we were speeding away from Nurton in a fresh breeze on a typically freezing Scottish night.

As the lights of the village grew bigger we strained our eyes, but couldn't locate a harbour; not to worry, we would just find a suitable beach. Motoring up and down parallel to the dark shore, closing it with each pass we searched the blackness for an appropriate landing point when alarmingly; we both heard a rolling rumble, getting louder. Before we could react, we were on a wave, broaching, heading for an unknown destination.

Fortunately though, we were both trained CD's! Lester hung onto the motor and yelled, fuck!!! And I grabbed a handle and did the same.

By pure arse, we only felt a mild bumping as we were deposited on a gently sloping rocky shore. Lester had tilted the leg, and we quickly hopped out into foot deep water and dragged the Gemini up to dry rocks where we secured the anchor and continued on our mission.

After a bit of a scramble over more rocks and past a few trees on a steep slope, we found a narrow path that led into the village. We headed down the main drag and quickly spied a post box, next to the village pub – we had been gone a little over 30 minutes.

Walking into the pub wearing bulky dry-bags, covered in heavy arctic-weather jackets, with black balaclavas folded on our heads and a diving knife on a belt around the waists, we quickly got everyone's attention. For a moment the half-full pub went quiet, and people stared, it was as though they thought we were about to commit some criminal act.

"Where are you boys from?"

Lester answered the barman's question with a friendly smile.

"Just in from the sea for a couple of pints mate."

This seemed to relax everyone, and their conversations resumed as our drinking commenced. We had three pints before Lester decided we didn't want to push it too far, and we headed back to the Gemini.

The little rubber boat was still there, but unfortunately, the sea wasn't. More precisely, it was further away due to the ebbing tide. After around 15 minutes of grunting, we had lifted/dragged the Gemini back to the sea and were soon speeding towards Nurton.

We were hoisted aboard 2 hours and 30 minutes after leaving. The First Lieutenant was very impressed.

"Excellent work McMahan, Macfarlane, you found a post box then?"

Lester told him what he needed to hear and then, when he was gone, we hurriedly removed our dry-bags desperately in need of a piss.

On one of these route-surveys we experienced rougher than average weather, and I got to experience a Mine Hunter in a Force 7 to 8. Apart from just battling through heavy seas, the memory that stands out was how we only 'existed' between decks in such conditions.

Meals were kept basic, but the simple act of taking food from a plate to your mouth was fraught with danger. As the bow dropped into a trough, any unsecured item would become weightless, and cutlery and crockery would end up tumbling. Somehow though, we managed to eat and go about other daily routines. The heads were an exciting experience during such weather and timing was everything! Depositing the 'load' had to be done when rising up a wave, followed by an immediate flush before the bow dropped into the next trough. Failure to execute this un-published RN drill correctly saw the load become airborne and strike the individuals backside.

Bracing in my bunk during similar weather one early morning I heard an unusual message come over the tannoy, it was Fish's voice.

"Navigator to the bridge, Navigator to the bridge."

The Navigator was third in command and usually tucked up in his bunk at this hour, as the First Lieutenant held the 'Morning' watch.

It turned out that 'Nigey', as our *Royal* Navy, MWCDO, First Lieutenant was called behind his back, had collapsed on the bridge wing. Apparently, this was a regular occurrence in bad weather though, as he had some rare form of seasickness that seriously played with his brain. Unfortunately for Nigey, apart from bumps to the head, this condition diminished the old man of the sea airs he would carry going about his duties in calmer weather, but hey, he was a *Royal* Navy, MWCDO, First lieutenant and therefore should be afforded all due respect.

During a period of relatively calm weather, something rare happened. Nigey came on a conning run, and was going to be diving too! I still had to prepare his CDBA, but there he was, on-gas, with thumb up to Laurie. We had Lester on board the Gemini as well, so I guessed that Laurie wanted the extra hands, just in case?

I was tending Nigey's lifeline, and to my disappointment, everything was going to routine during the relatively shallow 18m dip. He signalled that he was ready to leave bottom, I acknowledged the four-pulls and then reported to Laurie when Nigey gave one-pull to signify he'd left bottom.

The lifeline we used was marked at three-meter intervals with masking tape to indicate depth: 1 yellow is 3m, 2 yellow is 6m, 3 yellow is 9m, 4 yellow is 12m, and one red is 15m and then a combination of red and yellow continues.

As Nigey continued to ascend, I reported his progress.

"Fifteen meters... twelve meters... diver stopped travelling?"

Laurie turned his head at the abnormality of my report and listened in closely.

"Diver is now travelling down... fifteen meters... eighteen meters... diver's stopped travelling?"

Both Laurie and Lester were looking at the water, cogs rotating slowly, trying to work out what Nigey was up to. As a precaution, Lester began to pull on his fins, but then my report changed rapidly.

"Diver is now travelling up again, diver travelling fast!"

Securing the last fin-strap, Lester grabbed his CDBA and threw it over his shoulders just as Nigey, in all his *Royal* Navy, MWCDO, First lieutenant glory, broke the surface with a rather sizeable un-CD-like splash.

His facemask was half off at a 45-degree angle revealing a snotty beard and flappy lips. In his left hand was a lobster, with its crushing claw firmly secured to his right hand.

"It's all right PO, I breathed out on the way up!"

This was an incredibly dangerous situation, but it was all Laurie could do to hold back laughter.

"Any pain in your chest, Sir?"

Nigey had removed his mask entirely and was proudly showing the lobster to his divers; the fact his beared had great blobs of snot about it kind of lessened the effect of his triumphant return to the surface though.

"No, fine PO. Not bad eh chaps?"

Grabbing a lobster from underneath an FBR during a conning run was an example of a really cool diver, nearly killing himself on the return to the surface however...?

In case you haven't quite got the image of Nigey in your mind's eye yet, just picture Basil Fawlty with a beard.

Later that day I wrote up a new diving emergency procedure called 'Companion Lobster Drill' and pinned it on the crew noticeboard in the main drag.

A few weeks later I was tending Lester during a dip to 42m in freezing weather. He was on his way up, no FBR found, when suddenly I started pulling in slack lifeline. He arrived on the surface moments later with both hands on the spindle of his relief valve desperately trying to loosen the fitting. This had frozen closed, and Lester's counterlung was bulging.

Quickly recognising the problem, Laurie retrieved a pair of multi-grips from the toolbox and gas was venting shortly after. Laurie then shouted instructions to an attentive Lester, who was looking no worse for wear.

"Go back down to nine meters Lester; we'll do some precautionary O2 stops and see how you go. If needed, we'll go back to the boat and throw you in the pot."

With mixed-gas closed, Lester cracked his O2 reserve and descended. Radio calls were made back to Nurton and TC, and Heff readied our one-man decompression chamber, but fortunately, Lester surfaced without any immediate symptoms of decompression sickness.

Later that afternoon though he noticed a dull 'niggle' in his right wrist and emergency action was commenced to mitigate the effect of this early symptom of 'the bends'. We didn't put him in the pot though; instead, a helicopter was flown from Faslane, the RN's nuclear submarine base, where a CD team was stationed. Lester was winched up and flown at a low level to the base, where he was put into their more substantial chamber to complete a lengthy treatment finishing up around 10 pm that night.

He remained in Faslane the following day and was returned after a second nights 'observation' by the same helicopter. Despite the treatment he still had a significant headache, but as it turned out this was nothing to do with the therapeutic table though. Lester and Laurie were both former Faslane Team members, and as a result, Lester was not allowed to leave until the appropriate amount of beers had been consumed during a very long observation period with his former teammates.

One incredibly dull route-survey afternoon, in reasonably shitty weather, the Mine Warfare team was struggling to find targets. This was great for the divers as we lounged about keeping a low profile, but the *Royal* Navy likes to keep its chaps engaged to prevent mutinous thoughts developing.

"Away Gemini, away Gemini, this is a seaboat-drill, a seaboat-drill only."

In unison, the duty crew of Lester and me expelled an expletive at the futility of the task we had just been directed to undertake. We undertook enhanced 'seaboat-drills' day and night, all the time; it was what we did for Christ's sake, who the bloody hell was behind this brilliant plan?

Arriving at the Gemini, we saw Nigey on the bridge wing with a stopwatch in his hand. Surprise, surprise! He saw Laurie with us.

"No need for you to go PO let McMahan take charge!"

A moment later I was at the horse ready with the quick release attached to the boat-rope and Lester was cursing away as the Johnson refused to start. Then, for reasons known only to him, Nigey ordered the Gemini to be lowered fully, and he had the seamen on Nurton's bow release the boat-rope from their location.

We broached immediately, but still connected to the crane the port pontoon quickly disappeared into the pressure wave of water, and I found myself astride the starboard pontoon like a bucking bull rider as the water swirled around my thighs. The ordinarily unsinkable

Gemini was almost submerged and being dragged forward at around five knots as the lift line to the crane strained alarmingly.

I looked to Lester who was lower, face screwed up in pain, with swirling water up to his chest.

"Lester, you want to bale?"

He just shook his head while continuing to grimace.

Looking up to the boat I saw the PO Mine Warfare glance at us and then up to the bridge wing. Nigey was there, frozen, with hands locked on the rail, both mouth and eyes open wide.

"Go astern you cunt!"

The PO's urgent message registered with Nigey and he disappeared inside the bridge. A moment later there was a loud rumble, and strong vibrations as Nurton's screws were put full astern. The Gemini bobbed back to the surface in boiling white water, amazingly without damage, but then I saw why Lester had been grimacing.

His hand had been caught between the wire lift-bridle and the pontoon, he couldn't have 'bailed' even if he had needed to, and the back of his hand was now bruising up around broken skin.

Back on board, Laurie came to speak with us in the dive equipment store. He found us in a not happy state.

"He's a fucking idiot Laurie!"

Laurie, the senior NCO aboard Nurton, had a responsibility that we were acutely aware of, but sometimes struggled to accept. He had to support the Captain and therefore by default the First Lieutenant too. So he chose his words carefully.

"Mate, how's your hand."

Lester turned his eyes downward briefly and then back to Laurie.

"Fine."

"Good," Laurie continued, "Look, he fucked up Lester-"

Lester cut Laurie off with venom.

"He's one giant fuck up Laurie, and you know it!"

There was a moment of silence where Laurie processed his options, but he responded, diplomatically, as Coxswain of HMS Nurton.

"Ok mate, what would you have me do?"

Lester knew that mutiny wouldn't be a productive move and that Laurie, even if he pushed hard for action to be taken against the First Lieutenant would achieve little, other than threaten his own career. After all, this was the pre-Falklands *Royal* Navy, where the officer's never made mistakes, especially not in front of the chaps.

"Just keep him out of my way."

About an hour after the incident Lester and I were called to the Captain's cabin via a tannoy announcement.

"McMahan, Macfarlane, take a seat… please."

Please? A *Royal* Navy officer never used such language when addressing lower-deck chaps. Maybe the one-eyed, disgruntled opinion, of an apparently trouble causing AB was misguided? As we sat, knees almost touching the Captains in the very small cabin, he continued.

"Now, I don't know who was to blame for this afternoon's drama-"

Lester was having none of that and cut him off.

"Who's to blame?! Sir, the First Lieutenant, ordered the boat-rope to be released from the bow before I had the Johnson started!"

Lester had spoken with a tone very much on the wrong side of acceptable. The contempt he demonstrated would have justified the Captain bringing charges against him in any other circumstance, but he didn't. Instead, he just used both his hands in a gentle patting motion as he countered Lester's accusation.

"Now, McMahan, you can't possibly have known everything that was going on at the bridge at the time now, could you?"

Of course we didn't know! We were both reasonably busy trying not to drown at the time; nonetheless, the captain chose to keep whatever this valuable information was a secret.

Although it was evident to all aboard that someone had stuffed up and that the vast majority were confident they knew who this was, the official line remained the same; it wasn't Nigey. Any motivation I had to be a good little diver and put up with the First Lieutenant's bullshit vanished after that day, and fortunately, I was to receive my 'draft' orders for a Team a month later. Nurton had one more little adventure for me though.

I was halfway through a circular search in about 36m of zero vis when the search-line snagged on something. I signalled the surface, moved in and my fingers contacted a metallic box-shaped structure the same size as a buoyant mine's anchor. The thing that struck me immediately was that unlike a training mine, this one was covered in barnacles.

I signalled the surface again and left bottom with my hands moving over each other on the mooring wire. It was still zero vis, but I could feel my numbed palms catching broken strands on the wire as I continued upwards. I had no idea what depth I was at, but as my world began to turn dark green, I figured I was at about 5-6m when I noticed a dark shadow about 2m above me.

My heart rate seemed to have doubled, and I had stopped breathing. All I could see was a shadow, but I knew what it was.

Continuing, I crept up the wire and noticed rust particles breaking away and drifting in the light tide with each hand movement. Then at about 1m below it, I paused again.

A rapid mine recognition lecture flashed through my brain as I stared up at what had to be an old British Mk17 Acoustic mine above me. I knew this weapon had an explosive charge of between 300 and 500 pounds, but my focus was on the mooring-lever, it was armed!

When a CD locates a mine, he is meant to verify as much detail as possible before returning to the surface. During training we became familiar with the dimensions from our fingers to our elbows, the length of our knives, how long we were stretched out from fingertips to fins etc. so that we could measure mines and report the data to our dive supervisor. I did none of this! There was a bloody Mk17 above me, and it was armed for Christ's sake!

Arriving on the surface shortly afterwards, Laurie was naturally interested in what I had found.

"What you got Mac?"

"A buoyant mine Laurie, Mk17 Acoustic... I think?"

Laurie frowned.

"Think? What's the width of its band and what length are the horns?

My answer was not what he needed.

"Fuck Mac, you're meant to be a bloody CD."

He checked his logbook to gauge how much bottom time I had left and frowned again.

"Lester, get dressed and go check it out."

Several minutes later Lester returned to the surface. Usually a confident bloke regardless of what was thrown at him; his brief to Laurie reflected how I had felt upon seeing the shadow above me.

"It's a Mk17 Acoustic Laurie, and I'm certain it's live."

Laurie called up Charlie Brown, and we waited. Our initial apprehension had waned, and we were now relishing the opportunity to blow up a live mine.

This would be accomplished in one of two ways: Lester would first secure a pre-made canvas covered PE-4 plastic explosive charge around the middle of the mine, and then he would connect a length of detonation cord to this and bring it to the surface. On the surface, this 'det-cord' would be connected to a 'double-L' float with a small timer and detonator connected to it. Then with the engine running, the timer would be started, and we would get well clear.

The other option was to undertake a conning run with an MDW (Mine Disposal Weapon) in place of the icosahedron. This was essentially a big bomb. The MDW would be dropped next to the anchor and detonated in the same manner. The most practical choice for the mine so close to the surface though was option one, but it wasn't to be.

After leaving us sitting on top of a live mine for close to 30 minutes, Charlie Brown came up with a plan.

"Snoopy, this is Charlie Brown. Leave it where it is, we will just mark it on the charts."

An opportunity for the Captain and his team to do what their boat was designed for was allowed to slip by. What tossers!

News Headline:
A Ministry of Defence spokesperson confirmed that an old World War Two sea-mine had been located by the Royal Navy this week during training exercises north of the Firth of Forth. The mine is thought to be in a safe location, and the MoD is yet to determine whether it will need to be destroyed at a future time.

Author and Nigey in Norway on a NATO exercise, icicles on Nurton's Bow

Nurton's dive team on NATO 'holiday' in the Mediterranean
L-R: TC, Heff, Laurie, Author, Lester foreground

CHAPTER 3

Royal Navy Clearance Diving (How Not To Become A Civilian)

AFTER LEAVING HMS NURTON IN 1981 I was drafted to the Fleet Clearance Diving Team, or more simply, the 'Fleet Team' who were based in Portsmouth. This had been my first draft preference, but you never got your first preference, especially the Fleet Team? Normally, a diver fresh off a boat would go to one of the bomb disposal teams positioned in either the south of England or Scotland. He may also go to the Faslane Team where endless in-water screw (propeller) changes were undertaken on nuclear submarines to ensure they remained stealthy (slight damage on a blade could cause a screw to 'sing' on enemy sonar), but who would want the hours of mind-numbingly repetitive tasks this entailed? Anyway, after a year on a Team the once baby-diver, now 'CD-3', would complete a Leading Diver course and go back to another Mine Hunter as the 'CD-2'. With this achievement under his belt, he would then have a good chance of a Fleet Team draft before continuing his career with further promotion to Petty Officer; the first of the CD-1 qualifications. It was apparent that I had been very fortunate; especially after receiving advice from numerous divers that no one ever got the Fleet Team first pick.

The Fleet Team was the RN's quick response unit. If a diving related task came up anywhere in the world, the Fleet Team jumped on the nearest transport and went off to save the day. This type of operation is what I had dreamed of from my first dive as a school boy; it was not Jacques Cousteau, but this was better, and contained, in my eyes at least, far more prestige and opportunity.

I was introduced to the Team's Fleet Chief Petty Officer, or just 'Fleet Chief' for day to day working arrangements, on the morning of my first day. The highest-level CD-1, this rank is now aligned with the rest of the armed forces with the ubiquitous title of Warrant Officer. Mick Ferdinand had undertaken my CD aptitude when I re-applied for the branch after a couple of years at sea. He was a no-nonsense Chief Petty Officer back then, and I doubted he had changed with the promotion. Despite his rigorous discipline, I liked him. He was one of the most respected Fleet Chiefs in the RN, and I knew that I would learn a lot under his command. If you read Battle for the Falklands by Max Hastings you will discover more about his authority and capability – there is a picture of him there (the only FCPO-D), standing at the back of Margaret Thatchers 'team' comprising of mainly Cabinet Ministers, Generals, Admirals and Air Marshalls.

On my first trip away with the Fleet Team, nowhere exotic, unfortunately, just the isle of Rothesay in Scotland for a deep work up, Mick loaned me his dry-bag as I had yet to be issued one in the hurried departure. This was another rare event - things were looking pretty bloody good.

On this trip, I completed a standard work up to 55m but got to use The Kirby Morgan Band Mask (KMB10) for the first time. This was a great experience, especially having voice communication with the surface. What luxury. The mask, or more correctly 'hat' felt heavy at first. Its weighty moulded structure seemed to pull your head downwards. After a couple of dips though, with its spider-band adjusted correctly and growing confidence with the oral-nasal (like a fighter pilot's mask) instead of a standard mouth-piece, it felt normal, and I couldn't imagine why you would ever want to go back to SDDE. This equipment now appeared obsolete in comparison.

We followed robust pre-dive drills that included closing off the main supply from the dive-control-panel, the diver then 'purging' the umbilical by cracking a defog-valve at the front-right of the hat until the oral-nasal was sucked against his face with a breathing restriction. At this moment, simulating an air failure, the diver would then open a reserve-valve at the right-side of the hat to take a couple of breaths from the bailout cylinder on his back. Hearing the supervisor's words coming from two waterproof earphones inside the neoprene hood as he acknowledged these drills was strange too, but as the dives continued the 'comms' became standard, and I soon learnt to time my exhalations when communicating underwater to prevent words being obscured by bubbles passing the earphones. What a great piece of kit the KMB10 was.

CD2's and higher ranks would be diving to 75m. This was undertaken using a Zodiac, about twice the size of a Gemini, and this craft carried sufficient gas and umbilical for two divers and a standby – it was crowded. Instead of our usual mixed gas ratios of oxygen and nitrogen though, for the greater depth, the Fleet Team were using helium at a mixture of 80% helium and 20% oxygen. The purpose was to prevent nitrogen narcosis and, ultimately, reduce the chance of decompression sickness; it wasn't without risk though, and one of the Team Chiefs summed up the threat during a brief on helium hazards that got everyone's attention.

"Ok, apart from making you sound like Donald fucking Duck, remember that helium has a far greater expansion rate than air or other gas mixture you have used in the past. So, what this means is that an emergency free ascent is not wise, because you will not, no matter how controlled you believe you are, make it to the surface alive. Understood?"

Lester was on the Team too; he'd been drafted a month before me. This was to be his first excursion to 75m using helium, and watching him go on gas, I saw a similar set of eyes to when he had found the Mk17 mine.

Despite the anxiety of doing something new, a little bit more dangerous perhaps, I wanted to be a CD-2 so that I could dive to 75m on helium too. I knew that I was on the best Team to start the process of making it happen though, and so I just focused on listening and learning.

The dives continued for the two weeks we were in Rothesay, and the initial anxiety of something new passed as the new boys gained confidence. We hit the Rothesay nightlife pretty hard too, some small pubs and one small club, it was a great intro to Team life.

On one of the last dives, a CD2 called Ginge who was a former Saturation Team diver (the RN's experimental unit that used diving bells), and the official 'Boss' of the Fleet Team were diving together. The Boss was another *Royal* Navy, lieutenant and MWDCDO, fortunately of much higher quality than Nigey. Nonetheless, the Chief running the dive sought to have some fun with him.

They had completed a series of stops and were coming to the end of the last one at three meters. These were more extended stops and not just the precautionary ones we had undertaken during our air dives. The Chief called Ginge, independently, on the comms box.

"Ginge, I have given you extra time at the last stop. I want you to go over and open the Boss's suit inflation."

There was a moment's silence and then a chuckle.

"Ok."

A few moments later the Boss arrived on the surface spread-eagled against the rapidly expanding dry-bag. Ginge arrived in a far more controlled fashion a few moments later and closed the suit inflation that the Boss could no longer reach with his arms forced out wide. When they were both back on the Zodiac, they came off gas with Ginge looking sheepish and the Boss looking angry.

"Sorry Sir, orders."

Everyone laughed at the Boss's expense, but as he turned his head towards the Chief, his expression suggested that he didn't appreciate the joke as much as everyone else.

The Fleet Team had a scheduled trip to Crete in the eastern Mediterranean. It was to be a couple of weeks undertaking seabed searches and salvage exercises to show Britain's friends that she was always close at hand if help was needed. What this translated to for CD's however, was a summer holiday with some water sports; admittedly water sports with more chance of death, but good times nonetheless. Unfortunately for me though, there were no seats left on the Hercules transport as I had arrived after travel arrangements had been made. Mick gave me the good news but told me I would be 'loaned' to the Portsmouth and Medway Bomb and Mine Disposal Team in their absence.

Fortunately CD's reduced this grand title to the more acceptable, 'Pompy Bomb Team'.

Located in the same building as the Fleet Team at the far corner of HMS Vernon's parade ground, that faced Portsmouth harbour, we both shared a jetty and a couple of small boats. However, apart from occasional socialising, we pretty much kept ourselves to ourselves.

Although disappointed at not going to Crete, I knew I would get additional experience working with the Bomb Team boys. Unfortunately though, when being introduced to the Chief of the team, another no-nonsense bloke called Mo, I had a black eye that was a result of a drunken battle over a cheeseburger.

"Oh, are you one of those 'bovver boys' are you?"

He didn't look impressed at all. My drinking was getting a bit out of control, it had never stopped me getting my head wet, but ending up in a brawl over some irrelevant issue was becoming a more frequent occurrence. I lied, partially.

"No Chief. I've been training for the navy novices, and some sparing got a bit heated, that's all."

I had been training, preparing for my second navy novice championship. There were indeed spirited sparring sessions involved, but the worst I'd received from these was a bloody nose.

We held eye contact for just a second and then he dropped his head to look at a diary on his desk, apparently not enthralled with my explanation.

"Will it stop you diving?"

"No Chief."

"Good, we have a little job you can do this morning then."

An hour later I was in a cutter with Mo, another new Bomb Team diver and a CD-2. We were heading up the harbour to the frigate HMS Avenger. This ship had variable pitch propellers that had to be calibrated periodically. To do this, a diver was sent down to read a mark on the blade against a scale each time an engineer adjusted the blade's angle internally. It was a painfully dull task that had landed on Mo's desk because the Avenger had no Ships Divers on board. To make matters worse, it was a particularly freezing cold late February morning.

We were using CDBA rigged for O2. This meant I had a comfortable 60 minutes of gas with a standard reducer flow rate of 1.5Lpm. However, I could push this longer if I closed the O2 valve, opened the bypass (to allow direct high-pressure gas into the counter-lung) and then just cracked the O2 valve periodically as the counter-lung O2 supply was used up. This process would likely get me closer to 90 minutes, but as this was the endurance of the CO2 absorbent and CD-3's (my recognised title after time on Nurton) were not formally qualified to do this, I would just run off the reducer flow rate. Notwithstanding the formality of my decision, it was self-preservation and not rules that determined my choice, as I could sense Mo was waiting for an excuse to abuse the hell out of me on the trip up the harbour.

I had been in the water for close to an hour. I had almost completed the first lot of readings on the port screw when the hiss of gas from the reducer went silent. I cracked the reserve and signalled to come up. Mo was there, looking angry as I surfaced.

"What's the problem?"

"On reserve Chief."

Mo checked his log.

"Ok, put another set on and finish up this set of readings, ok?"

I was bloody cold. Visibility was so shite that I had to get my mask right up against the scale on the screw to read the marks and I was busting for a piss.

"Yes Chief."

When the last reading was taken I came out of the water, and the other new diver hopped in. Mo passed me a brew, and I took over tender duties for the other bloke.

After just half an hour or so this bloke signalled to come up; on the surface he asked for a torch to better read the markings, and Mo exploded. I think he actually liked this bloke too; he probably would have killed me if I'd said anything at all.

Later that week we got a job up the coast. Someone had found 'some old bombs' on a deserted section of beach while walking their dogs. We loaded up the 'bomb-bag' and other Explosive Ordnance Disposal (EOD) gear into one of the Bomb Team's blue Land Rovers with its distinguishable red wings (Fenders for US and AUS readers). A team of four including another Mo, but this one was a Petty Officer, a CD-2, myself and another CD-3 cruised up through Kent and to a Coastguard building near a remote chalk cliff face.

The Coastguard bloke pointed us to a path, and we picked up the heavy bomb-bag (a backpack containing a range of explosives), another bag containing detonators and tools, and then headed off to find the bombs.

It was a steep and long walk down to the base of the cliff, but we could see the point the Coastguard bloke had pointed out, 'a large chunk of rock, freshly fallen', about 500m further up the rocky beach.

On arrival at our destination, a boulder the size of a typical shed, we found about ten milk bottle sized bombs; they were most likely old WW2 practice ordnance that aircraft had dropped against the target cliff. This sort of stuff was being found all the time, not very dangerous as ordnance goes, but there was so much of it the Bomb Team undertook an annual 'milk-run' around Coastguard stations to collect the lot for one big collative disposal/bang at a military range. Taking these heavy bombs back up the cliff was not something Mo was contemplating though.

"Empty the bomb-bag Jan."

The CD-2 did just that, and Mo began prepping the ordnance for detonation.

Arranging the first five bombs in a line side by side, Mo removed the brown wax-paper cover from a stick of PE-4, the standard UK plastic explosive, and cut it into strips with his knife. These were 'shaped' onto the centre of the bombs, and another stick of PE-4 was used to complete the first row. He then placed the remaining five bombs on the PE-4, directly on top of the first lot. More PE-4 was wedged in and around the pile, and some premade quarter-pound blocks were linked with detonation cord to complete preparations.

We then walked a distance of about 300m back towards the path, to another large boulder, timing how long this took. Returning to the bombs, Mo cut a suitable length of fuse, ignited it and timed how long it took to burn out. Happy with the duration, he measured a longer length and cut this off the roll. He then connected detonators to more detonation cord, spliced these together, to the main charge and then connected the fuse.

Checking we were all ready with remaining equipment packed, he then ignited the fuse. We walked backed to the large boulder and took shelter behind it. About 1-minute and 30-seconds afterwards there was a deafening boom.

After a check of the area to verify there was no unexploded ordnance remaining, we headed back up the path at a reasonably lively pace thanks to the reduced weight of the bomb-bag. The Coastguard bloke met us at the top.

"Shit, that was a big explosion!"

Mo looked him in the eye.

"Yes mate. All ordnance is safe until you forget it's dangerous, even little bombs like those. Be sure and report any other stuff to us the moment it is reported to you, ok."

Handshakes were undertaken with the positive acknowledgement of the coastguard's input; therefore assuring that we would get more trips up the coast in the future. We then proceeded to spend out 'subbies' (subsistence allowance) in the local town, maximising their value by sleeping in the shed of the Coastguard station.

After returning to Pompy, we pretty much replenished the stores and were off again. This time it was to a coastal army base where locals had found a large bomb on sand flats at low tide.

Chief Mo and the Bomb Team's Boss came on this job, plus a gaggle of CD's in two Land Rovers. We loaded what gear we thought appropriate onto an army 3-Ton truck and were driven out onto the sand flats at low tide. We drove for about a mile and came to a halt about 10m from the exposed tail section of a standard 'dumb-bomb' from the Second World War.

It looked to be a 100-pound bomb (about a meter in length) judging by the size of the tail, and the Boss gave us orders.

"Right chaps start digging and let's get it exposed."

Mo had another idea.

"Sir, we could always-"

"Thank you Chief; I know what I'm doing!"

Despite being abruptly shut down, Mo just shrugged his shoulders and smiled.

After about 30-minutes of digging where we only managed to produce a hole a foot or so deep due to water and sand filling each shovel load almost immediately, the Boss turned to Mo.

"Chief, you were going to suggest something?"

Mo had us replace the shovels on the truck. He took two quarter-pound blocks from the bomb-bag and linked them with 2m of detonation cord, tying a thumb knot at each end. He then buried each block about half a meter each side of the tail section and finally cut another length of detonation cord and spliced this to the original. He had been working for just 5-minutes when he turned to the Boss.

"Do you want to connect the detonator, Sir?"

"No. You carry on Chief."

"Very well Sir. Can you take the truck and the boys 400m clear please, I will join you shortly."

After Mo's casual stroll back to the truck there was a delay of about 1-minute before a mound of sand and water vapour burst upwards. It was accompanied a second later by a loud bang reverberating over the mud flats due to some low overcast cloud, as the mound of sand fell back to the ground.

We drove back to the area to find a hole about 1.5m wide and 1m deep. The bomb was completely exposed in the centre of the hole, and there was no water seeping into it. The Chief smiled but said nothing. He and the Boss then worked together to place a wedge of PE-4 on the bomb, which was believed to be another practice weapon, and we retreated to a safe point again to observe a second boom.

A theme was undoubtedly being revealed concerning the capability of *Royal* Navy MWCDO's when compared to their subordinate None Commissioned Officers, but I wasn't surprised. As I've mentioned before, this was the pre-Falklands RN, perhaps somewhat complacent after decades without real combat. During this time my Chiefs and Petty Officers would often suggest that a vast majority of RN officers obtained their commission, not because of ability, but because of what 'daddy did' – Nigey, perhaps an extreme case in point, demonstrated the typical consequence of what the Chiefs alluded to.

Looking back, the types of officer this system produced can be likened to some of the pompous caricatures from the TV series, Black Adder.

I was living in a flat about 10-minutes jog from HMS Vernon's front gate. This had me closer to the nightlife in Southsea where typical dives like Johanna's nightclub met the needs of drunken sailors.

Waking late one Saturday morning, I checked my watch and saw that I'd had a good sleep in. It was just after nine, and I was contemplating what I would have for breakfast as a moment of clarity sent adrenalin rushing to my extremities. It was Friday!

Dressed in running gear moments later I was sprinting towards Vernon. I entered the main gate before 0920hrs and continued across the parade ground. The Team weren't there, extended morning sport at the gym, good; I would say that I'd gone for a run.

"Where have you been?"

It was one of the CD-2's. I told him the truth, which turned out to be a big mistake. I was in Mo's office later that morning; you never, ever let alcohol stop you doing your job. You are always ready to dive at 0800hrs!

"Yeah, well I'll let Mick deal with you. He's due back on Monday."

My meeting with Mick wasn't nice. Apart from him threatening to kick me off the Team if anything like this ever happened again, I felt like a prick for letting him down.

The warm welcome he had shown me on my first arrival was a thing of the past. I continued to dive and try and make amends, but there was to be no quick fix.

We had a couple of dips over the next few weeks, one to free a line on a navy hovercraft and another undertaking submarine salvage training. This involved connecting air-lines to a huge submerged buoy and then after turning appropriate valves, re-floating it. These were useful tasks, but more importantly, my head was remaining under Mick's radar.

As the weeks ticked over, I came up with a plan to ensure I would never be late again. It involved sleeping at Vernon in the 'Diving Guard' mess after a night on the piss. This was the Team's room in the base accommodation building; we had the only key as it was for our exclusive use to support operational matters.

One Saturday morning (definitely Saturday this time) I was in a deep slumber as the sun shone in through the Diving Guard windows at around 11 am. I'd had a big night, and my run-ashore clothes plus remnants of a Chinese takeaway were strewn across the floor when I heard a clicking sound as someone tried to open the door.

"This room appears locked Master."

Instantly awake, realising it was 'Commanders Rounds' and that the Master at Arms and an entourage of staff were escorting the base Commander around for his periodic inspection, I then relaxed again; I had the only key.

"Don't worry Sir; I have a key."

I could hear the Master rummaging through the many keys on the large ring he carried. Do you big fella? This is the Team's room, and I have the only one.

The sound of a key entering the lock and then the clicking of a bolt being withdrawn caused an adrenaline release higher than I had experienced in quite some time. I instantly feigned sleep.

"There's a man asleep there, Master."

"I'll wake him, Sir!"

"No. Master, that man may have a reason for being in bed. Find out who's in charge of him and have this person report to me."

The Fleet Team was on long-weekend leave. Mick was called at home and had to come in and explain to the base Commander why one of his divers had trashed the Diving Guard mess. Suffice to say, I was off the team on Monday morning and back at the dive school – considered penance for any CD-3 budding to become a CD-2.

Life lessons are often hard. This one was reasonably big for my 21-year-old body to take. One of the most respected divers in the RN thought I was a dick; he was correct, but worse, this would spread around the branch like wildfire.

I caught up with Laurie and Lester during the week to discuss my options.

"Well Mac, I reckon you're fucked!"

Thanks, Laurie. Their combined advice was for me to suck it up and get on with things. My career was going to be set back a year or so, but it wouldn't be the first time this had happened to a diver. They suggested I put in for the Faslane Team, because of all the CD Teams they attracted the heaviest drinkers. This was indeed an option to get back to a Team more quickly, but the thought of endless screw changes still didn't appeal. The only other option was another year on a Mine Hunter after my penance at the school was completed, before starting the whole promotion process again. What to do?

This was all happening in August of 1981. At the time the British Armed Forces were being subjected to significant defence cuts, and there had been calls for voluntary redundancies. I had received some calls from a former CD mate, now a civilian, working for a company called Northern Divers based out of my hometown of Hull in the north of England. He was making at least three times the money he had as a CD and said that the work was a piece of piss. I filled out the necessary forms.

A month later I was standing in front of the same Commander, Master at Arms and the Boss of the dive school to see whether he would approve my discharge.

"Now, Macfarlane, I understand that you have had some troubles these last few months, but" He turned to the Boss of the School, who nodded subtly "Essentially you are considered a valuable member of the diving branch and we are sure that you can overcome these difficulties. Are you sure this is what you want?"

"Yes, Sir."

The Commander paused, studying the documents before him.

"Once signed Macfarlane, I won't be able to reverse this decision, and the navy will not let you return, you do understand this?"

"Yes, Sir."

I left the room feeling as though a huge weight had been lifted off my back. I had already scheduled an interview with 'Northerns' during some upcoming leave and was advised that my discharge may take several months to process. I couldn't wait.

Remaining at the school as paperwork was processed my two final dives in the RN were interesting. I was undertaking second-dickie duties for a Ships Diving Officers course, and we were in week-three, ships bottom searches. The SDO course was pretty much the same as a general Ship's Divers course, but we had to be polite and couldn't administer the same level of pain as cooks, sailors, electricians and general bottle-washers received.

We used a line called a half-necklace for ships bottom searches – the line was taken to the keel and then swum the length of the ship's hull one side at a time in search of limpet mines. Divers left the surface by numbers. Number-one was 'keel-man' and spaced at arm's length towards the surface other divers connected to the half-necklace. The amount of other 'numbers' leaving surface after this diver depended on the depth of the keel and or the visibility. In the Far East for example, if anchored in crystal clear tropical waters, just two or three divers may be required to sweep the hull of a typical destroyer. At the head of Portsmouth harbour though, where the mothballed frigates of the 'reserve fleet' were moored, the half-necklace required sufficient divers so that their sweeping hands touched to ensure limpet mines could be located in what was typically no more than 1-foot visibility.

Another challenge for diving recruits here was the tide and buoyancy control. Anything more than half a knot and the divers were working hard to maintain position without pulling their mates, or sinking away from the hull. If they were to come out of position on the half-necklace, that they were all physically attached to (by a metal clip) in the limited visibility, chaos ensued as divers were pulled by their buddies and fingers grabbed at razor-sharp barnacles to maintain position. When this occurred, the novice divers were recalled to the surface, towed by Gemini back to the bow, given a polite briefing on procedure and then sent back down to do it again. A further complication presented itself when the half-necklace reached the stern, and the screws and rudders had to be both searched and negotiated.

I was acting as standby diver on the second day of ships-bottoms. The half-necklace's position, indicated by a member of the course swimming on the surface holding onto a surface marker float, was approaching the stern. It was the second attempt for the current group of divers, who had now been in the water for over 30-minutes.

"Four pulls on the necklace PO."

Bagsy Baker, the PO CD-1 running the course shook his head, frustrated.

"Ok, call them up."

The day wasn't going well. This lot was yet to complete a full sweep of the ship.

One diver surfaced and then went back down again, fins appeared on the surface and flapped about (a big no-no). Something was wrong? I had my twin-cylinder 'Aquarius' air set on my back as the surface swimmer spoke again.

"I think they're stuck PO."

"Away standby diver!"

My fins were already on and with mask hurriedly pulled into place I was following the half-necklace line down within three seconds of Bagsy's call.

What a shit fight! Somehow they had got the half-necklace around the shaft and through the 'A' frame. Half the divers were pulling one way, half the other in their attempt to surface.

I was trying to pull the keel-man and his group of divers back down and around the shaft, but there was some wild kicking going on, and I wasn't having much success. The kicking was getting more frantic too, suggesting that panic was taking hold. Knowing that they must be low on air, especially after hearing a high-pressure transfer of gas from main to reserve cylinder (equalisation), I broke a significant diving rule and pulled out my knife to cut the necklace.

Equalisation was achieved by breathing from just one of the diver's twin cylinders at the start of a dive - the 'main' cylinder. When this was breathed down sufficiently, the diver would experience a breathing restriction and open the valve on the other 'reserve' cylinder causing air to transfer, or equalise, between both cylinders. Once the sound of high-pressure air moving between the two cylinders was completed, indicated by silence, the reserve cylinder was closed again. When this equalisation process was completed twice the diver would surface, ensuring sufficient air had remained in his set for the last part of the dive.

As mentioned in the first chapter, I had failed this simple process during my diver aptitude test while wearing weighted boots and as a result, knew firsthand how panic had quickly overwhelmed me. Therefore, it was concern that some of the divers on the necklace were approaching similar panic that influenced my decision to cut the line.

When the necklace parted, both sides of the line were pulled upwards, and I followed them to the surface, where thankfully, all divers were recovered without further incident.

Bagsy challenged my use of the knife, not overly happy at my actions. I countered by explaining the situation and reinforcing my concern asked what he would have done in the same case. He accepted I had acted appropriately, given the circumstances, but suggested I didn't make a habit of it.

The final dip was in the pot. On the morning of day-3 of deep dips, one of the students complained of a niggle in his right wrist. We hadn't left Vernon at this stage, so we hopped in the base's chamber for what turned out to be a 6-hour precautionary treatment. The student was okay but would be completing his training with another course.

Processing my discharge papers had dragged on and on, but I finally left Victoria Barracks, in Portsmouth, in late February 1982.

My interview with 'Northerns' had been a success, and I started work as a commercial diver a couple of weeks later.

News Headline:

Five weeks later - The Ministry of Defence is recalling members of the Parachute Regiment and the Royal Marines from leave following the invasion of the Falkland Islands by Argentinian armed forces. The Royal Navy is hurriedly loading ships as a task force prepares to sail south, with some special operations units already on route to Ascension Island, which is located about halfway to the Falklands in the mid-Atlantic.

CHAPTER 4

Northern Divers (Different to the Navy - Mates off to War)

A LONG-STANDING COMMERCIAL DIVE COMPANY owned by a former CD-2, 'Notherns' undertook both offshore and onshore work from offices in East Yorkshire and Aberdeenshire. Their headquarters consisted of a couple of prefabricated offices and a large warehouse backing onto the river Hull, a dirty brown sludge that flowed through the town of the same name and then into the much larger dirty brown river Humber. The navy had prepared me well for onshore commercial diving.

My first dip was to be under a harbour tug located at Immingham Docks, west of the town of Grimsby on the south bank of the Humber. Grim-sby summed up the shit hole that was Immingham Docks of the early eighties. Opened in the nineteen hundreds, they looked as though no rubbish had been picked up since, let alone upgrades to modern equipment.

We were there to inspect the tugs Kort Nozzle, a large propeller within a short ducted-tunnel (the nozzle) that increased the propellers efficiency. It was a routine inspection to check for blade damage between their tips and the inner surface of the nozzle.

Getting dressed in a zip-entry dry-bag (luxury), and donning a commercial weight belt with supporting shoulder straps (cumbersome and heavy), another luxury was the KMB10. Previously I had only used it on deep dips. One difference that was a little concerning though was the lack of fins. Rufus, a forty-year-old Hull boy and supervisor with

Northerns, had advised that fins might be all right for navy jobs but, 'int commercial world they just get int way mate.'

Not wanting to push my preference to wear fins in the new environment that I hoped to succeed in, feeling somewhat naked, I stepped off the 2m wharf without them. Despite the heavy weight belt I resurfaced without drama, the air in my dry-bag supporting me well enough and I swam breaststroke to the stern of the tug and descended after venting minimal air from my cuff. Able to keep contact with the hull, I soon found the Kort Nozzle and commenced a standard inspection.

It was a short dive, but I had broken the psychological barrier of something new. More importantly, Rufus was happy, and I settled into the routine of being a commercial diver. A week later we would be heading back to the Immingham Docks for a regular job that Northerns undertook.

Watching the news the night before our return trip, the third story in got my attention. Apparently some Argentinian scrap metal workers had landed on a remote British island called South Georgia, never heard of it, and high-level political talks were underway to put an end to their planned removal of steel from an old whaling station. The part that got my attention though was the report that the navy was sending their Antarctic research vessel HMS Endurance from the Falkland Islands, never heard of them either, to remove the scrap workers by force if necessary. I knew a sailor on the Endurance; he had competed in the navy novices boxing with me. He'd told of the cushy times aboard the survey ship compared to a traditional warship, and that they always had a detachment of Royal Marines on board being so far from home – just in case. Maybe some scrap metal workers were about to get their arses kicked?

Entrance from the sea to the Immingham docks was through huge lock gates sitting in around 30-feet of water. These giant gates were at least 50-feet high, top to bottom, and were opened and closed by machinery pulling on anchor cables attached to either side. Northerns were contracted to inspect this cable and to clear any debris from the base of each lock gate a couple of times a year, or if a problem opening them ever eventuated.

My job then was to descend against the harbour wall, made of stone blocks, in the usual zero visibility and then to follow the wall to the gate to commence the first task of rubbish removal. Unfortunately, the closest we could set up our dive station meant that I would have a 'walk' of around 50-feet to reach the base of the lock gates. Not believing this to be much of a challenge, I pulled on the usual gear and descended 20-feet down our purposely-positioned ladder and dropped into the shitty water.

I had a new supervisor this time, another forty-something Hull boy called Gordon. He was a very experienced diver, but one not apparently interested in sharing anything much with the new boy unless it was a need to 'just get on wivit mate' so we could 'get t'slather shop' for a few pints on the way home. The standby was another old hand and Hull boy called Bob, 30-ish; but he looked as old as Gordon. These blokes obviously spent more time in the 'slather shop' than a typical CD!

Another point I forgot to mention was the lack of a bailout for shallow dives. When I'd questioned this, I was on the receiving end of some more piss taking.

"Fookin navy! Need their fookin ands owldin all't fookin time by looks of it."

As I stepped off the ladder and swam over to the wall, with no fins, I was conscious of the lack of weight on my back too. But hey, the pay was a damn sight better, and it was just something new. I would get used to it.

With my right hand on the wall feeling one stone after the other as I descended, I noticed my downward speed increasing rapidly. I was blowing against the nasal-plate of the KMB10 continuously and wondered where the bloody bottom was? Gordon had told me it was 'bout twenty feet mate, just get on wivit', but I was sure it was deeper than that judging by the amount of pressure on my ears and dry-bag.

I smacked into the bottom a moment later and ended up on my back. Lying there assessing my situation, I called the surface.

"Topside, diver one's on the bottom."

There was no reply.

"Topside, topside, this is diver one, I'm on the bottom."

Still nothing? Comms must have shit themselves.

Reaching for my umbilical I gave one pull to signal arrival. The umbilical was tight initially, but then I was given more. They must think I want some slack? Oh well, this isn't the navy; I'd best get on with it.

Awkwardly rolling over in the darkness in an effort to stand up, the pressure on my dry-bag reinforced its presence. Imagine wearing clothes that are too small; you can't bend your knees or elbows fully, pressure everywhere. It wasn't unbearable, but as there was no suit-inflation that was fortunate. Finally, on my feet, I put my right hand against the wall and maintaining contact commenced the slow plod towards the lock gates while holding onto the umbilical with my left hand.

'Did Gordon say not to bother with signals?'

Asking myself all sorts of questions, I moved slowly over years of debris now resting at the bottom of the dock as the back of my knees and other folds of skin pinched against the pressure. There were old prams; bits of wooden pallets, a chunk of steel, breezeblocks, what I thought was an old cupboard and a bunch of other stuff my mind just labelled as shite.

Taking another step forward, probably 20-feet from the ladder and 30-feet from the lock gate, my left hand was pulled backwards. The umbilical had snagged.

Not a big issue, I pulled it towards me hoping to break it free.

'This wouldn't have been necessary if I had a navy tender' I told myself, then asserting, 'but this was different, that's all, suck it up!'.

Despite assertive pulls the umbilical wouldn't come free, so I began backtracking to the snag to free it, when suddenly; my inhalation caused the oral-nasal to crush hard up against my face. I had no air!

Instinctively my left hand came up to the dial-a-breath and began winding. At the same time my right hand went for the defogger and cracked this too, but both devices failed to provide the air I needed. There was still a vacuum in the oral-nasal, and I had barely any air left in my lungs. Fear made itself known as adrenaline stung my bladder, but more instinct made me release the defogger and grab the reserve. The moment I cracked this valve though, I recalled Rufus's words from my first dip.

'We don't use bailouts on shallow dips mate; they just get int fookin way.'

Fuck!

One last option remained. The regulator had a manual purge button; maybe the dial-a-breath was broken? Moving my right index finger to the centre of the regulator I pushed this hard. Nothing happened.

Perhaps 3-seconds had passed since my first breathing restriction. Every valve on the KMB10 had failed, I had no comms to the surface, I was wearing a bloody heavy weight belt that couldn't be ditched quickly, my tender wasn't doing his job and my umbilical was fouled. The no-nonsense advice passed on by Fleet Chief Petty Officer John Dadd, The head of Horsea Island dive school, reverberated through my mind.

"If you take shortcuts in this game boys', one thing's certain. You'll end up dead real quick."

Back in Oban three-years before, SD-28 had come up with an ingenious plan to use only full cylinders of mixed-gas when operating the portable 'booster pump' to refill our smaller CDBA mixed-gas cylinders. The booster pump had two, one meter long handles that two divers pumped up and down to transfer the gas from large cylinders to the smaller ones. This job was a pain in the arse, made much more difficult when the large cylinders were almost depleted of their contents. It was back breaking work that made us stay longer than desired at the end of daily operations.

Under our truck was a pile of cylinders marked FULL and M.T. (empty). In between these was a pile of cylinders not quite M.T., but very close to it.

We obviously wanted to use the FULL ones to ease our pain, but as both Psycho and John Dadd (visiting from Horsea Island) were adamant that all cylinders were to be completely emptied before a full one was used, we had a problem.

Smart guys that we were though, one evening after recharging was completed we cracked the almost M.T. cylinders, just a fraction (no tell-tale noise), knowing they would be completely M.T. by morning. The perfect crime, that would ensure selection of FULL ones at the end of diving the next day. How clever were we? Not very as it turned out! You see we hadn't worked out that both Psycho and John Dadd had done a whole lot more diving than us and that they likely knew we were to try such a trick. The next morning we suffered.

Up above Oban is a folly that looks like a mini-Colosseum. Under a kilometre from the wharf as the crow flies, it is much longer by road and path. We were directed to unload all the dive tenders equipment, Geminis, large cylinders and all, transport it all up the windy roads and paths leading up to the folly while wearing dry-bags and thick woolly undersuits. To top off the pain, the sun came out as we struggled through the punishment. Sun in Oban, really? Give us a break!

When up at the folly we then had to re-charge all the sets that Psycho and John Dadd had kindly emptied for us. Once this was completed, we returned all the gear to the dive tender where operations for the day began. We didn't leave harbour though. Instead, we rigged sets for 12lpm and did a shore dive on the end of a lifeline. The water was only a couple of meters deep at the end of our lines meaning rocks had to be grabbed to maintain negative buoyancy – for if a fin was seen on the surface, we were in for yet more punishment.

We finally finished the day about 11 pm and I for one never cracked another cylinder ever again. But numerous shortcuts could be taken when diving, and at Northerns, I had a list that was growing.

In the seconds following the air failure, I distinctly remember my mind processing a whole lot of information. Included in this bombardment of options was a voice telling me that my death would be used as a lesson for future CD's, 'if you ever take shortcuts you will end up like Mac Macfarlane, he…' but I wasn't ready to die just yet.

I had dismissed removal of the weight belt as an option though. With its two shoulder straps and a large pin located between a series of metal eyes at the waist, even if I got it off quick enough it was likely to foul on my umbilical as I tried to shake it free, not to mention the umbilical was still snagged. Another option was to ditch the KMB10 and swim up, but with the pressure on my dry-bag producing slightly negative buoyancy and not wearing fins I doubted this would work either. Instead, my buzzing mind decided to walk back to the ladder by following the umbilical. But this too was a dumb choice that would never work! Even so, my racing mind figured that if I lost consciousness having the KMB10 in place should prevent water entering my lungs (therefore making resuscitation more effective) if my elite surface crew ever realised I was in trouble?

Perhaps 5-seconds had passed since the air failure. In the midst of my desperation, I elected to use the remaining air in my lungs in the hope of alerting the surface – despite the comms failure.

"No gas, no gas, no gas…"

I pulled another couple of steps closer to the umbilicals snag; my lungs were stinging with pain as the build-up of CO_2 begged me to breathe. When suddenly, vast volumes of air came blasting into the hat. The neoprene hood of the KMB10 pulled upwards with the enormous quantity of air now inside it, and I had to pull it down assertively to keep it in place. Quickly shutting off the valves, I felt my umbilical pull tight and break free of the snag. I started travelling up, fast!

Black...black...dark brown...surface; Immingham docks never looked more beautiful! I was being pulled on my back with a gloomy grey sky above producing a light shower of rain.

I bumped into the ladder and turned around. Gordon was a couple of rungs down and moving towards me. I climbed out to my waist, pulled off two of the spider-band connections and pulled the hood over my head.

"What's your fookin problem!?" Gordon challenged.

My fucking problem!

"I had a complete gas failure, that's what! None of the valves worked either!"

I could see cogs turning in Gordon's head.

"What number ats that bastard?"

I turned it around to look at the face.

"Seven."

"Oh, that's Billy's owld hat; if it does that again just bash fook outa reg. It happens once int'while."

Welcome to commercial diving Mick. It was not the navy, and you had better start looking out for yourself if you hoped to see the benefit of all the money you were now making. Despite my internal proclamation, I put the hat back on and completed the job. What could possibly go wrong?

The news story that had gained my attention had continued to build over subsequent nights. Now, in an emerging crisis for the British government, some Argentine soldiers had landed on South Georgia before Endurance's arrival, and by all accounts, they were there to protect the scrap metal workers.

Argentina had just given the finger to Britain's Prime Minister, Margaret Thatcher. Additionally, some warships in Gibraltar for Exercise Springtrain, NATO's annual war game, were being recalled to Britain. It looked like the government would have its hands full sorting this little diplomatic mess out.

Late in my fourth week with Northerns we were tasked with clearing a blocked water inlet to a power station. This inlet was a concrete tunnel about 5-feet in diameter that connected with another shitty brown river. To clear the pipe, full of shitty brown river mud, we were going to use a fire hose. The nozzle connected to this had two handles made of concrete-reinforcing-bar that were set in a block of concrete the size of a standard telephone directory. The weight was there to aid the diver to control the nozzle underwater.

Descending in my KMB10, still without fins or bailout, I moved down a ladder into a large concrete pit on the power station side of the inlet. I hopped into the water about 10-feet below the upper edge of the pit, and the fire hose was lowered to me, and then swimming over to the wall where the inlet was located, I left the surface.

It was shallow, about 15-feet, but no light made it past an inch in depth due to the level of mud in the water. On reaching the bottom, my feet sank into knee-deep mud, but I couldn't feel the concrete floor of the pit. In front of me, all I could feel was mud, no inlet, so I started sweeping with my free hand.

With my hand just above head height, I felt a curved concrete edge – the top of the inlet. Except for this everything else was mud. It was as though the power station was severely constipated and in need of an enema. It was about to get one!

Taking the nozzle in both hands, I braced my legs in the mud and leaned forward.

"Make it hot."

The simple command used for activation of any equipment from air lances, cutting or welding gear and was actioned immediately. As the water jet rushed forward, I was forced backwards, and it was a major struggle to control the hose even with its added concrete ballast. After about a minute I wanted to check my progress.

"Make it cold."

Dropping the nozzle to the mud, I reached forward to the curved edge I had found before. This was now more prominent, and I had cleared about a foot of mud from inside the inlet-tunnel. Running my hands around the edge, I could feel about half of the tunnel's circumference and was confident I could make this work.

"Make it hot."

After about 10-minutes of battling away, I had cleared a meter of mud from the tunnel entrance and was able to get inside and brace against the solid concrete. This bonus gave me more control, and I pushed forward.

It took 90-minutes, but finally, there was no more concrete as I broke free into the river.

Returning to the surface, when I came off air I found that mud was caked to the inside of the hood, my hair, nostrils and ears. I had been told early in the navy that diving was like underwater labouring, but I doubt the person giving this advice ever envisaged this shitty job.

On Monday the 29th of March we were tasked with a salvage job at Goole docks located towards the head of the Humber. Apparently, a ship maneuvering from its berth had reversed into a 100-foot long barge that had subsequently sunk at its berth.

As we drove up the M62 towards Goole that morning, news on the radio was implying a chaotic situation developing in the South Atlantic. Lord Carrington, Britain's Foreign Minister, was in talks with the Americans, John Nott, the Defence Minister, was in negotiations with Armed Forces Commanders and Argentina's President Galtieri was apparently telling them all to go and fuck themselves.

A decision had to be made over South Georgia, and it looked like, from the strategic perspective of a disgruntled Able Seaman at least, that action, and not words would be required to resolve it; but so far all the British government appeared to be doing was talking. Apparently, HMS Endurance had been ordered to return to the Falklands and then back to South Georgia as the high-level indecision continued. What a bloody fiasco!

With a hint at what was probably feared by the government though, a CD mate still in the navy (waiting to 'get outside' through the same process I had taken) had called over the weekend to tell me that his volunteer redundancy had been put on hold, 'for some fucking reason.'

Arriving in Goole the owner of a salvage company who had sub-contracted Northerns to recover the barge, ironically called Salvager, met us at the wharf. He was about 60-ish, nuggetty, ham-fisted, the sort of bloke you gave one glance and knew he'd been doing this type of work all his life.

"I have a lift barge due tomorrow. For now, we can get the inspection done and start rigging lift lines. The ship that hit it was stuck in astern, impacted at about five knots too, at the starboard bow."

This was going to be a challenge that would take some time to complete. I was in for a long cold couple of days.

Another new diver to Northerns who had just returned from a stint offshore would be working with us. Steve was a nice bloke about my age who had finished his training the year before at the commercial school in Fort William, north of Oban. He and I would rotate through the water and Griff, another old hand Hull boy who enjoyed the slather shop, would manage the surface and liaise with the salvage company owner.

A reasonable crowd had gathered as we prepared to dive thanks to the local radio and newspaper providing daily updates of the 'dramatic events' since the sinking.

I dived first, but without fins again, descending where the stern was positioned judging by a broken mooring line still attached to the wharf. About 15-feet below the surface I contacted the deck of the barge and moved up the port side, which was positioned about a meter from the dock wall. It was a typical river barge with flat upper deck, half a dozen large hatches and a small wheelhouse at the stern. Some of the hatch covers were missing, but as I continued towards the bow, the port side appeared undamaged – as was expected.

Turning aft from the bow along the starboard side, I noticed significant damage almost immediately. I could feel jagged steel that had been pushed inwards over an area larger than my extended body. At the centre of this large indentation was a hole about the size of an average fridge. This had penetrated the hull at the bow and corresponded with reports of the collision and that, 'it sank bow first.'

On return to the surface I gave my report to Griff, the salvage company owner and a couple of port authority people waiting with the even larger crowd than before I'd dived. We were the main news story of the day in Goole, the drama unfolding in the South Atlantic had apparently been pushed to the back burner.

As we prepared to position some wrist-thick lifting wires, the rain became heavier, and the once enthusiastic crowd diminished and then finally disappeared altogether. Their departure was probably due to the methodical pace at which we worked, akin to watching paint dry, the worsening conditions and realisation that nothing exciting was going to happen for quite some time.

As we continued to set up on the surface, Griff gave me some good news. I was officially a full-time employee with Northerns. Up until that point I had just been a casual but apparently reports from Gordon and Rufus to Tony Starling, the owner, had all been positive.

I'd had just a brief chat with Tony during my interview process. He was around fifty, a very likeable individual who was keen to hear about the modern diving branch. He told me that Northerns were bidding for a contract to remove WW2 ordnance from a Libyan harbour and that if he was successful, I was to be part of that job. Exciting times indeed, with a massive bonus for the hazardous work too; I could live with the differences to the navy.

We completed our set up, and Griff confirmed the plan before I hopped back in the water.

"Mick we need the first wire passed through the rudder aperture. When you're in position we'll lower it to you, ok?"

The rudder aperture was a very narrow slot where the keel rose up to the stern. The large rudder took up most of this space, there was no propeller, and we would use it to anchor the aft lift wire. This seemed like a pretty straightforward job that I was sure your average BSAC diver could accomplish.

"Not a problem Stew, should take about twenty minutes."

Everything started well. I positioned at the outboard side of the aperture with a rope line in hand and had the boys lower away as I pulled in to guide the steel wire towards my position. Comms were good; I wasn't wearing a bailout or fins, but was becoming more comfortable without them (fins not bailout) and had an excellent minds-eye image of the job in front of me as I pulled the rope through the tight space of the aperture. Then the rope fouled... keeping this part of the story simple (the task wasn't), I eventually returned to the surface with the wire in place. Griff, with roll-up hanging from the corner of his mouth and apparently keen to get to the slather shop, took time to comment on my performance.

"Not bad Mick, but twenty minutes? I think you need a new watch mate."

I had been in the water for a little under three hours.

Northerns was indeed very different to the navy. Not just safety wise, although this remained an issue for me. The other difference was a simple one and perhaps a bit obvious, at Northerns I was just a diver.

Let me explain. In the navy, although my title was Able Seamen Clearance Diver, this did not mean 'just a diver'. The 'seaman' part meant that I had to clean toilets, paint ships, do guard duty and, rarely thankfully, march on a parade ground. Furthermore, someone typically resembling a Monty Python upper-class twit would always reinforce that being a diver was a secondary duty.

'Remember Macfarlane; you are first and foremost a seaman of the *Royal* Navy.'

So, although I thoroughly enjoyed the Clearance Diving aspect of navy life, I could have done without a fair chunk of the seaman part. Therefore, despite the higher risk of underwater death at Northerns, all I had to do was dive, and dive regularly for much higher pay. I was having a ball! But it wasn't all beer-and-skittles.

On day two of the job, Steve got in the water about half-past nine after discussion with the salvage operator and equipment positioning was completed. He was going to place a line under the bow and through 'fairleads' on the deck. His job was going to be harder than mine though, as the keel was in the mud and he would have to work the heavy wire underneath it.

I was acting as his standby, Griff his tender, and we watched as he worked away into the early afternoon. We were both bored out of our brains as the location of his bubbles fizzing to the surface showed his progress with the job. It was slow. We paused for a short bite to eat and got on with it.

Another difference I noticed to navy diving where we typically dived for no more than an hour before being relieved was that with Northerns, if you were the diver, you dived, all day if necessary until the work was completed. This had pros and cons. Steve's next job was to connect the fore and aft lift wires to the 'big rig' of the lift barge now moored in the dock with its crane positioned over Salvager.

This was to be another of those simple-in-theory tasks. You know, just hook four wire eyes onto the hook, winch in, barge raised to the surface, job done. He had been in the water for an hour when the comms box sparked up.

"Topside, diver one, Griff I'm going to need some more rope and Mick to give me a hand."

Griff looked at me and then raised his eyebrows.

"How much rope Steve and what do you need Mick for?"

There was a pause. Watching Steve's bubbles, I could almost see his brain formulating a response.

"About five foot should do it. I don't need Mick right off, but when I ave shackles rigged I'll need im to help pull up ont line, so I can get em dunup."

Steve was working fairly hard; his breathing through the comms box was quick and correlated with the amount of bubbles coming to the surface. The shackles he was talking about were big heavy bastards too! A man's grip would just about get around their circumference, and the pin would have made a good club.

We passed him the line, and about half an hour later he was ready. I swam over to the large hook; or rather the collection of wires supporting the hook that was about a meter below the surface and took the length of 5-foot rope from Steve's outstretched hand after he tapped my leg with it.

I wasn't exactly sure what he was doing, but guessed that he wanted me to hold a shackle by the hook as he fitted the pin - the two lift wire eyes each had a shackle fitted so they could reach the large hook.

I could feel Steve with my feet as he worked away, still in zero visibility, even though he was just a meter or so from the surface. Another half an hour went by.

"Diver one, topside, how's it going Steve?"

The owner of the barge, who was paying a lot of money for the salvage operation, had turned up and was looking impatient standing alongside Griff.

I was beginning to feel cold after just a short time bobbing about on the surface, Steve must have been bloody freezing, and divers don't think straight when they are cold. His movements had been slowing, indicating to me that he was running out of ideas, but he didn't want to admit defeat and hand over just yet, so he persevered. Griff caught my eyes.

"Mick, you want a dip?"

I knew the question would be coming at some stage, but no, I didn't. It was about 3 pm on a particularly cold East Yorkshire winter day; there was intermittent rain and a low overcast making for an exceptionally gloomy atmosphere. All I had been thinking about was getting out of the dry-bag, having a piss and then a few pints after we knocked off. Worst case I would be starting again tomorrow if Steve hadn't finished the job.

Fuck!

"Yeah, ok Griff."

Griff looked relieved and 15-minutes later, after a piss, I was swimming over to the hook.

Descending down the crane wires, I found that Steve had connected up the two aft wires to the hook with their shackles. The forward shackles, connected together, were still hanging with their wires about a foot below the hook, attached to the closest shackle by the 5-foot length of rope he had requested.

Giving a tug on this rope, I immediately 'saw' that Steve had been making things hard for himself. Where he had secured the rope meant that the shackle would be pulled up on an angle, making it very difficult, if not impossible to align it sufficiently to get the pin inserted when the open holes of the shackle were pulled above the inner surface of the hook.

Half our problem was the length of the lift wires. They were not quite long enough, hence the need for shackles, and even had we lowered the hook to the deck of Salvager the wheelhouse would have presented an obstacle further hindering the wires length. We were stuck doing this suspended mid-water.

"Topside, diver one, Griff can you get me two, eight-foot lengths of rope mate?"

"On its way Mick."

I secured an end of each rope onto the eyes of the lift wires and then took these up, above the main hook, pulled in to take the weight and then secured them both, then removed the old 5-foot length of rope. Returning to the first shackle, I removed the pin and pulled the shackle clear of the eye, then re-fit the shackle (inverted) over the hook and replaced the pin; repeating the process with the second shackle.

I now had the two shackles sitting on the hook, pins lowermost, wire eyes about a foot from each connected by a length of rope. All I had to do now was pull up the eye to the correct height, connect the shackle to the eye and bobs your uncle.

"Diver one, topside, how's it going Mick.

When Griff called, I was at the precarious stage of trying to position the first shackle pin. I had the lift rope tied around my foot applying tension to adjust the angle and height of the eye sufficiently, as I wiggled the wire with my left hand. The shackle pin in my right hand was threatening to fall as I struggled to push it through the wire eye that was being pulled closed by the same force I was using to hold it in place. I was concentrating so hard I didn't have time to talk.

"Diver one, Mick, this is Griff, how's it going?"

"Hang on!"

I just couldn't get the eye wide enough. Fuck! I was so close. It wasn't going to work though; I would have to re-rig the rope line.

"Working on it Griff, connecting up the first shackle, shouldn't be long."

Hopefully, that was sufficient bullshit to keep the owner off his back.

Using the original 5-foot length of rope, I secured the first wire eye to the hook. Then I retied the other rope below the eye (should have done it this way the first time) and repositioned myself to try again. As I pulled up this time (pushing downwards with my foot), the eye was coming to the shackle, open wide and ready to receive the pin. Yes! As the eye passed the height of the shackle pin, I unscrewed it and pushed it through with relative ease, quickly screwing it home.

"Topside, diver one, Griff first shackle's secure, doing the last one now."

"Roger that, Mick."

I began rigging the second line the same way, but when I unscrewed the shackle pin with my numb hands, I dropped it!

Fuck, fuck, fuck!

'Settle down wanker, it's made of steel and has sunk directly below you to the steel deck of the barge.'

"Topside, diver one, Griff, give me four meters of slack thanks, mate."

I felt the slack and with the rope line secure I hung from the hook keeping my body as straight as possible and then dropped. Impacting the deck a couple of seconds later, I continued down to my knees and began a cautious search with my hands, fingers mentally crossed. Endless circular searches proved a dividend though, and I found the pin on the second sweep.

With pin firmly in one hand, I moved along the deck to one of the aft lift wires and used this to assist myself back to the hook to complete the task.

With everything in place, I completed a final inspection of all wires and shackles and returned to the surface. It was dark, and streetlights were on. I had been in the water for 3-hours and 40-minutes. I was bloody freezing!

The owner had gone home, which was good because he didn't witness what happened next.

The crane commenced a cautious winch-in, and we began to see the wheelhouse appear. Some fog was rolling in around the docks too, adding to the tension. Just when the decks were becoming visible though, the large hook of the crane reached its stop with Salvager, decks just below the surface of the water, not quite salvaged. The wires would have to be re-rigged!

I completed six more dives on that job, two of which were more than three hours duration. We were there for four days only, but I logged over a thousand minutes. As a comparison, it had taken me around 4-months to record the same amount of time after qualifying as a CD, and that was diving with every available opportunity.

That Thursday night celebration in the slaver shop was a big one. But with sore heads the next day, the 2nd of April 1982, comprehending the news that Argentina had taken the Falkland Islands by force was even harder to process. Were we going to war? The only war I had ever really contemplated involved 'instant buckets of sunshine' and either a swift end or a painfully bleak outlook in a nuclear winter. However this war played out though, I shuddered at the thought of a bunch of Nigeys' leading people I knew into battle.

As Britain's task force comprising of around 100 ships began departing from various ports the following Monday. I boarded a train to Aberdeen for a period of secondment to Northerns Scottish operations.

After a night in a sleeper compartment, I woke to the sound of squeaks and whistles as the train made its slow approach into Aberdeen station. Walking through the ticket barrier, I made eye contact with a 40-something solidly built man with red hair.

"Hello, Mick is it? I'm Hamish; did ye have a pleasant journey?"

Hamish was one of the Aberdeen dive supervisors. He had a very heavy Scottish accent that I could just follow, missing every third or fourth word.

We loaded my gear into a long wheelbase Land Rover and headed north out of the city and onto a coastal road. After driving through some small villages, we arrived at a small yard containing some prefabricated offices. Hamish took me inside and introduced me to Derek Tynemouth, Northerns Aberdeen manager.

"Hey Mick, welcome to sunny Scotland."

Derek was in his early thirties, didn't look as though he had spent his life in a slather shop, and had a persona that made the new boy feel welcome straight away. His midlands English accent was a damn sight easier on the ear too.

"So, you're an ex-CD Mick. It looks like you got out just at the right time judging by the shit fight on the news at the moment."

Derek was another former CD-2 who had left the navy after his second stint on a Hunter. We discussed likely scenarios for the diving branch, which included 'compass-swims' for 'beach-clearance' amongst the standard EOD operations.

Beach-clearance was a task CD's completed covertly to ensure there were no obstacles at intended landing sites. We practised this type of operation during the baby diver course using a compass-board while swimming on O2. The process we followed was not dissimilar to that used by WW2 frogmen who attached limpet mines to enemy ships.

Working in pairs, we swam from point 'A' to point 'B' and then onwards. The process required us to surface periodically to take compass bearings, which had to be done very stealthily so as not to alert the enemy – in our case Psycho, who was tracking our progress from the Dory.

With one diver remaining submerged, the diver with the compass board would ascend slowly as his buddy paid out on the buddy-line. When the compass board diver's eyes broke the surface, he would pull on the buddy-line, and his buddy would hold him with just half a head visible as the new compass bearing was set. When completed, 1-pull was relayed, and the diver was pulled down, slipping from view with hardly a ripple.

On such a dive at around 3 am one cold night with a good mate, Smudge using the compass board, I was following along with not much to do. We were in the middle of live-in-week; the final phase of O2 training at Horsea Island designed to verify if recruits really wanted to continue with the course. Our minds and bodies were somewhat strained, all the more so as the endless cold sapped strength and motivation.

To complete live-in-week, a recruit had to ignore this hardship and continue on robotically. This was essential, but also dangerous if the recruit switched off too much.

Finning close to the bank as we ascended to a suitable depth for Smudge to take another compass bearing, I bumped the bank. This collision resulted in my suit inflation connecting with a rock, and I was suddenly wide-awake as air rushed into my dry-bag. Quickly closing the valve, but not quick enough, air filled my legs, and I was pulled upwards feet first.

Tucking into a ball I desperately tried to vent my dry-bag, but the inevitable happened, and I broke the surface with a noticeable splash. As I urgently continued venting, I heard the alarming sound of the Dory's engine revving fast as Psycho closed on my position. As the last of the air escaped past my cuff, I saw Psycho standing in the Dory, arms raised above his head holding his 'whacking stick'.

This weapon was a sawn-off paddle wrapped with neoprene on the striking end. Psycho used this to issue summary punishments, the neoprene meaning he could swing with full force and not kill an under-performing recruit.

As my mask slipped below the surface, aided my Smudge's assertive pulling, I saw the whacking stick coming down fast. It struck my head with noticeable force, but I was quickly out of harm's way thanks to Smudge. We continued with the task without further incident, but I was to receive a serious dressing down as we recharged to commence the next dip at 5-am.

Knowing that CD's would likely be undertaking such tasks in the coming weeks, I reflected on Psycho's teaching methods: old school yes, overtly aggressive yes, but essential? Considering that CD's may well face a bullet and not a whacking stick if they broke surface during upcoming operations, absolutely!

Derek introduced me to some other divers, and we prepped some equipment for a job due to start the next day. Hamish and another diver, Patrice Lebbo and I would be heading to Aberdeen to start removal of an old slipway.

Patrice, a 5-foot 8-inch fit looking Frenchman with a round face and blond crew-cut, was a former 'Para-Commando'. I had never heard of this unit and asked if it was like the Foreign Legion. Read the next bit with a heavy French accent.

"Ha! The Legion is made up of a bunch of un-disciplined psychopaths that would kill each other just as quickly as the enemy. No. We were similar to your marines or paratroopers."

Patrice had a cheeky grin and was forever telling stories about Para-Commando operations in Africa where he fought the 'Nig-gair'. Obviously not one for political correctness, he was nonetheless a good diver.

The slipway we were tasked to remove consisted of two ramps about 20m wide that extended into the water about 30-40m. The old wooden beams running into the harbour were about 2-foot thick and covered in mud. At their deepest point they were at about 20-feet, maybe 25-feet underwater. Shallow, but we would have to expose them to get the slings fitted and to ensure excessive suction wouldn't overload the crane as the beams were pulled from the mud.

To clear the mud, we would be using an 'air-lift'. I had trained with these at Horsea Island during 'tool-week', but the equipment I had used then was a baby compared to the monster I saw being prepared on the wharf.

There was a 30-foot long drainpipe, but half a meter in diameter. Attached to the side of this was another pipe, smaller in diameter than a normal drainpipe, with its opening attached via a 90-degree elbow to the 'working-end' of the air-lift. An airline from a large compressor was connected to the smaller pipe and air was pushed down this and then into the larger pipe to make it work. As the air was pumped into the larger pipe, it then rushed up to the surface, inside the pipe, expanding rapidly thanks to Mr Boyle. And as this occurred, an area of low pressure was created at the working-end of the air-lift and this, in turn, caused anything in the immediate vicinity to be 'lifted' by the 'air'.

The navy air-lift I'd used was a relatively small plastic pipe that I had control of with a small valve at the working end, basically pretty easy to operate. To control the beast on the harbour though I would relay directions to Hamish, via the comms box, who would then use a radio to direct the crane driver to move the air-lift as I required.

Getting dressed on the wharf closest to the slipway, I noticed that there was a bailout with the KMB10. Happy days. Putting this on my back and then fitting the weight belt, Patrice picked up my umbilical, and we began to move over to the ladder when Hamish spoke.

"Are ye nay taking fins with ye, Mick?"

He was holding a pair in his hands and looking at me as though I was a child who had forgotten their lunch box.

"Oh, ah, yeah, cheers Hamish."

He saw the surprise in my eyes and grinned.

"I guess ye're used tay the Hull way o doing things by noow, aren't ye?"

Again, my expression must have said it all.

"Doonay worry Mick, fins and bailouts are standard equipment up ere."

'Finning' away from the ladder, feeling truly confident for the first time as a commercial diver, I lined up with the nearest wooden beam 30-feet from the slipway ramp and descended.

Touching mud first, a short sweep of my hands located the 2-foot thick beam, or more precisely, about six inches of it prominent above the mud. I finned deeper, following the beam until it disappeared into the harbour bottom.

"Topside, diver one, Hamish I'm ready for the air-lift."

"Diver one, topside, roger Mick, it's on its way doown."

Up above I pictured the 30-foot long pipe being lifted by the crane and slewing out over the harbour to above my position, with Hamish directing the crane driver to where my bubbles where.

"Diver one, topside, in the water noow Mick, it's directly above ye."

Straddling the beam with my knees, I felt above my head, and about a minute later I contacted the air-lift. It was moving very slowly downwards as Hamish was no doubt being cautious. The air-lift was going to land about 3-feet to my right though. Picturing my position in relation to the crane, I called Hamish.

"Topside, diver one, Hamish, slew right, three feet."

"Slew right, three feet?"

"Roger, right, three feet."

"Diver one, topside, slewing right, three feet."

How good was this! I even had someone who knew how to communicate and appeared genuinely concerned about my welfare too. By the time the airlift had moved to the required position, it was still 1-foot above the beam. I waited until this was 3-inches above and then called 'all stop'. Feeling around the opening of the pipe, I confirmed it was in the correct position and then checked my umbilical was clear.

"Make it hot."

I felt vibration in the air-lift that I was holding in a single-arm hug with my head against the pipe and could hear the sound of low pressure air rumbling away. It was a bit of an anti-climax though! I had expected a deafening roar and without this noise wondered how effective the air-lift was.

Moving my spare hand down to the bottom of the pipe, I cautiously eased two of my gloved fingers inside. Bam! It was as though a giant hand grabbed at them and adrenaline stabbed at every cell in my body. I pulled my hand back instantly, accompanied by a slight yelp, but fortunately, the only damage was my glove being ripped off to be rocketed up the pipe.

"Diver one, topside, are ye well Mick?"

I was breathing a little bit more rapidly, but apart from that everything was fine. It was nice to have a supervisor paying close attention to my every whimper though.

"Topside, diver one, all good Hamish, just shifting the air-lift."

I wasn't about to tell him I was a dickhead, but he had kind of worked out I was new to this type of work.

"Diver one, topside, that's why we have the crane, Mick."

The air-lift was very effective. Within an hour I had exposed the first beam to its end and was becoming much more comfortable using the crane via Hamish too. The air-lift was replaced with a sling, and I fitted this to the upper end of the beam and then surfaced, moving clear.

Seeing the massive wooden beam being pulled from the harbour was very satisfying, but watching Patrice at work the next day was even more so.

The water and mud blasting out of the top of the air-lift were like a giant broken fire hydrant. The roar this made accompanied by the sound of the compressor was thunderous. And where the air-lift disappeared into the harbour the brown water was churned up white as water and debris returned from its short flight. The power of this equipment was awesome but most impressive was the knowledge that down below a 5-foot 8-inch cheeky Frenchman was working the mouth of the beast.

From this job, we were heading inland to Loch Sloy to inspect the base of a dam wall and some fittings that were leaking in a hydroelectric power system. Loch Sloy was in the mountains on the west side of Loch Lomond and was a day's drive from Aberdeen. We loaded up vehicles and one trailer with a load of equipment and headed west.

Around 5 pm we pulled into a hotel a kilometre or so north of the tip of Loch Lomond. It was a classic country pub with some basic rooms, a mountain behind it, a few tourists, and some locals in for after work beers. This charming little place was to be our accommodation for the duration of the job.

After a quick dump of bags, we met at the bar. Hamish introduced me to another diver who had been with the Aberdeen branch of Northerns for about a year; he was an ex-CD like me and had served on the Faslane Team before getting outside.

With both of us holding similar views about the leadership of the RN, as the beers were consumed we soon entered a slagging session about our former commanders. This was a great form of entertainment. He told stories of former 'bosses' who demonstrated the equivalent capability to Nigey, and I reciprocated. He'd had one or two alarming near-misses too and gave blow by blow accounts of how simple fuckups had nearly ruined his day, but as we chatted away, he began to slag off the Fleet Team as a bunch of show-ponies and so I responded with equal force about the knuckle-draggers from Faslane. Before we were too shit faced though, we entered a serious discussion about the next few weeks and what this meant for mates heading south.

We both thought a war was inevitable, despite the US sending their Secretary of State (Alexander Haig) back and forth between Buenos Aries and London in a seemingly endless shuttle to find a diplomatic solution; Galtieri was just too much of an arrogant, egomaniac, twat to back down.

Although we didn't know for sure, we were positive the Fleet Team would be on their way, and that other Teams would no doubt be on standby to travel too (actual details of the Fleet Teams operations can be found in a book, *Diver* written by former CD-2 Tony Groom). What we knew for sure though, was that the biggest mobilization of Britain's armed forces was underway since the Second World War and they were heading to the bottom of the world to fight a battle with an enemy who was close to home. Even for disgruntled CD-3's, we knew this was not how you set up for success, and recent telegrams we'd both received that had reminded us we were on 'Immediate Reserve' and where to report 'If Mobilized' suggested that the government were also concerned about the potential outcome.

In a brief moment of sincerity we agreed that we would 'go' if called, but seconds later we were back to the slagging game.

"The dickheads would have a tough time finding us hiding up behind Loch Sloy though."

The drive up to Loch Sloy's dam wall the next morning took about 35-minutes. Heads were moderately sore, but fortunately, we were not going to be diving, just setting up the equipment required for the 50-foot descent from the dam wall to the water below it.

After one of the other divers, Eric had backed the trailer along the narrow roadway we commenced unloading gear next to a relatively small platform overhanging the loch side of the dam wall. To get to the water, we would be using a simple winch system permitting us to descend in a cage. The winch system, fitted to a steel frame, was lashed to anchor points on the platform. The final product resulted with the cage being suspended over the water with an inch gap to the platform.

We set up the panel, gas and umbilicals in the trailer and had the comms box in the back of a 4WD. All our personal gear remained in the vehicles, which included a SuperLite-17 for the diver and a KMB10 for the standby.

One of the dam's operators showed us inside the wall via a door in a centrally positioned concrete tower, where he pointed out a series of rollers from an internal walkway. Apparently, these were some sort of sealing system, but they weren't working as they were meant to be. Our task was to approach them from the other side and deposit a large amount of sawdust to complete the necessary sealing process. How this was meant to work I didn't know, but the task appeared simple enough, and so I didn't give the outcome much thought.

We were back at the pub by 3 pm and so had the danger of an even bigger night. Fortunately, though, we came to a collective decision to go for a walk up the mountain that greatly mitigated fuzzy heads the next day.

As we prepared to dive, some ships of the task force were already leaving Ascension Island on their journey south. I found myself thinking about mates serving on some of those ships, or divers who were probably on their way to Ascension Island by plane. I didn't envy them, not one bit, but I had more immediate concerns.

"So, Hamish, what's the plan if I need assistance?"

I was about to go on air wearing the SuperLite-17 and enter the cage, the slow-moving cage, which would take a while to deliver the standby; my new ex-CD mate, Chris, if I needed him. Hamish smiled.

"The plan is tey deliver Chris to ye by the cage. It's nay perfect, but ye have a bailout, and the job is less than thirty feet deep. Recovery will be one at ay time in the cage if needed. Are ye happy we that?"

Hamish delivered his plan evenly. It was far from perfect, but there was logic in his risk assessment. Essentially, all I was undertaking was a shallow dip and some minor underwater labouring. What could possibly go wrong?

I carried a couple of spanners and a short length of rope with me in the cage as I was lowered to the water. We had been advised that a small grate was blocking access to where we needed to deposit the sawdust and my first job would be to remove this and secure it out of the way.

After a short swim to the dam wall, I descended in the amazing visibility of around 15-feet. I followed the wall down in reducing visibility and arrived at an angled grate with visibility now about 5-feet, at a depth of 26-feet; the precise depth was reported by Hamish who was monitoring my progress on a Pneumofathometer. The 'Pnuemo' was an open hose attached to the umbilical and connected to a gauge on the panel. Hamish simply opened a valve which blew any water out of the Pnuemo hose, then shut the valve to let ambient water pressure push back up the hose to indicate my depth. In a worst-case scenario, Hamish could also increase the pressure to the Pnuemo to supply me an alternate air source.

This was my first time using a SuperLite-17, which was essentially a KMB10 with a solid hat. It had been noticeably heavy on the ride down in the cage, but once in the water the air it contained removed this hindrance and reinforced the need for its weighted handle attached to the top of the hat.

There was only one section of grating; it was about a meter square with four nuts securing it in place. I started on one of these, but it felt as though it would never budge. Moving along to the next nut, the spanner had an immediate effect, and I removed the nut and placed it on a lip of concrete above the grate. Working my way back to the stuck nut, Hamish's voice came into my ears far more clearly than with the KMB10.

"Diver one, topside, Mick I d'nay hear ye purging the hat?"

Hamish was obviously concerned about a CO_2 build up inside the confined space of the helmet. I thought the oral-nasal was supposed to take care of CO_2, but having never used the hat before I was happy to take Hamish's advice.

"Topside, diver one, roger Hamish, purging now."

I cracked the de-fog valve and let it run for a couple of seconds as bubbles escaped past non-return valves to the water around me.

After tapping the first troublesome nut firmly with the spanner and then trying again, it reluctantly came free. The grate weighted around 70-pounds, but with a bit of grunting I got it off the bolts, secured the line and moved it to the side. I then returned to the surface and collected a bag of sawdust from the cage, descended to the grid and slit the top of the bag with my knife.

The dam guy had told me to just poor it in from the grate, and the 'suction would do the rest'.

As I upended the bag, some of the sawdust descended further, but more than half of it just floated around me. Surely there was a better way?

"Topside, diver one, Hamish the first bag is in, but half is floating around me. Should I get the next one closer?"

"Diver one, topside, standby Mick."

I was called back to the cage and lifted to the dam wall. The dam guy wanted to check how things were going via the internal walkway and wanted me out of the way in case he had to operate equipment.

To my surprise the sawdust was doing as advertised, but more was needed. We emptied about 20 bags that day and 20 the next morning. The dam guy was happy and we packed up for the return to Aberdeen.

Back in the yard, we continued with some routine inspection work, but on Monday 22nd April we began readying equipment for an underwater concreting job. Northerns had a regular contract to repair the Aberdeen harbour wall. This was a long structure made of large boulders and concrete blocks that were regularly pounded by North Sea storms. The sea is a powerful beast, and the consequence of repeated wave action was dislodgement of boulders causing 'holes' to appear at the outer edge of the wall. Our job was to plug these holes before they had the chance to threaten the integrity of the wall itself.

Hamish and I headed down to the harbour on Tuesday to meet with the port authority representative to firm up start-plans for the following day. We met a young Billy Connolly look-alike, complete with a wild beard, but with broad shoulders and a bit of a beer gut. This was the port guy whose name I think was Robert.

"Ah s'oyu th'boys fray Nortns here fa tho job, ah?"

Thank God Hamish was there to translate!

"Aye, that's us."

"Okay, am Roert, thay arhbor mayger. Wail ave a gren doon tamora mornan, who much quipment da ye ave com'n doon?"

Hamish continued to discuss the operation and what we would be doing for around fifteen minutes. Well, at least I think he did; I still struggled to understand Hamish, let alone port Billy Connolly.

As we were leaving the office and heading over to the car, Hamish turned to look me in the eye.

"Mick, did ye understand what he said?"

I shrugged my shoulders.

"Not a word Hamish."

Hamish smiled.

"Neither did I."

With vehicles and trailer loaded we drove down to the harbour for an early start. Seven 'holes' had been identified, and we estimated at least a week's work to complete the repairs.

The radio that morning, the 24th April, was full of chest pumping rule Britannia messages. The Royal Marines had re-taken South Georgia without loss, and a wave of euphoria was sweeping through the British media, who for the main part had no idea of the actual conditions the armed forces were facing. Reading in a newspaper later that week, however, there was a hint of reality. Whiteout conditions had caused the loss of aircraft, and pure luck had prevented detonation of mines as Marines pushed towards their objective. Furthermore, the need to rescue Special Forces from a Gemini because an engine had failed (fucking shite Johnsons) had all suggested that this was not going to be a "walkover", as stated by the task force commander.

I was lowered into the water by a cage. It was the easiest way to clear the large boulders, and the cage could then be used to transport the equipment I needed.

The first hole was 5m wide. To repair this I was first going to build a wall of sandbags filled with concrete across the front. The boys on the surface loaded up bags and these were lowered to me in the cage. I simply laid these out like bricks and hammered lengths of reinforcing-bar between the bags. It was a slow and monotonous task, but at least I had a couple of feet visibility and gained some satisfaction from seeing the structure take place.

When the sandbag wall was high enough, the cage was replaced with a small hopper full of concrete that was lowered behind the wall. Using a shovel, I emptied the last of the concrete that defied gravity to fall through the gate and then repeated the process again and again, until the concrete was level with the sandbag wall. I didn't see the end of this job though, as I was called back to Hull to prepare for another that was to take place in the English Channel. I was back on the sleeper heading south before the weekend.

By the time Northerns had things sorted for the trip south to the English Channel we were into May and any doubt that full-blown conflict with Argentina could be avoided was long gone.

Sea Harriers had bombed targets at Port Stanley, and a nuclear submarine had sunk the cruiser, General Belgrano. This victory first created more euphoria, but then in some quarters, anger, as it was determined that Belgrano was heading away from the Falkland Islands. Despite the media challenges to this decision it is worth noting that surface warships will change course often if submarines are a threat, and so the Belgrano's course change may simply have been one of many. Either way, as a result of this action the bulk of the Argentinian navy, perhaps realising it wasn't a one-sided game, promptly returned to port and stayed there for the remainder of the war. Moreover, the decision to sink the Belgrano significantly reduced the threat for the thousands of men and (some) women aboard British ships relying on a fragile logistics chain such a long way from home.

By the time we had checked into the small seaside hotel at Lydd-on-sea, east of the bleak and wind-swept beach at Dungeness where an old nuclear power station was located, British forces had landed at San Carlos Water. Before these landings though, Britain had sustained significant loss after the Argentinian air force launched an Exocet Missile at HMS Sheffield in response to the sinking of the Belgrano. The impact, explosion and subsequent fires the Exocet produced killed many personnel and ultimately saw the Sheffield sink during a tow to safer waters. I think for much of the British public (and government) this was an, 'oh fuck, they can shoot back' moment of acceptance as to what was actually unfolding 'down south'. Consequently, the prior rule Britannia euphoria of the British media vanished overnight as the harsh realisation that victory was not a foregone conclusion hit home. Reinforcing this fact as British land forces pushed out from the San Carlos beachhead, the navy continued to sustain intense air assault from a determined and courageous foe.

As the battle in San Carlos (named 'Bomb Alley' by sailors) continued, aspersion and blame began to surface as weapons systems designed to protect the fleet, and those ashore proved ineffective or just failed. The frustrating and terrifying outcome of these deficiencies saw the loss of more ships and many more lives.

Contributing to the losses was the army's reasonably new Rapier surface to air missile system that experienced a range of technical issues. These included difficulty engaging aircraft attacking below certain elevations; such as, if it was positioned on a hillside and a jet was at sea level. Additionally, the Navy's Sea Cat and Sea Slug missile systems proved about as useful as they had during a NATO training exercise I was part of in the late seventies.

On this occasion we were tasked to shoot down a propeller powered pilotless target aircraft, or PTA, travelling from a known direction, at medium-altitude, at relatively slow speed - this was obviously not the attack profile chosen by the Argentinian air force. Nevertheless, as the hum of the propeller approached the ship (designed for air-warfare), the missile systems were brought to action, but unfortunately, it took four PTA passes and four Sea Cats before the PTA was hit. The admiral, captain and officers of this ship, the Flagship of the First Flotilla, rejoiced at their success during a shipboard cocktail party in the Bay of Naples afterwards. Although this was a splendid occasion full of tradition and formal dress, I don't think much was said about the performance of their Sea Cats, or it's big brother, the Sea Slug. This missile simply nosed over into the sea after its booster rockets were jettisoned, permitting yet another PTA to fly on past the weaponry of their air-warfare destroyer.

Alarmingly, this result wasn't anything new. Supervisors of mine who had completed close to 20-years service in the Royal Navy confirmed that this was not an unusual outcome of the once-a-year live fire exercises undertaken by the First Flotilla.

Despite the above, it is not debated that the hills around San Carlos, chosen to protect ships from Exocet, had created difficulty for radar systems to acquire and lock onto attacking aircraft. However, the continued missile system failures saw much of the fleet in San Carlos resort to WW2 weapons including Bofors 40mm guns, Oerlikon 20mm Machineguns and General Purpose Machineguns during air attack. Notwithstanding the courage of sailors, soldiers and occasionally civilians operating these weapons, had it not been for Harriers intercepting many of the Argentinian aircraft the harsh reality was that the Royal Navy would have sustained even greater loss.

Two newer missile systems however, reflected some proactive Royal Navy action to remedy the failings of obsolete weapons. Positioned on different ship types, a short notice plan to use Sea Dart (medium range) and Sea Wolf (short range) as a combined attack and defence system proved reasonably successful, but the relative infancy of such tactics contributed to yet more disaster. HMS Coventry (Sea Dart) was sunk and HMS Broadsword (Sea Wolf) was damaged during air attack due to (as commonly reported), a frustrating combination of computer errors and ineffective communications when both crews were under most stress. Notwithstanding this reasonable hypothesis, the fact that two Sea Harriers were assertively requested to 'hall off' as they were about to engage the attacking aircraft, perhaps provided opportunity for further analysis of this disaster. Unfortunately though, this command decision was not widely publicised.

Reading between the lines of daily press updates in 1982 and statements from those involved in books and blogs, plus hearing first-hand accounts from former colleagues, it was clear to me that the anger and frustration of many lower-decks personnel (and some officers) was obscured in the official reporting of the war. Which for the main part, especially after victory had been achieved, remained rule Britannia and plaudits to Royal Navy commanders.

Explaining the 'challenges' the British had encountered against the Argentinian air force after the war, one officer, quoted in Max Hastings *Battle for the Falklands*, stated that the reason was simple.

"We had been geared to fight the Soviet Union..."

Hastings didn't challenge this ridiculous statement, but seriously, did the Royal Navy, or hopefully just this one moron, really believe that the Soviet Union would only attack from an altitude where RN missiles would be effective, or that Soviet pilots wouldn't display similar determination and courage as the Argentinians? Possibly, but this assertion may simply reflect the ongoing threat of the Cold War and not wanting to publically acknowledge such failures to the Soviet Union.

With regard to the sinking of HMS Coventry and the decision to 'hall off' jets that had the enemy aircraft in their sites, *Hostile Skies* by former Sea Harrier pilot Flight Lieutenant David Morgan, indicates the level of distain his fellow pilots had for Royal Navy surface warfare officers:

"...Neil and Dave arrived back and were spitting nails... walking across the flight deck, helmets were off, arms waving. When I saw them in the crew room they were beside themselves with anger... Neil was always calm no matter the provocation, but they were both in a high state of agitation and cursing the stupidity of the surface navy in very specific terms... We had just lost a ship as a direct result of a couple of idiotic decisions... This sort of decision was lamentably common in peacetime exercises when missiles always splashed targets... Unfortunately ships warfare officers seemed to believe their own propaganda..."

Perhaps the ultimate failing during the war occurred at Fitzroy Inlet. The transport ship Sir Galahad, with Welsh Guards embarked, had anchored there due to bad weather while on route to Bluff Cove to offload soldiers closer to Port Stanley – the capital and ultimate goal of the task force. Seeing this occur in broad daylight, a Royal Marine Major had pleaded with a senior army officer on Galahad's stern ramp to disembark his troops due to the significant risk of air attack, but the officer refused, citing breach of procedures.

Having been at anchor for several hours at a poorly defended forward location, and without the predicted cloud cover to protect against air attack, I suspect ego, army/navy rivalry and basic communication failures contributed significantly to the disaster that ensued.

There has been much written about this event, including the challenge of moving troops forward without the support of Chinook helicopters that were lost after the transport ship Atlantic Conveyor was sunk. Similarly, the compounded pressure of worsening weather as winter approached and the impact this would have had on troops if significant delay were to occur, are perhaps equally contributing factors to the real-world challenges decision makers were presented. However, as a micro-analysis of how the blatant threat of air attack was not appropriately evaluated (or worse, ignored) after Galahad had anchored, I have included the Royal Marine's words below, which are readily available on the Internet:

"...The officer wouldn't listen to me as I held a lesser rank. He'd failed to grasp that peacetime rules no longer applied and that he needed to disembark his troops immediately due to the genuine danger they were in. In a fit of anger, I told him that he was behaving extremely irresponsibly and that my career in amphibious warfare reinforced the need to disembark his troops, which I could have done in as little as twenty minutes. However, regardless of the rationale I provided, he continually refused, and sadly, three to four hours later I was to be proven correct..."

Virtually unopposed, Argentinian jets bombed Sir Galahad, and as explosions and huge fires engulfed the accommodation at the stern of the vessel, the reality of war hit home. Sadly, devastatingly, many men who'd been assigned to the final push towards Port Stanley had been killed (50+) or wounded (150+), which ultimately placed a greater load on other land forces. These men, Royal Marines, Para's and Special Forces, who'd already marched (and fought) through 60+ miles of peat, rain and snow, would now have to assault the final mountains without the expected reinforcement. Furthermore, considering the upcoming battles would now be undertaken with their medical support facility at Ajax Bay inundated with casualties, well, it likely played on the minds of soldiers already pushed well beyond normal limits.

Although it would be easy to lay blame for this catastrophe with the senior army officer who refused to disembark his men, surely the captain of Sir Galahad must share some responsibility? After all, it was *his* ship, and therefore *he* must have understood the risk? If you accept this logical consideration, why then did the captain not assert his authority and order the army to disembark?

The Royal Navy didn't appear to find fault though, and for his actions to take charge and evacuate personnel following the bombing, and no doubt for the bravery of his crew who assisted, the Sir Galahad's captain was awarded the Distinguished Service Order (DSO) for:

"...Leadership and courage in the face of great danger..."

While not debating the assessment of this officer following the attack, conversely, the combined failures of both army and navy to act upon the reality of the situation, as described by the Royal Marine, may have leant weight to examination of systems that produced such disastrous decision making.

Ultimately, though, the disaster at Fitzroy Inlet may simply reflect the brutal consequences of human (and technology) frailty during any war.

Having lost a former colleague in this conflict and seeing one badly burnt, despite my personal feelings, if there were a British villain here, perhaps anger should be directed to the government of the day and its immediate predecessor. After all, they had neglected the Falklands for some time, were withdrawing MoD resources from the South Atlantic and were well into programmed and widespread defence cuts by April 1982. And without casting too broader net, it is perhaps this overt action that gave sufficient incentive for the Argentinians to act in the first place. Consequently, when the crisis erupted the British government was left with two choices: debate forever knowing that diplomacy would fail, as would their time in power; or give defence Chiefs an impossible task.

Regardless of my analysis, history will show the Royal Navy's actions leading up to and during the conflict helped to secure victory against insurmountable odds. I would agree with such holistic analysis, but unless individuals and organisations are willing to *genuinely* acknowledge their shortcomings, there will always be a (failure to learn).

We pulled up in a Dungeness roadside car park and were met by a local fisherman. He and his son launched their small boat from the shingle beach using a winch and a series of rollers. After boarding this, we motored for about a mile to a large steel structure that resembled a mini oil platform 'jacket'. This skeletal frame was protecting four very large water-inlet-stacks that provided cooling water to the nuclear power station via underground pipes. This structure was old and in danger of falling down, and so we had been sub-contracted by a demolition company to help pull it down. The purpose of this first visit then was simply to get eyes on the job to evaluate the conditions we would be working in.

On first impression, as we closed to within 20-meters of the jacket, it was huge, but not having been on an offshore platform before I was assured that this was just a 'baby'. The other significant observation was the tide. It was racing between the legs of the jacket, swirling over the huge cross beams to create whitewater. We would not be able to work in such currents and therefore would be restricted to periods of slack-water between the tides.

When bidding for this job, Tony had quoted the hours it would take us to complete the sub-sea demolition and fortunately his experience had specified 'hours in the water' and not hours at the site. As a result of this inspection, it was agreed we would dive during available slack-water, at least twice a day for an average of one to two hours per slack period depending on the strength of the tide either side of the slack-water. It was going to be a long job.

My first dip, undertaken from the demolition company's 70-meter long barge positioned next to the jacket, commenced with around half a knot of current running. I was tasked with clearing mussels from the connecting bolts of pipework attached to the first leg. Bracing firmly with one hand and moving slowly as I worked a wire brush and knife alternately to expose the bolts. Eventually, the tide eased, and I pushed on. This was mundane work personified, but as we were working at a higher daily rate of pay than normal, I could live with it. The purpose of my task was to prepare the bolts so that Gordon could 'cut' them with a 'Broco' cutting torch.

The Broco was a simple handpiece that the diver would slot a 12-inch ultrathermic rod into. Oxygen was pressurised through the handpiece via an umbilical and then out through the rod. When ignited, the resulting temperature at the tip of the rod was around 10,000F. The cutting power of this temperature was enhanced as the diver pulled a trigger on the handpiece to direct high pressure oxygen through the rod to its tip to easily burn (and blast) through the steel bolts I was exposing.

As the days went by we were making very slow progress, but by the end of week two we were ready to start dismantling the structure. Prior to lifting any of the crossbeams though we had to protect the water-inlet stacks, as these provided crucial cooling water to prevent a 'china syndrome' meltdown scenario occurring at the power station. To protect these 20-foot high structures, special 'table-tops' were being constructed. The table-tops were 30-foot high, four-legged frames built from rigid-steel joists (RSJs) and covered with heavy steel mesh. These were to be lowered by the barge crane and guided into place by a diver - me.

Waiting for slack-water that was two hours away, Gordon suggested we take the inflatable boat to the beach for a break.

"Ow bout a trip to slaver shop wile we wait f'tide?"

I managed two pints, and the boys had three of four, but two hours later I was kneeling in the dark on the bottom of the English Channel at the corner of four 30-foot long cross-beams surrounding one of the water-inlet stacks. With an arm on the larger vertical riser, I alternated my other arm from inside the corner of the steel structure (where the leg of the table-top was to be positioned) to above my head, to feel for the leg.

"Diver one, topside, should be just about there now."

Ensuring I was clear of the inside of the structure, I circled my hand above me and my fingers brushed the bottom of the RSJ leg coming towards me.

"Topside, diver one, I have the leg. About a meter to go, keep coming down slowly."

With my thighs braced against the 'outside' of the cross-beam, I maintained a grip on the RSJ and dropped my other arm to the corner of the structure to gauge how close the RSJ leg was. In its current path, it was going to land on the cross-beam at my thighs.

"Topside, diver one, slew left one foot."

"Diver one, topside, slew left one foot?"

"Roger, slew left one foot."

"Slewing left one foot."

I immediately felt the RSJ pull away from me as it continued in its downward travel. It was about 6 to 8-inches above the crossbeam, almost there, when I had a moment of uncertainty about its position relative to the corner.

"All stop."

"All stopped."

Leaving my position of relative safety behind the cross-beam, I let go of the RSJ and leaned forward and down to check the base of the vertical riser. In doing so, I had placed my KMB-10-covered-head directly between the very heavy steel table-top's leg and the inner side of the jacket.

I had only been there a couple of seconds when I felt and heard a strange vibration through the jacket itself. What was this? Lifting my head back to the vertical, cocking it to one side in the darkness trying to hear the sound more clearly, there was a sudden and deafening clash of steel on steel. With an instant adrenaline release, I swept a hand forward to relocate the RSJ, only to find it hard up against the vertical riser where my head had been just seconds before. Fuck!

"Diver one, topside, looks like the tide's turned earlier than we thought. How's it going?

The tides had been fairly unpredictable, often resulting in early knock-offs and trips to the slaver shop, but up until this point I had never been in the water when one changed so aggressively. Luck, for more than one reason, had placed the RSJ in a perfect position. I called for the table-top to be lowered fully and when it was in place, I checked each of the other corners before finally disconnecting the lift slings.

On return to the surface, we had a brief discussion about the change in tide, but I decided not to tell Gordon how stupid I had been. It was time for the slaver shop anyway.

This job was dragging on and on, and so on a spur of the moment decision during a rare weekend break back in Hull, I went to the travel agent to check out airline prices to Australia. I had been offered work diving on something called the North West Shelf in Western Australia and wanted to see if I could afford it. Despite spending my pay on more beer than I now believe humanly possible to drink, to my surprise I had more than enough saved up. And so less than two weeks later with a one-way ticket in hand and about two thousand pounds in the bank, at age twenty-two I waved goodbye to my family and boarded a night flight to Melbourne.

Left: descending in KMB10 beneath some haphazardly placed electrical cable
Right: a 'Northerns' dive container located on the barge next to a table-top

What can possibly go wrong

Left: table-top construction
Right: table-top readied for lowering

Left: KMB10   *Right: SuperLite-17*

CHAPTER 5

Yellow Beard (Explaining Some of the Previous Chapters)

I HAVE USED THE EMPHASIS on Royal (*Royal*) when referring to the Royal Navy once or twice. This stems from a Monty Python movie that I thought captured the absurdity of some pre-Falklands Royal Navy officers very well.

If you haven't seen *Yellow Beard* (1983), the famous British actor James Mason plays the role of a very pompous and despotic commander of a square-rigged sailing vessel. He's always impeccably dressed, has no interest in any of his sailors' wellbeing, and issues summary punishment perhaps not appropriate to the misdemeanour.

"Nail that man's foot to the deck!"

In the same movie, Eric Idle plays a Naval Intelligence officer tasked to capture Yellow Beard (Graham Chapman) who is hiding out on Mason's ship. Idle, on a pursuing ship, has not been successful, but nonetheless has a junior officer document a message to be relayed to the Queen by carrier-pigeon. As he frantically writes, the junior officer looks confused, but challenges the authenticity of Idle's message once the dictation is completed - I paraphrase their engagement below.

"Johnson" Idle addresses the junior officer "write down this message for the Queen."

The junior officer jumps to attention,

"Sir!"

"Your Majesty," Idle begins "I have engaged many enemy ships… fierce battles… expect to capture Yellow Beard and retrieve his treasure very soon…"

The junior officer is looking perplexed.

"What is it, Johnson?" Idle asks with malevolence.

"Err, Sir, that isn't, technically speaking, err, quite accurate."

Idle, looking down his nose with all the superiority of his position responds in a manner validating the words of Sir Winston Churchill, the future First Sea Lord of the Admiralty.

"Johnson, that is what *we* in the *Royal* Navy, call a *lie*."

Before I'm sent to the yardarm for my un-patriotic slur against the great man please see the following quotes from Churchill himself.

Quote 1:

In a speech to the House of Commons on January 23, 1948, Churchill stated the following,

> *"For my part, I consider that it will be found much better by all Parties to leave the past to history, especially as I propose to write that history."*

This is often misquoted as,

> *"History will be kind to me, as I intend to write it."*

Quote 2:

As for recalcitrant sailors of the seventies and early eighties who had the audacity to question an officer over a dubious process, to then find themselves subjected to the ubiquitous fall-back, "because it's naval tradition man;" let us see what Churchill thought about naval tradition.

British diplomat and author Harold Nicolson (1886-1968) comments in his diaries about an occasion when Winston Churchill was at the Admiralty. Apparently, the Board objected to some suggestion of his because it would not be per naval tradition. Churchill responded vehemently with the following.

> *"Naval tradition? Naval tradition? Monstrous.*
> *Nothing but rum, sodomy, prayers and the lash."*

Reading between the lines in chapters of this book where I discuss things navy, you may have formed an opinion that I haven't got much of a kind word for the officers who commanded me. You would be partially correct. That is not to say that I didn't serve with officers who both inspired and led their men by high example. Unfortunately though, for the five and half years I served, these people were rare exemptions. To redress the balance though, let me discuss two of them.

Sub Lieutenant Charles Patrick (not his real name) was a junior officer aboard a County Class Guided Missile Destroyer when I served during the mid-late seventies.

The first time our paths crossed I was on gangway duty during a leave period. He was 'Officer of the Day' and responsible for the daily admin and general running of the ships work parties that included the gangway crew of Boatswains Mate and Quartermaster.

He approached me during the dog watches (4 pm to 8 pm) with a request to paint an area of superstructure around the gangway before my second watch of the night; the morning (4 am to 8 am), was finished. The request could have been an order, maybe it was, but by the time we finished speaking I knew I would carry out the mundane task as he had requested, and do a good job too.

At the time I thought the difference between Patrick and other officers was simple, he had respect for me.

I was, at the time, just a Junior Seaman (Sonar), something most *Royal* Navy officers found on the sole of their boots and cleaned off with a stick. My assessment of Patrick back then hasn't changed today, but naval tradition ensured he was a rarity.

Patrick's genuine leadership was reinforced during an expedition involving around 15 of the ship's crew to climb to the top of the highest mountain on the Island of Madeira. Now a full Lieutenant, Patrick was accompanied by another typical officer, a young 'Suby' who was the son of some well-to-do.

It was hot and hard climbing where some of the sailors, not as fit as they thought they were, began to struggle. The Suby was full of the 'buck up chaps' naval harangue, but Patrick was the opposite. He stopped regularly, ensured people had enough rest, and even got everyone's opinion where a navigation decision was required (this was the navy ashore remember) before making a final decision on which track to take. As a result, all of us enjoyed the expedition immensely (only getting lost once). Had the other officer been in charge it might not have been the same judging by his inspirational quips along the way.

"Yes, but as an Ordinary Seaman you're expendable, Macfarlane."

Really, arsewipe! I'm a Ships Diver that serves some purpose on board, what the fuck do you do?

"Aren't we all, Sir?"

After leaving the ship, I never served with Patrick again. But I heard through the grapevine that he had changed career path to aviation and ended up flying as an observer during the landings on South Georgia where he was mentioned in dispatches for a significant rescue and the sinking of a submarine. If you ever read books on the Falklands air war, there are one or two; you will probably work out who he is and get to see a good product of the Royal Navy. He ended his career at the rank of Rear Admiral, making a successful transition to civilian life. Interestingly, his opinion was sought on the MoD's preparations for deployment to Helmand Province in 2006. During a radio interview in 2010, he identified flawed planning that relied upon lessons from Borneo, Malaya and Northern Ireland, instead of 'radical and progressive ideas', which were needed. These probably didn't fit with tradition though.

Another officer was from the same ship. Commander Carl Harrington (not his real name) was second in command; a solidly built man, who moved about the ship with purpose as though he never had a minute to waste. I never had any direct communication with him, but he was someone who the lower-decks respected from afar.

I was, however, to hear what some of the other ships officers thought about him when I was rostered as duty Land Rover driver (the ship carried its own). I had been tasked to drive half a dozen officers to a social event one night, and when they piled in the back, they were all a bit giggly from pre-drinks in the wardroom. Commander Harrington wasn't with them, but his name came up when I asked for directions at a country lane intersection north of Portsmouth.

"I say, what would Harrington do chaps."

Laughter erupted.

"Damn it, man, go left, and move quickly!"

More laughter erupted as they enjoyed the Harrington impersonation. This didn't stop until we reached their venue, by which time Commander Harrington had a back full of knives. These men had character traits to potentially outdo James Mason.

The first time Harrington addressed me directly, well, addressed a whole bunch of sailors actually, was after a replenishment at sea, or RAS.

A RAS, as the name implies, is when a ship takes on stores from another ship. It is undertaken while steaming along, lines passed between both ships, with a collection of sailors pulling on more lines working up a sweat. It can be very hazardous, and a complete pain in the arse, but decades of naval tradition (there are some good bits) ensures that it appears routine when observed by persons not familiar with the processes involved.

We had been at it for a couple of hours bringing over pallet load after pallet load and were working well as a team under the coordination of a couple of Petty Officers. Finally, lines were released, and the ships broke away from each other.

As we were packing away equipment, looking forward to a stand-easy (drinks break), Commander Harrington appeared amongst all the carnage of ropes and pallets, and we were mustered on a clear area on the flight deck.

"Ok gentlemen, I have some statistics for you. The fleet record for pallet transfer in one hour stands at 54 (I don't remember the actual figure, but it's not important). Through your tenacity, guile and sheer hard work you have smashed that record by achieving 59 pallets per hour, for two hours straight!"

The flight deck erupted in cheers. Harrington, stern-faced, held up his hands requesting silence.

"But I don't want you to leave here today thinking you're good, because you not!"

As the flight deck's buoyant mood slumped, Harrington continued immediately.

"You're *damned* good!"

The cheer that followed was louder than the first, but Harrington just turned on his heels and left without further comment.

I have met many an individual who believed they had the motivational ability of Harrington but were not within in a mile of him. Like Patrick, he was genuine; he respected the men beneath him and gave praise, but only when recognition was due.

If you read other books on the Falklands, look out for the Commander of a frigate that harassed the enemy over several nights in hazardous circumstances. Harrington proved very useful to the campaign and was decorated accordingly.

CHAPTER 6

Port Emergency Service (Bodies, Rabbits and Chemicals)

In September of 1982, the diving job I had been offered in Australia failed to become a reality. A few days after arriving in Melbourne I had walked into the office of the Professional Divers Association of Australia and spent five minutes with the head of this organisation, three of which he was on the phone speaking to someone else.

"You could try Oceaneering in Sale, but there isn't much on there at the moment. Best bet is to head over to the Middle East, plenty of jobs there mate."

After paying this bloke $200 for the privilege of becoming a member of the PDAA, probably the real reason to offer a job to someone on the other side of the world, I left his office somewhat shell-shocked. There would be no high paying dive job coming my way, and my relatively small bank balance had just taken a big hit.

Fortunately, my parents were from Melbourne, I know, I know, what were they doing living in England? Good question. Anyway, they left Australia in the late fifties and stayed there as Dad's career took off much faster than it would have back in the somewhat Luddite white-Australia-policy-centric-land-down-under of the fifties.

Speaking of mum and dad, they'd given me a good childhood that had, along with the navy, prepared me very well for the rest of my life. My mum featured strongly in this preparation as she subtly reinforced lessons from previous generations – try hard, respect others and get on with it. Three prominent memories spring to mind: she was a concert violinist who occasionally played solo performances in front of huge crowds, she also won the parents 200m running race at a school sports day, made brilliant hedgehog-cakes and was the go-to splinter remover for all the kids in our street.

Although mum and dad had provided a good start in life for my brothers and I, can you imagine being an Australian living in England and watching your boys grow up with pommy accents? Must have been strange. Whatever, my parents' circumstance worked for them, but their birthplace ensured that I had plenty of support in the form of Australian aunts, uncles, cousins, friends and one grandparent when I needed it most.

I lived with my 80-year-old, church elder, grandfather for the first few months. This kind and wonderful old man, who I had seen on only a handful of occasions while growing up, put up with a 22-year-old entry-level-alcoholic-former-sailor remarkably well. More importantly, he helped me type up resumes and apply for diving jobs as I helped out around his unit. Unfortunately the jobs I applied for didn't eventuate, but at least I was off the grog and getting my fitness back with daily runs and upper body workouts.

During these few months 1982 moved into 1983, I met members of the extended family I had never seen before, visited my aunt and uncles farm, had meals with people who had previously just been names on Christmas and birthday cards and then one morning I met the daughter of my dad's stepsister.

Anne was brilliant. Although I was very grateful for all the love and support from Grandpa, I needed to experience Australia as a 22-year-old. She introduced me to some of her friends and took me to nightclubs, and life was good, but it didn't take too long for the sailor in me to take over. After one night out with Anne, I was dropped back at Grandpa's place at about 6 am in a state of wobblyness, and there he was, standing by the front door looking incredibly worried. I felt really bad and realised that I had to find a place of my own.

Anne helped with this indirectly by introducing me to a friend of hers who worked for Melbourne Diving Services, a sports diving organisation. Shortly afterwards I started work as a Divemaster and travelled to Portsea, on Port Phillip Bay, most weekends to take students on jaunts over shallow reef and ventures into 'Portsea Hole', a 30m deep mini amphitheatre less than a kilometre from the beach. This was brilliant, not commercial diving, not commercial pay, but something new and exciting nonetheless – and the visibility was amazing!

One of the students had a spare room and was looking for a tenant and so about a month after starting work with MDS I moved out. Grandpa was worried, but I assured him things were going to be ok. I had actually enjoyed my time with him, the chalk and cheese difference between us gave me a new perspective on life that I am still grateful for today.

One of the MDS boat skippers, a bear of a man nicknamed 'Moose', worked for the Melbourne Port Emergency Service, the PES. He told of firefighting, diving and all sorts of emergency service operations that sounded pretty cool. More importantly, though, he told me there was a rare recruit intake scheduled for the next month. With this knowledge in hand, I picked up my running and swimming and attended a selection test one crisp April morning in 1983.

Located on North Wharf road just out from the Melbourne CBD, the PES headquarters looked like a fire station. Several vehicle bays contained more than the standard fire 'pumper' though. There were cranes, rescue trucks, foam tankers, large foam cannons and an array of equipment to combat any likely wharf related event. And across the road, there was a rescue boat, dive barge and oil pollution vessel.

I was advised to wait in a foyer with around 30 other blokes and felt the usual anxiety knowing I was about to undergo a crucial physical test. Some of the blokes in the room looked pretty damn fit, and we had been advised that just two positions were on offer. As my palms moistened thinking about the run, swim and other challenges to come, I was glad I had put in the extra effort leading up to this moment. Swimming four times a week I would do 2-kilometres each time and sometimes twice a day, not Olympic training, but I was perhaps swimming better than I ever had in the past. My runs had been pretty much daily, but short, no more than five to six kilometres at any one time, although the pace was quick.

Standing on North Wharf road with the others and an Emergency Service Man (ESM), pronounced 'S' 'M', wearing running gear like the rest of us, this bloke gave a short brief.

"Right, we'll stay as a group until we reach the Harbour Control building, then you blokes can take off."

He pointed to a tower in the distance. This was to be a short run of about 3-4k. By the time we turned at the tower around ten blokes had dropped off the pace the ESM had set, and the rest of us surged forward.

Within half a kilometre I was in a pack of around six, about a hundred metres ahead of the rest, but with less than a kilometre to go there was just two of us. The bloke with me, later to be nicknamed 'Slopstick', started to pull away and I couldn't keep up with him. He crossed the finish line about 150-meters ahead of me, and the nearest bloke behind me was a similar distance away. The swim was next.

Split into two groups we were given another brief while standing on the edge of the wharf, all of us now wearing speedos as the first of many shivers were becoming evident. The wind was making for a somewhat crisp morning and the brown Yarra River 15-feet below us at around 16-18-degrees Celsius was hardly inviting.

"You will line up straight from here and when I say go you will swim to the stern of that ship."

This was going to be a short swim of around 400-meters, but the cool water would provide a reasonable test for the muscle conditioning of those participating. Thank God I had been training in an unheated outdoor pool. Nevertheless, another ESM dressed in a wetsuit carrying fins and a PES ambulance close by was an ominous sign.

"All clear? Right, in you get."

There was apprehension form some of the participants as they obviously wanted to avoid the cold for as long as possible, but this was not the purpose of the test. I pushed past them and leapt in, the icy chill causing involuntary gasping straight away. There were about eight others with me as a similar number hesitated on the wharf's edge.

"Go!"

I was glad the ESM running the test wasn't a 'group hugger'. As we took off, the weak bastards on the wharf found themselves way back in the field by the time they finally jumped in.

Powering forward there was just one other bloke with me; I could see his eyes looking my way as we turned to breathe. This bloke, 'Chris' was a good swimmer and we were pushing each other along, but with about 50-meters to go I edged away and finished about 10-meters ahead of him.

Back at the PES headquarters, we had some simple fireman's carry drills to undertake, but the hard part of the test was over. Slopstick had come first in his swim too, and so I thought that he and I were looking pretty good. Of the other blokes, Chris had come about forth in the run and so I guessed he would be in with a chance too, just the interview to go.

Sitting down in the office before three senior PES officers I was not at all comfortable. My strength was hands-on work, not formal processes. When they asked questions I gave answers I thought appropriate, but with hindsight, I just talked a load of shite. Later in life when on the other side of the table I had dismissed people like myself without a second thought for better efforts than I had given. Nonetheless, at the end of the process, four of us were called into the Officer in Charge's (OIC's) office at the end of the day.

Standing there with me was Slopstick, Chris and another bloke called Dave who I couldn't remember seeing during either run or swim.

"Right", began the OIC "we'll keep this short. We have chosen Splashman, Dowlands and Hunter is a reserve. Thank you gentleman.

As I walked from the first-floor room and down to the foyer, I was devastated. I tried to make sense of the decision, but couldn't. Slopstick (Splashman) was fit as fuck and a former Australian navy CD – good choice. I had beat Chris (Hunter) in the run and swim, but maybe he had performed better at the interview – ok, fair decision. But who the fuck was Downlands (Dave)? I couldn't remember him at all from the testing. Either way, my first chance at a solid entry into emergency service work, and a job that involved diving had gone. I had blown the opportunity for being a dumb bastard at the interview. I was shattered!

Returning from Portsea the next Sunday evening to a new flat that I shared with my first Australian girlfriend, she was waiting at the door, smiling, holding a telegram.

> *'Due to unforeseen circumstances, the PES requires an additional recruit. If you are still interested in the position, please call...'*

The following Monday I started recruit training with Slopstick, Chris and Dave (who turned out to be a good bloke by the way). My delight was tempered slightly with the news that the position had arisen as a popular ESM had been killed in a car-verses-tree accident that weekend while driving to Sydney. Either way, I was bloody relieved and looking forward to the next ten weeks of basic training.

Our instructor, a forty-something old school operator, called Alf, was brilliant. He had an open manner and encouraged participation in discussion. Listening to his examples of fire, chemical and rescue work around the wharf was brilliant, we were going to be trained to do this work too, and I loved every minute of it.

Much of the first few weeks involved firefighting drills and theory. The discussion and practice were maritime-focused, and we spent a lot of time on an out of service roll-on-roll-off ship tied up at North Wharf. We became very familiar with Breathing Apparatus (BA) and learnt how to use an O2 set called BG174. This device gave much longer duration than air sets, and we would use it to search for missing persons in the rabbit warrens of decks and passageways of commercial shipping. Towards the end of this first ten weeks, we were introduced to a bloke called 'Dirty Dave'. Dirty as in covered in it usually and perhaps a little bit on the nose.

An ESM, Dave was somewhat eccentric, but with a very bright mind. He had set up a training facility under the enclosed section of a bridge near Station Pier. This vast space contained tunnels, simulated offices and engine-room spaces, and was used to evaluate ESM's whether they were recruits or on 'on-shift' operators.

One of our first challenges was to squeeze into a pipe, in complete blackness, which provided only enough space for the BA-wearing recruit to inch forward using hands and feet. With BA scraping on the roof of the pipe we followed the bloke's feet in front as another came behind us – if you had claustrophobia this was a near-impossible challenge.

Surviving this, we were sent into a more substantial pipe that permitted movement on all fours. Tasked with locating and recovering dummies, again in blackness, but with BA masks off, we crawled over sandbags, moved past dangling ropes and wire and shivered in and out of water. Occasionally coming to branches in the pipe system we found dead ends and had to reverse our course. The tunnel system was immense.

At one point a hatch was opened, and Dirty Dave dropped in a flare causing smoke to rapidly fill the confined space.

"Best get on air you blokes, hard to breathe in smoke."

Needless to say, the drills were challenging, but they ensured successful recruits would be able to cope with the real-world challenges of maritime fire and rescue.

In the final week of training, Alf had organised a visit to the police communications centre to provide a holistic perspective on emergency service operations. However, when the van pulled up outside the old Melbourne Morgue, we quickly realised the comms-centre visit had been a ruse. As part of ESM training, all recruits were required to witness a post-mortem examination to prepare them for the real world of operations.

Without making this too macabre, the old morgue was like a medieval step back in time. There were bodies piled on top of each other in a freezer, cadavers on steel tables in a cool-room awaiting their turn and the most fun room, four tables where morticians were preparing bodies. One of these blokes walked us through the process.

"Ok, we need to expose the chest cavity."

Using a scalpel, he slit from bottom of the neck to the abdomen and then made lateral incisions to fold back the skin on the chest. Then using bolt cutters, yes, nothing fancy, just stock standard bolt cutters, he cut through ribs and revealed the organs beneath.

We were undertaking this observation with a bunch of police recruits too. By this stage, one police recruit had fainted, and another couple had left the room, I was not exactly enjoying it either, but was following advice from a navy instructor from years before.

"If something is not nice, keep busy and ask questions to keep your mind focused."

The mortician had pointed out that the lungs he was removing were 'healthy' compared to some others, but I had no idea of anything different.

"How can you tell?"

The mortician appeared pleased with the question and dropped the pile of meat into a dish; turning to the table behind him he lifted another lung, much greyer in colour and presented it to the group.

"See this one; this bloke was a heavy smoker. Watch."

He squeezed the tissue, and black tar oozed out. He then smiled, returned the organ to its rightful owner and prepared to inspect the brain.

With scalpel in hand, he sliced around the top of the head level with the forehead, to literally 'scalp' the corpse and peel the skin down over its face. Then, with Bunning's angle grinder in hand, he cut through the top of the skull. This didn't come away entirely though, and so using a hammer and chisel he finished the job with an audible crack of bone.

Sorry, this is macabre.

Anyway, he collected the brain, weighed it and then pointed out specific structures inside the skull.

All right, enough!

Needless to say, post-mortem examinations are not my thing, but for emergency service recruits they serve their purpose.

About six months later after serving a period of time in the PES maintenance section doing all sorts of shit jobs, I was rostered onto 'D' shift to become an operational ESM. The PES had five shifts and we worked an incredible roster of four on and six off. That was two 10-hour day shifts, two 14-hour night shifts and then six whole days off.

Shift work consisted of training, more training and occasional turnouts when a job came. Additionally, as ESM's we had the responsibility for overseeing safety at Melbourne's tanker berths. Whether it was chemical, oil, or gas, we would meet the ship on arrival, reinforce the safety requirements to the Master or Chief Engineer and then enforce these necessities through deck patrols and gate security. This was the one aspect of the PES that I did not enjoy, mainly because it was boring as batshit. Can you imagine 14-hours on a chemical tanker with nothing but the hum of machinery and the smell of toxic gasses ever present as you either plodded around a deck or sat in a security hut? For me, it was soul destroying.

On one of these patrols, I heard the sound of an angle grinder? No, surely not. This was a chemical tanker loading highly flammable and toxic product from Melbourne's Coode Island tank farm – this place was later to erupt into a two-day fire that significantly challenged all of Melbourne's firefighting resources.

Coming down from the bow to the loading-arms I was searching for the origin of the sound, and I noticed liquid dripping from the vicinity of the enormous loading-arm pipework. At first, I thought it was a leaking fire main, but the sickly sweat toxic aroma that was growing ever stronger sent adrenaline to my fingertips. Then the sound of the angle grinder hit me again, and I spied the culprit about 30-meters away near the accommodation.

Pulling my Emergency Life Support Apparatus (ELSA) from the pouch on my chest I pulled the clear visor over my head, and air rushed in pushing the toxic properties away. Within seconds I found the chord to the angle grinder and pulled it out, and then clear of the dripping liquid upwind, I removed the ELSA and called the PES watch-room to explain the situation.

Keeping this incident simple, the ship stopped loading, the Master got a severe kick in the arse, and Coode Island got a reprieve for about eight more years before the inevitable happened. As an example of 'inevitable', we had visited one of the tank operators for a brief on their firefighting systems. The manager showed us two pumps, one electric and one diesel driven. These pumps were to supply foam to the top of the tanks in the event of a fire, and he was giving us the brief as part of ongoing safety and preparedness arrangements should we have to respond at some stage in the future. After isolating the lines to the tank, he pushed the button to start the electric pump.

'Click, click… click.'

The battery charge apparently wasn't sufficient to get it running.

"Ok, not to worry, this is why we have the diesel back up."

'Click, click…click.'

The PES gave this bloke a kick in the arse too. However, it was with some tainted satisfaction after such PES services had been wound back over subsequent years, and the MFB had taken responsibility for the port, that a lightning strike to a tank caused a fire that quickly became out of control. Whether the failure of equipment contributed to the fire escalation during the Coode Island disaster of the early nineties is debatable, but for ESM's made obsolete through a bureaucratic process, it reinforced the valuable service they had provided to the Port of Melbourne for decades.

Early one night shift we got a call to Station Pier, there was a body floating between this structure and Princess Pier, about 600-meters further along. Pete Buckler and Harley Clarke donned wetsuits and waded out into the shallow water about 60-meters to recover the body as Brian Locke (my boss), and I waited on the beach.

A couple of media vans pulled up and as the boys completed the last 20-meters or so images were being played live on the evening news. This was unfortunate because Harley's voice echoed across the water.

"Fuck me, Brian, she looks like an old girlfriend of Pete's!"

Luckily this wasn't picked up on news bulletins, but the boys laughing at Harleys joke was. Nothing was said about it afterwards, but it was a good lesson in public perception. Despite the joke being a stress release process that operators utilised without much thought, it could have been very confronting to a family member or anyone who did not understand the challenge of dealing with death as part of their job. This sort of humour was regular though, and another example perhaps reinforces its needs.

The boys had responded to a suicide in a large port authority garbage compactor. The body was, well, 'compacted' and they had to remove it after photographs and evidence had been collected. Picture a face squashed to half its size and similar distorted body parts that the boys were confronted with, not nice. To break the tension, one of the ESM's spoke.

"Fuck me, boys; he must have been under a lot of pressure."

Back on the beach with light all but gone, the body was deposited, not covered, and the media had gone. Brian advised me I was to stay until the coroner's van arrived and that he would be heading back to the station and would send a ute back to collect me – we were a long way from our primary area of operations.

The gravely and partially muddy beach was deserted. It was dark, but street lighting provided sufficient vision. And there I was standing, a deceased woman (the corpse was wearing stockings) at my feet waiting for the coroners grey panel van to arrive.

Despite not over-enthusiastic about the task I had been given, curiosity made me look at the body. The legs seemed quite normal, but the head and torso were swollen. The head was particularly grotesque. The flesh had lifted from the bone, and the nose and part of the mouth had been eaten away, hair and seaweed were entwined and matted over the skin, and empty eye sockets appeared to float over the bone like a bizarre mask.

The morgue experience helped with this encounter, but I can still recall that face over thirty years later. Why would anyone want to be a mortician?

A regular body recovery job involved the West Gate Bridge. At one point I think we were averaging six jumpers a year from this structure, but most of these never made the papers. I believe this was purposely the case to prevent others following suit from the largest bridge in Melbourne.

After impact with the water, a body would either float, sink to the bottom to stick in the mud, or drift downstream underwater to appear later.

During one underwater search at the bridge, an ESM called Herman found what he thought was a head. He tentatively recovered this and brought it back up in the zero visibility. When handing it to the dive supervisor, there was a bit of laughter as the head turned out to be a half empty sandbag.

The first jumper I went to was a floater. We pulled him on the boat with a lot of effort as he was a big man. While our boss called the watch-room to advise of the incident, we were informed that police wanted to talk with us to work out what might have happened. An old hand ESM called Barry came up with a plausible explanation after retrieving the corpse's wallet for investigation purposes.

"Got it, boys, this poor bastard's only got two bucks to his name."

One of our bread and butter jobs was to 'Assist First Aid'. The port had its first aid stations around the docks, and one officer manned each of these. Typically, these blokes responded to accidents on ships where people had fallen in holds, had sustained crush injuries or other trauma, plus regular medical episodes. Where the injury or illness was significant, we were called upon to carry the casualty to the wharf under the guidance of the First Aid Officer (FAO). The carry involved the use of stretchers, lifting systems and often, just plenty of muscle. The regular practice I had moving big men in stretchers was to prove invaluable later in my helicopter rescue life when winching to ships, but one of these experiences was perhaps not the best demonstration of good practice.

We had responded to a wharf where a ship was approaching to berth, Alf was our boss on this job, and we had the FAO plus a 'civil' Mobile Intensive Care Ambulance (MICA) there too. One of the seamen was having breathing difficulties as a result of a possible heart attack and the moment the ship was secure the FAO and MICA blokes were going to board and we would follow along as usual with our stretcher.

Angled away from the wharf as it approached, the bow of the ship had ended up in the wrong position on the narrow berthing area and progress had paused. As this delay continued the crew on the bow were describing the worsening condition of their mate and tension was high.

"He's hardly breathing; his face is like a ghost too, we need you on board now!"

The MICA blokes were keen to move, but without a gangway, there was little that could be achieved. To maximise support, Alf had us throw up a line and the crew pulled up an oxy-viva resuscitation unit to the bow, but they didn't know how to use it and continued to plead for support!

As the frustration of the delay intensified, the captain began to back away from the wharf to reposition the ship for another go at berthing. This would mean another five minutes at least before the FAO and MICA blokes could board and the frustration in their eyes was acute!

As the ship began to move away, Alf handed me the line that was now secured to the bow guardrail just eight feet above me thanks to the low tied.

"Get up there Mick, and don't fall in!"

Relying on a unique navy skill, I reached up high on the rope and shifted my hands upwards to swing across the meter of boiling water as the ship went astern.

Spending a short time as 'First-Swing' for the 'B' crew of the Portsmouth Command Field Gun crew in 1979, my job had involved swinging across an 18-foot simulated chasm as part of a display the navy provided to the public once a year. As First Swing, I had been one of an 18-man crew who dragged and lifted a field gun up, over and through fixed obstacles simulating the Royal Navy's support to besieged soldiers at the town of Ladysmith during the Boer war. The last time I had done this was six years previously, but essentially, I was very comfortable on a rope and Alf knew this.

My feet smashed into the hull and using upper body strength I 'walked' up to the rail. Helped over by the waiting crew, I collected the Oxyviva and was taken to the cabin of the sick seaman.

He was ghostly white, struggling to breathe and his face was covered in sweat. Quickly opening up the Oxyviva I selected the therapy to high flow and placed the mask over his mouth and nose. I only had basic first aid skills at the time, but at least the PES made us confident in the use of O2. With my fingers mentally crossed I attempted to reassure the patient and his colleagues, but I was out of my depth and thought this bloke was about to die. Nonetheless, I kept up appearances by attempting to take a pulse and looking confident. Thankfully though, a few minutes later the FAO and MICA blokes came into the room and took over.

I don't know what happened to this bloke, but hoped we had made the difference. Still, he was a big man who did not appear to have placed health and fitness high on his list of priorities in life, so regardless of our intervention he was likely on the decline anyway at some time in the future.

Our/my actions that day would have seen a severe arse kicking by safety Nazis this day and age, but were still probably unnecessary actions even back in the reasonably old school world of the early eighties. A statement from a MICA officer during my NSCA days perhaps sums up emergency response and risk-taking best.

"Some people are going to die no matter what you do mate, so never risk your life or those of others unless there are exceptional circumstances".

Wise words.

Due to the nature of cargoes coming into Melbourne, it seemed like we were forever practising or responding to some type of chemical incident. Typically this involved a shipping container being dropped, or a forklift-tine being driven through a storage container or drum by mistake. As a result of this type of event, the operators of the equipment bolted (rightly so) to avoid inhalation or any other form of contact with the chemical. Upon arrival then, we were often confronted with the frozen moment of a hurried departure.

As such an event may have required us to move equipment and vehicles part of our training included obtaining, crane, forklift and articulated vehicle licences.

During forklift training, I learnt a unique skill and lost a bet at the same time. Our instructor challenged us to pick up a 50-cent coin with the tines, and we all had a good go, but no matter what we tried we couldn't do it. When the instructor said he could do it and suggested that we were hopeless. The bet was made. Laughing, he simply lowered the tip of a tine onto the edge of the coin to apply sufficient pressure. Then, reversing slowly, friction caused the coin to first lift up and then flick back on top of the tine - piece of piss. I never had to use that trick operationally but spent a few hours in a gas suit driving a forklift into a container to move bulky items so we could get to the source of the liquid leaking past the door. As I mentioned before, this was not joyful work.

There had been a spate of firebug activity in Melbourne in early 1987. They had been targeting a variety of industry, and as a result, the PES was tasked to patrol Coode Island 24/7 as a preventative measure. The thought of 14-hour night shifts driving around the tank farm, or more precisely the river side of it, on your own, in search of some nutter was not to the liking of the unarmed ESM's. We challenged the safety aspect of this task and recommended that it be a two-person job, but as that would have cost more the OIC declined our proposal, and we were put to work.

Behind the tank farm was a grassy riverbank about 30-meters wide with a small track running along a cyclone fence bordering the tanks. Some weird people came fishing here despite the risk of chemical run-off into the river. How they put up with the constant toxic smell was beyond me, but perhaps they had lived in the area so long they no longer noticed it? Anyway, this area, about one kilometre long was to be our place of work for the foreseeable future.

On my first night shift, I took over from an ESM who held the record for killing rabbits. These had been in plague-like proportions when the job started, but now, just one week in, they had become scarce as ESM's broke the monotony of the 14-hour nights cleaning them up with S12, the small PES station wagon we were using to patrol the area. In addition to the lack of rabbits, there was another change too. The once lush green grassy riverbank had been subjected to extensive circle work by board ESM's, and as a result of rubber, rain and over-enthusiasm it now resembled the Somme on a bad day.

After having my tea in the wharf security hut, I began my patrol. Pickings were slim, a light rain was falling, and I doubted I had a chance of getting any rabbits. Trying a new tactic though, I parked up in an area of grass where the tank farm was split midway by a small road. Hiding here, with lights out at about 10 pm, I waited…

When I thought sufficient time had passed, I turned the ignition and accelerated forward as fast as the little four-cylinder would allow. By the time I reached the intersection of the riverbank, I was moving! I turned left, turned on the lights and correcting a loss of traction with a flick of the wheel I focused ahead. About 10m in front of the car, there was bunny-boy and his mates.

They bolted in different directions immediately, and so I locked onto the nearest who was fleeing for the fence.

Really bunny-boy? I don't think so!

I was closing fast, the car still accelerating despite wheels spinning in the ankle-deep mud. Almost, a bit more, Damn! Bunny-boy ducked under the fence and into the tank farm.

In the midst of my disappointment, I suddenly realised that I was about a meter from the fence and still closing towards it at speed, and so to avoid a collision I turned the wheel easy right. Nothing happened! I turned the wheel harder, but still nothing happened. There was just too much momentum and mud! With a horrible crunch, the front fender smashed into a vertical pole supporting the cyclone fence. This was not good.

Reality smacked me in the face. My wife, Mandy, was over eight months pregnant with our first child, and I was about to lose my job. Quickly getting out of the car I surveyed the damage. It wasn't good! The fender was bent inwards, and the wheel appeared to be bent inwards too. Fuck!

I bashed the fender to release it from the fence, but some of it just wouldn't separate. Back in the car, I reversed, bouncing it back and forth with wheels spinning as load came to bear without much success either. Fortunately though, after a few minutes of controlled panic, the vehicle separated from the fence. This structure was bent slightly, but not so as you would notice – in the dark at least – I had more significant problems.

I got back in the car and just sat there, shitting myself, for about fifteen minutes, wondering what to do.

The way I saw things I was going to be sacked first thing in the morning when the OIC got to work, so I had nothing to lose. I looked at the radio handpiece for about a minute then picked it up. With a quick change of heart, I threw it down.

'No, that would be stupid.'

Naturally, stupidity won over, and I picked up the handpiece again.

"Port emergency, port emergency, port emergency, this is S-twelve, intruder sighted climbing over the tank farm fence mid-section... I've had a bit of a collision with the fence too."

There was a moment of silence as the PES watch-room operator, a Maori bloke called Vince, moved to the headquarters radio.

"Is that you Mick, I guess you want the boys down there, hey."

I acknowledged his confirmation call and just sat there. It took about another five minutes before I heard the first siren.

Melbourne's emergency services were geared up for firebug attacks. Any sighting would result in a large-scale response, and as I waited, more sirens joined the chorus.

What the fuck had I started?

Hearing the first one getting closer, I jogged around to the intersection and met a responding police sedan.

"He went that way!"

I yelled and pointed urgently, and the cops took off. Next was an MFB pumper.

"He's bolted, the police are after him. He didn't get into the farm."

The fireys must have cancelled the alarm as other sirens faded too, but after driving back to the security gate, S2, the PES primary pumper turned up with Brian and the boys. Covered in mud, the car was a bit of a giveaway.

"You been chasing rabbits, Mick?"

Brian didn't say much, but he suggested I clean the car before coming back to the station.

It was time for the morning parade at the PES. There were about five groups of men standing before their officers, with the Chief and OIC addressing them all. I had cleaned the car, but was unable to conceal all the damage and so driving in through an archway to the rear of the area where the parade was taking place, just 2-meters from the OIC, S12 wobbled and squeaked from the front left as I moved slowly passed the lot of them.

After the parade, a pulse-increasing PA was made.

"ESM Macfarlane, report to the OIC's office."

Entering his room I was told to sit as he looked through some paperwork. He kept me there, sweating, for some time. Then he looked up, steam issuing from his ears.

"Well, what happened?"

I had prepared a story to match the radio call and stuck to it. He challenged several points, but in the end, dismissed me with the directive to write out the account formally.

I was the luckiest bastard on the planet, not smart, just dumb arsed lucky. The OIC knew precisely what had happened, I was sure of it, but for him to acknowledge this, he would have to report to other emergency service leaders that one of his ESM's was a dick. As this would obviously reflect poorly on his leadership, I guess he chose to accept my story. For some time afterwards, though, I suffered. ESM's would regularly pass me making bunny sounds, it wasn't particularly funny, but what could I do. Simply put, it was a reminder of life lesson 101 – you are responsible for your actions.

On the plus side, at least I could keep my family's head above water, so that was good, but after four years with the PES I was becoming frustrated with the lack of decent jobs and was about to make a career move that would change my future forever.

Sitting in the watch room one Sunday, I read an article about a team of blokes from Gippsland in Victoria's east. They parachuted, dived, flew in helicopters and this organisation, the NSCA, were currently recruiting for a new intake.

CHAPTER 7

NSCA Pararescue (Freddo's Vision)

MOST AUSTRALIANS WOULD PROBABLY HAVE little, if any memory, of headlines that dominated the Australian media during March and April of 1989. In fact, even for those old enough to remember the massive police manhunt that spanned not only Australia but overseas as well, the saga surrounding the collapse of the Victorian division of the National Safety Council of Australia, (the NSCA), has probably blurred into other financial disgraces of the late eighties. But to compare the NSCA to such organisations would be unjust; it wasn't a Bond Corp, and it could hardly be compared to the empire of greed ruled by Mr Skase.

Unlike the people controlling those organisations, the NSCA's leader didn't use his funds for personal gain; in fact, he was quite the opposite. There were no mansions in the hills, no European villas, and no Impressionist artworks. And except for just two sports cars purchased for NSCA executives, all NSCA funds, no matter how procured, were used for only one purpose – saving lives.

The key-figure in both police and media inquiries at the time was a Mr John Friedrich – the Executive Director of the NSCA. He was missing, and a massive manhunt had been launched to find him, and an estimated $300,000,000 of missing NSCA funds.

The focus of police and media was West Sale base; the headquarters of the NSCA situated about fifteen minutes' drive from the country town of Sale, in Gippsland, east of Melbourne. From West Sale base reporters showed the Australian public the enormous and varied collection of rescue assets that the NSCA possessed. There were helicopters, fixed-wing aircraft, fast rescue boats, all-terrain vehicles, as well as parachuting, climbing and other rescue equipment. And just across the Gippsland Highway from the base was a vast stables complex with an indoor arena to rival anything Australia had to offer, complete with horses and dogs that were trained for mountain searches.

At Welshpool, a coastal town around an hours' drive away, there was the 'NSCA navy' consisting of an offshore rescue ship, dive launch and a couple of fast rescue craft. The rescue ship, a converted rig tender, had a helideck, recompression chamber and the latest navigation equipment complete with a Dynamic-Positioning system that allowed the ship to stay in position on the open sea without anchors. The ship was also equipped with the latest Side-Scan sonar and underwater search and tracking systems that were used in conjunction with a six-man submersible rescue vehicle and two remotely operated underwater search vehicles.

But all this equipment was just the Victorian operation. Friedrich had expanded the Vic Div. operations interstate, and at smaller bases in NSW, QLD, NT and SA; the NSCA – a not for profit organisation – had amassed a massive collection of search and rescue assets far exceeding anything that both State and Federal governments had to offer.

So why had Friedrich built such an organisation? Who had operated the equipment? And how had it been financed?

The many reporters covering the demise of the NSCA mentioned this equipment and its 'state of the art' nature, but they barely commented on the type of people Friedrich had employed to use it, or what they had achieved with it. Instead, and possibly of more interest to the public at the time, they went into great, although very much assumed detail about the missing money and the whereabouts of the 'mysterious' John Friedrich.

"This is bigger than Texas," suggested a senior detective running the police investigation. He was referring to the yet to be confirmed massive deception John Friedrich had been conducting for over eight years to acquire the funds needed to build and run such an organisation. The task ahead of him and the appointed liquidators was going to be massive.

However, as the search for Friedrich continued, it became apparent that he had used shipping containers that were allegedly full of very expensive rescue equipment as collateral to justify huge loans from many of Australia's leading banking institutions. He had these positioned at each of his bases and would fly bankers from base to base pointing out the many containers, occasionally stopping to open one or two, to reveal things such as the latest mine-rescue, or perhaps the latest dive-rescue equipment. But of all the containers the NSCA owned probably less than five percent had anything of great value. The rest, well, they were either used to store drums of aviation fuel or were merely empty – Friedrich's skill at deception and perhaps the bankers' greed hadn't allowed time for detailed inspections.

As the years went by banks were enjoying the substantial interest payments Friedrich was making on his many loans, and by the late eighties, seemingly endless processions of suit-clad salivating-gentleman would visit West Sale seeking even more of Friedrich's business. Despite his polite smile and friendly mannerisms, Friedrich treated these people with contempt by developing a system of false invoices to justify even more loans to ensure their money kept pouring into NSCA accounts.

Despite Friedrich's ability to efficiently manipulate greedy bankers, the high costs of operating such a sophisticated and ever-expanding operation meant that he couldn't always meet the banks repayments, and by mid-1988 Friedrich had been robbing 'Peter' to pay 'Paul' so much that he would often work late into the night to make the books balance before a board meeting. But it didn't take much whiteout/whitewash on Friedrich's part to ensure board meetings ended in smiles and handshakes because the simple fact was the NSCA's board of directors loved Friedrich! Why wouldn't they? He had expanded the operation into a huge concern in minimal time and had just about every government agency visiting our bases. The directors, all of whom had rescue craft named after them, had perhaps been blinded by the huge wave of prestige and ego they'd been riding and didn't ask critical questions of Friedrich until it was too late – but they were not alone in this oversight.

After an extensive search, Friedrich was caught in WA, about an hour south of Perth not far from the town of Rockingham. He gave himself up to police without a struggle and was taken back to Melbourne for questioning, suggesting to police at the time that he had 'just needed time to think'.

By the time of his capture, the media had discovered more about what they believed to be his history: he had apparently arrived in Australia from New Zealand on a false passport and had left; or rather, a person with his passport had left, pretty soon after. There was a suggestion that he was a German called Friedrich Hoenburger, an embezzler who had faked his death in Germany and then disappeared with a large sum of stolen money. The Federal police had not confirmed this, but they and German authorities were investigating the reports.

There were also hyped-up media accounts suggesting the NSCA was involved in drug running operations and arms smuggling to raise funds for its 'overseas' operations. Some reporters, with wild imaginations, even suggested that the NSCA was a CIA front to gain intelligence in the Asia Pacific region. Apparently, the NSCA was a means of keeping a covert eye on 'areas of interest' such as Pine Gap.

Hyped-up speculation aside, the police had a solid case for Friedrich to answer regarding his apparent fraud and the missing millions from the company he had been the Executive Director of. However, if the police did believe he was guilty of this massive fraud, and that he was possibly an illegal immigrant wanted for embezzlement overseas, why then, and this has always amazed me, was he allowed out on bail? Moreover, why was he permitted to run another aviation operation in North Queensland – allegedly to research a proposed US Space Port?

Many months after his capture and shortly before he was due back in court to give full details about the NSCA's operations, he reported to police that some attempts had been made on his life. There was one attempt in a Melbourne hotel and another at his Gippsland property. Police were still investigating these incidents when his body was found on a hill not far from his home.

A former NSCA colleague of mine found Friedrich's body on the hillside. There was an old rusty revolver by his side and a fatal, disfiguring, wound to his head. Friedrich had apparently committed suicide rather than face questions that would ultimately show him to be nothing but the exceptional fraudster that many believed him to be. Although this supposition had merit, to some former NSCA staff things didn't seem quite right. Friedrich, a man who had apparently faked his death previously to escape prosecution, and had proved himself capable of entering and leaving the country undetected, just wasn't someone to use anything old and certainly nothing rusty – so why the old revolver? To those questioning the suicide assumption the upcoming investigation, or perhaps Royal Commission, was eagerly anticipated because after all, why had the government awarded military contracts to an apparent illegal immigrant with a criminal record?

Friedrich had lived with a vision. It was to produce the best rescue service in the world: a 'Rolls Royce service'. To those of us who had experienced the 'Council' in action and for many of the Australian services and agencies that had worked alongside us, it was obvious that he'd succeeded. The service that Friedrich had established was built around something called Pararescue: a rapid response, long-range capability that delivered teams of doctors and medics to anywhere on land or sea, day or night. NSCA Pararescue teams had proved themselves in an operational sense and had surpassed the capabilities of the Australian Defence Force and that of the US Air Force on every occasion the bodies had met in both competition and training exercises. We were in fact at, "…the forefront of open sea rescue…" and we "…had no peers…" according to the best of US military rescue.

Therefore for those of us who, despite upturned lives, still respected Friedrich for his achievements there were many questions left unanswered when, in what seemed like a heartbeat after the funeral service, the police quietly closed the case. It was as though in the eyes of the Australian government, Friedrich and the NSCA had never existed…

Prime Minister Bob Hawke circa 1986 on one of at least two flights in an NSCA helicopter.

CHAPTER 8

NSCA Pararescue (Have a Good One)

IN THE SUMMER OF 83-84, a few mates and I decided that we should go and experience skydiving. I had never really thought much about the challenge of doing this; yeah it may involve testing my exposure to heights, but seriously, how hard could it be?

Back in 1975, as a 15-year-old at a school fair, I was with a bunch of mates watching as a small plane orbited high over our field. We were getting impatient waiting for the skydivers to jump out and were full of ignorant, testosterone-fuelled remarks about the inadequacies of the jumpers. Or engineering science teacher, Mr Wigham, was with us too, occasionally rolling his eyes at some of our more outlandish remarks.

When the jumpers finally appeared there was a considerable anti-climax as their chutes opened just seconds after leaving the plane. We had expected to see smoke trails for around thirty seconds or so, like when watching the Red Devils at military air displays. To make matters worse though, only two of the three jumpers landed anywhere near the marker flag in the middle of the field, with one jumper landing a good 100m from this in amongst the crowd. We giggled like, well, school kids at their pathetic display.

Mr Wigham, perhaps appreciating the challenges of the low cloud and gusting winds more than his young charges, commented on our observations.

"Hey, boys, those men just jumped from a real airplane. You talk big here on the ground, but I bet you would chicken out if you ever had the opportunity to do it."

Heading up the highway north from Geelong that late summer morning in 1984, I had been in Australia for close to a year and a half. With me in the car was Geoff Dunham, my flatmate and dive buddy at Melbourne Diving Services (the SCUBA school and club we both attended) and Cathy Tucker, Geoff's girlfriend. The previous weekend we had watched some of Geoff's mates undertake an advanced stage of the course we were about to try. These blokes were supposed to be doing 'dummy ripcord pulls' as a lead up to their first freefall, but all three of them buggered this up and pulled their reserve handles instead. One came down with a bundle of canopy between his legs, another with his main and reserve deployed fully with him hanging between both, but the last bloke somehow managed to deploy his reserve inside his main. This was quite alarming! As we watched, the main partially collapsed and then re-inflated all the way to the ground, threatening to collapse both canopies in the process. How could they stuff up such a simple task?

As we approached Meredith, the small country town where the skydiving school was located, my mind was drifting back to Mr Wigham's words. Then, recalling the images of the previous weekend, I found my palms moistening slightly as the first inkling of doubt crept into my head. Hmmm, what could possibly go wrong?

Pulling into the small airfield parking area - an open grass space near a couple of hangars and a small office type building, we spied Rod Thompson, a mate from the Port Emergency Service. He was with his new girlfriend who was also going to be jumping. We said hellos, talked shit for a while, then joined around eight others as a skydiving instructor named Richard called us into the building to commence training.

Richard was a well-spoken man in his mid-twenties with a dry sense of humour. He had an eloquent way of describing parachuting procedures, including the anxiety we were likely to experience after boarding the small Cessna aircraft for the climb to 2500 feet, our jump height.

"As I point to you, indicating that you should move over to the door, you may feel apprehension."

The morning consisted of theory where we were shown how a parachute was supposed to work (my apprehension was building) and the way in which we were meant to steer it to the ground for a safe landing. A safe landing was the obvious choice, but variations of landing procedure depending upon wind strength and direction before ground contact suggested that 'safe landing' was not a goal achieved by all?

As the day progressed, we practised standard and emergency drills, the latter raising doubt about the likelihood of success if I had to execute such maneuvers. Richard's directions went something like this:

"Ok, you identify that you have a parachute malfunction. Immediately, you bring your right hand to the reserve handle and your left arm across the top of the reserve container."

We were using chest-mounted reserves as back up to our static-line opened 'round' parachutes on our backs.

"Then, after determining the direction of rotation, you pull the reserve handle, collect the canopy as the container opens and throw it in the opposite direction of your rotation. After doing this, you will shake the lines now rapidly entangling around your legs and then keep on shaking the lines until the reserve canopy has wrapped around your face. Once this has been completed, you simply empty the contents of your bowel until finally being put out of your misery when high-speed contact with the ground occurs."

At the completion of training, it was late in the afternoon. Richard selected four students for the first and last load of the day. The rest of us would be coming back the next morning to undertake our jumps.

As the little plane climbed into the remaining light of the day, we watched attentively, anticipating each step in the process we had recently been taught. An Irish guy with the clichéd name of Paddy was first out. His canopy deployed ok, and we watched as a moderate wind pushed him away from the centre of the airfield. As he closed on the ground it was apparent he was well off target, and we watched in alarm as he closed on the only power line within range of the field. He was going to hit it, there was no doubt, and other instructors who had remained behind were yelling instructions to steer him clear, but a round canopy has little maneuverability!

Paddy collected the power line with a large flash! Instructors jumped in a ute and headed at high speed to where Paddy was dangling, suspended about 8-feet from the ground in a perfect silhouette with the rapidly developing red sunset behind him.

Not surprisingly, the remaining jumps were cancelled, and Paddy was recovered, alive, not electrocuted, but very wide-eyed. Not much was said about this incident, but we were advised to be back at the drop zone by 8 am the next day.

The next morning, somewhat apprehensive to use Richard's words, we climbed aboard the little Cessna. Richard positioned us facing rearward with him at the rear of the plane. I was last on board and would, therefore, be first out. As we rolled down the undulating grass runway I was acutely aware that there was no door and conscious that the only thing keeping me on board was my grip on the airframe – later I was to cringe at the cowboy training this school undertook.

As we climbed to jump height, Richard pointed out specific heights.

"One thousand feet!"

As he yelled, he pointed to his altimeter. This was the signal for us to look at the ground and become familiar with various sights and landmarks to aid our recognition on the way down. Finally, though, the plane levelled and commenced a straight run over the small airfield. My heart rate up to this point had been relatively high, but when Richard pointed to me and yelled,

"You're on jump run!"

Fear, like I couldn't remember experiencing ever before, filled my body. To truly understand this level of terror you must have sat in an open doorway at 2,500-feet. Imagine you are in a plane and someone opens the door and asks you to dangle your legs over the edge. The ground looked so close. It was hard ground too, that my flesh and bone body would impact violently, painfully, terminally, if my parachute failed to operate and I didn't follow the complicated procedures in the event of a malfunction. The knot of tension in my stomach was growing intensely as we closed on the exit point, not that I was looking down.

My hands were fore and aft on the doorframe, body slightly twisted with half my arse in space. My head was up slightly too, looking at Richard who had positioned in front of me as the airflow buffeted my body.

I heard him call "power off" and then a moment later the plane's engine throttle back. His eyes locked with mine as he nodded and yelled, "Go!"

The next few moments were a blur. For a Nano-second, I remember his face and the wing above me. Then there was a deafening rush of air, and a white void as I continued to fall with arms and legs stretched wide. In the midst of this confusion, I was counting aloud, but not really aware of my actions.

"One thousand, two thousand, three th-"

The deceleration was not as severe as I had imagined it would be, but as the canopy deployed above me I became aware of my rapid gasping and strained groans. These involuntary reactions were generated in part from the realisation that I was not going to die, but also as a component of my hyper-tense body entering a period of recovery.

The simplest way to describe the exit from the plane until canopy deployment was, BLOODY TERRIFYING!

Hanging there, beneath the canopy, about three seconds past before I continued with the drills we had been shown. I reached up and located two wooden toggles that controlled the steering lines. These simple devices were connected to lines that closed holes, or 'modifications' at the rear of the round parachute. By closing a hole on one side it caused air to propel the canopy in a slow rotation as it escaped from the other hole, but not much else. The forward speed was negligible, meaning that I was going to land somewhere within a small cone below the point I was dispatched – if there was no wind.

By the time I was descending past around 1500-feet I had my bearings. My once sensation overloaded eyes could now see the hangar and other drop zone buildings. Importantly, I could also see the windsock and smaller 'streamers' positioned closer to the target area. I was about 250m from the desired landing point, but heading away from it at an angle of around 60-degrees. Pulling on the right toggle, I aligned myself with the target area and gauged the range. I had about 220m to go and was now below 500-feet.

'I'm going to make it,' I thought confidently.

How wrong I was! Still, around 200m from the target area, reality sunk in. I checked below and to my alarm saw the only pile of rocks within 2-kilometres of the drop zone. I briefly thought about turning, but Richard's words jumped into my head and so I prepared for landing.

"Don't attempt to turn when low. All you will do is increase the rate at which you hit the ground."

We had been advised that usual ground impact was about 18-feet per second, 'like jumping off the roof of a house'. Increasing the possible pain associated with such impact forces was obviously not my intention, so bringing my feet and knees together (to prevent fractured bones) I braced for contact with the rocks.

Any moment now… not long… I looked down between my feet. One moment the rocks were getting close and then all of a sudden they rushed up to meet me. Pain smashed my senses! The soles of my feet and my left side where on fire. Fuck that hurt!

I just lay there for a second or two, and then slowly began wriggling my toes and then moving my legs. The pain was easing though, and I don't think anything was broken. Remembering Richard's words again, I slowly stood up to indicate I was ok. Was I though? Either way, I gathered up the canopy and walked back to the target area where Geoff was close to landing.

The prick was only 30m away, and above him, Cathy and Rod looked as though they would land at a similar range, all on nice soft grass too.

It turned out I had been used as a wind-drift indicator. Like Paddy the previous evening; the cowboys of Meredith elected to use me instead of a paper 'streamer' to gauge wind-drift to determine the best exit point. Geoff, Cathy and Rod benefited from this, and after their grass landings, they were keen to go again.

"Are you in, Mick?"

For some stupid reason, I said yes.

This time the terror was far worse as I knew what was coming, but at least the landing (on grass thankfully) wasn't as bad. We went back the next weekend too, but bad weather prevented us jumping. I was glad. I never mentioned it to the others, but as far as I was concerned, I had completed my last jump. It was too bloody frightening. Why would anyone want to do this for fun?

Shortly after this little adventure I met a five-foot-nothing, university educated, very cute librarian. Opposites do attract. I am confident in this because after 30+ years of marriage, Mandy and I are living proof. In the background to the adventures in this book, we dived in numerous locations, walked across mountains and ventured to exotic places around Asia. Our two kids, probably like anyone else's, also ensured we have had additional challenges along the way. Jess was caught up in civil unrest whilst doing volunteer nursing in a remote Kenyan village, and Lachlan missed flights, ran out of money, and never answered his phone whilst in places like Cancun. Adventures aside, Mandy has been there for me, often to her own detriment, keeping me honest, and I doubt I would have achieved as much without her. An example of this was her re-writing my application for the NSCA. My effort was terrible, and frankly, wouldn't have got past the first review. Mandy's effort, and her ongoing support, not only ensured I got a foot in the door, but helped me to confront the challenges you will read about in this chapter and the rest of the book.

Just over four years following my failed experiment with parachuting, I was sitting near the head of a boardroom table after completing selection testing for NSCA Pararescue. Around the room were heads of department from Training, Parachuting, Diving, Medical, Physiotherapy, Psychology and the Executive Director himself, John Friedrich.

During the preceding days we had been tested physically and mentally, and of the original 300 applicants from around the country, 15 had made it to the interview stage.

Friedrich began. He had my resume in his hands, as did the panel members.

"Ok, err, Mick, did you enjoy the last few days?"

"Yes, thank you."

I was feeling very awkward. I had worn a jacket and tie, but everyone else was dressed casually. Friedrich looked at the closest head of a department.

"Medical?"

"Fine John."

He continued around the table with similar responses and finished with Parachuting. This bloke looked me in the eye.

"Why did you stop skydiving, Mick?"

It was a fair question for someone who had aspirations of leaping out of a plane for a living, but I had prepared for it.

"I tried to continue, but when we returned to the drop zone, the weather was always bad and prevented us jumping. After a while, I thought I was going backwards and so I just concentrated on my diving."

"Happy Potsy?"

Friedrich received a nod of acknowledgement and then looked at me; I had a collection of documents in my hand.

"Err, what do you have there, Mick?"

"Confirmation of the qualifications I have recorded in my resume."

Friedrich waved his hand in dismissal.

"We've checked those already. Anybody else?"

The panel shook their heads, and Friedrich looked at me once more.

"Err, why the change from the Port of Melbourne, Mick?"

"I wasn't getting anything out of it and wasn't going anywhere with it."

The answer had just popped into my head. Friedrich smiled, and I was excused.

During part of the drive back to Melbourne and the hospital where my wife and newborn daughter waited, my mind wondered about the day I would have to put on a parachute again if I was successful, and my palms moistened on the steering wheel.

Around six months later after completing most of the land and marine training components, the six successful candidates of the NSCA Pararescue Rookie-6 course were handed to the Sky Gods to commence the first component of jump training, Accelerated Free Fall, which was commonly abbreviated to the phonetic, AFF.

In the eighties, most parachute training commenced with static-line at 2,500-feet and students slowly progressed to freefall of extended delays as ability and height was increased. The Sky Gods were probably the first in Australia to turn this long-established process on its head, literally, by starting training with an initial jump from 16,000-feet. The rationale for this was the number of fatalities or serious injuries occurring with first jump static-line students. The Sky Gods had determined that a novice was highly unlikely to undertake precise emergency drills due to sensory overload, I couldn't agree more, or execute drills too late for them to be effective. For those of you old enough to remember the eighties you may recall news reports corroborating their concerns:

"The reserve parachute failed to open" or "the parachute didn't open in time to prevent the student from impacting the ground".

So with safety in mind, the Sky Gods used AFF to expose students to the sensation of freefall first. With the added height of 16,000-feet there was also time for the student, strapped to the instructor initially, to practice pulling dummy handles and then observe standard canopy openings. This important familiarisation was followed by a one-on-one direction on how to control the parachute to a safe landing. AFF is commonplace these days, and it's unlikely that you will ever find a school teaching static-line unless you join the military.

The NSCA Sky Gods were a team of primarily four: Banjo, Potsy, Dinky and Johnny. All PJs, they also represented the NSCA at skydiving in four-way relative-work competitions. Four-way is a discipline where after leaving the aircraft the team would complete as many formations as possible before the mandatory canopy deployment height. Competing as the 'Forth Force', the Sky Gods had been Australian champions for some years. Not only had they beaten the best sports jumpers in Australia, but they had also beaten the best military teams in similar competitions and at their first world championship had placed sixth.

Another Sky God, although not a member of the Forth Force, had a similar ability. 'Truck' was a Vietnam veteran and former Special Air Service jump-instructor. Also a serving PJ, Truck's primary role was to teach us accuracy. As Australian champion in this discipline, plus being consistently in the top three in the world, we were acutely aware of the expertise Friedrich had gathered to support this next phase of our training.

The theory and practice before our first jump, however, was not what I had expected. We revised aircraft emergencies, briefed and practised exits, and then we donned a harness for the climb to altitude; the whole process taking no more than 30-minutes.

Maso (another member of Rookie Six) and I were sitting on the floor of Juliet Echo Yankee (JEY), one of the Council's two relatively large single-engine turboprop Cessna Caravans. Not C-130's, but a damn sight cheaper to operate with rapid turnaround times between loads to 16,000-feet. With us were Dinky and Banjo who would be acting as our Tandem-Masters for this first Jump. The brief we'd received was pretty simple.

"Hold an arch after exit and then check the canopy when you feel opening shock."

For the rest of the jump, I sensed the primary requirement was to stave off screaming as we adjusted to the new sensation of freefall.

The climb up to altitude in JEY was noisy, a little cold, and a perfect opportunity to practice 'stress management'.

Before commencing hazardous training (so very early in the course), we had attended sessions with the Council's psychologist. Gavin, at around the fifty mark, had grey hair and spoke with a soft, friendly voice as you might expect; but he also had a sense of humour not associated with that first impression.

"Good weekend Gavin?" I had asked one Monday morning.

"Yes, Mick, I spent most of the weekend making love to my wife, so bloody great, actually."

Gavin's wife, plus other medical staff were within earshot of this remark and didn't bat an eye. Gavin was indeed gifted with unique skills to deal with the range of personalities PJs presented. Moreover, his research into 'Critical Incident Stress' ensured he had the expertise required to both mentor operations personnel and manage the effect of their work-related activity. His first session with Rookie-6 wasn't going to plan though.

What can possibly go wrong

We were all laying back on beanbags with our eyes shut. Gavin had asked us to think of a place that always made us happy: a holiday location, favourite pub, the ocean, whatever brought a smile to your face. The intent of this was to build coping mechanisms for when a challenge was coming our way, i.e. on your way to leap into a bushfire, preparing to dive for bodies in zero visibility or, climbing to your first freefall from 16,000-feet etc. The trouble with the session was probably due to the age and ego of the men on the beanbags who had collectively, through one eye open smirks, formed the opinion this was all a little bit too arty-farty. Gavin continued.

"Focus on this place now, remember how it made you relax and unwind…"

A snigger escaped one of Rookie-6, then another. Gavin changed tact.

"Alright! Listen up!" The aggression in his voice silenced us immediately. "I don't care where you've been, or what you've done in the past!" His voice softened slightly "This job you are training to do, will, not maybe, but *will*, present you with some demanding sights and challenges. If you can accept now that these challenges will fuck, you, up, you'll deal with them a lot better when they occur."

With our egos put back in their respective boxes, Gavin now had our full attention and continued.

"People who believe they will cope no matter what, are generally the ones who need the most help. Remember this boys', because Pararescue will challenge you."

Passing 10,000-feet my mind was on a Maldivian beach. The image of sugar-white sand, turquoise water and overhanging palm trees from our honeymoon were not entirely blocking out the door that would shortly be opened, but they were doing enough.

Looking around the cabin I saw that Maso looked like I felt, Dinky was reading a book, and Banjo, with eyes shut, was rehearsing emergency procedures. Putting his book down, Dinky passed me an O2 mask, and I took a couple of breaths in the reduced atmosphere of the unpressurised cabin. I passed the mask to Maso, and we continued up.

Arriving at 16,000-feet, now connected to the front of Dinky's harness by my own, we edged towards the door in a rehearsed maneuver. Dinky was outboard of me as I eased up, reaching for a handle on the roof above the open door. With both hands on this, my head and shoulders were above the roof of JEY in the airflow. In the periphery to my left was the blur of the propeller, and everywhere else was a blue void in the crisp, clear sky.

I found myself surprisingly calm. I think Gavin's training had helped, but moreover, I believe it was the professional approach leading up to this point that had kept my pulse in check.

I swung my left leg as per the brief and voiced my actions into the 80-knot airflow:

"Out, in, arch!"

On the arch call, I released my grip and formed a hard arch position, arms and legs in a spread-eagle beneath Dinky. My first conscious thought after letting go was that there was no sensation of falling, just a deafening rush of air and immense pressure on my body - stick your head out a car window at 150kph, and you will get the idea.

As we continued to fall, I knew Dinky was there, but couldn't feel him. I was having a ball.

'Hey, you're in freefall; did you hear me, you're freefalling! You're that little dot in the sky. Yeeharrrr!'

My excitement dissolved though when I began to realise we were getting closer to the ground.

'Fuck, I hope this works...'

The deceleration that followed was significant, and pressure on my leg straps was intense. I looked up immediately and watched the canopy deploying above us as, to my immense relief, the parachute opened fully at the briefed height of 5000-feet. Dinky was talking, but my ears were still partially deafened from the roar of air. Wiggling my jaw, I got some function back and picked up on what he was saying.

"...Bad spot. Look over that way and you will see we're a long way from the base."

I couldn't see where he was pointing to, there was just a lot of grassy paddocks, but I acknowledged him anyway as he continued.

"Ok, quick steering lesson, then I'll take over and get us a bit closer. Take these."

He handed me the two webbing loops connected to the tandem-rigs steering lines and talked me through a series of turns. Sitting in the harness felt fine, and the steering process was not complicated. Quickly though, he took them back, and we continued towards the ground.

As this approached, memories of that first sports jump came flashing back, and my pulse rate increased; the relief though, when we gently bumped onto a lush grassy paddock was both wonderful and encouraging. AFF-1 was complete.

I left JEY in the same manner for AFF-2; still strapped to Dinky, but this time I was not along for the ride. I had to perform altitude checks, and dummy ripcord pulls at designated heights. Following the brief, I voiced my actions internally as I moved my head (and eyes) from up to down.

"Horizon, ground, altimeter."

With the last action, I focused on the device attached to my chest strap. The needle was moving, approaching 12,000-feet. It was time for a dummy ripcord pull. Turning my head right slightly, I called "see", and focused on the handle positioned at my right side for this purpose. Calling "feel" next, I brought my arms in from the arch position simultaneously, one going to the handle, the other symmetrically opposed touching my head. During this simple action my arms were buffeted and deflected slightly in the airflow (like an arm outside a car). The final part of this drill was "pull", but I left the handle in place, as per the brief, and brought my arms back to an arch.

Completing three of these drills, I pulled the handle on the last, and the canopy deployed, once again at the height of 5000-feet.

Dinky gave me control and talked me through some more procedures: brake checks and stall limits. The first of these involved turning into the wind, looking between your feet and gauging the speed relative to ground movement. You then pulled both steering lines and watched as the speed reduced. When there was no longer any movement, you had reached full-brake for the relative wind speed. Going beyond this point could produce a stall, not good at low level, as Dinky demonstrated with plenty of sky beneath us.

"Ok watch this. See we have stopped, that's full brake. If I pull further... look upwards, Mick."

I looked up to the canopy. It buffeted for a moment and then collapsed. We dropped like a stone. Dinky released the brakes and pumped the lines, the canopy re-inflated quickly, and we continued towards the target area at West Sale, but not before losing about 150-feet during the stall.

"So, brake checks are important. You will do them a number of times during each jump before setting up for landing."

With AFF-2 completed we were handed over to Truck for flight planning and landing drills.

When in competition, Truck's accuracy and that of his rivals was measured in centimetres. Aiming at a plate-sized target it was a given that the leading jumpers would always hit this, so to determine the best, an individual's foot-strike was vital. If they managed to do this dead centre of the plate, they would record a zero score, off centre and their score would be recorded in centimetres from the centre. Winners had very low numbers or even zero at the end of a competition. To support preparation for such competition, Truck spent time with Gavin because confidence in oneself was an equally important factor in the range of jumping skills required. He also had free access to a Cessna Caravan for repeated practice jumps too, which helped, but at that elite level, Gavin's teachings probably meant the difference between just being accurate and being champion.

Truck first took us through performance characteristics of the ram-air (square) parachutes we would be using. The X-300, compared to today's handkerchief-sized sporting rigs was like a tractor compared to a sports car, but we needed the extra canopy to support all the equipment we were expected to carry when on operations.

With seven cells, or hollow partitions between two layers of rip-stop fabric, air filled these spaces travelling from front to back producing a rectangular wing when the parachute was fully 'inflated'. The air escaping from the rear of the cells produced a forward speed of 25-knots and, by closing off end-cells with the brake lines, this speed could be reduced as required. If just one end-cell was partially closed, the canopy would rotate slowly allowing for heading change. However, if the turn were aggressive, the rotation (and 'G' forces) would increase rapidly causing the PJs blood to rush to his feet as the canopy banked to an angle of around 60-80 degrees. Such rotation also resulted in rapid height loss too.

Another method of control was the front-risers that were connected to the array of parra-cords that in turn connected to the canopy. If one of these were pulled down the leading edge of the canopy would flatten, causing a stall of that area of 'wing', and the PJ would spiral very steeply towards the ground. Pulling both front risers increased forward speed slightly above maximum, but also resulted in a higher descent rate.

So, with this knowledge on board, Truck walked us through post canopy opening drills.

The first step was to 'check target' and 'check wind'. Sighting the 'pit', a gravel mound about 8m in diameter, the PJ would first gauge his distance from it. Then, turning into the wind, a brake check was completed at the same time as determining the 'wind cone'.

Picture a line upwind from the pit to where the PJ was suspended under his X-300. If he is directly in line with pit and wind, provided he is not too far upwind, it is relatively easy to steer back along the 'windline'. If however, he is crosswind, he will have to steer, or 'crab' back to reach the pit before the wind pushes him past it. Therefore, the strength of the wind and the maximum forward speed of the X-300 will determine a variable 'wind-cone' which the PJ needs to be inside to reach his target. The greater the wind strength, the narrower the cone, and zero wind will produce a circular wind-cone all around the pit.

With this first check out of the way the PJ remains inside the wind-cone and completes a series of checks aiming to fly over the pit at around 900-1100-feet. Depending on the wind strength he will then fly downwind, past the pit before turning back into wind following a half-light-bulb type path to ensure he remains on-line for the final approach to the pit.

During this final approach, subtle adjustments are made on brake lines to gauge speed to an aiming point at which the PJ will pull both lines down to 'flare' before landing. A flare is a procedure to stall the wing; and if this is successful, the PJ will make contact with the ground as though he has just stepped from a bus. Flaring late, however, may cause a significant impact as the canopy drives the PJ into the ground. Equally, flaring too early may cause a stall at height with subsequent painful impact. Because the likelihood of such error was high on first solo jumps, Truck took us through Parachute Landing Falls, or PLF's.

Just like army jump training, we practised over and over again with feet and knees together, elbows inwards protecting our heads as we rolled to the ground distributing contact evenly along our bodies. When Truck was happy we could do this regardless of our direction of travel, he wished us well and smiled.

"Don't worry boys, if you stuff things up, Dinky will come and visit you in hospital."

We were back with the Sky Gods the next day for emergency procedure training.

Suspended in harnesses from the roof of the hangar, that held us belly to the ground, we ran through drill after drill as the Sky Gods spun us and yelled at us to try and throw us off. Each drill started with the 'see', 'feel', 'pull' sequence and then continued with the ubiquitous parachuting count.

"One thousand… Two thousand… Three thousand…"

If everything went to plan, we should be experiencing opening shock at this point, but for the emergency drill of a high-speed-malfunction, we continued.

"Four thousand."

Rotate head and shoulders twisting from the waist to 'disturb' a potential vortex holding the canopy's pilot chute behind our back.

"Five thousand."

Malfunction!

"Look"

Identify the chrome reserve handle and the soft green cut-away pad.

"Locate"

Bring both hands in symmetrically and take hold of both devices.

"Punch right."

Push your right hand, holding the cut-away pad, out to its full extent.

"Punch left."

Push your left hand, holding the reserve handle, out to its full extent.

"Arch"

Form a hard arch to ensure belly to earth as the reserve deploys.

"Check"

Ensure both cut-away and reserve wires have been pulled out completely.

"Clear"

Remove any wire remaining.

At this point, in theory, the reserve should be deployed, and the PJ would continue the descent as per the flight plan, the only difference being the colour of the canopy. Not the standard Pararescue yellow, but black; the dark colour reducing the effect of ultra-violet light damage (or if you believed the media, 'for covert operations'). The more

UV damage a canopy received meant more porosity and therefore less lift and, not what you want during a malfunction, slower openings.

Other malfunction-types could occur after the main canopy was opened. With these, we had to identify, for a novice, subtle variances such as a line-over. This was when a single or group of para-cords ended up over the main canopy. For the PJ below when a line-over occurred things weren't that different; he had slowed, could probably steer his canopy, but critical performance was lost that may result in heavy ground impact.

Additionally, there were not so subtle post canopy deployment malfunctions to consider. There was a range of potential causes, but the result was the same; a spin developed that the PJ wouldn't be able to control requiring immediate execution of emergency procedures. The Sky Gods reinforced all the above before the final aspect of emergency training was undertaken.

"So, whatever a malfunction resembles, you will, without further thought, immediately execute emergency procedures!"

For the umpteenth time, we ran through the sequence on the ground just to be sure we had it squared away.

Before heading out to JEY for AFF-3 though, we went back to the classroom and sat down in front of a TV. Here, we were subjected to around 20-minutes of canopy deployment sequences captured by cameramen as their canopies unfolded above them. The final part of this involved watching a bunch of skydivers acting along to the words of the song 'Jump' by Van Halen. There was even one skydiver 'standing by the record machine' in a bar and finally the same guy mouthing the lyrics in freefall; it was quite funny and helped relieve building tension.

We would be undertaking AFF-3 one at a time, exiting with a Sky God either side holding onto our harnesses and their cameraman, 'Sparksy' filming the jump for debriefing purposes. Banjo gave one final piece of advice as I headed out for my jump.

"If after pulling your ripcord you identify a canopy that looks any different to the videos you've just watched, or either of your two tandem openings, you will execute emergency procedures immediately. Clear?"

I was.

The climb up was halted at 14,000-feet due to the cloud, and I moved to the door wearing my own parachute. I was anxious, but as before, sufficiently under control to focus on procedure. Standing with hands on the rail I had Potsy to my left, Banjo to my right and below him, hanging in space with one hand on the rear door handle, Sparksy with a camera on his helmet.

I looked towards Potsy who nodded slowly mouthing the word 'OK'. Following the out, in, arch drill we dropped away, immediately turning upside down. Holding the arch as briefed we returned belly to earth, and I commenced the height checks, and dummy ripcord pulls as before.

The first of these drills were completed at 9000-feet, I was behind schedule and my tension increased. We were in and out of cloud too, and my goggles had fogged up, then all of a sudden my body started to pitch from head to toe about an axis at my waist. No matter how hard I tried to stop this with my arch, it just increased!

I felt a fist smash onto the top of my helmet. Then another, Banjo was giving me the signal to 'calm down, relax, you are too tense'.

In such a tense state a falling body becomes rigid and 'pig-roots' on the pressure of air beneath it. The simplest way to correct this action was to relax.

Simple? Yeah right! My alarm was increasing, I only had partial vision due to fogged up goggles, but another bash on the head followed by two more in quick succession, fortunately, had the desired effect. Relaxing, well trying to relax, I focused on the drills and the pig-rooting reduced, just a bit, but at least I didn't get any more bangs on the head.

The deployment or 'dump' height was 6000-feet to ensure I had both plenty of time to manage a malfunction and to practice steering.

I had been told not to worry about the pit though, just to focus on being into wind at around 500-feet and landing with a PLF, regardless of how well I thought my flare might be.

As the altimeter needle passed 6,500-feet, I brought my hands in.

"See, feel, pull, one thousand, two thousand, three thous-"

The deceleration was much the same as with the tandem and my head cocked up to...

"Check-canopy".

I actually yelled the words. It was there, deploying just like the movies we'd watched. What a most beautiful sight. I quickly got on with the drill.

Check target!

I was about 1000-meters from the pit and off wind-line by around 600m. Turning into the wind, I completed a brake check; I then turned back, well outside the wind-cone to run, crabbing, towards the pit. Although a novice, I knew I wasn't going to get there. Nonetheless, I continued in the general direction, continuing to crab across the wind completing brake-checks as I descended to verify whether the wind strength was changing at the lower altitude.

Below me and about 100-meters ahead, I saw both Banjo and Potsy spiralling down, fast, with bodies well to the side of their canopies. They landed about 400m from the pit and, as briefed, I used them as my target.

I passed overhead them at about 900-feet and continued downwind, gestimating the correct distance. Turning back into the wind on final approach I knew that I was too close though, the angle was too steep. I pulled on the brakes to half and commenced a series of 'S' turns in an attempt to lose height as per Truck's briefing. As I was doing this, I saw the chase car (a small 4WD) pull up at Potsy and Banjo's position. Potsy retrieved two large red paddles and held these above his head signifying my brake line position and that I should follow his arm movements. He had me complete another 'S' turn and then extended his arms fully up (brakes off) for the final approach to landing – sufficient speed is required to achieve a successful flare.

He was walking backwards quickly, with arms still up, as I was going to overshoot their original position by around 20m. Finally though, with the ground getting very close, he pulled both arms down smoothly until the paddles were by his hips. I reciprocated and felt my sink rate reduce rapidly. Seconds later, with feet and knees together, I completed a soft PLF onto the grass. Standing immediately, I then pulled on one brake line to fully collapse the canopy in the 12-knot breeze. How good was that!

The boys completed their AFF-3s over the next couple of days, and we all enjoyed watching each other's movies, commenting like the experts we weren't on body position and hand movements.

AFF-4 was with just one instructor and Sparksy. Banjo had given me simple advice to defog the goggles, which involved turning your head to the airflow so that air could enter through a small mesh vent. This simple advice significantly improved my confidence as I think the lack of vision had been the primary cause of my tense body.

Remaining ahead of the game with the height checks and dummy ripcord pulls, I confidently dumped at the lower height of 5000-feet.

My flight plan was executed more efficiently, and I'd had a reasonable spot too, but as I turned on final though, I knew I was going to miss the pit by at least 100-meters. Nonetheless, I concentrated on the landing; this time without paddle assistance and completed another soft PLF. AFF-5 remained.

On this last jump, we were to exit the Caravan independently. Sparksy would drop away with me, and Potsy would follow. I was required to complete the same drills, but also to steer onto a heading ('point north towards the mountains') and complete a series of back-loops to verify I had control in freefall.

I was stable very quickly after exit and by twisting my body at the hip; I aligned with the mountains with minimal effort. It was back-loop time.

Potsy had told me to concentrate on drill sequence and not the normal actions to roll your body if you were say, in water or on a trampoline.

"From the arch, tuck your knees up sharply. This will immediately flip you over in the airflow. Once you turn over, immediately go back into a hard arch; then, once stable, re-align with the mountains."

Passing 14,000-feet, I brought my knees up for the first time. I felt a moment of increased acceleration as I inverted and then quickly arched, emphasising the angle of my head upwards. In a blur of rotation, I was stable again, the mountains were there, a few degrees to my right, so I corrected heading and checked the height. 11,000-feet. I repeated the process about three more times and saw the height was still above 8000-feet. Potsy was in front of me and twirled an extended index finger, beckoning me to do it again.

Stable once more, Potsy was even closer with his hand extended and a huge grin on his air-buffeted face. I brought my own hand in for a brief shake while grinning like a child. How brilliant was this!

Checking the altimeter, I was past 6000-feet and so waited a moment longer before executing the drill. I had a good canopy deployment and set up for a reasonable flight plan. The spot wasn't great again (more clouds), and we landed about a kilometre away, but this time I completed my first stand-up. Awesome!

Unfortunately, though, the fun of AFF was over, and we were about to commence the real work of PJs, static-line from 2,500-feet, with increasing challenge and a focus on accuracy.

The rationale for static-line was real-world conditions on a SAR task. Simply, SAR's didn't occur on bright, sunny days. There was a good chance of low cloud, rain and strong winds, so we needed to be close to earth to see the target and to ensure an accurate spot, i.e. an exit point to position us correctly within the wind-cone. Over-water this was especially important as we would be carrying 80kg of equipment and the static-line would ensure canopy deployment immediately after leaving the aircraft.

After more theory and ground practice that included the 'grab a fat chick' exit position, we headed out, all six of us, to JEY. The grab a fat chick position included legs too; picture a head high beach ball and a PJ, in a vertical plane, with arms and legs wrapped around it. This was how we were to leave the aircraft. The Sky Gods had determined that this position, with airflow on our backs, maximised stability and therefore effective canopy deployment when carrying large amounts of equipment from the small doors of our aircraft. But this first jump was to be clean-fatigue, i.e. no equipment, just the X-300.

With all seats removed, we sat on JEY's floor, in pairs, facing the rear and connected by a lanyard with a karabiner as the Caravan climbed to height.

Banjo was wearing a parachute too; he knelt by the roller door and lifted this up, locking it in place on the roof once we were at jump height.

Wearing a green Nomex flight suit, similar gloves, Protec helmet and GP boots I stood up (in a noticeable stoop due to the low roof) when requested, as did Maso. We were half a pace back from the door and would be dispatched as a pair on this first run. Banjo had secured our static-lines to anchor points on the floor, and waiting there, we both checked each other's reserve pins, leg and chest connections. These were Quick-Eject-Clips (QEJ's) designed for rapid release of our parachute harnesses after water entry. Knowing how effective the QEJ's were though, it prompted an almost obsessive-compulsive routine of multiple QEJ checks before exit.

Banjo, with head out in the airflow and aligned with the body of JEY was conning the pilot into the wind over the pit. The con consisted of simple heading corrections.

"Five right... Straight..."

I saw the pit pass beneath us, and it looked so bloody close compared to the view at 16,000-feet, as a result, my pulse rate increased. In a moment of distraction, I twisted to Maso who had a hand extended, open palm upwards. I smacked my hand down on his.

"Have a good one!"

We yelled in unison, repeating the low-five and then I turned back to Banjo. He moved from the door and beckoned me forward. As I cautiously eased into the stooped exit position, Banjo took my static line, and I waited as he did a final check.

I was bent forward from the waist to fit in the low door, with my feet on its lip and hands braced on either side of the doorframe. It was cold, had been raining, not a particularly lovely winter day in East Gippsland. Banjo's hand smacked against my arse.

Pivoting on the ball of my left foot, I rotated rearward into space grabbing a fat chick.

"One thousand... Two thousand... Three thousand... Four thousand..."

Falling vertically, as planned, I twisted my body instinctively as per the emergency drill.

"Five thousand!"

My brain hadn't computed the seriousness of this number yet, but automatically, I continued with the drill.

"Look"

I sighted the handles.

"Loc-"

As my hands were coming in, I felt opening shock, albeit not as violent as freefall.

"Check canopy!"

Up above the canopy was deploying, but slower than expected. I reached up for the steering lines and pulled them down as the 'slider' slid down to the four webbing risers above my head.

A small square of rip-stop fabric, the slider had the para-cord lines threaded through metal eyes at each of its corners. The purpose of the slider was to slow the opening so as not to overstress the canopy, or the PJ. We had been briefed on its function, had seen it work on previous jumps, but I didn't expect such a difference with the relatively low-speed opening of static-line compared to the terminal velocity of freefall. Whatever, I still had to get to the pit.

I was in the wind-cone, but close to the pit and still at 1800-feet. I had to lose height quickly. Pulling down on the right line, I commenced a sharp turn. Holding this as 'G' forces picked up I felt the blood rushing to my feet as I angled well away from the vertical. Checking the altimeter on my chest, I saw 1400-feet and eased the turn to level off facing downwind for a run over the pit. My judgement wasn't good though, and I passed overhead at 1300-feet.

Running downwind, I gauged the distance required to lose sufficient height for a good final approach and then commenced the turn back. When on final approach though, I saw that I'd buggered it up. The angle to the pit was too shallow – I was too far away.

I landed standing up, quickly turning to deflate the canopy in the 15-knot breeze and collected up the canopy for the 40m walk back to the pit and the waiting Drop Zone Safety Officer (DZSO), Dinky, who had been monitoring my performance. He smiled.

"How was the snivelly opening, Mick?"

Apparently my exit, executed very well according to the debrief I received from Banjo, had something to do with the slow or, 'snivelly' opening. It was a shit-happens moment though and had I cut-away (used my reserve) it would have been deemed the correct decision. Putting that one in the not nice experience box, we continued with more clean-fatigue accuracy practice.

On that first jump the furthest from the pit had been around 100m and the closest, a Rookie called Maff, was about 2m from the gravel. Accuracy was everything now, and over the next five jumps we all got inside the required 10m and progressed to land equipment packs.

Operationally the packs contained a sizeable medical kit, including intravenous fluids, drugs and the usual airway, wound and fracture management gear. We also had survival and navigation equipment suitable for seven days of unsupported operations. Although unsupported ops was a standard operating procedure (SOP) we prepared for, they would be highly unlikely as supply drops would always be available; unless there were atrocious weather conditions of course. What could possibly go wrong?

The contents of our land equipment packs for training were more basic, consisting of just large water containers. Depending on how full these were, a Rookie would be carrying between 15-25kg extra as they waddled to the door in a shallow stoop.

For the climb to jump height we sat on the packs and when directed to stand we attached them to the X-300 before static-lines were secured. Stepping through the shoulder straps first, the jump-master would then connect quick release clips. These were different to the QEJ and were stitched into both the parachute harness and to attachments on either side of the pack. When fitted correctly the pack was in front of the PJs legs, the top suspended level with his thighs.

A final connection was to the rear of the parachute harness and consisted of a 2m webbing line. Once under canopy, the PJ would drop the pack via the quick releases to have it suspended by this line; the intent being to reduce the chance of leg injury in the event of a heavy landing.

I was behind a Rookie-6 bloke called 'Frommy' who was in the door with the pack suspended between his open legs waiting for the smack on the arse. Our height was just 1900-feet, not part of the plan, but due to necessity; it was a shitty day with 22-knots of wind and rain, and we were skimming below the cloud base. Despite this, patches of lower cloud would pass the door causing Potsy to direct the pilot to go around for another run. Braced in the cabin against the turbulence, with 20kg suspended from my harness, the difference between freefall and PJ operations became very apparent.

Finally, with Frommy gone, I moved into the open door and received a smack on the arse straight away. I hurriedly pivoted, and this caused an over-rotation as I fell away. On opening shock, my head was pushed forward as significant 'line-twists' prevented movement. Quickly though, they unwound, and my head was freed. Looking up,

I saw the canopy was deployed, but noticed the slider was still up, held by more twisted lines below it.

Line-twists were a common occurrence and not a severe emergency. The PJ would kick in the opposite direction until they unwound, but until this was achieved he couldn't steer the canopy.

With the twists freed, the slider dropped, and I commenced the drills.

Fuck! I was at 1500-feet, and directly over the pit. Releasing the brake lines I dropped my hands to the pack release clips at my waist, pushing the levers downwards. Catching the pack's straps with my feet, as briefed, I kept my feet at 90-degrees to hold onto the pack ensuring maximum stability during maneuvering. Then, with hands back on brake lines and looking past the pack to gauge wind speed, I found that just a small pull was required to stop forward movement. I decided to stay where I was and adjusted the brakes slightly in the 22-knot wind to keep my feet over the pit, but as I descended further the canopy started to buffet – it was jumping up and down what felt like half a meter in the gusting wind!

"If you feel any buffeting apply half brakes immediately. This will pressurise the cells and prevent the canopy collapsing."

Good safety tip! Banjo's words had jumped into my head, and I did as taught. The only problem though, I began to drift back, away from the pit.

At 300-feet I was probably 40m downwind, but as the buffeting had eased at little I released the brakes and tipped my feet forward to drop the pack. I managed to close to about 30m before a messy landing had me tripping over the pack's lanyard, falling on my back and then hurriedly trying to collapse the canopy as it pulled me along the wet grass.

Without a doubt, that was the most challenging jump of this phase. I think everyone at least touched gravel once during those four jumps and that was good because we were moving on to confined area landings.

Leaving West Sale for an unknown destination, we had been given simple instructions. Identify the target, pick a final approach point and follow the drills you have been practising.

I was first out of the last pair, with Goose (more on his name later) following behind me. Bent over in the door I could see the Longford Pines dirt runway as Dinky conned the pilot over the target – a day-glow pink cross laid out at the centre of the runway where a gravel road intersected it. The runway itself was about 5-meters wide with a cleared area extending about 20 to 30-meters both sides of the runway. Either side of the cleared area were pine trees, and these also ran alongside the gravel road. As we passed over the target, I saw the last of the second pair running in on final up the narrow road into the wind. Good plan. I would do the same.

I had a good exit and opening and commenced flight plan checks comfortably inside the wind-cone. Turing finals in the light wind I realised I had more speed than desired and would fly high over the target. Moreover, without immediate correction, I would also end up in the pine trees!

Commencing 'S' turns with a three-quarter brake, I managed to avoid the trees, landing about 5-meters from them and 20-meters upwind of the target. Some of the boys didn't have as much luck though. One bloke collected some head-high young trees at the perimeter of the cleared area, and another landed short on the gravel road with canopy entangling in low branches. Still, we were pretty pleased with our first effort. All of us choosing the same approach had got us within a reasonable distance, and nobody had ended up suspended in the trees. Looking skyward, we saw that Dinky had hopped out behind us.

There was the legendary Sky God on final approach running up the middle of the runway, flaring to hit the centre of the target in a perfect stand-up landing. He quickly gathered his canopy and came over to where we were standing. He wasn't happy.

"What the fuck was that! You have a whole fucking runway, and you elect to run up a dirt track terminating in a dead end? Boys, in case you hadn't fucking noticed there is less than four knots of wind, probably less than two knots now. I suggest you switch on because this was the only easy target you are going to get."

Egos back in their respective boxes once more, we headed out on confined area jump number two that afternoon.

I was to be first out and watched and listened intently as Dinky pointed out a property in amongst open paddocks. There was a road at the main entrance with a power line running alongside it. The main house was detached from a large shed and two smaller buildings in an 'L' shape. Between the house and the 'L' of the buildings was a small paddock with chest high fences measuring about 50-meters by 70-meters, although a portion of this was unavailable due to the proximity of the buildings. In the centre of the paddock was the day-glow cross.

On jump run, we passed over the buildings and continued over open land. Scanning the area, I realised that I would be turning final behind the buildings and would have to fly between them, albeit above, before landing. If I were low though, I would have to break away to avoid hitting the buildings and would miss the target.

Don't be low!

My flight plan went well. I passed over the target running downwind at just under 1000-feet, but turning finals I realised there was a dog-leg, i.e. a dramatic change in wind direction. It was now coming from my left shoulder.

Shit! Turning right 90-degrees to run downwind again, I twisted my head in an effort to watch the buildings. Satisfied I had given myself enough room I turned back, carefully watching the altimeter. I was at 300-feet running in on final, slightly out of wind, aiming to clear the 'L' shaped buildings before adjusting into the wind for landing. I crossed over the buildings at 50-feet, paddock fence at about 40-feet and landed within 5-meters of the target. It was by far the best jump I completed during the confined area phase. The last of these however…?

Once above 1000-feet, Banjo started getting us ready. I was in the second pair, second out. The target was a small island in the centre of a large dam. Probably 30-meters long it was about 10-meters wide at its widest point. Banjo was smiling as he beckoned us to the door.

Turning finals I dropped my equipment pack. My chin was resting on my chest ensuring no head movement to aid the accuracy of my final approach course corrections. There was a reasonable wind on my face as I lined up for the widest part of the thin island. The surface wind was too much for an effective flare in a crosswind landing I figured, so timing was going to be everything. Below me, I could see that one of the boys (Troy) had made it and another was in the dam (Maso) being picked up by a safety boat.

Goose, below and ahead of me, suddenly broke to the right and steered for the paddock to the side of the dam. He had been too high and would have gone in the water on the other side for sure. I was confident I would make it.

Adjusting my aim for the closest point of land on the island, I didn't want to overshoot; I braked sufficiently so that my flare would begin over water, 10-meters from the island. This was going to work. Here comes the water… the island is where it needs to be… and, flare.

Suddenly I was thrown forward smashing into the water face first, coming to rest 5-meters from the island. Doh! With my immense concentration, I had forgotten about my equipment pack, which had made for the perfect anchor. Fortunately, the water was only a meter deep though, and the only real damage was pride.

One other member of Rookie-6 (Jimmy Two-Heads) made a successful landing, but Maff, turning downwind late on final approach smacked into a foot or so of water at the edge of the island reasonably hard. He was uninjured but received a stern warning and reminder about 'target fixation' and the importance of into wind landing. Night jumps were next.

What can possibly go wrong

Moving from day to night operations produces raised anxiety no matter what the discipline, it's a primeval human emotion that has to be managed.

Taping small light sticks onto the top edge of our altimeters we left just a centimetre of yellow glow exposed. This was sufficient to illuminate the display, but not too much to destroy night vision. Banjo had briefed us on the procedures, essentially the same, but with reinforcement of no turns below 500-feet in case our depth perception was inaccurate. The chase car would be at the target with lights indicating surface wind direction, and a light stick would mark the target itself. We were to overshoot this if high and were 'not to attempt late turns'. I don't think anyone needed the extra reinforcement, but the point was locked in as we boarded the plane.

We would be jumping from 4000-feet, clean-fatigue on this first jump, and leaving in singles on each run. I was second out.

Seeing Goose disappear into the black void was both weird and confronting. If he'd had a malfunction, Banjo wouldn't have known and if he had a double malfunction the DZSO may or may not hear the thump as he impacted the ground.

'Shut the fuck up and focus!'

I got my growing fear under control as we rolled around the circuit for my turn. The most prominent worry I had was not being able to see the canopy and therefore not being able to identify a partial malfunction. Also, if I had a malfunction, would I be able to see the handles?

'Maldivian beach, Maldivian beach, Maldivian beach…'

Banjo beckoned me forward.

I had a perfect exit. Checking canopy, I also had more than enough visibility to see it deploy correctly and so quickly turned my attention to the flight plan.

The world below was black, but the main highway to Melbourne had some traffic that gave perspective. Moreover, the base tennis court lighting was on too, producing an almost green beacon, and so with sufficient references, I was able to sight the chase car positioned in the centre of the grass area between the runway lights and pit.

The flight plan was surprisingly normal, and I completed a stand-up landing 20m from Potsy who had been standing a couple of meters from the target light stick.

All of Rookie-6 arrived in similar circumstances, and we conducted a quick debrief and then were off again, but this time with equipment packs from 2,500-feet. This jump produced identical anxiety while waiting my turn to exit, but we all arrived in the area of the target to satisfy the Sky Gods requirements. Land jumping was complete, only seven water jumps to go.

Left: Frommy and Rick wearing PJ harnesses at a crash site after securing the scene. Right: Jacques jumping with dog from JEY, the static-line can be seen pulling out the parachute from it's container.

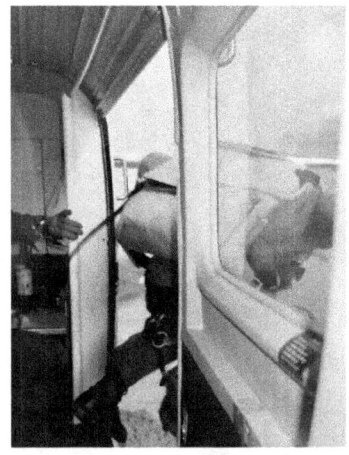 

Left: leaving the Caravan with land equipment, the first PJ's canopy is visible in the background. Right: X-300 with land equipment pack on toes, slider above PJ's head and seven 'cells' visible.

Left: Exit trainer – Troy 'grabbing a fat chick'. Right: Potsy guides Maff to the 'target' on AFF number 4 – Truck's accuracy training worked.

CHAPTER 9

NSCA Pararescue (Water Jumps and Beret)

AS A DEVIATION TO THE Rookie-6 program, I had split company with the rest of the boys when they did their diving course. During that phase of the program I went off to Melbourne to complete my medical training, and we were about to be split up again due to something called Freddo-Factor. Banjo came to talk to me after we finished night jumps.

"Mick, Freddo wants you water qualified on Monday, that will mean seven jumps in one day. Are you happy to do that?"

Previously the longest day involved four jumps. The weather had kept us behind schedule, and so we had pushed on to catch up, that was a long day. Seven jumps?

"Yes, ok, but I haven't actually used LAR-5 yet Banjo."

"You will be doing that tomorrow, including water equipment pack swims, and Dinky will take you for exit-trainer drills first thing on Monday morning, ok?"

"Yeah, fine."

As I walked away to the base accommodation, my brain processed what I had just agreed to. LAR-5 shouldn't be a problem, it was a simpler, more compact version of CDBA. The equipment pack swims involved breathing from LAR-5 while finning on the surface towing a heavy 'water equipment' pack behind you. Sounds basic, but the boys told me of the kilometres and kilometres they swam in the Bass Strait with their instructor, Eric, an-ex-RAN Chief diver pushing them on, and I wondered how much of this I would be put through on Saturday morning. As for the exit-trainer, this was a zip-line that we travelled down while doing emergency drills. Up to this point, it had been a somewhat alarming experience stepping off from 30-feet above the concrete below, more so than leaving an aircraft, but now I would be doing it with 80kg of gear.

On Saturday morning I was heading over to the pool as the Bass Strait was not happening, apparently, due to more Freddo-Factor in play, when Freddo appeared in a doorway and called me over to an office. With him was a new Council employee, a recently retired Victoria Police Commander. This bloke was part of the grand Freddo plan of influencing people in the right places, but on first impression, he appeared like a pompous individual who Freddo was barely putting up with.

"Mick" Freddo began "Keith believes that you shouldn't be undertaking water jumps until you have completed the full dive program with Eric. He thinks that you will not have the necessary water skills."

Freddo smiled and then the new employee looked me in the eye.

"What do you think, Macfarlane?"

Keith, the former police Commander, was a tall man. He was staring down his nose in a similar way the best of the *Royal* Navy had in the past. I remained as professional as I could.

"Eric runs a very effective course John, but I am quite comfortable with re-breathers and am happy to undertake just the 'acquaint' dips to become familiar with the LAR-5."

Cop-boy was about to speak, but Freddo got in first confirming that his plan, the pool, would be the one we followed.

"See Keith; Mick's an ex-CD for Christ's sake. Now..."

Freddo waved me away as they continued their discussion.

LAR-5 was pretty straightforward. The only real functional differences were a less effective bypass (a button to push), and the counter-lung was smaller too. After a couple of laps up and down the pool, it all felt pretty 'normal' though.

I completed a 2k swim towing the water equipment pack and to conclude with I was directed to climb a cargo net and a webbing ladder up to the 3-meter platform positioned over the deep end of the pool.

With the LAR-5 connected to my chest via 4 QEJ's onto the PJ harness I was wearing, climbing up the cargo net was a challenge. My instructor, a hyperbaric medicine bloke called Hooter, made me do it while on gas too. Back in the water, I prepared to climb the webbing ladder.

This device, customarily packed flat into a pocket on the left side of the PJ harness, would be used to board yachts from the water. To do this a PJ would first pull a lanyard from a right side pocket and attach this to the guardrail of the yacht. This action ensuring he remained 'attached' to the yacht if it was underway – I had all this to look forward to on Monday. Climbing the ladder was challenging, but not impossible. Using leg muscles and coordinating movements was vital, but with this completed I just had the exit trainer to go before commencing the water jump challenge on Monday.

I met Dinky at the base of the 30-foot tower at 0730 am on Monday morning. I was wearing a 7mm yellow council wetsuit and had the PJ harness fitted with a slim, Secumar life jacket over the top. Dinky had the rest of the water jump gear.

The LAR-5 went on first and then I climbed up the ladder to the steel cage platform that resembled the inside of a SAR aircraft. After pulling up the rest of the gear, Dinky assisted me to don it. The X-300 was followed by the water equipment pack, this one was positioned behind my legs but attached by similar quick release clips. Finally, a one-man liferaft was attached to the PJ harness between the bottom of the X-300 and the top of the equipment pack. The only things missing were operational items such as radios, fins, mask etc., but I felt the weight nonetheless.

Dinky attached me to the exit trainer wire, and I positioned in the doorway that was fabricated into the cage.

"Whenever you're ready, Mick."

The concrete, just 30-feet below, was as intimidating as previous exit trainer drills. I fell about a meter before the weight came to bear on my leg straps. This was accompanied by an uncontrolled 'oomph' as the air was forced from my lungs as I commenced the emergency drills while sliding down the 60-feet of wire.

By the time we had packed up the gear and were at the Ops building, it was 0830. We climbed aboard JEY without delay for the transit to Welshpool Base, a small dirt strip with a series of prefabricated buildings and a couple of hangars.

Taxying to a halt close to the main building I saw a range of fish bins containing LAR-5's, next to these was a number of X-300's and water equipment packs. On-shift PJs were standing by and the moment I stepped from JEY, Dinky directed me to the duty Jump Master, Chris.

"Ok, Mick, let's get you ready."

Five minutes later I was in the back of a Beechcraft Super King Air; a twin turboprop aircraft converted for SAR by Council engineers - this was soon to be replaced by the Dornier 228, which I would be pleased with due to the extra room it afforded.

Sitting on my water equipment pack we crossed the coast running towards Wilsons Promontory. I was braced against mild turbulence with my hands on each side of the cabin and my head, bent forward, pushing on the roof. It was a crystal clear winter day, July the 25th 1987, my 27th birthday.

Chris was cleared to open the door, pulling it inwards and sliding it forward to lock it in place. The opening was narrower than a Caravan but slightly higher too. We had completed just one practice jump from the King Air during the initial land equipment phase; it was a squeeze into the door, there was a higher speed on exit, but primarily it was just another platform to step from. The vista greeting me after the door was opened, though, was surreal.

There was 'Wilsons Prom', a key tourist destination of rugged low mountains, covered in a dense forest all ringed with white sandy beaches. The water was a deep blue, glistening in the rare winter sun too – what a birthday present!

We were heading to Rabbit Island about halfway along the promontory on the eastern side. Orbiting the area briefly, I saw the NSCA's primary vessel, a converted oil rig tender called the Blue Nabila (nicknamed the 'Blue Pig' by PJs), a couple of ribs and a small orange blob - the target life raft for the first jump. We were rolling out onto jump run.

Chris dispatched a 3-minute floating smoke flare to give me wind indication and then I was called to the door. God, it was hard to move! Waddling into position I was conscious of the extra air pressure on my body with the increased jump speed, but on feeling the smack on the arse I just fell forward.

The undisciplined exit had me almost face downward and the powerful opening shock that followed, before I had called 2-thousand, sent stars to my eyes. I swung violently as the canopy deployed, catching my bearings while breathing deeply. Recovered, almost, I checked the target and turned towards it, failing to undertake the required brake check.

I was in a state of awe I guess? The vast blue expanse of the Bass Strait and the alarming exit, they had thrown me off. I passed over the raft but continued downwind too far. Turning back into the wind, I remembered the water jump drills that I had yet to complete. Not good!

Quickly disconnecting my chest strap, I then pulled the LAR-5 twin-hose from its Velcro restraint and past the retaining strap around my head to commence the two-minute breathe down to expel nitrogen from my system. Next, I dropped the pack and then recovered my brake lines. I was going to land short, by a whopping 200-meters!

Water entry was fine though, and I quickly operated the two leg QEJ's to dump the X-300. As I was pulling my fins free from the water equipment pack outer stowage, a rib pulled up alongside. Banjo was not looking happy.

"What the fuck was that? I didn't see you do one bloody wind check!"

As I continued to pull on my fins under the disapproving gaze of two on-shift PJs in the rib with Banjo, I offered the only suitable defence.

"I fucked up. It won't happen again."

"It better not. Right, you best get swimming!"

I reached the raft and climbed aboard, hauling my equipment pack up behind me. A Bell-412 arrived shortly afterwards, and I was winched up, leaving my equipment for the rib crew to manage.

In the helicopter was a crewie nicknamed the 'Gobbaldock' after a TV add creature that loved potato chips. The nickname was a bit harsh I thought, especially as the Gobbaldock gave me a water bottle once we were transiting back to Welshpool.

I stepped from one aircraft to the next and 15-minutes later we were back over the ocean with me braced against the turbulence in a kind of Groundhog Day moment.

Jump number two was to be a repeat of the first. I had a much better exit and completed the flight plan as per the brief. We had no altimeter for water jumps (saltwater would not be good for them), but the other jumps had given us the required judgement of height. Turning final with all checks completed, I was aligned pretty much flawlessly and splashed into the water 7-meters from the raft.

Banjo was there as I boarded the raft and made a comment.

"Better. Yacht boarding next. Remember to land sufficiently up current."

The helicopter arrived after about fifteen minutes, and the Gobbaldock winched me aboard. I was feeling good at this point, not tired, and after the first fuck up I was now confident that I was on top of things too. During the transit back I saw the Gobbladock's watch and noticed that it was 1140am. Shit! Where had all the time gone?

Back at Welshpool, there was a slight delay as PJs transferred wet jump gear from a Bolko-105 helicopter to the waiting JEY. JEY was transporting this gear, collected from the Blue Pig via deck landing, back to West Sale to be washed in fresh water and hung in the para-loft drying room. Seeing all this activity, I had a holy-shit moment; just how much was being spent on my birthday?

Chris had given me a couple of tips on King Air exits while wearing water equipment and we were working well together, getting on with the collective jumping task with minimal discussion. When boarding the King Air for jump number three though, we had a kind of 'morning Ralph', 'morning Fred' moment from the coyote cartoons that made me laugh. I think Chris thought I was losing it.

Seeing the Council's yacht Eneseay, without a sail, drifting along in the 1-knot current as I scanned past the open door, I quickly revised the brief I had been given.

"Land up current from it! Even at just one knot, you will struggle to keep up with the gear you are wearing. Judge its movement through the water too and land on the downwind side, but not too much. Quickly get your fins on and be ready with the boarding lanyard. Aim for midships, but make sure you get it connected quickly!"

At the 1500-foot brake check, I was positioned nicely and turned back towards the target. I was aiming to fly over the yacht about 200m ahead of its bow and so allowing me to close this distance to around 50-100m on final. I would also adjust the landing point during the final approach to ensure I landed on the downwind side.

With all drills completed I kept my chin on my chest while breathing from the LAR-5 and splashed into the water about 50m in front of Eneseay.

After ditching the X-300 I checked on the yacht, it was about 35-meters from me, closing on a good line. By the time I had my fins on it was 20-meters away and I adjusted my position to intercept it at the bow.

There was just a lazy one-meter swell rolling through making for almost perfect conditions. I reached to my right side, located the red webbing loop and 'punched right'. The white webbing lanyard pulled from its pouch, and I took the karabiner in hand gathering up a meter of slack in the other.

The bow was a meter away. In my periphery, I could see someone on the forward port side rail watching me, but my focus was the rail at midships.

Trowing the karabiner upwards, it missed. Fuck! Finning back quickly alongside the hull, I gathered the lanyard and tried again, this time getting the Karabiner over the wire rail just aft of midships. Coming to rest, it had dropped halfway to the deck, and I finned upwards aggressively with hand extended grabbing the Karabiner to pull it back down. Back in the water I quickly connected the Karabiner to the lanyard and let it pull tight. Then, relaxing my finning action as I was now being pulled along with the yacht, I located the left loop and punched left. With the ladder in hand, I pulled up on the lanyard while finning hard and hooked the Karabiner to the rail.

I was breathing bloody hard into the LAR-5 mouthpiece as I began the climb and was wondering about CO2 poising, but the drill was to climb with LAR-5 in case you were smashed back into the sea. As I came over the rail, I spat out the mouthpiece and was about to recover my equipment pack when the Eneseay's skipper, Roy, offered some advice.

"Next time attach it to a stanchion and not the wire, you cunt! The stanchion's stronger!"

As I took this in, I saw the other crew included Maso and Maff, who were looking slightly sheepish under the command of the pirate-like Roy. I recovered the pack, and the boys helped me repack the boarding gear just as the sound of the 412 was heard approaching from the north.

"Leave your pack with us and get back in the water for the winch."

Sir, yes Sir! Roy was ok, but on first impression when he was on *his* yacht, he could be perceived as a tad despotic.

Jump number 4 was to the yacht again. Accuracy was good, and the boarding was much more to Roy's liking, but transiting back to

Welshpool the Gobbaldock had to nudge me before landing as I had dozed off. The combination of physical and psychological effort was apparently taking its toll.

As we climbed into the sky for jump number 5, I was acutely aware that I was becoming too relaxed. My tired brain was accepting the jumps as routine, and this was not a good state of mind. I managed to dig deep, telling myself to buck-up, and as I moved to the door I was reasonably switched on again. However, it didn't prevent me catching an equipment pack quick release on the doorframe.

I was unaware this had happened, but on opening shock, the pack, attached by one side only, swung back through an arc and contacted my thigh at speed. The pain was intense. I had never broken a bone before but suspected that might have happened.

With stars before my eyes, I was thankful I had a good canopy. The pain lasted throughout the descent, dropping to around a seven-out-of-ten by the time I hit the water; this time next to a one-man life raft of the type fighter pilots would use.

I completed a double-lift of the PJ playing a pilot and returned to Welshpool with pain hovering around five to six.

As I exited from the 412, the pain was constant four, and I moved to the replacement equipment with a mild limp. This was discussed briefly, but we pushed on to jump number six.

For this jump, I would be exiting at 1500-feet. This was considered the lowest 'safe' altitude for the X-300 in training, but would be pushed to 1000-feet on operations if required. The intent of the low height was obviously visibility in low cloud base because if we couldn't see the target, the likelihood of putting PJs into the wind-cone was low. And if we weren't in the wind-cone in strong winds, we wouldn't make the target, no matter how good a swimmer we were.

Stooped in the doorway, the ocean looked very close. Being a thousand feet lower than the previous jumps the Blue Pig looked bigger, obviously, but my brain quickly processed the detail as we ran over the yacht. In theory, there was still time to cut-away if a malfunction occurred, but any glitch that hindered normal or emergency drills would be exacerbated significantly due to the rapidly depleting sky beneath us and good old-fashioned terror.

'Focus on the drill, focus on the drill!'

With this in mind, I pivoted from the door on my left foot following the smack on the arse. The opening shock was normal, and after checking canopy, I completed a quick brake-check and then turned to the target. I was about 200-meters upwind at just above 1100-feet.

With brakes off I crossed ahead of the yacht at a height below 800-feet and turned away from the yacht's path, turning final way too close. I completed a couple of tight 'S' turns at three-quarter brake, but was still going to land upwind of the yacht, and I still had equipment drills to do.

Leaving the LAR-5, I released my pack, undid the chest strap and then came back on the brakes to land in the water a few moments later.

I was about 60-meters ahead of the yacht and about 20-meters upwind. I had to get on the downwind side if I wanted any chance of boarding!

Leaving the leg QEJ's, I pumped my brake lines to keep the canopy inflated and, thankfully, Dinky's brief proved correct.

"If you do land upwind, use the canopy as a sail."

With the canopy remaining in the air, the moderate breeze that had picked up during the day pulled me backwards reasonably quickly, and I crossed to the downwind side of the yacht as it closed to just 15-meters from me. I promptly ditched the X-300 and then set about donning fins. By the time this was complete the bow was on me, and I noticed the roll of the hull was greater as I finned backwards to keep pace.

This more significant roll helped though. As the hull rolled towards me I kicked up to get the lanyard secured, it worked well, and not breathing from the LAR-5 was far less of an encumbrance too.

Banjo pulled up in the rib as I was resetting my gear with the aid of Maso and Maff.

"One more to go, Mick, then you get a maroon beret."

The realisation that I was about to become a PJ was an anticlimax. Without big-noting myself, this was because I knew that I had put in the hard yards to get to this point and knew I had earned it. However, this was quite a contrast to the first time I saw a pair of jabbers descending to West Sale during selection, where I had watched as the first guy landed in the pit and the second missed it. This second bloke had kept his canopy inflated as he ran half a dozen steps to jump into the gravel to 'land' again. His mate had called bullshit and laughter followed. I had watched this with a degree of awe, wanting to be one of these blokes more than anything else in the world.

Keeping the last jump simple, I started in the King Air wearing a flight suit and had to don all the gear as per an operational task. We were back to 2500-feet, and I jumped to a Jet Ski that had been positioned in the water from the Blue Pig. Trials were underway for Jet Skis' to be deployed from the air, but as these were ongoing, practicality (and safety) determined use of the simpler deployment option. Nonetheless, I parachuted into the tourist destination marine park, wearing really cool dive gear, and was required to demonstrate prowess on a Jet Ski and then have fun on a yacht. When evaluating the entire experience, I wondered just how much thrill-seeking members of the public would pay for it? But there I was being paid, and it was my Birthday too!

That final jump completed, which had included medical diagnosis and treatment of a casualty while being assessed by a PJ doctor; I finally boarded the Caravan for the trip back to West Sale.

Upon arrival, my world turned back to relative normal. I helped with gear cleaning and then waited as people returned by road from Welshpool. I had been told that I would be assigned an operational base and would be heading off in the very near future. You can perhaps understand my confusion then when Banjo spoke to me later that evening.

"Mick, you are going on two weeks leave. When you get back we will be having a training week with the Townsville, Willytown and Wollongong teams; once that's completed, you'll get your beret. Ok?"

Freddo-Factor was in play again and entirely out of Banjo's control. From what had been all hurry, hurry, we need Mick qualified, had changed to hurry up and wait – it wasn't worth worrying about though, it was just Freddo being Freddo.

It worked out well in the end though. After months apart while I was training, Mandy and I had a leisurely two weeks to find a house to rent in Gippsland – I was being posted to West Sale. We settled on a weatherboard place with a big back garden in a quiet Maffra street, and when I returned to work three Monday's later, there were additional SAR aircraft on the hardstand.

Morning sport was notably more energetic as the rivalry between bases was tested. It was good to meet the other PJs and hear about water jumps off Magnetic Island in Far North Queensland, or jumping into the snow in New South Wales, but they were at the base for major training exercises, and so we got on with equipment preparations straight away.

Early on Tuesday morning, I took equipment by road to Welshpool, and by the time we got there three helicopters and one King Air were already parked up, and people were moving with purpose. A jump roster had been organised, and I was slotted on load three of day one and load six of day three. After these jumps, I would be officially qualified. Maybe... who knew what Freddo would do next?

On my first jump, I was paired with 'Pecky', a Townsville Jabber and former Special Forces (SF) soldier. Our Jump Master was Boney, another Townsville/ex-SF Jabber and we were tasked with a simple yacht board, i.e. no medical exercise.

I was number two to Pecky, a stocky bloke with a good sense of humour. After the mandatory 'have a good one' low five amidst mild buffeting, we both focused on Boney. He pulled back from the door, and I was happy to see Pecky waddle similarly to my previous efforts as he got into position.

As I moved in after him, my inner voice had a constant loop running at the back of my head.

'Land next to him, you are a team of two, land next to him, you are a team of two.'

After opening shock and a good canopy, I checked target and Pecky simultaneously and then put the target on the back burner. If Pecky missed, I would miss too. I *was* going to land next to him.

Pecky had turned back into the wind and was now about 50-meters ahead of me and about 200-feet below. He started a gentle spiral as we were close to the yacht and still too high. I pulled hard on my right brake line and commenced a blood draining spiral straining to keep eye contact with Pecky. I knew that each spiral lost about 200-feet in altitude and if I hoped to catch him I had to lose height quickly.

Rolling out from the second rotation he was 40-meters ahead of me and about 20-feet below, now running towards the yacht. I dropped my equipment, undid the chest strap, but just put the LAR-5 strap around my neck without going on gas as it was a mild day and the sea was hardly a challenge.

As Pecky turned onto final, I turned early to intercept his track and rolled out behind him, now just 20-meters to his rear. I was adjacent to his track by around 20-feet too, meaning that he would land closer to the yacht.

Pecky entered the water ahead of the yacht's path, downwind side, with the yacht about 25-meters away. After last-minute adjustments on final, I splashed in 10-feet from him and hurriedly got on with boarding preparations.

As I positioned by the yacht, Pecky was commencing his climb up the webbing ladder. I hung onto the base of this and secured my lanyard and then, saving time, I just climbed up Pecky's ladder.

We were recovered by winch and a crewie called Bill, another ex-navy bloke. The transit back to Welshpool was uneventful, but after leaving the noise of the 412, we dropped our gear in freshwater bins and headed for a brew.

"Good jump Mick, cutting the corners worked well and using my ladder saved time too."

Pecky's remarks were short and delivered without much thought, but they meant more to me than he could ever know.

Between this jump and my last, I hung about doing minor tasks, talking shit and generally just savouring the moment. This was such an awesome job. I've said that already haven't I? Anyway, I found myself wondering how my life would have turned out had I not trashed the diving guard mess at HMS Vernon? If I had stayed in the navy, I would have probably ended up going to the Falklands War, taken promotion afterwards and never even heard of the NSCA, let alone get the opportunities I was now being afforded. Shit happens for a reason I guess?

Maso and I were paired up for my last jump. It was Maso's seventh too, and we were going to complete a medical exercise for his final assessment.

"Have a good one."

Grinning like school kids for just a moment, we quickly focused on the task. Jet Herbert was Jump Master this time and he was giving final corrections to the pilots via intercom. Seeing him pull the flare igniter and drop the smoke out of the door, I began shuffling forward just before he beckoned me.

I had a good exit, a couple of line twists, but after a quick flick of my legs, I was into the drills. I spied Maso on my second wind check and saw that he was positioned well.

Turning final I landed with the yacht about 35-metres away, and as I put on my fins, I watched as Maso splashed in close by. Legend!

Once I had connected my lanyard to the stanchion, I paused and removed the LAR-5, clipping it to the lanyard. Removal of the weight and bulk made attaching and climbing the ladder so much more comfortable, but the LAR-5 remained easily retrievable should I need it.

Up on board, I pulled up my equipment pack and then the lanyard and the LAR-5. Maso was connected by the time I had recovered my gear and had removed his LAR-5 too. I told him to use my ladder, helping him over the rail before leaving him to recover his equipment as I headed off in search of our casualties: a physio called Julie and a PJ, Flat-Nose McCall.

We left our packs, just filled with water, on the deck and proceeded below to where a duplicate set of medical equipment was ready in a bag for our use.

Julie was laid out on a bunk, on her back, feigning injury. There was black makeup on her face simulating both burns and smoke inhalation from the exercise fire. Closer to the ladder was Flat-Nose. He was holding his arm, simulating pain and a possible fracture; he was breathing ok though, so I proceeded to Julie as Maso came down the cockpit ladder.

"Maso, possible fracture with him, burns over here. Can you look after the fracture and call for a medevac, I'll look after this one."

Maso acknowledged me, and I got to work with Mal, one of the PJ Doctors, watching our progress.

I completed a set of observations on Julie as Mal interjected with the simulated blood pressures, temperatures, pulse, respiration rates and general condition reports. She had partial thickness burns to 30% of her body and full thickness to 10%. She had lost fluid through simulated broken blisters but was breathing ok despite inhaling smoke.

I opened up some burns dressings and applied them to the affected areas and then prepared a giving-set with normal saline. In my periphery, I could see that Maso was immobilising the fracture and was about finished. As I readied a cannula for the IV, Maso headed up on deck to make the call.

Julie had good veins. As I presented the IV needle, she gasped, breaking from her acting.

"Mal, he's actually putting it in!"

Mal smiled.

"Don't connect the giving set Mick, just tape the cannula in place. Ok, Julie?"

Julie didn't look super happy but went back to her role-play. As I listened to Maso's call, which advised the medivac would be arriving in about ten minutes, I completed another set of observations on Julie.

"What else could you be doing now, Mick?"

Mal was staring at me, clipboard in hand with pen poised. Fuck, what had I missed? Running out of ideas, I attempted to lighten the mood. Placing my hands on Julie's knees, I eased her trouser covered legs about an inch apart.

"Internal vaginal examination perhaps, Mal?"

Mal stifled a laugh and Julie's stern face cracked into a smile. Quickly regaining control, Mal offered some advice.

"How about a space blanket to ensure Julie's core temperature remains normal Mick? Remember, burns can quickly produce hypothermia, and often it's the simple things we do that make a difference."

Hurriedly doing as Mal suggested, Julie was wrapped in silver as the sound of the approaching helicopter entered the cabin. Our casualties were remaining on the yacht for another exercise though, and so as the helicopter approached overhead Maso and I had a final check of our gear and noticed that only one LAR-5 was on deck.

"Where's yours, Mick?" Maso shouted above the noise.

"That is mine Maso; it's connected to my lanyard where I left it."

Maso's face revealed a horrible pit of the stomach feeling as he remembered what he'd done. He had connected his LAR-5 to the ladder, but not through a rung, and it had worked its way down and off the end as we had been on board. It was now conducting a solo swim somewhere in the Bass Strait. A please-explain was coming Maso's way.

Later that afternoon, back at West Sale I received my maroon beret, a collection of PJ wings and some new uniform shirts in a very unceremonial exchange. This concluded with Freddo's two bobs worth, "don't let me down" and that was it, I was an NSCA PJ.

The rest of Rookie-6 had medical training, tree falling, and sailing (with the joyful Roy) to go before they received their berets.

On this occasion they were all sitting around the boardroom table as Freddo dished out the maroon symbols of success, sliding them across the table. He paused when he got to the last one though, Maso's, and turned very serious.

"There is the matter of a five thousand dollar LAR-Five missing at sea, Masy."

The room went quiet, the buoyant celebration of a moment before instantly gone.

"Come with me."

Maso followed Freddo outside. Once they were gone, Frommy, not happy, suggested mutiny.

"If he sacks Maso boys, fuck it, we all quit. Yeah?"

Fortunately, it didn't come to that. Back out in the corridor, Freddo was looking into Maso's eyes, still not smiling.

"Well, Masy, what happened?"

"I fucked up John."

Maso chose the right words. Freddo smiled and handed over the beret. Rookie-6 were now fully fledged ass-kicking PJs.

On the jumping theme, there are a couple of episodes that are worth mentioning. Frommy completed what was to be the second operational

Pararescue jump after being stationed at RAAF Williamtown for less than a month. A civilian light twin-engine aircraft had crashed in the outback. He and the senior Williamtown PJ, Rick, jumped to it, but unfortunately, there were only bodies at the scene. They received positive recognition for their effort from police though, which had included scene preservation, photographic evidence collection and coordination of oncoming emergency services.

On my forty-first jump, Jet Herbert was Jump Master and Ross, one of the first qualified PJs, was paired with me. We were conducting a trial of a new land equipment pack that had a larger medical box and some other equipment. This arrangement meant that a sleeping/casualty mat was repositioned from the side to the top of the pack. The width of this item meant that there was barely a centimetre clearance when in the door.

The boys had given me the privilege of doing the first test jump, and I moved into the door quickly after Jet had told me to go when I was ready. I left with a standard pivot on the left foot and immediately felt something catch on the door. It was the mat, but I wouldn't know this for sure until advised later by Jet.

The minor obstruction caused me to rotate significantly, and upon opening shock, I saw the result of this unplanned action. One half of my canopy was inflated perfectly; the other was hanging like a bunch of washing, flapping in the breeze. I knew immediately that it was a malfunction and that a spin was developing, but I also knew that I had exited at 4000-feet, a standard practice for something new.

I could feel something hooked up behind me and thought it must have been one of the main risers. So, with height to spare, I began pulling and bouncing in an effort to free it, but quickly abandoned this desperate measure as the spin rate increased.

Less than three seconds had passed since the opening shock, and I commenced the drill.

"Look"

I could see the silver handle of the reserve, but where was the cut-away pad! Scanning the area rapidly I saw that just a portion of it was visible, as the hooked up riser had altered the position of my harness causing the pad to twist under the webbing.

"Locate"

Bringing my hands in, I reached under the webbing and got a good hold of the cut-away pad as my left hand waited on the silver handle.

"Punch right"

The acceleration down was intense.

"Punch left... One thousand... Two th-"

Upon opening shock, I looked up to see the most beautiful black canopy. A moment later I was suddenly aware of buzzing extremities as adrenaline continued to circulate after preparing me for the emergency actions. I took a couple of deep breaths before proceeding with the flight plan.

Landing about 10-meters from the pit I had reasonably recovered from the initial terror of the malfunction and collapsed the canopy as per usual, as one of the para-loft riggers, Michael, came jogging over. These blokes signed for each rig they packed, and he was apparently concerned about what had gone wrong.

"Shit, you got the reserve out quickly, what happened?"

Although my pulse was not entirely under control, I managed some PJ cool.

"I didn't like the colour of the first one mate."

Cool aside, I was directed straight back to the loft to get another rig. 15-minutes later I leapt out again, clean fatigue this time, but almost had the exact same drama following another over rotation. Nothing caught this time; I was just plain and simple shitting myself and had become too rigid on exit. I completed one more jump though, and fortunately, this one was textbook.

Upon landing, I was directed to see Gavin. I resisted, saying that I was okay, but was told to go nonetheless. Walking into the medical centre I was very embarrassed; I had to go and have my hand held as I saw it and PJs didn't do this, they merely 'hardened the fuck up' and got on with things.

Gavin broke the ice with a grin.

"Hey Mick, they told me you got the reserve out pretty quickly as the spin developed?"

I gave brief answers to all his questions, wanting to get out of there as quickly as I could. But with hindsight, this meeting was the best course of action I could have taken. His final advice, in the five minutes I was with him, prepared me very well for what was to come and has helped me through a number of other challenging post incident periods.

"Look, Mick, you may have some flashbacks tonight and during the days and weeks to come. This is all pretty normal, shows you're human. If you're still having them in a month or so come and see me and we'll talk about it some more, ok?"

I did have flashbacks. I could see that bundle of washing in broad daylight as I spoke to people on totally unrelated topics, but within a month they had all but gone.

When I look back at all the post-traumatic suicides that have occurred with other emergency services since that time, I wonder if some of these could have been prevented had pragmatic advice from someone like Gavin been available.

I have never considered myself a talented jumper. I had to work at it every time; whereas some of my colleagues took to it like a duck to water. My challenges resulted in some interesting exits and average landings in the 94 jumps I completed before the Council went into receivership. On the 64th jump though, a night currency jump, I was to have my fifteen minutes of fame.

We had stayed back after daily operations for one currency jump each. The off-shift PJs were in too, and everyone was doing the usual piss-taking as preparations got underway.

"Are we going to see a specky exit from you tonight, Fairlane?"

"Get fucked, Dudley!"

It was pick on Mick night!

Of the ten PJs there, Dinky and Truck were expected to kick arse in the mini competition, and I don't think I was getting any short odds.

I was out last in the first load of five. I had sighted the light stick early and spied Dinky's canopy below me as I turned final in the moderate moonlight. He overshot the target by about 2-meters, and there were no other canopies within 15-meters of him.

With chin on chest, elbows in and eyes locked onto the light stick, I continued with fine steering adjustments. When I commenced a smooth braking action to flare, I was still downwind and my forward speed and sink rate reduced as I'd hoped. Then, with an explosion of elation, I smashed my left foot onto the light stick for a perfect stand-up.

"Yes!!!"

Collapsing my canopy, I saw no need to be modest about my achievement, and spying the six-foot-three frame of the 'Big Dud' I let fly.

"Fuck you, Dudley! Did you need a taxi to bring you back to the target?"

Up above the second load was preparing to jump, Truck would be out last. Of the first four, the closest was under 10-meters and the furthest, a woeful 70-meter effort!

All heads were up, looking for Truck. He was sighted turning final and seemed to be positioned very well… what else? As he closed the pit, we saw the familiar, relaxed figure suspended in the harness. He commenced his flare, extended his right foot for the well-rehearsed strike… and missed the light stick by about 8-centimetres. Holy shit! Truck missed?

As we were putting the gear away back in the hangar the piss taking had been re-directed to the bloke who had landed 70-meters away, as it should have, accuracy was everything. However, when Truck passed me with rig in his arms, his simple comments made this night one to remember.

"I guess you're getting the hang of this now, Mick, good jump."

Left: Banjo and Bear demonstrating Pararescue to Thai Military. Right: 'Top Tongue' gearing up. Below: Bear and Flat-Nose McCall in a PR shot wearing full water equipment.

Top: Author about to land during a water jump. Blue-Pig and orange wind indication flare to left, Wilson's Prom and Rabbit Island in background

Top: Author on board yacht with helpers assisting to re-pack boarding gear prior to helicopter retrieval. The Jet Ski used to approach the yacht is bobbing alongside.

Pecky's Crew from RAAF Tindal training hard in the Territory

Rick's crew from RAAF Williamtown on another King Air water jump

CHAPTER 10

NSCA Pararescue (Helitac)

WEST SALE WAS AN OLD WW2 base that, until the NSCA's arrival, was a sleepy, somewhat overgrown old airport with a collection of small hangars primarily used by a local flying club, and occasionally helicopters supporting oil and gas operations. By the mid-eighties, however, it was a hive of activity where 'Jabbers' could be seen descending by parachute, rappel line or winch wire many (and any) hours of the day or night. Jabber is an abbreviation of 'Poo-Jabber,' a derogatory term developed from the official descriptor by an NSCA Operations Officer named Norm. Norm obviously believed, and reinforced to anyone who would listen, that Para-Jumpers (PJs) had a preference for men over women. With a degree of irony, Jabber became an acceptable term even among PJs themselves, and later to others moving in NSCA circles who knew nothing of its origins, believing it had something to do with syringes carried in their medical packs.

After completing my PJ course the year before (1987), I had by now been involved in many fixed-wing searches as part of a three-man PJ crew aboard an NSCA Dornier 228 aircraft. Most of these missions were to track down marine distress beacons, but unfortunately for keen PJs they usually ended up as a false alarm due to inadvertent activation. On one of these missions, however, the outcome was different, resulting in a supply drop of life rafts and equipment to a capsized yacht crew in the Bass Strait.

The intent of the supply drop was twofold: firstly, to provide immediate support to survivors and secondly, as a precursor to dispatching PJs by parachute. On this occasion, however, the survivors were, unfortunately, safe enough and well enough, and most importantly, close enough to shore to deny us the chance of a water jump. Instead, we watched from top-cover as another PJ was winched by helicopter to recover the survivors.

I say 'unfortunately' because up to that point only six PJs had ever completed operational jumps, and the Bass Strait job was the closest I had come to joining this prestigious club.

I had undertaken other rescues though. One that springs to mind was via helicopter not long after completing 'Rookie-6' training.

On this particular job, I had been lowered to a young boy who had been lost for two nights and was feared dead due to the extreme cold of a Victorian late winter. There had been one or two dramas on the task, including a close encounter with a wire crossing a paddock on the first night and a low fuel status requiring a quick decision from the pilots' (Chris and Kingo) at the moment of rescue. However, the satisfaction of returning this boy to his parents safely, albeit a little cold, had confirmed to me without any shadow of a doubt that being an NSCA PJ was the best job in the world.

Back at West Sale, having just completed a usual hour-and-a-half of morning sport, Maso, who had been posted to West Sale too, and I headed to breakfast with the on-shift crew consisting of Jump-Master (JM), Down-The-Wire-Man (DTWM) and Aircrewman (AC). Maso and I had the roles of PJ-1 and PJ-2, whose primary function was first and second out of the door on any Pararescue related task.

On the walk up from the gym I cast a glance towards the mountains that were once again, disappointingly bright and clear. Usually, that would be a good thing for an East Gippsland summer day; typically colder than desired, with a chance of rain, but coming towards the end of the fire season I was yet to see smoke, and therefore the opportunity to challenge myself in the PJ discipline of Helitac was waning.

"Another shitty day at the office, Maso" I quipped, "What has Jet got slotted for training today?"

Maso looked twenty feet ahead of us to where Rod 'Jet' Herbert, our team leader/JM, was walking with 'Flat-Nose' McCall, the duty DTWM.

"Fucked if I know." Maso then looked to the mountains with a similar evaluation as mine, "You reckon we'll get a Helitac job this summer?"

I just shrugged my shoulders. Although it had been warm enough with recent temperatures being consistent high twenties to early thirties, we lacked any decent northerly wind that would aid rapid escalation of a fire and therefore a subsequent need for our Helitac services – good for those who lived and worked in the bush, bad for over-enthusiastic Jabbers.

After breakfast, we headed over to the hangars to commence the morning routine of SAR equipment checks. On the way, I passed Brian Randal, the man in-charge of the NSCA's airborne firefighting operations.

"Reckon we'll get a job this summer, Brian?"

He looked at me with a friendly smile that revealed just a hint of frustration as he no doubt got this question several times a day from unfulfilled PJs.

"Be careful what you wish for, Mick."

Brian had overseen the development of a service that was, at times, considerably undervalued by professional agencies called upon to support massive wildfires. For several years now (way back in the mid-eighties) the NSCA could deploy a team of firebombing helicopters, plus Helitac aircraft and large fixed-wing firebombing aircraft to support the much more significant (although predominantly ground-based) government-controlled operation to fight bushfires. The NSCA helicopters were supported at remote sites by 4WD fuel tankers that towed their own sleeping/cooking quarters. The operators of these trucks could accommodate all NSCA crews involved, often in relative luxury compared to other services involved. This capability meant the NSCA could set up a remote base providing an intense and prolonged attack to a large fire flank or, provide rapid support to ground teams and members of the public who needed assistance. Our capability was achieved by arrangements between NSCA and Canadian wildfire services that saw each other's aircraft and personnel exchanged between opposing fire seasons.

This is what I had hoped to gain experience in, even though it was looking more doubtful as each day passed. Nevertheless, early into preparations for a pool training session to practice yacht-boarding techniques, we were called to the operations office unaware that the fire gods had smiled upon us.

"There's a fire developing to the east of Snowy Plains airstrip and Helitac support has been requested."

Norm delivered his brief without any emotion, but my mind was immediately racing with procedure revision, emergency drills, and equipment re-familiarity.

Maso and I were assigned to a Bell 212 helicopter that was being reconfigured for Helitac. The aircrewman was there, an ex-navy bloke called Lucas, and we sought his advice as to what needed to be done.

"Just grab one rappel bag each out of the store, and the chainsaw bags too boys, there are checklists in each."

Lucas had been my 'crewie' on that first winch job and had taken us for basic rappel training during Rookie-6. This had concluded with a rappel from 120 feet to verify we weren't afraid of heights and could control our speed during a long descent. We were good in both criteria, but the 'racing' your mate down factor during this drill had resulted in some late breaking to prevent heavy ground impact.

Despite wearing thick gloves, such breaking had produced significant friction and subsequent burns to fingers as break lines were pulled assertively to avoid embarrassment.

Lucas's laidback yet controlled approach during our training was achieved by having real-world experience, and Rookie-6 had got on well with him. So as the familiar anxiety of a new operational task mounted, seeing him there that morning provided welcome reassurance. By the time Maso and I had the requested gear by the helicopter, the other members of the Helitac crew were there too.

The standard rear-crew for such tasks included two professional tree-fallers - local blokes who did this as a second job to supplement their beef and dairy properties - and one Forestry manager representing the Victorian government. Dave and Harold, in their mid-thirties, were a pair of clichéd country boys who liked a drink, but they were reasonably competent with a chainsaw too.

I had spent a day with both of them cutting Mountain Ash as part of my training and as a result, had gained a healthy respect for the uncertainty associated with determining which way a tree would fall when cut down. You see despite an excellent initial wedged shape cut (or scarf) that was used to control the direction of travel, sometimes the tree had its own ideas.

Harold had asked me to stand with my back to a tree and then look upwards through the branches towards the crown, i.e., the bulk of branches and foliage at the top of the trunk. The purpose of this task was to determine where the crown was prominent to estimate which direction the tree may fall and therefore, decide where the scarf should be cut to assist the direction of travel.

"What do ya reckon Mick?"

"Err, that way." I pointed confidently to the east.

Both of the boys chuckled at my professional assessment. Still laughing, Harold moved up against the tree, looked up and then an instant later pointed to the west. He was about to speak when Dave looked at him in disbelief.

"Are you on drugs mate?" Dave suggested as he moved into Harold's vacated position against the trunk. He looked up, then looked at Harold, shook his head and then took a couple of steps to his left, proclaiming, "North."

Dave was the leader of this duo and his solid frame, no-nonsense, are-you-a-fucking-wanker contempt for anyone who challenged him without legitimate reason was evident.

Not surprisingly then, Dave fired up his chainsaw and cut the scarf at the base of the tree, facing the north. He repositioned on the opposite side and commenced the back-cut to intersect the scarf and as he had just about completed this, we heard the initial crack of timber as the tree began to move. Alarmingly though, just a second later, we hurriedly dived clear as it fell to the *south* with a deafening crash.

That little misdemeanour aside, the actual purpose of a Helitac operation was to support the much more extensive firefighting mission and was a process that had proved its' worth many times. Helitac involved the rapid deployment of a small team to remote mountainous regions to prepare a helipad on a ridgeline ahead and to the flank of the fire front. Once completed, large numbers of volunteer fire-fighters, specially trained in cutting firebreaks, could be quickly flown into the helipad to begin their work. Provided the fire remained manageable, i.e., low winds, Helitac was a useful tool for the government-appointed Incident Controller to deploy. However, another requirement for success was that each cog in the bigger operation ran smoothly, but this was out of our control.

As the 212 accelerated forward, still close to the ground, I glanced towards the pilots and watched how the flight controls were manipulated so effortlessly. The subtle, yet precise movement always impressed me and seemed in complete contrast to the acceleration and power as we climbed away from the grass cross-runway of West Sale.

The 212 was essentially a twin-engine version of the Vietnam-era Huey. Modern additions included weather radar, radio altimeter, a sophisticated navigation system and a more complex communications system. Fortunately, though, one thing that remained from the Huey era was the ubiquitous 'wocka-wocka' sound the two rotor blades produced as their tips advanced forwards breaking the sound barrier. In part, this sound is what made it a 'real helicopter', not dissimilar to the effect produced by the sound of a throaty V8 – it meant business, and everyone for miles around knew it.

In the rear cabin, there was one row of five webbing seats facing forward. Maso and I sat on the outer of these next to the sliding doors, inboard from us were Dave and Harold, and between them was the Forestry guy who we had not been introduced to at this stage. In front of us was Lucas, sitting on a mound of Helitac equipment that was secured to the floor. This equipment included five 'rake-hoes' - a horrible back braking tool used to clear fire breaks. Lucas was attached to an anchor point on one of two purposely fitted 'posts' by a webbing lanyard called a 'wander-lead'. All in all, it was a tight fit, but I could see ahead and was looking for the fire that we would soon be dropping into. However apart from a bank of cloud to the northeast, the sky was clear. Where was the fire?

As we continued up and into the mountains, my mind ran through upcoming drills as I continued to scan for the fire. Then suddenly, my ignorance was shattered and my pulse increased. The bank of cloud I had been observing, now covering most of the northeast horizon as we flew closer to it, was the fire! It was huge, and we were about to rappel into it!

The pilots had commenced descent, and the Forestry manager was talking to them on a headset. There was occasional pointing, which Lucas joined in on, but all I could see out of the window was smoke.

We were much lower now, orbiting a ridgeline to the west of the fire front and I saw flames for the first time. To my surprise and relief, I saw that despite the massive bank of smoke, the fire front consisted of low, slow-moving flames that appeared to be no more than knee height. There were occasional flare-ups though where flames consumed smaller trees, but these died down as quickly as they began, and so as we continued to orbit my pulse rate reduced slightly. After all, we had trained for this. 'Just do what you have been taught', I told myself.

This worked only temporarily as when Lucas turned around and pointed to Maso and me, signalling for us to connect to the rappel lines, my pulse picked up yet again.

Lucas opened both doors, sliding them all the way back onto stops to reveal a large opening to the terrain 200 feet below us as the 212 banked around the ridgeline. Rolling level again, Lucas commenced conning the pilots towards the chosen ridge as Maso and I re-checked our harnesses, equipment and descending device for the umpteenth time. Looking across the cabin we made eye contact briefly and smiled, but just for a second, this was very real, and any attempt at bravado was lost.

The 212 settled into a hover about 20 feet off the treetops and approximately 130 feet above the ground below. The fire was about two kilometres away as we stepped out of the machine onto the skids, leaning in towards the cabin, break lines secure. Lucas dropped our rope bags and confirmed they had cleared the tree canopy to reach the ground. Looking over my shoulder as he did this I could see a small 'hole' in the tree canopy below us that he had selected for the rappel. It was tight, with some considerable branches to negotiate, but we had rappelled into similar holes during training.

On one of these rappels, just for an added challenge, the rappel rope was purposely dropped onto trees requiring us to first tie-off, and then free the rope before finally continuing the descent. After the effort to do this in training I was happy the ropes had made it to the ground.

Maso and I both had eyes locked on Lucas. He was talking to the pilots via intercom with both hands in a relaxed-surrender position. Then, when he began slowly moving his hands up and down, pivoting from the elbow, we eased the friction on our break lines to slide backward while keeping our feet connected to the skid. When Lucas brought his hands back up sharply, palms open, we re-applied friction to stop in the 'L' position with our arses pointing to the ground, level with the skid. Lucas's lips were still moving, but all we could hear was the deafening turbine-wine from the engines. Any moment now!

As we waited, the pilots were undertaking a final scan of engine instruments to ensure the machine was operating as it should, because an engine failure while in the hover would require aggressive action if the aircraft were to be saved. This meant that the pilots would either dive forward in an attempt to get sufficient speed to fly away on one engine or, decide to 'settle' into the trees below. That is pilot talk for a crash! If we were mid-rappel, either course of action would result in Lucas immediately releasing our lines to prevent our bodies impeding the pilots' action by entangling in the tree canopy. This final scan was a good thing then, but it left us waiting, tension building, for just a second or two longer than you would have liked.

Lucas's hands suddenly chopped downward! I released my break, letting my feet slip from the skid as gravity took over. With my head cocked to the left and down I saw the canopy closing rapidly. Applying sufficient friction on the brake line, I slowed just enough to ensure I would not contact the mass of branches at the crown, then once clear I picked up speed, conscious of the emergency drills that could be implemented without warning. About 30 feet from the ground I began breaking and spied Maso in my periphery for the first time. We were level and both slowing rapidly. I felt just a small amount of heat through the glove as my feet connected with mountainside. No time to relax, I quickly detached from the line and held my descending device up as verification to Lucas that I was clear.

As Dave and Harold arrived around a minute later, we took some of their equipment and watched as the Forestry guy began his descent.

Finally, Lucas lowered the last of the gear and then less than three minutes after arriving in the hover, the 212 was gone.

The contrast of environment was dramatic. A moment earlier we had been in our own private cyclone of wind and turbine wine, with the smell of burnt Jet-A1 filling your nostrils, but now there was silence. Although we could hear sounds of birds and the snap of twigs beneath our feet, it was the sudden focus on a different smell that ensured we moved with purpose... smoke.

"Righto' Harold, I'll start this side you take the other mate."

Dave was apparently in charge, despite the Forestry guy's authority in the National Park we had entered. As the boys set up their saws, Maso and I grabbed a rake-hoe each and waited for instructions. The Forestry guy had quickly disappeared down the ridgeline, presumably to check on the fire, and so we decided to wait for his return before wasting energy randomly clearing vegetation.

A moment later the saws exploded into life, and not long afterwards the first mountain ash came crashing down. The boys were about 30 feet down the slope both sides of the ridge and working quickly. As the Forestry guy returned another tree was cleared, and Maso and I were beckoned forward.

"Come with me please, I'll get you to start a trail over this way."

A 'trail' was a meter wide path cleared of any combustible material that, amazingly, was a means of stopping a fire in its tracks. This process did, however, require a small fire, like the one we were encountering, and by stopping, read slowing. Either way, it provided maximum opportunity for fire bombers to concentrate their attack in one area, which if coordinated well, proved very useful.

We walked fifty meters or so downhill along the ridgeline to where he pointed out a one hundred meter line through the scrub running parallel with the area the boys were cutting the helipad. Beyond the area he was pointing to, the sky was full of smoke, and it was coming our way. The trail we were cutting was not to stop the fire though; it was a safety measure, in a worst-case outcome, to protect our helipad.

Maso and I worked together, hacking and scraping at the vegetation to produce the required trail. It was slow progress, and we were sweating like buggery within a few minutes.

We had completed about two-thirds of the trail when the boys came to assist after completing their helipad, and with the trail finally finished we headed back uphill to the ridgeline.

Upon return to the position we had rappelled into the devastation either side of the ridge was impressive. The boys had felled around twenty trees each and the mass of timber each side of the mountain resembled a bomb blast. But it had achieved the desired result, producing a 20-meter wide gap in the tree canopy for helicopters to safely approach and depart from. In the centre of the pad-area was a cleared space large enough to comfortably accommodate the skids of a 212-sized machine, although on the slightly uneven ground. Dave was happy with his work though and impatiently challenged the Forestry guy to get on with his.

"Hey, you called up the base yet mate, because I don't hear any helicopters coming this way?"

The Forestry guy appeared a little intimidated by Dave, who when frustrated flexed his frame and sent piercing daggers with his steely-eyed glare.

"The choppers mate!" Dave continued as a result of further inaction from the Forestry guy, "The fire isn't getting further away ya know!" He persisted.

Dave looked at Harold and shook his head, but at least the Forestry guy was speaking into his radio now and would no doubt soon provide us with an ETA of the first aircraft. His body language wasn't positive though, perhaps secretive, and he turned away from us as further whispered communications were made. Finally, he turned back to face us.

"The first one will be here shortly."

"Shit hot." Dave acknowledged sarcastically.

Harold just chuckled, and Maso and I looked on slightly confused at the unfolding situation.

Ten minutes later a Bell Jet Ranger flew over the helipad quite high and commenced an orbit. This was a machine about half the size of the 212, and after a third orbit, the Forestry guy's radio relayed a message from the pilot that we couldn't quite hear.

"Understood."

With the curt response to the orbiting pilot's message, the Forestry guy turned to face Dave.

"He would like you to cut some more trees on the southern slope to extend the overshoot and, would like you to assemble a landing pad from logs at the centre of the-"

Dave cut him off.

"He wants what? Are you fucking well shitting m-!" Before Dave could finish the Forestry guy interrupted.

"Another couple of trees, that-"

Dave cut him off again!

"Yeah, I know what you said mate, I just want to know why he wants a pad big enough to land a bloody 747?"

The Forestry guy began to speak, but Dave ignored him.

"Come on Harold, beer's getting warm."

With saws in hand the boys commenced more devastation producing handiwork, and ten minutes later the required tasks were completed, with Maso and I helping to roll logs.

As the jet Ranger pilot commenced his final approach, we all watched as the relatively small machine slowed, and then came to a hover around 60-80 feet above the pad. He was there for no more than ten seconds when the machine dipped at the nose, and he accelerated away, climbing back to around 500 feet above the ridge to commence a safe orbit. Not long afterward the Forestry guy had another whispered radio conversation.

"The pad's not big enough. You're going to have to cut more logs in order for-"

Dave lost what little patience remained.

"Just tell that cunt to fucking well land! We need crews in here now, or the fire will be on top of us."

Forestry guy, neutral faced, turned away and commenced a reasonably lengthy communication. Finally though, when he turned back towards us, he looked defeated, but to his credit, he showed more courage than I thought he possessed.

"Just a few more logs, that's all he wants?"

Dave stared in silent disbelief for a few moments, but nothing was said. We were on our feet rolling more logs as requested reasonably quickly, but tension filled the air now, along with an increasing amount of smoke. We had been on the ground for well over an hour.

More communication between ground and air resulted in the helicopter approaching once again. As this was happening Dave's expression was intense, and he offered advice to Maso and I before the sound of the Jet Ranger was too loud.

"If that cunt tries to fly off again just grab the fucking skids, boys."

Dave had a fire in his eyes and the Forestry guy, who'd overheard these directives, was about to speak but had second thoughts.

We watched again as the helicopter descended to just above the logs we had positioned. Tentatively, the pilot eased the machine down. One skid touched lightly, but then the machine immediately lifted back into the air about a meter above the pad. On the next attempt both skids made contact, but with a similar outcome. Only this time the pilot climbed rapidly, too quickly for Dave's plan to be executed thankfully, and he positioned the helicopter in another high orbit.

As the noise of his departure began to fade I became aware of the wind, it had increased, blowing even more smoke our way; but it was the sound of crackling undergrowth, not smoke, that got our attention very quickly.

"Fuck it!" Dave announced, "Come on boys, grab them hoes!"

Moving quickly towards our trail it was very apparent that things were not going well; I know that sounds a bit obvious, but until that moment and despite the challenges encountered, I had been reasonably confident that all would work out well in the end. This confidence faded rapidly when we sighted the fire a short distance from our trail, and in places jumping over it!

The fire was actually several kilometres in length, but in our little world, the 100m of the trail was all that mattered.

We followed Dave's lead in a rapid attempt to rake another trail where the fire had jumped. It was obvious we were fighting a losing battle though, as every few moments a small tree was engulfed in flame and the fire marched steadily forward uphill towards the pad.

For the first time, I felt fear tiptoeing around my senses, but this increased significantly when I saw apprehension in Dave and Harold for the first time.

"Fuck this Harold, let's start a burn."

With zippo lighters in hand, the boys moved with purpose lighting up the undergrowth on the upward slope to begin a back-burn up the hill towards our pad. Our trail was forgotten, but we still raked away like madmen to protect our rear. Despite the speed at which we raked, flames were leap-frogging ahead of us to the next bit of scrub as more small trees erupted on both sides and flames occasionally extended to the crown of some more substantial trees. This was bloody frightening! Although the back-burn was slowly taking effect, the fire was rapidly outflanking us, and I felt radiant heat hit like a blast furnace every time a tree lit up. Then all of a sudden there was a deafening roar above, followed immediately by an explosive downpour. Masses of red liquid fell from the tree canopy, and for a moment it was like we were in a tropical downpour as the red liquid, a chemical fire retardant called Foscheck soaked both the surrounding foliage and us.

Quickly looking up I saw the firebomber banking hard to avoid the rising terrain, I don't know who called him in, but guessed Forestry guy had finally done something useful. The firebomber had arrived in the nick of time; the yellow belly of the NSCA aircraft made for a bloody marvellous, morale-boosting sight.

A combination of back-burn and Foscheck had kept us safe. And so with stunned expressions and not much to say we commenced a slow plod uphill through the charred and smoking ground. By the time we got to the helipad the fire was moving upward along the ridgeline and down the other side. The pad was still there, charred but intact.

Although it had created significant challenges and real fear, this fire had been a relative baby. It had picked up speed partly due to the increasing wind but also because of the sudden increase in incline towards the ridgeline. Even so, for the most part, it had remained below the main tree canopy and would no doubt continue its course until either rain or further human intervention had a definitive effect.

No doubt another Helitac crew would be tasked again, but that was the least of my worries as we scanned around the smoky hillside; for me, the concern was not about the fire, it was more selfish - how were we going to get home?

Close to last light we all turned our heads skywards in unison as the beautiful wocka-wocka of a 212 was heard nearby. A few minutes later it came into view banking hard over our position. What a lovely sight!

Completing just half a circuit the pilots', Captain Barry Kingsford, or just BK usually, and his co-pilot Simon 'Cow-Lips' Stevenson conducted a routine approach and landed on the pad without any fuss.

One thing I was to learn early in the Council has proven correct throughout my aviation experience: some people profess to be pilots, and then there are those who can fly. Fortunately, the Council employed the latter.

Having a beer with the boys that evening at Snowy Plains airstrip, thanks to the Council fridge in the fuel truck's trailer, I reflected upon Brian Randal's words. He was right; running up and down a hill with a rake-hoe, even on a good day, is not something you would wish for.

News Headline:

Fire authorities advise that attempts to suppress the flank of the Snowy Plains fire were unsuccessful today, the rugged terrain and weather change proving too much for firefighters, who had to be evacuated from a remote site.

Left: Rookie-6 L-R: Maso, Frommy, Troy, Author, Maff and Goose.
Right: Rookie-6 undertaking 120' rappels from a Bell 212.

West Sale Base 1988: Swan Airship being trialled as a fire observation platform, authors parachute (circled in red) after scoring one of only two jumps permitted.

What can possibly go wrong

Bell 205 fire bombers on route to a fire circa 1987.

CHAPTER 11

NSCA Pararescue (Lake Eppalock)

ABOUT TWO WEEKS AFTER QUALIFYING as a PJ I was at home, our new home, in the town of Maffra about twenty minutes' drive from the base. It was Saturday morning, and Mandy and I were re-arranging furniture in our daughter's bedroom. My phone rang, it was the senior West Sale PJ, Banjo, who asked me a question.

"Mick, with your diving background are you able to help out the Sale council with a small job that has come up?"

No preamble, cut to the chase, this was the Council I was getting to understand a whole lot better.

"Probably, what sort of job Banjo?"

This same understanding had taught me that you never knocked back an operational task either.

"They believe that some stolen drums have been dumped in a river about two k's out of town and wanted us to go and check. I said I would get back to them."

"That sounds pretty straightforward Banjo if they know where the drums were dumped; otherwise, we could search indefinitely. Are there any other divers available to help out and do you know what's inside the drums?"

About two hours later I had parked an NSCA FWD with suitable dive and search equipment in it's tray by the side of the river (muddy river) in question. Furthermore, the local shire representative had assured me that the drums (two 40-litre white ones containing something he wouldn't confirm) were, 'about there'. Not overly confident about the position he had given, I sought confirmation.

"Ok mate, just to make sure we find the drums then, I will do a search from there to there."

I pointed about 20m up and downstream from where he was pointing. Then further explained how I would position a search line from one side of the bank to the other, about 15m width, and then swim either side of this moving the line a meter at a time to cover the 40m in question. He seemed to appreciate that if the drums were there, this was a reasonably thorough process and that I should find them even in the zero visibility.

Two NSCA marine operators arrived to assist, and we got on with it, but found nothing. Was there anything there in the first place?

Banjo appreciated the effort though, and on my next day shift, John Friedrich pulled me aside.

"Err, thanks for getting your head wet on the weekend Mick. I, err, understand the local shire were not exactly helpful in their guidance to the right section of river?"

Apart from a few moments during Rookie-6 I had barely spoken to Freddo and was still very cautious around him.

"No worries John; I always enjoy a dip."

He paused and then smiled, the Freddo smile indicating that either pain or good times were coming your way.

"Err, Mick, I plan to expand our subsea capability soon, would you like to be part of that?"

Expand? What the hell could that mean? Was the weekend job some sort of test? There was only one answer.

"Yes John, I'd be glad to be involved."

He smiled again, good times, and turned away.

Less than three weeks later the duty SAR crew were tasked at night to a light plane crash in Silvan Dam, east of Melbourne. Apparently, the pilot had flown low level over the dam and put a wheel in the water, resulting in catastrophe. Amazingly, one of the passengers survived, swimming to shore to raise the alarm.

The SAR crew in the Dornier were of little use in the almost suburban location, but they remained as top-cover while the helicopter crew flew a low search pattern over the lake using their Nightsun searchlight and the Forward-looking Infrared (FLIR). No other survivors were located, but the FLIR operator identified a possible heat signature from the aircraft's engine. This position was relayed to authorities, and an underwater recovery operation was readied for the next day.

I was loading dive and search gear into a Council 5-Tonne Mercedes truck well before first light. The boys from Rookie-6 were all there too having just finished their dive training with Eric, the ex-RAN Chief CD, who worked for the Council mainly driving a large rescue boat as part of a new RAAF contract supporting Williamtown fast jet operations.

Freddo had fast-forwarded my training as he saw no need to waste time (and with some irony, money) having me undertake the four-week program that gave PJs necessary scuba skills and an intense introduction to LAR-V, the re-breather we used when water-jumping. After hearing the boys' stories of compass-swims at night between islands of the Deal Group in the Bass Strait, speed dressing and general anguish, it was clear to me that RAN Chiefs were not dissimilar to RN Chiefs.

We arrived at Silvan Dam around 8 am and followed a gravel road around the edge of the heavily treed 'lake' to where a handful of police vehicles were parked up in a cleared area. A police sergeant, Geoff and his colleague, Charlie, were in charge of the operation and we were there to assist – officially this time because occasionally Freddo had us turn up unannounced.

There was one body to be located and the aircraft which, when found, was to be lifted to the surface. The cops would be undertaking a circular search at the site of the FLIR target, and we were given the job of searching between this point and shore. Apparently, the survivor was sure his mate was with him most of the way to the beach, but as he'd swum at night over an area covering approximately 300m, the position was uncertain.

A Council marine operator I had not met yet, Pete 'Nords' Norder, was on the job too. He was Eric's assistant, and the boys' had described him as hard but fair. Nords seemed like a good operator at first glance and the way he effortlessly organised the boys' set up for the search provided an example of his real-world capability.

I wasn't needed on the first dive, so I waited with the gear on a narrow beach, where Banjo and Potsy had turned up shortly after to take charge of the Council side of the operation.

As discussed in previous chapters, both Potsy and Banjo were very capable skydivers, but except for LAR-V, they were entry-level divers.

"Is there anything we can be doing to assist here, Mick?"

Banjo looked slightly perplexed. Our team was just sitting there, 200m from shore and there wasn't much activity. Circular searches are, without doubt, boring as batshit. Nords, with the limited gear available, was undertaking a series of overlapping searches to ensure we covered the entire area.

I suspected Freddo was on his way and that Banjo wanted some options.

"Nords has the boys doing circular searches Banjo. He will work back towards the beach covering our allocated search area, but it's a slow process."

Banjo looked like he wanted more options. There were no real ones without additional equipment, but I gave him an overview of 'jackstay' searches, so he had ammunition if Freddo pushed.

"Another option in this situation, with the correct gear, is to run two weighted lines out from the shore a couple of hundred meters and have divers swim up each dragging a search-line between them."

As I continued with the brief, I could see that Banjo saw both the benefits of the jackstay search that would undoubtedly snag the aircraft in the limited visibility, and also acknowledge the lack of gear we had available to achieve it. I offered another option.

"We could also do an 'arc' search from the shore. This is pretty simple, but with a diver on a lifeline, we can cover one-hundred-and-eighty-degree arcs to the length of the line. It would include the shallows, and the line would either snag the aircraft, or the divers could extend the arc a meter at a time with each sweep to look for the body."

Resigned to the fact that Nords had the best available solution underway, Banjo, Potsy and I continued with the operation in waiting mode.

Later in the afternoon I had just completed my stint on the search-line and had handed over to Billy 'Goose' Peterson for his turn.

Goose, as Rookie-6 had unfairly named him, was voted most likely to die during our rock climbing training. Goose was just as capable as the rest of us, but we figured with all the high-risk training we were doing someone would probably end up dead sooner or later. Goose had been out of the room at the time and so by default he became the character from Top Gun. At least his blond hair fit the part.

I was Goose's tender. Sitting there in the pleasant sunshine 'feeling' his progress around the shot with my hands relaxed on the lifeline, I was a million miles away, when suddenly the line pulled tight.

"One pull from Goose, Nords."

I was about to continue my report when one pull was repeated several times in quick succession. Nords, supervising this dive, was about to order the standby diver, Maso, into the water when Goose appeared on the surface, regulator out of his mouth.

"I've got him!"

His eyes were reasonably wide, so I had no doubt he had located the body we had been searching for, but we needed him to secure it to the lifeline in order to complete the recovery.

"Good work Goose, now go back to-"

He cut me off.

"I've got him here!"

With that said, Goose produced a corpse from beneath the water in a somewhat comic recovery effort. Its arms were upwards in a frozen and unsuccessful struggle to stay afloat and these, plus the head and shoulders, were quite stiff.

"Where do you want him?"

This was Rookie-6's first body. We secured a line around the chest and held him in the water out of view of the shore, just in case family were there, and called the cops on the radio. They motored over to us and took the body back to the beach.

Later in the afternoon, the cops found the aircraft and diving was suspended as a salvage plan was put together. We gathered on the beach around a police 4WD as one of the sergeants, Charlie, began discussing how best to lift it to the surface. There were a number of lift-bags, including a type called 'salvage bags' which had their own steel 'strong-back' designed to maximise the lift of an object in shallow water. As aircraft didn't crash into dams that often, there was a degree of uncertainty as to the best course of action.

"Attaching a standard bag to the propeller is an easy solution as this pulls the aircraft through the sky."

Charlie didn't need to know I was just repeating the words of a PES diver called Spider who had recovered a plane a few years back. I continued with more of Spider's words and some of my RN and commercial experience combined.

"We could position the strong-backs either side of the fuselage too, tying them off and together so that when the salvage bags are inflated they will bring the aircraft up in a level attitude. Key is when it reaches the surface; we need to be ready to secure it."

All eyes were on me, and many heads were nodding agreement. Charlie turned to his diver who had found the aircraft.

"What do you reckon, Pete?"

The job was a big success for Rookie-6, we were to receive pats on the back and felt proud that we had stepped up when called upon. However, if Freddo wanted to expand his subsea capability, he would need to increase the level of diving training he currently afforded PJs and purchase more appropriate equipment.

A month or so after this job I was at home with a long-time friend (another Mandy) and her husband (George) visiting from the UK. We had been having a wonderful time reminiscing about our adventures growing up together when, as was becoming the norm, the duty Operations Officer called. Freddo had requested my attendance at the West Sale pool to view some new equipment.

30 minutes later, entering the pool building, I spied a man I had worked with not long after arriving in Australia. Russell Girvan ran his own electronics business and, back in the early eighties, he had supplied an Underwater Damage Assessment Technology (UDAT) camera to a small commercial company I was working for as a casual. With this system, I was to spend many hours under tankers and oil rig supply vessels filming every square inch of their hulls as part of an 'in water survey', saving considerable dollars in dry-dock fees for the client and making a tidy sum for my boss.

Russell had a newer, far shinier, toy for me to play with this time though. Jet Herbert was there too as he was an electronics technician by trade before becoming a PJ. Another bloke, Steve Hayman, an ex-RAN ship driver and current head of the NSCA Marine Section was there as well, plus a smiling Freddo. Introductions were made, and Russell gave us an overview of the Phantom S2, Remotely Operated Vehicle, or more simply the 'ROV'.

"A bit different to the UDAT Mick, in addition to the colour camera and SIT (silicone intensified target) camera, this has a Mesotech colour sonar and Simrad tracking system."

I was looking at a sleek white housing held inside an alloy frame. It was about the size of a high coffee table, had two vertical thrusters and two fore-and-aft thrusters. Mounted on the housing were the colour camera and SIT camera, which could see in extremely poor visibility, plus the sonar and tracking gear. In addition to these items was a small manipulator arm that could move in multi-planes. Designed for inspection work primarily and with a depth rating of well over 1000 feet, Russell pointed out that we could deploy the ROV quickly to any location with a suitable power source.

The boys had already connected a red umbilical and were checking the functions of the control 'boxes' nearby. I had already forgotten I had friends from the UK awaiting my return (sorry Mandy and George) because simply put, this equipment shit on anything I had ever used as a CD!

After just a few moments of seeing the ROV in operation, I knew Freddo was a man of his word, and that he was indeed expanding the Council's subsea capability. Over the next few weeks, Jet, Nords and I took the ROV to Port Welshpool for open water trials, and it surpassed our expectations. Nords and I knew nothing about electronics, but Jet did, so we just concentrated on operational procedures. If it broke, we had Jet, what could possibly go wrong.

During the period of our ROV trials, I was tasked on a night SAR to Adelaide. A plane had crashed a couple of miles offshore from the airport, and we were there to support the search, but it was unlikely we would jump due to the crash datum's proximity to land. We dropped two time-expired RAAF LU2A parachute flares to assist a line of vessels undertaking a search for survivors though. These flares usually turn night into day, but a simple glitch on our part – not securing the required static lines for activation (Doh!) – meant that our role in the night's activities was limited.

The night search was called off early in the evening, and we headed to a hotel to wait for first light. Of course 'waiting' meant checking out Adelaide nightlife. As we partied away, another Council crew were loading the ROV onto a second Dornier that was scheduled to arrive before first light. It was bringing Nords and a couple more PJs, but no Jet unfortunately as he was tasked elsewhere and wouldn't be available.

Nords and I were assigned to ROV operations and headed off to the Special Tactics and Rescue (STAR) headquarters of the SA police first thing in the morning. We were introduced to the sergeant in charge of this group and his team. They were an impressive lot, with that fit-as-fuck presence and the, 'don't waste my time' arrogance of elite operators lurking just below the surface. Unfortunately, at this early juncture, the feeling wasn't mutual.

"So, is this camera of yours going to be of any use boys?"

The sergeant was smiling, but it was apparent that he'd been told to accommodate the 'blokes from Victoria' by someone senior when he was flat out organising the day's events. In a similar position, we would probably have responded the same.

"It's being transported to the wharf at the moment, but the ROV is a good bit of gear, and we can easily operate it from the boat you blokes have."

He still wasn't impressed, and so Nords and I just tagged along as his blokes loaded their equipment. As this was underway, we watched in slight amusement as the sergeant communicated to his team with whistles and nods of his head. Seriously! He would look at a piece of equipment, get the attention of a couple of operators with a whistle, point with his head at the relevant equipment and then turn to a vehicle, whistle again, a short pipe with tongue on the roof of his mouth, and the operators moved the equipment as required without a word being spoken. Apart from finding this funny, it was also indicative of a very close-knit team who obviously worked very well together.

We followed them down to the pier where we commenced loading our gear onto the police launch when finally there was a change of mood. The ROV out of its transport box was pretty impressive.

"Fuck! I thought you blokes were bringing over one of those 'swimming cameras', this looks bloody expensive."

He didn't need to know Nords and I had minimum time driving the thing, and so we waffled on about the ROV's capability without pushing the bullshit too much. Unfortunately though, while still tied up to the pier undertaking pre-start checks, flicking on the required switches etc., the controls and monitors failed to work. Not good!

Undeterred and fortunately both skilled in the art of smoke-and-mirrors, Nords and I headed off to our transport container with the pretence it was a routine glitch. When out of earshot though, we quickly determined we were buggered unless we could get hold of Jet, fast!

I called West Sale operations from a public phone about a 100m up the pier and got John 'Waldo' Waldron, the very capable senior Ops-Officer.

"Jet's not here Mick, sorry. I'll page him for you and get his number. Call back in ten minutes."

Not wanting to go back without a result I waited five minutes and called again. Waldo had the number ready.

Jet, chuckling as he spoke, walked me through a simple sequence and assured me this would make the ROV work. So, with a degree of confidence, plus crossed fingers, I headed back to the pier. Jet, the legend, saved our sorry arses!

With the ROV fired up, Nords and I continued the brief like we were seasoned professionals as we headed out to the search area.

Later that day Nords and I were in the police vessels cabin driving our ROV in front of the boat. Police divers were managing the umbilical as the boat followed along the search line, and senior police were looking at the image of the seabed as our state-of-the-art ROV covered the area far quicker than any diver could.

Overhead the Dornier was conducting a more extensive, low-level search, which occasionally crossed our track causing people to look up. There was indeed a huge area to search, and we were expecting to be there for a few days.

The Dornier had a couple of Jabbers in the back feeling worse for wear due to a hangover and turbulence they were being subjected to.

With them was a gaggle of specially trained 'Air Observers' from the Department of Aviation who, like the Jabbers, were scanning the shallow ocean for signs of the light-twin aircraft that had crashed. In the front of the Dornier, acting as co-pilot, was Captain Rowan 'Smudge' Smith. Smudge, like the Jabbers in the back, was regretting the amount of beer he had consumed the night before as he was close to throwing up. With sweat on his brow, he turned his head to avoid the glare from the sun and to make sure the spew-bag was ready. Sighting the bag, his peripheral vision observed more endless ocean below him when suddenly, there it was!

"Chatey, eleven o'clock directly below, light-twin sighted in about thirty feet of water. Marine marker, now!"

Chatey was the jumpmaster of the crew and was positioned next to the open door with Mk58 marine flare close to hand. He dispatched it immediately, and the flare landed in the water about 50m from the target. The senior Air Observer, sitting with four others on Chatey's side of the aircraft was amazed.

"I've been an observer for years but didn't see a thing as we flew over. How did you spot it?"

Smudge, listening on the intercom, gave what became a legendary and future stock standard response for PJs whenever questioned about something Pararescue by an outsider who didn't fully understand. "It's just what we do mate."

Back on the police boat Nords and I were hurriedly recovering the ROV so we could reposition to the marked location about a kilometre away. By the time we were on scene 50m from the flare on the vector provided by Smudge, the police divers were about ready to leap into the water. They helped with the ROV first, and then a couple of them hopped over the side.

We had the ROV on the bottom without delay; sonar fired up and were scanning for the aircraft. Very quickly we saw the definite shape about 20m away and flicked back to the camera, and there, directly in front of the lens was a STAR force diver with index finger beckoning us forward. There was around 10 feet of visibility, and we followed him, like a loyal puppy, along the seabed until the aircraft came into view.

Just as we were pulling up to the tail section, Smudge relayed a request from the senior Air Observer.

"Can you confirm the registration please?"

The ROV monitor was displaying the tail markings for all to see.

"Yes mate, that's Victor, Hotel, Echo…"

That night South Australian and Victorian news had a 10-minute lead story retelling the 'dramatic events of the last few days' and how, for South Australian viewers, 'a specialist rescue team from Victoria had bla, bla, blaa saved the day'. There was extensive vision of the Dornier, the ROV, PJs and pilots, which was undoubtedly enough to keep Council PR going for months. But the bit that made us laugh the most was a couple of seconds of Nords and myself on the back of the police boat, returning to shore, waving arms urgently and pointing towards the horizon.

Nords had spotted a media boat on our return to harbour and gave me some rapid training.

"Quick Mick, point in that direction. They love colour and movement on the evening news."

Returning to West Sale, we were invited into Freddo's office and were welcomed with a big grin (this only meant good times) and given a sneak peek of another expansion to our subsea capability.

Unlocking a desk drawer he pulled out a military manual and a similar industry document. The latter was the operating guide for a Perry Submersible PC-1804, a mini-sub with a diver-lockout capability. The other document was for the escape system of a Collins Class submarine, only just about to enter service with the RAN (where did he get that?). We were, apparently, about to go into the sub rescue business.

The PC-1804 was scheduled to arrive in the next few weeks, and all were pretty excited about this new tool and couldn't wait to start training. Then one hot sunny day we were called to the Ops Office.

"Ski boat has sunk at Lake Eppalock, near Bendigo. Police have requested the ROV and diving support."

Over the preceding weeks, Jet had been organising special containers for all the ROV equipment, and fortunately, we were able to pack up reasonably quickly. The rescue truck containing a variety of dive equipment, a duo-com two-man recompression chamber, a rib rescue boat in tow and a gaggle of PJs with a 4WD and second rib was on the road a few hours after we left.

Lake Eppalock in central Victoria, in 1988, was reasonably full and close to 30m at the deepest point. The ski boat we were coming to locate had apparently flipped somewhere in the deep section and police divers, already on site, were running out of available bottom time due to the rapid accumulation of nitrogen at their working depth, hence the request for the ROV.

Geoff, the police sergeant from the Silvan Dam job, was running things. We met at his van in the middle of a collection of other vehicles, including those belonging to the family of three missing persons, which included a boy aged three.

Apparently, the father of this young boy had custody of his son for the weekend; divorced for some time, he had taken him skiing with a bunch of mates who all had a few beers on board. Men, alcohol and boats (despite unofficial RN guidance) are not good for safety, and the inevitable had happened. To make matters worse, the young boy wasn't wearing a life jacket. Understandably then, there was a degree of tension at the site between family members as we went about our business.

Geoff's divers had covered a reasonable area to this point, but the nitrogen they had absorbed into their bodies mandated a 48hr stay out of the water to avoid decompression sickness. They had more divers on the way, but for now, the ROV was key to locating the boat.

Despite Jet's electronic knowledge, he'd called for Russell's assistance. This was a good decision as we only had a tiny boat to operate from and the gear had to be somewhat jury-rigged with a small generator to accommodate for lack of space. As we headed out to a buoy the police had left in the position, I was amused to watch Jet and Russell tweaking switches and checking manuals. We were still pretty new at this and their brow-wiping in the 35-degree heat was adding to the challenge.

The ROV was 'driven' down to the bottom using its vertical thrusters, but once there the colour camera proved useless in the dirty water. Jet selected the SIT camera and with a brief flicker the monitor produced a black and white picture. Using this and the sonar, Jet and Russell began investigating targets. After half an hour of finding nothing but rocks and tree stumps, a solid and very straight line appeared on the screen. They couldn't work out what it was but thought it might be part of the boat. I offered my two bobs worth to the debate based upon a statement made by my RN sonar instructor eleven years before.

"There are no straight lines in nature Jet."

The police boat was called over, and we had a brief discussion about the find. They agreed it was worth investigating and their remaining diver descended the ROV's umbilical. About ten minutes later he returned to the surface, minus his lifeline, which was now secured to what he hoped was the boat we had been looking for.

"It's fucking black and cold, but I'm pretty sure it's the ski boat."

Geoff was happy enough with the report.

"Good work Dave, come on out mate." Geoff turned to us, "Well, we're out of divers for a while now. I'll tie a buoy to the lifeline and let's head back to the beach and talk about salvage."

The ROV had proved its worth. It was now back to standard diving and a little imagination to determine how to raise the boat.

By the time we reached the shore, the familiar sight of a Brock Commodore was perched on a prominent section of higher ground, and the rescue truck and other equipment were rolling in too, Freddo had arrived.

"Err, Mick, what's going on?"

He was eager to get up to speed, and as Jet and Russell were busy with post dive checks on the ROV, he'd latched onto me.

"We've found the ski boat with the ROV John, but there are still three bodies to locate."

A contented smile appeared on his face. I continued.

"The police are going to discuss salvage of the boat shortly, but we'll be diving as their blokes are out of bottom time…" I pointed to the marker buoy, "…It's over twenty-five meters out there."

"Good. That's why I had the rescue truck brought along; you can use the Drager gear."

The gear Freddo intended me to use was designed for firefighting. It was primarily a single cylinder 300bar, reasonably low volume set, and one not equipped with a reserve system – a warning whistle doesn't cut it underwater. Although the first stage regulator would support augmented air delivery as ambient pressure increased, the low volume of the cylinder meant that we would have limited bottom time, i.e. not nearly enough! Although these sets weren't suitable for the task, the other option, 200bar scuba sets didn't present much of a choice, especially as the standard gauges would be useless in the zero-vis reported by the police.

"Ok John, I'll go and check on the police and their lift bags, and confirm what time they want to dive."

"Anything else you need, err, Mick?"

Some decent dive equipment would be good, I wimped it.

"No."

Freddo turned to find Banjo, his face all business, he was obviously about to take charge of the operation.

Geoff was in his van checking through a dive log.

"Hey Geoff, how's it all going?"

"Not bad mate. The boys are getting the bags out now; you diving?"

"Yeah."

I was thinking of a way to tell him our gear was shite and that I would like to borrow one of his large twin-sets, without making the Council look bad. This was going to be tricky.

"Hey, err, Geoff, what's the chance of borrowing one of your sets? I've used plenty of twins in the navy mate and would be far more comfor-"

"Err, hello, boys."

Freddo was standing behind me. I couldn't see his face but knew he wasn't smiling. I turned around, and he continued; there was a smile, but it wasn't a good one.

"Err, Mick just use a Drager set, they're 300bar you know?"

Geoff shrugged his shoulders and looked uncomfortable. I took the gutless option.

"Err, ok. Geoff, we best have a look at those bags then."

One of the standard parachute-type lift bags was selected, and there was a group discussion about its use for this type of recovery. By the time all had put their two bobs worth in; the bag had been rolled up tight to exclude air for the descent and secured with a line. Attached to the webbing at the neck were a wire lanyard and a rope one, I would use the most appropriate to secure the bag to the boat. Also, connected by another line was a single air cylinder that I would use to inflate the bag via its neck (or throat) opening.

This equipment plus, Kevin 'Bear' Hartley (standby diver) Louise Bradley (tender/supervisor), Flat-Nose McCall (driver/standby diver tender) all boarded our rib for the drive out to the buoy. Freddo came too, and Geoff headed out in another police boat. We all secured alongside a police boat already in position, and I gave the Council team a short brief.

"Ok, when I have the bag secure I'll put a small amount of air inside to lift it clear. This will let me check the connections." I had their full attention and continued on. "Ok, Louise, I'll give you two-pulls when I make the bag positive. You should have a good idea where it's going to come up from my bubbles, and I will ascend well clear, OK?"

There were more nods, but Bear was looking a tad concerned, poor bastard. If I required his services today, I wasn't expecting much. Nothing against Bear, he was a bloody good PJ, but shallow scuba training and LAR-V hadn't prepared him for this type of task.

"Bear, when you see the bag hit the surface move in quickly and secure the support line. If the bag fails, we don't want to have to do this again, ok."

Bear gave a positive response, and I could see he was rehearsing the shallow dip we had briefed where he would attach the five meters of heavy line to the boat for security. Louise was looking relaxed and had my lifeline ready, but line tendering wasn't rocket science, especially for an experienced commercial diver like her.

I had crunched up some numbers and added a decent fudge factor to work out how much air I would get at 25m, the depth of the boat. This conservative number was 15-minutes, not a lot, but sufficient for what I had to do. Who was I kidding? This was bloody stupid, and I knew it. If a leak developed, the regulator shit itself, or a range of other realistic dramas eventuated I wouldn't be having much fun. I put my stupid decision to dive down to Freddo and Jabber pride. Simply put, I wanted to impress him and also show experienced Jabbers that I could step up when things became other than routine, but this was the dumbest decision I had come to in a long time. Whatever. It was time to get my head wet.

The moment I rolled into the lake I realised my first mistake. I had weight for saltwater not fresh and was bloody heavy due to the reduced water density, too late to worry about that though. Kicking my legs madly to stay afloat and breathing too quickly inside the full-face mask of the Drager set, I looked to Louise for confirmation I had no leaks, an essential check before I descended into the black world below. Her head was turned away from me talking to someone else though... *come on, do your job...* Fuck it! Very conscious of my depleting air supply, I ignored Louise's authority and swam the short distance to the buoy, grabbed the line and left the surface without the leak check. Mistake number two.

The water was a dark green and became a pitch black within 10 feet of the surface; I was plummeting like a rock. With one hand on the down-line I opened my body like a skydiver to try and create more surface area in an effort to reduce the descent rate. I couldn't gauge how effective this was, but judging by the constant blowing against the nose clip to relieve the pressure building on my ears, it probably wasn't working too well. The other thing I noticed was the temperature change. At the surface, the water had been a pleasant 26 degrees Celsius, but the moment it went black this plummeted rapidly.

I smashed into the bottom and rolled onto my back. Remaining in this position, I quickly tightened my weight-belt and harness straps that were now loose as a result of routine wetsuit compression. Rolling over onto my knees I was conscious of how negatively buoyant I was, this would aid working but may present a challenge when returning to the surface. With the down-line still in hand I swam/crawled towards the target, and in less than a minute I found the coiled lift bag and cylinder that had been dropped down the line previously. Moving carefully over this partially neutral mass so as not to become entangled, I pulled it forward along the down-line and bumped into the ski boat.

Super conscious of my breathing and sure I would get a restriction any moment, I slowed my respirations as much as I possibly could and worked along the boat towards the transom.

The rudder was intact, and the propeller was still there, good. I reached out, sweeping my arm back and forth and located the rope lanyard attached to the lift bag. Quickly passing the lanyard several times around the rudder-post and the small 'A' frame holding the prop-shaft, I connected the lanyard back to itself with a shackle. The bag was secure.

Twisting around, very cautious of the lines and entanglement risk, I felt for the lift bag and the rope securing it. I had seen this rope on the surface and knew what it looked and felt like, but the cold, water pressure and zero visibility played with my mind. Which line was it? I ran my fingers over the bag a few times, then finally satisfied I had the correct rope (there was only one), I untied the knot.

The two meters of heavy-duty plastic bag began unrolling straight away. I assisted, with one hand on the securing lanyard and the other pushing away the invisible plastic 'blanket' that kept trying to engulf me. I wasn't very successful though, and every time the bag fell back on my head my breathing rate picked up.

'Slow down dickhead and switch on!'

I mentally ran through the options.

'Just put a squirt of air in the bag and let the buoyancy lift it clear, idiot!'

Ignoring the bag, I retrieved the inflation cylinder with one hand and brought it to my other hand at the throat of the bag - so far so good. However, when I tried to get the scuba cylinder's valve inside the throat, the 8-inch opening wouldn't seem to accommodate it. No matter how I pushed, the valve just wouldn't fit inside?

'Come on you weak bastard! I thought you were a fucking diver?'

With the subtle prompt from my inner voice, I changed tack. Positioning the cylinder between my knees, I used both hands to open the throat and bring the opening over the valve.

Yes!

Moving the fingers of my left hand, I located the valve and cracked it once, then twice. A moment later I felt the bag pulling up as the air tried to take it to the surface.

Following the now vertical lanyard back down to the transom I checked the security of the attachment and shackle – all was good. It was time to inflate the bag some more and send it on its way. However, despite the urgency of the task I didn't want to tangle up with it for the express ride to the surface. So at an expeditious, yet methodical pace, I ensured I was clear of the rigging and that my lifeline was behind me. All good. Time to signal Louise.

I pulled on the lifeline expecting to feel her grip on the other end of the rope respond in kind, but all I got was more rope? I pulled again and again, but with the same result. Experienced commercial diver my arse! Giving up on Louise, I moved back to the bags throat and pulled the cylinder in close.

This type of recovery could be completed in two ways. Either the diver puts sufficient air in the bag and keeps clear as Mr Boyle does the rest for a hurried trip to the surface, or, the diver stays with the bag and operates a relief valve to control the ascent. In the black world I was in, option one was the only choice.

With knees on the lakebed next to the transom and rigging, I gave a couple of squirts into the throat. The bag moved slowly upwards, and I extended my legs to stand on the tips of my fins.

'Was that enough air to keep it moving?'

Trusting my instincts I gave a couple more squirts, and then suddenly, I felt movement, fast movement and my fins were no longer touching the bottom. I pushed back away from the boat and bag, praying my lifeline was still clear. Thankfully it was. Forgetting the God I didn't believe in until I needed him again, I started kicking hard as my heavy weight-belt was making itself known now that I was no longer holding onto the bag.

After thirty seconds worth of aggressive leg action, I felt the first strained breath as the regulator drew on the depleted contents of the cylinder. In an automatic response my right hand dropped to my waist and operated the quick release of the weight-belt. Ballast gone, my progress toward the surface improved significantly, but the next, harder breath, ensured adrenaline still buzzed at my extremities.

Although I knew that the remaining air in the cylinder would expand on the way to the surface, in the black cold world physics was the last thing on my mind. I continued to kick hard, hyper-alert and monitoring my lungs for overpressure; until finally black became light green, and I commenced a slow exhale to the surface.

I was freezing, but arriving back on the surface still sweltering in the summer sun, the smack to the senses was quite a contrast to the last 14 or so minutes of my life.

Quickly orientating, I saw the dive boat a few meters in front of me and turned swiftly around with a flick of my fins. There was the bag, half of its orange shape bobbing gently after its explosive arrival moments before. Bear was alongside it with thumb held high, signalling to the crew that the line was secured. Thank Christ for that!

I swam the short distance to the boat and passed my set up to the smiling faces, which included Freddo's and Geoff's. Geoff spoke first.

"How'd it go?"

"Piece of piss mate."

Freddo could afford a new weigh-belt, and we could discuss the reality of the dip over beers.

During the motor back to the shore Freddo began to sing my praises. I interrupted him.

"Well actually John it wasn't particularly clever, you see I almost ran out of air on the way up."

I smiled, trying to soften the challenge to his comments.

"Err, Mick, that's not a problem for a professional diver like yourself now, is it? I mean, if you have a drama you pull on your line and ask for more air, and the standby brings it down to you, hey?"

Freddo was all smiles, and on a roll, I tried again.

"Yes, but a dedicated reserve system would make the job a lot easier, and safer."

He held eye contact for a second or two, long enough for me to realise I had pushed it too far.

"Ah, redundancies? Mick, I've talked with Eric about this..." he turned to face the others, "...and he disagrees with you."

Is that right? A Chief Clearance Diver doesn't believe you need a reserve system. I was going to lose this battle though and accepting it; I shrugged my shoulders.

"Well, it's just my view John..." My voice trailed off in defeat.

The salvaged ski boat was towed to shore and lifted from the water using a crane mounted on the back of our rescue truck. As water was sloshing over the transom, I had a dreadful thought. I didn't check the boat for bodies! The family were close by watching every step of the operation, and if a lifeless child spilled out onto the beach, it would be devastating. As the water flowed, a single child-sized life jacket spilled onto the ground causing the family to gasp and cry. The tension was high, but fortunately, operations were suspended for the day.

We spent the night in a Bendigo motel with plans to continue searching for bodies at first light. Bear and Flat-Nose were assigned the role of divers for the next day, and Banjo was to be standby. Over dinner, they had stoically joked about what joy this would be, and so the following day I took them aside for a 'no-shit' brief.

"This is bullshit boys'. The gear Freddo wants you to use is not suitable, and you'll have bugger-all endurance at the depth and temperature you're diving in. What do you want to do?"

Although not an NSCA diving supervisor at this point, my question was a bit of a cop-out in the responsibility department. The gear was shit. I knew it, Freddo (I suspected) knew it, and everyone else knew it, but I was passing the buck to Bear and Flat-Nose.

Although it was plainly visible they were anxious; I could see the cogs ticking around as they processed the same real-world factors I had the other day. Unfortunately for them though, PJ pride and not wanting to let Freddo down won out. They both agreed to dive.

"Ok then. I know you know how to do a circular search, that's the least of my concern, and if you don't complete it, I don't care. From the moment you leave surface, I want your focus to be on emergency actions for a breathing restriction. So, at the first hint head up, and if you find this too hard drop your weights immediately. Understood?"

The boys', dumb-arse Jabbers like me, both gave a positive thumb up.

As we moved out towards our boat there was increased activity on the edge of the lake. A police boat was on its way in, and the divers were holding something over the side? I don't know how it happened, a mother's sixth sense perhaps, but a woman started moving purposefully through the people on the beach. Her eyes were wide, and her mouth was opening slowly as she passed us. Some of the family members tried to hold her back, but there was no stopping a mother on the way to her son.

As the divers carried the small frame of a three-year-old boy from the boat to the beach, with his wet mop of blond locks partially covering his face and his arms outstretched in the final death throes of survival, I heard the most haunting scream build to a howl. Everyone on the beach stopped and turned towards the poor mother about to be reunited with her boy. She collapsed on the bank, pushing aside offers of comfort, wailing inconsolably.

It was a sight I hoped never to see again, as my mind immediately put our daughter's face to the boy. For a second I wondered what my wife was doing at that moment and wanted to be home with them both.

The sight of a body before you were about to dive, and one recently drowned, was not the best motivation for a dip into 25m of cold black water. But to the boys' credit they sucked it up, and we headed out to the dive site.

One Council rib was moored in position already, and we tied up to that. A shot-line was positioned with a float on the surface and Bear prepared to enter the water first.

As he finned out to the buoy, Banjo, in the water by the ribs pontoon keeping cool at 'immediate notice' whispered up to me.

"What do I do here exactly, Mick?"

This was a bloody nightmare!

"If he needs assistance, just follow his lifeline down and help him up."

I whispered my response, not wishing the police diver who was driving our rib to overhear how unprepared we were. What I should have done was call a halt then and there. We were now several bad decision steps into an unfolding disaster.

Bear left surface, and I followed his descent with my hands on the lifeline. Louise was actually supervising, but wasn't contributing a whole lot. Nonetheless, I reported Bear's progress.

"On the bottom and he's moving out on the search line."

I had suggested eight minutes bottom time was a maximum due to dives Bear and Flat-Nose had (allegedly) completed in preceding days, wanting him out well before he ran out of air. The cop wasn't stupid though; he knew we were using smoke and mirrors; the anxiety in people's eyes was a bit of a giveaway too.

As Bear continued on his search, I watched the clock; it was coming up to seven minutes. Bugger it, that's close enough. I gave him the signal to return to the shot and then to ascend.

Once on the surface, arriving in a controlled state, Louise and Flat-Nose helped him with his gear, and then Flat-Nose got dressed. As Bear finished reporting to Flat-Nose what the conditions were like, he turned to me and whispered that he had a slight breathing restriction a meter or so from the surface. Fuck!

Another warning ignored, we put Flat-Nose in the water, but as he was leaving the shot to start his search, Banjo looked up at me positively. Well, who knows, maybe we would get away with it?

At about the five-minute mark I received one pull on the lifeline. This was quickly followed by four more. I answered the 'I want to ascend' signal with my heart rate increasing rapidly. Did Flat-Nose have a breathing restriction already?

I could feel Flat-Nose's progress and that the lifeline was coming up at a controlled rate, but then suddenly it pulled tight, then went slack and I hurriedly pulled in heaps of loose rope. Shit! He appeared on the surface 5-meters from the boat shortly afterwards rising to his chest in an explosion of water and bubbles. Before the water had time to settle the cop, a senior constable, was first to react appropriately.

"Is he well?!"

My first reaction had been an expletive, and it must have alarmed the cop, but after seeing several uncontrolled assents in the RN, I fully appreciated the seriousness of the situation.

"Flat-Nose, are you well?"

He was 15-feet from the rib, and his mask and regulator were still in place. Spitting the regulator clear and pushing the mask from his face he yelled loudly.

"Fuck no!"

For some reason, the lifeline had parted, and so I couldn't pull him in.

"Banjo, get him!"

Banjo moved quickly; perhaps five seconds had passed since Flat-Nose's arrival at the surface. Within fifteen seconds we had him at the side of the rib, but only then did I notice his face was covered in blood! His gear was dropped, and we hauled him over the side when he screamed again.

"My fucking shoulder!"

As he screamed my focus remained on the blood around his lips and nose. The rapid breathing and pained expression combined with the blood brought back an image of the Royal Marine's accident too; Flat-Nose's shoulder pain was the least of my concerns.

The senior constable was at the back of the rib standing next to the controls of the twin 75hp outboards. As Louise and Bear continued to position Flat-Nose on the deck, I turned to the cop.

"Start her up mate."

He responded immediately, and I turned to the others.

"Louise, call the beach and tell them to ready the duo-com. Bear, help Banjo up and then untie us from the second boat."

On the beach, PJs had been standing by for a worst-case outcome. As part of this planning, the duo-com was at immediate readiness with a PJ assigned as an attendant. Although we never really expected to execute this role when diving, PJs often undertook it during recovery of 'bent' commercial divers or people suffering from 'gas gangrene' who required recompression as part of their treatment. In such situations the PJ and casualty were loaded into the two-man chamber, then this was loaded onto a twin turboprop King Air aircraft to be flown to Adelaide hospital for a Transfer

Under Pressure (TUP) to a more extensive chamber where medical staff were waiting.

After yelling the instructions, I dropped down to Flat-Nose who was lying on his back on the rib's deck. His mouth and nose were still covered in blood, and his face was screwed up in pain. The image of the Royal Marine from nearly seven years before was front-centre of my memory, and I knew that if we were to prevent expanding gas bubbles blocking blood flow to Flat-Nose's brain, we had to move fast. Then Louise spoke, challenging my request.

"The duo-com, what for?"

What? I couldn't believe the arrogance in her voice. Just where had she gained her commercial qualifications? I snapped.

"Just tell them to have the chamber ready Louise, and do it *fucking now!*"

I lifted Flat-Nose's legs up onto the side of the rib and then fitted the oxy-viva therapy mask to his blood smeared face. The cop had the rib moving quickly towards shore, but as we entered the shallows, he slowed down for a professional approach to ensure no hull or engine damage was sustained.

"Fuck the motors mate, just tilt them up and run it onto the beach."

He did as I requested and we bumped to a halt with about six inches of water at the bow.

We quickly lifted Flat-Nose from the rib and assisted him to walk back to the Council 5-Tonne truck containing the duo-com. The boot was off, ready to get him inside and back under pressure, with Maso, as duty attendant, ready to go. Following close by, Louise voiced her opinion with an assertive tone.

"It's probably nothing guys."

All attention turned to Louise as Flat-Nose just stood there, bloodied mouth and nose, face still screwed up in pain, chest rising and falling rapidly. After all, she was a senior hyperbaric attendant, respected commercial diver and supposedly the one in charge of this operation. My anger boiled over once more.

"I don't give a shit Louise! If he has a gas embolism, we need to blow him down now!"

I couldn't believe her stupidity. Despite not backing her statement up with an alternative explanation, so what, even if Flat-Nose didn't have a barotrauma, wasn't bent, it was just a chamber ride. Moreover, if he had sustained a pressure injury and we didn't recompress him immediately, he could die, or worse, become a vegetable. I ignored her.

"Maso, hop in. Boys, get Flat-Nose on the stretcher. Let's go!"

I won the debate. With the boot end of the duo-com locked in place, I rapidly recompressed Flat-Nose and Maso down to 30m. Maso, now sitting in an 'L' position with Flat-Nose's head positioned at his lap on the duo-com's stretcher, was equalising rapidly with one hand and preparing equipment with the other.

After five minutes on chamber bottom, Maso reported that Flat-Nose's shoulder was still very sore, but the bleeding had stopped, and he appeared to be breathing ok now. This was both good and bad.

When recompressed, a diver will likely have the initial barotrauma symptoms reduce as the pressure takes effect. So if the pain is still present when on chamber bottom it is probably not a pressure-related injury. In Flat Nose's case, the absence of bleeding was a cause for concern, and his shoulder pain would need further evaluation.

As you can imagine, Freddo had taken great interest in proceedings. He advised that an aircraft was on route to Bendigo airport from Sale with Dr Ian Maxwell on board. Ian was the Council's senior medical officer, and with many years of hyperbaric medicine behind him, he was just the bloke Flat-Nose needed.

As we waited for Ian's arrival, Louise begrudgingly took control of the duo-com and continued with the appropriate therapeutic table. It looked as though things would settle down for a while when another drama eventuated, the heat.

"He can't get his suit off, can you pass in some scissors and some more water please."

It was Maso's fourth request for water in fifteen minutes. We passed the items through a small airlock, but as before, when the iced water arrived inside it was lukewarm. The boys' were suffering. Maso, performing a partial contortionists act in the very tight space, cut away at Flat-Nose's wetsuit and then his own flight suit. He described the conditions as 'stinking hot, like a furnace'. The extreme heat was hazardous and could easily cause severe hyperthermia resulting in overheating of the body's cells and ultimately organ damage or death, but we had limited options.

Although the truck's canopy was offering some shade, we had draped wet towels over the chamber to ease the internal temperature; but they weren't very effective. The boys' selection and training for Pararescue was going to be tested! During these processes, time in confined space and accepting hardship was something you put up with, or you went home; but hours in a duo-com, in extreme heat, with an injured mate? They were doing it very hard indeed.

About two hours after we had blown them down, Freddo's Commodore appeared with Ian and the two pilots who had delivered him. He had a box of drugs in tow and looked his usual calm self.

I explained what the dive involved, the incident facts, plus what I saw and the actions taken post surface, reinforcing that I believed Flat-Nose's shoulder was the main problem at this point.

Louise passed on details of the table she had been following and where she was up to, and then Ian turned to a small window and depressed the intercom switch. He used Flat-Nose's real name.

"G'day Ryan, how do you feel now?"

There was a half-hearted electronic chuckle from inside the chamber.

"Lucky to be alive." Flat-Nose followed this with a more serious appraisal though, "My shoulder still hurts quite a bit."

Flat-Nose then re-told the story from his point of view for the benefit of Ian. He'd had a breathing restriction on the bottom and done as

I had requested – drop everything and ascend. During the ascent, the breathing restriction became worse, and he dropped his weight-belt but also inflated his buoyancy jacket with its small CO_2 cylinder. As he accelerated to the surface the lifeline, hooked under his shoulder, had suddenly pulled tight stopping him with a significant jolt about 3m from the surface. He found himself trapped, hardly a breath of air left, in a dark green world about to die if he couldn't get free. He'd reached for the knife secured to his calf and quickly cut the lifeline free, and then a moment later he had exploded onto the surface. We were to find out later that his lifeline had become entangled in the unique shot-weight the police used. This device had a small swivel arm to aid the rotation during a circular search, and Flat-Nose's lifeline had become entangled around this.

Ian continued his assessment.

"Ok Ryan, the pain in your shoulder. From one to ten, how would you describe it initially?"

"Twenty-Five!"

There was humour to Flat-Nose's response, but everyone listening knew how frightening the situation must have been. Ian had good humour too.

"Ok, I'll take that as a ten. How about now?"

Flat-Nose indicated a constant seven, with painful flare-ups to eight if he moved his arm. Ian continued with his assessment.

"I'll give you something for the pain soon. Now, can you take a deep breath in for me please?" Ian had his face against the window, watching closely, "And out… any pain or discomfort then Ryan?"

"Just my shoulder as my chest rose with the breath, ok apart from that."

"Thanks, Ryan" Ian acknowledged, "Ok, just breathe normally. What I need you to do now is count back from one hundred to zero in increments of seven. Off you go."

Flat-Nose's response to that request drew more laughter from the crowd.

"Fuck! I'd have trouble doing that on my best day."

Despite the maths challenge, Flat-Nose worked his way down to zero and confirmed to Ian no cognitive impairment was present; a likely outcome if expanding gas bubbles had prevented oxygen reaching the brain.

After the assessment was completed, Ian determined that the shoulder pain was likely caused by the sudden trauma to his armpit after the abrupt stop, but an x-ray would have to confirm the extent of the damage. The blood on his face though? It was put down to a massive reverse sinus squeeze. This was likely caused by plugs of mucus building in the cavities of the skull while at depth, which had trapped air that rapidly expanded during his hurried ascent. At some point, the increasing air pressure forcibly expelled the plugs causing significant damage to small blood vessels, which in turn produced lots of blood - but fortunately, no ruptured lung.

As Ian was giving his appraisal, Louise had a smug 'I told you so' expression for all to see, but it just made my contempt for ability as a diver grow even more.

'If in doubt, you throw them in the pot!'

These were words Psycho, Bob Oulds, Mick Ferdinand, John Dadd and every other RN dive supervisor I'd worked with. Somehow Louise's training hadn't provided the same reinforcement.

Despite relief over the lack of barotrauma, Ian was also very concerned about dehydration and hyperthermia. He had Maso take regular observations of Flat-Nose's vital signs and asked if he could get a cannula inserted to start an intravenous drip. Even though he had practised this as part of the nine-month PJ program during a secondment to a Melbourne hospital, Maso's contortionist ability was limited. Very quickly this request was cancelled, and it was doubted whether even a skilled anaesthetist or critical care paramedic could have achieved success in such a tight space.

Notwithstanding the level of discomfort, Ian had decided against transport to Adelaide as the time to do this compared to the time remaining for completion of the therapeutic table offered little reward for the added risk. The boys continued to drink lukewarm water as their decompression continued.

I was very relieved that Flat-Nose had received a shoulder injury only and that his lungs hadn't been damaged, but there was still the issue of Council diving equipment and enhanced training for PJs. So, no time like the present to get the point across.

Around the chamber were a gaggle of Jabbers, Ian, the pilots, Louise and Freddo. I turned to Freddo.

"John, we could probably get some new equipment brought down to the base to have a look at. Something with a reserve system, it ma-"

He exploded.

"Redundancy! There you go again." His rage softened a little, "Look, I told you Eric doesn't think they are needed, these things happen from time to time."

I wasn't ready to back down.

"Yes, but even if they do, with a reserve system it is far safer, and there will be no need for a free ascent."

I had raised my voice to the wrong side of acceptable, and people were noticeably backing away. Freddo locked his eyes with mine.

"Well, I guess *redundancy* is the key issue here."

Fuck, was he talking about my redundancy? Freddo turned to Ian.

"Ian, what do you think?"

Ian had been with the Council from the beginning, he was a tactful man, but he said enough.

"There are pros and cons for both John. But, in this case, a reserve may have benefited?"

Freddo paused, his eyes drifting between the two of us. Finally, there was a hint of a smile.

"Well, err, I will have to talk to Eric some more on the subject."

Freddo moved off to his car, equipped with one of the first reliable car phones of the eighties and did just that.

Eventually, the boot was removed, and the two semi-naked jabbers emerged. The floor of the duo-com was soaking with sweat and Maso's hacked up flight suit was hanging over the rim; Freddo saw this and turned to Maso, who was still holding the scissors.

"Err, Masy, what have you done to that suit?" He had half a smile "You owe me five hundred dollars."

As the rest of us started packing up the gear, Flat-Nose went off to the hospital for x-rays and Maso, invited to ride in the Brock Commodore, headed into town with Freddo – this, a ride in Freddo's car, was acknowledgment for doing something good.

Maso described an interesting conversation with Freddo during the drive into Bendigo that revealed his influence at the time, but it never made the light of day during later court proceedings.

"On the way into town, Freddo opened his briefcase and produced a letter. It was a job offer from the Victoria Police asking him to run their Air Wing. I can't recall the signatory, but can recall the letter and guarantee it as being genuine."

Just why did the police close the investigation into the demise of the NSCA so quickly?

I was thankful I still had a job after the raised conversation with Freddo, but a few beers would help ease the remaining worry. Bear, slightly tongue in cheek, suggested I was crazy to argue with him as he, "may have taken me back to his room for a *workover*?" He was referring to the growing rumours that Freddo was bisexual, but after laughing at my potential plight, he turned serious.

"Good work today 'Fairlane' you're a good operator."

I didn't feel the general satisfaction after receiving a compliment from someone I respected, quite the reverse actually. Had I had the balls to speak more assertively at the outset I probably could have convinced Freddo to allow me to use the police twin-set. And furthermore, had Flat-Nose or Bear been killed, or me for that matter, I doubt people would have been signing my praises.

News Headline:

Police divers and other emergency workers involved the recovery of a ski boat and bodies from Lake Eppalock suffered a setback yesterday when a diver had to be treated for the 'bends'. Mr John Friedrich, Executive Director of the National Safety Council of Australia, advised media personnel that it was, in fact, a minor event and that his staff managed the situation as per their procedures.

Duo-com recompression chamber: the attendant sits up the back with legs extended under the stretcher. The casualty lies on a stretcher with his head in the lap of the attendant. The 'boot' at the right is then fitted.

Silvan Dam job:
Police divers with the recovered plane and Rookie-6 in background.

NSCA Duo-com being 'mated' to larger chamber. The boot is removed inside the larger chamber by medical staff and the casualty is transferred under pressure.

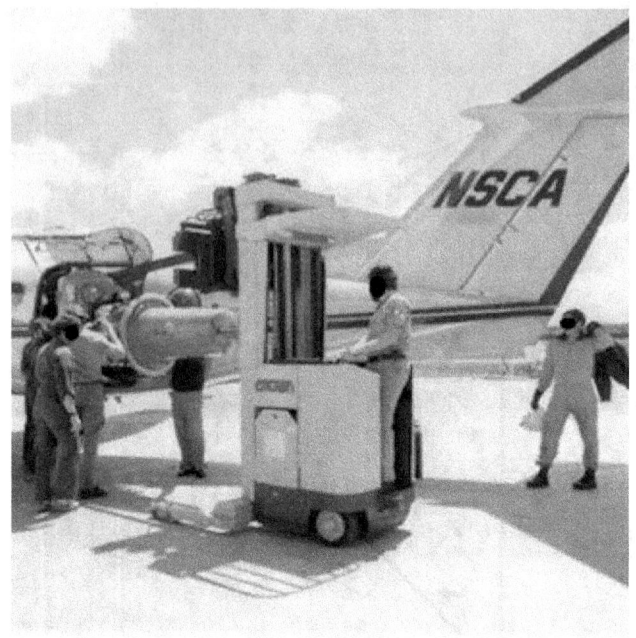

PJ and patient being loaded aboard the King Air for transport to Adelaide hospital. It was a very tight squeeze and interesting for the patient during take-off and landing.

CHAPTER 12

NSCA Pararescue (Subsea Expansion – Rookie-7 and Commercial Training)

NORDS AND I WERE ASSIGNED to the Rookie-7 dive course, which was to be an extended version of those before it. Freddo, good to his word, had organised for PJs to be trained as commercial divers. What this meant was Rookie-7 would complete a 16-week program to qualify as 'Australian Standard Level-3' commercial divers. This meant, 50m utilising both scuba and surface supply. On this course, they would also undertake salvage training, utilise tools and complete a range of tasks that would prepare them for the type of work predicted for Freddo's subsea expansion.

During the same course, I would be trained by Eric and formally signed off as an NSCA instructor/supervisor, and Nords would get the upgraded qualifications. There was one little glitch in the entire plan though, Freddo-Factor.

"Err, Eric, I know, but we don't have the time. I want the program completed in six weeks, Ok."

Freddo-Factor was something you got used to, but it didn't mean you enjoyed it, and poor Rookie-7, to their detriment, was about to experience Freddo-Factor for the first time. The level-3 program mandated that they accumulate a minimum amount of minutes underwater at various depth ranges as part of the qualification process. When 16 weeks were available divers spent reasonably long cold periods underwater, but six weeks? Individual motivation was undoubtedly going to be tested.

A couple of months before, Nords and I had hosted two sales representatives from rival diving equipment suppliers, one from Drager and the other from Interspiro. Freddo had approved new equipment trials, and we were to make our recommendations.

The Drager equipment was new, high-volume, 300bar and positive pressure. On paper, it looked like the sort of gear we needed. I had never heard of Interspiro before.

Despite Drager being a familiar brand with the latest cylinder design, its full-facemask was relatively bulky and old-fashioned. This was disappointing, but it was still an improvement on what we were currently operating with.

The Interspiro rep showed us his equipment next. It was also 300bar but had a range of high and low volume cylinders and a harness that was plumbed so that a surface supply umbilical or buddy-hose could be easily connected. Moreover, the mask was incredibly low volume and contained an oral-nasal that directed exhaled air across the faceplate (it never fogged up) and could be fitted with through-water-comms too.

We tried both sets in the 4m deep West Sale pool and afterwards I described the Drager mask as being like an 'upmarket bucket on your head'. We both favoured the Interspiro set that was designated, AGA - pronounced 'Ar-ger'.

Despite our immediate preference, before going to see Freddo we took both sets to Welshpool and gave them a bit of an open water work out, but our view didn't change.

Freddo smiled at our choice, but insisted that Drager was the set we would buy – this fascination with Drager perhaps indicated his true origins? Not giving up though, we raised all sorts of rational as to why the AGA set was better, but he was having none of it. Eventually, after lengthier, yet still cautious debate, a call was made to Eric and sanity prevailed.

I found myself in Freddo's office about five weeks after the first trial signing a purchase order for $250,000 worth of equipment and spares. My hands were sweating slightly at the enormity of the sum, but Freddo's brief statement as his eyes bored into mine reinforced my responsibility for the decision to select AGA.

"Don't let me down."

Unfortunately, the delay in approving the AGA purchase meant that it wasn't available for the start of Rookie-7, but we got the basics out of the way with regular scuba gear and then headed down to Welshpool and the Blue Nabila, the Council's flagship.

Known by PJs as the 'Blue Pig', this former offshore oil rig support vessel wallowed like one too and would have rivalled a Mine Hunter for its capacity to dance on its berthing lines while secured to a wharf in a calm harbour.

Joining us on the Blue Pig were two Victorian police divers that Freddo had invited as part of his plan to build relationships in the right areas. These blokes, both competent individuals, were somewhat apprehensive as they came aboard, because even the police had little idea about the inner workings of the NSCA. To a degree, there was an unknown mysterious aura around the Council; politicians loved us, but they didn't fund us, yet there we were with gear better than anyone else, doing some fantastic operations. But where did the money come from?

Barry, a police sergeant, and his mate soon realised that we were just a bunch of emergency workers like any others that, when not running around with work activity, liked a joke and a drink just like any others and their barriers came down.

The Blue Pig left Welshpool and headed into the Bass Strait. We turned east and began our passage north to Nelson Bay, north of Newcastle, where we would make the most of some protected (and deep enough) waters to start accumulating bottom time.

During the passage north, we delivered lectures and Rookie-7 commenced a work-up in the Pig's pot. And so one mid-morning, with the Pig doing its usual pitch and roll into the north-easterly breeze, the boys of Rookie-7 arrived at the chamber bottom of 50m for the first time.

Depth and pressure, like other constants, will have a variable effect on different people; therefore even when worked-up a diver may still experience uncertainty or twitches of fear as nitrogen narcosis begins to take hold. When such symptoms are identified in-water the only course of action is to ascend if a diver wants to maintain control... but in a pot? Well, it's not so dangerous, and, despite one or two consequences from being exposed to the 'narc's' it is good education. An example of 'consequence' is the challenge of communication due to the subtle voice changes pressure causes; the result of which ensures students get their money's worth.

The giggling coming through the pot's intercom as Rookie-7, led by Barry, repeatedly calling "one-hundred-and-eighty" as if getting a maximum score in darts kind of told the story. The singing and adolescent games continued, but every minute or so whatever they were doing was interrupted with another chorus of, "one-hundred-and-eighty!"

The fixation with this number was the approximate calculation of 50m into feet, and the boys, in their slight narc'd state speaking like a collection of wannabe Donald Ducks, thought this number was incredibly funny. It was a shame such fun had to come to an end.

The Blue Pig's engineer, 'Zaggy' also doubled as the chef. Of Italian origin, Zaggy was known for both his humour and temper. The latter was being tested as the potatoes he had sent through the airlock for Rookie-7 to peel were now being thrown around the pot, unpeeled, to the joyous sound of, "One-hundred-and-eighty," as the Blue Pig potato rebellion continued unabated.

Despite the narc's, the game had gone too far, and appropriate punishment would have to be administered. What to do? Nords and I thought a bit of speed-dressing would be relevant and sought Eric's advice.

"Ok, but remember to reinforce why we do speed-dressing. It's not as a punishment; it's training to prepare them for rapid donning of equipment in the back of an aircraft."

Eric was quite serious. Despite being a former Chief Clearance Diver, he didn't see the need to make people suffer unnecessarily and had, in fact, stopped some of the 'old school' methods utilised by instructors like Psycho.

During my CD course, a pair of divers was required to be dressed in neck-entry dry-bags within 2-minutes. Failure to do this saw the task repeated, again and again. More than once during speed-dressing, Psycho had us enter the water in whatever state of undress we were at ensuring our suits flooded and we froze. He did this even if we were well within the required time limit. Not exactly true sportsmanship, but that was old school Psycho.

Despite Eric's modern take on training, he knew that discipline on a dive course was equally important.

Exiting the pot, narcosis seeming like a distant memory (actually, true narcosis behaviour isn't remembered), Rookie-7 knew they were about to suffer. We lined them up on the deck and spent about 20 minutes pulling on wetsuits and taking them off again. They were always, 'two fucking slow' and we started again and again. Fingers began to blister, and nails were ripped, and the once happy faces were no longer smiling. Calling things to a halt, Eric addressed them all.

"We can have fun on this course boys', but don't forget its serious training you're undertaking."

Anchored in Nelson Bay, we commenced accumulating minutes. The equipment we used was Kirby Morgan Band-Mask Mk10, or more simply

KMB10. This was a surface supplied set that commercial operators had been using for close to two decades. As I mentioned before, my first experience with it was during time with the RN's Fleet Clearance Diving Team as the navy introduced it as 'new technology'.

It had a large faceplate built into a plastic moulded mask that housed a second-stage regulator. A neoprene hood was fitted to the mask with a band-clamp adjusted by a screwdriver and then the diver 'zipped' this onto his head and kept it in place with a broad 'spider-band', which clipped onto appropriately positioned studs on the mask.

The regulator had an additional control called a 'dial-a-breath'. This was a valve the diver could rotate to increase the amount of air available with each inhalation or, if required, leave a constant flow of air into the mask. The regulator had no mouthpiece though; instead, the diver breathed from an 'oral-nasal' that when in place looked similar to a fighter pilots mask. Adjustable from the outside, a nasal-plate could be pushed under the nostrils to support equalisation, and for comfort, it was pulled forward clear of the nose when not in use – much more comfortable than the ubiquitous nose-clip of old school full face masks.

Other essential features of the KMB10 were 'defogger' and reserve valves. At the top right of the mask was a forward facing valve that when opened sent large volumes of air across the faceplate. This obviously cleared a misted up faceplate, but it also provided extra air if the diver had a problem with his regulated supply. The reserve valve was located to the side of the defogger and was connected by a short hose to a 'bailout' cylinder worn on the divers back.

All in all, KMB10 was a tried and tested workhorse that the poor blokes of Rookie-7 were going to become very, very familiar with.

We had positioned two shot ropes at a depth of 20m off the stern of the Blue Pig and had single divers undertaking circular searches to mitigate umbilical snagging. But after the first day, Eric advised this wasn't going to meet Freddo's timeline and so circular searches were canned, and we just put two divers onto each shot with not much for them to do other than collect minutes. This was boredom personified and morale was taking a noticeable dip, but they needed the minutes.

Nords and I gave them rope ends to complete a range of splicing they had been practicing, and we even came up with a song composition game where the rookies had to make up words to the tune of 'Sitting on the dock of the bay' using plastic slates. The novelty of this didn't last long though and we were soon seeing more and more early-stage hypothermic rookies climbing up the ladder not exactly loving life. The only break in monotony was a change to LAR-5 for a compass swim, but the boys were doing it pretty tough, day and night.

Eric approached Nords and I one evening after a couple of Rookie-7 had been to see him in private early in the second week.

"How do you feel about helping with gear preparations so the course can get a bit more downtime?"

He saw the frowns appear and knew the reason for them, so he explained.

"Hey boys, I know this isn't normal, but they're struggling because of Freddo's needs, ok. We are cramming so much bottom time into the day some of them are close to cracking, but they're good blokes who we don't want to lose."

Eric was right, of course, they were working hard, or more realistically they were doing bugger all and would probably love a good work out. Although it went against the grain, we both agreed to Eric's plan for the remainder of the week.

Initially, there was a noticeable pick up of morale, but within a day they were on a slide again. Worse though, we identified a couple of blokes who abused our support by slacking off when all hands were needed. We spoke to Eric about it, and he agreed it was time to stop the experiment.

This was a challenging time for me, as I had never held a full-time training position before. I soon realised there was a lot more to training than just shouting at people and making them suffer; you had to use your judgement within the confines of a syllabus to get the most out of individuals, knowing that in the close-knit world of operations there were unique personalities, strengths and weaknesses.

Thankfully we left Nelson Bay with all Rookie-7 still on the course, they were miserable, tension was in the air, but they were ticking the required boxes to achieve the minutes and skills needed. It was time to take them deeper.

Anchoring off some high, relatively sheltered headland we prepped for the first dives to 40m, which were to be followed by 50m dips. We were now using another mask, or 'hat,' called SuperLite-17 in addition to the KMB10. As discussed before, this was essentially a KMB10 with a hard 'hat' instead of the neoprene and spider-band. Another piece of 'North Sea' gear, the boys all had appropriate photos taken in the SuperLite-17 with steely-eyed expressions to impress their mates/girlfriends.

Over the preceding weeks, the boys had learnt to operate the dive 'panel' which controlled the gas supply to up to three umbilicals. Large air cylinders were connected to the inlet side of the panel, and a manually operated valve for each umbilical reduced their high-pressure air. It was the panel operator's job to adjust the reducer to keep line-pressure appropriate as the divers descended. At first, this job was daunting, but Rookie-7 got the hang of it as a typical 'panel report' before diving indicated.

"Diver one: main-cylinder open at the neck (205bar) and open at the panel, reserve-cylinder closed at the neck (200bar) and closed at the panel, reducer set to 10m, outlet valve open. Diver two: main-cylinder open at the neck (195bar) and open at the panel, reserve-cylinder closed at the neck (205bar), and closed at the panel, reducer set to 10m, outlet valve open. Standby Diver: main-cylinder open at the neck (175bar) and open at the panel, reserve-cylinder closed at the neck (190bar) and closed at the panel, reducer set to 0m, outlet valve closed."

The divers were lowered in a steel cage, only exiting if currents permitted, and more minutes began to accumulate. The boys were showing genuine confidence in any task we presented them at this stage, and when hats were removed after dips, smiles were reappearing, but not just due to shorter duration dives. They were becoming a slick operation, and after a week and a half of deep diving, they had accumulated the minimum minutes required. We headed back south for Wilsons Promontory and the protection of Refuge Cove, and it's shallower water to undertake salvage training.

Starting with a lecture on lift bags and lift bags of opportunity, I discussed how 44-gallon drums could be used and even how sealing a submerged object and filling it with air may be an option. Weight in water compared to weight in air calculations were practiced, and simple fudge factor rules were ingrained – if it weighs 1-Tonne, use a 2-Tonne bag. If you don't have a 2-Tonne bag, use two 1-Tonne bags. But this course was about practical skills, so we got them in the water quick-smart.

During this week Rookie-7 used the Pig's crane to lift objects, they swam free carrying lift bags, they used surface supply and scuba to lift objects, and they rigged items so that they could be towed to shore. By the end of that week, there was just 'surface decompression' to go.

Not used much these days, surface decompression was a process where a diver was brought to the surface and then transferred directly to the ships decompression chamber to complete his stops in dry, none-wave-effected and relatively warm conditions. The final part of this training for Rookie-7 involved a variation called 'detached' surface decompression.

This was used for operations where a mother ship deploys a smaller craft for diving, like any Mine Warfare conning-run for example, and the bottom time required to complete a task pushes the diver into mandatory and extended decompression. Another example of the relevance of detached surface decompression is to support diving emergencies (see chapter 11). The process of detached decompression requires a disciplined crew and by the time they had finished the needed drills Rookie-7 had met the criteria, with just one or two yelled words of encouragement from Eric.

Six weeks of pain and suffering over, we were secured at the Welshpool Wharf packing up the gear with the Rookie-7 boys in preparation for the return to West Sale. Eric called Nords and me to his cabin, and as we sat down, I noticed he wasn't smiling.

"Take a look at these."

We both took a handful of the post-course critiques and began to read, my mouth fell open shortly afterwards and remained so as I continued to read on.

'The course was run by a second world war has been' and *'the assistant instructors seemed more interested in having a good time than helping with our instruction'* and even more damming *'the use of bastardisation is not necessary'*.

The comments pretty much continued in the same vein, although there were some positive remarks too, *'the lecture on lift bags was very beneficial'*, but such statements were a minority.

Eric appeared to be in a mild state of shock. He had trained RAN divers for many years, had taught the previous Rookie courses without complaint – in fact, PJs pretty much held Eric on a high pedestal despite some of them not particularly enjoying diving.

I was shocked too. We had held meetings with Eric every evening to discuss how the boys had performed during the day; we looked for ways to produce results and agreed on all activities and actions throughout the course. Importantly, we were also acutely aware that the Nelson Bay episode was soul destroying and had tried to mitigate its effect on morale. Although the course hadn't been run in Scotland, in winter, I was very aware that any inactivity encourages mind games that aren't there when you are being flogged by fin swims. The simple fact, though, was that they'd needed the minutes, there were no other options, and their remarks were perhaps reflective of the hard time they'd had - yet some comments had a degree of bitterness that indicated more.

"Do you think we could have done more?"

Despite his words, Eric's face had doubt written all over it.

"I mean, we were having brews while they were in the cold prepping gear, one of us could have been out there with them?"

"Probably Eric" I began "but if they can't suck it up without someone holding their hands now, how would they cope on their own operationally?"

Despite my words, I was beginning to think Eric was right. After all, I had vivid memories of the anguish I'd experienced after completing a second jackstay swim on my Ships Divers course one snowy day during the winter of 1977.

Having suffered a wet-dip on the first dive, nothing new, my undersuit was saturated by the end of the second; water was collecting at my calves like sloshing gumboots. I was well into the violent shivering stage of hypothermia and close to throwing it away when finally we had to surface due to low air. The course Petty Officer (PO) was there, smiling away with snow swirling about the little Dory dive-boat.

"Ok, quick change around and we'll get one more dip in before lunch."

The thought of recharging my set and then entering the lake for another 40 minutes of pain was too much. I was just working up the courage to tell him I wanted 'off course' when he had a change of plan.

"Sorry boys, I forgot the time. Get out and changed for lunch."

The fine line between a 'one-percenter' either keeping you going, or bringing you down, is a challenge that anybody regularly exposed to extreme situations would acknowledge. Although Nelson Bay wasn't

Horsea Island or Oban in winter; the psychological challenge of repeatedly freezing your arse off is the same anywhere, especially when immersed in poor visibility with your core temperature plummeting downwards.

We continued to discuss our performance and came up with options for Rookie-8, due to start in around four months' time. We concluded that Rookie-7 had a tough dive program, but this alone didn't warrant the comments. These were put down to the majority of the boys being fresh out of university and perhaps used to 'different' teaching methods. Either way, it was a good life lesson for me, and it allowed me to grow as a trainer. Eric wasn't quite finished though; he looked us both in the eye and smiled.

"They want to know if we are coming up to the Welshpool pub for end of course beers. I can't, catching a flight back to Newcastle; boys?"

Nords spoke first.

"They can get fucked on that!"

With some reservation, I said yes. I actually wanted to look them in the eye and have them say it to my face, but I wasn't enthusiastic about the inevitable confrontation.

By the time I reached the pub, the two cops had gone. I grabbed a beer and sat down at the crowded table next to the eldest member of Rookie-7, a former soldier and cop, Daryl. There were no formalities and Daryl spoke first.

"Mick, it took balls coming here tonight; shows character."

As a former police sergeant, Daryl had been keeping a low profile behaving like a rookie should. But now, he was demonstrating the maturity and experience he had in bounds.

"You probably didn't like some of the critiques mate?"

His eyes were locked with mine encouraging me to speak, and our area of the pub had gone reasonably quiet as the remaining Rookie-7 blokes tuned in. I cleared my throat and then scanned their eyes.

"You're welcome to your comments boys, but you should remember that Eric is a respected member of the NSCA, and I won't even begin to talk about his standing in the navy. You think you had a hard course, that we bastardised you?"

I paused to moisten my mouth; there were a couple of looks of confusion and a couple containing anger, I continued.

"If this is what you think boys, a good tip for you, don't ever try out for navy diving because you wouldn't last five minutes."

The room was quiet. I completed a slow scan, trying to gauge who had made which comments, then continued again.

"Whether you realise it or not, you have just received excellent training that has produced some very good divers. But a word of warning, one day you might not be in such good company you'll have a wanker as a tender, and you'll get in the shit. When that happens, the only thing that will keep you alive is the training you got here, and the ability Eric has instilled in you."

I was on a roll and kept going.

"This course is about Pararescue, and the PJs you *may* end up in a plane with one day; trust me, they think the sun shines out of Eric's arse! Now it's entirely up to you, but you may want to be a bit more objective when making comments after your next phase of training."

A couple of the eyes looking my way were seething, some were embarrassed; the seething eye brigade was about to speak, but Daryl stopped them.

"Thanks, Mick, we appreciate you coming and your honesty. Now, my shout."

I did talk to a few of the boys individually, and they expressed concern at out-dated teaching methods and the endless cold at Nelson Bay. All I could do was apologise for that part of it, going over the Freddo-Factor with them again, but suggested that when they had their berets if they still felt the same way to voice their opinions then.

Nords in blue wetsuit taking Rookie-7 for another LAR-5 dip – wind is gusting to 50 knots

Rookie-6 with Nords and Eric on the Blue Pig Deck, not everyone completed the program.

Eric's Rescue Boat, 'Bill Jinkins' winch training with Williamtown Jabbers

CHAPTER 13

NSCA Pararescue (Sub Rescue)

AFTER MUCH WAITING THE PC-1804 was ready for us to commence training. It was big. Weighing about 13 tonne it was primarily a yellow two-compartment decompression chamber with ballast tanks and thrusters all contained in a black steel crash-frame. It had a large window up the front, about a meter in diameter, and a small conning tower (measuring about 1-foot tall) with smaller side-plate sized windows and a hatch for entry and exit. Inside were the pilot's compartment and via a vertical hatch a diver-lockout compartment, with a further hatch opening to the sea at the floor via a small cylindrical 'trunking'.

Freddo had flown the designer of the craft and Perry Submersibles Chief engineer to the base for a week of tweaking and adjusting, and we finally sat down in the classroom for day one of theory.

Including Nords and me were several others on the 'sub-team': Goose and Jet, plus another PJ from the Townsville base, 'Boney' Mahoney and a new Council employee, Noel 'Tiny' Wilson, an ex-RAN air traffic control officer who was also qualified as a commercial diver. Steve Hayman was in charge of this team, and he had added three extra before we started training: Jack Newlands, the First Officer of the Blue Pig and two former Bass Strait saturation divers recently hired, Greg and John.

We spent much of the time that first week going over the PC-1804's systems: hydraulics, gas, electrical, scrubbers, trim-tanks, ballast-tanks, lighting, manipulator-arm, sonar, communications etc. It was fascinating stuff, and the two yanks could answer just about all we needed to know. The only time they seemed reticent though was when a particular operational process was raised, such as 'how do you traverse laterally?' The response to this type of question was becoming a bit of a joke amongst the team.

"Ahh, yeah, we'll probably wait until George Bezack gets here and let him answer that one."

The mysterious George Bezack was often mentioned. He was the Chief Pilot for Perry Submersible and was scheduled to arrive in the next few days to support training. The regular deferral to him had produced images of a John Wayne type of character; you know, cigar firmly wedged in the corner of his mouth, confidence busting out of a barrel-chested six-foot-twelve frame, "Yeah, that's right son, I'm a sub driver!" We were all looking forward to meeting this 'legend'.

On Monday morning at 8 am of the second week, we headed up to the huge maintenance shed to meet George Bezack at the sub where he was scheduled to give us a brief on 'submarine mating'. This was not aquatic humping, but locking onto a downed submarine for rescue purposes.

You can probably imagine our surprise then, when walking into the shed, we spied some nerdy looking bloke standing by the PC-1804's manipulator arm. He was wearing half-mast purple trousers and a red T-shirt over his five-foot-eight skeletal frame. His hair was the sort combed once a month, but no doubt looked as messy afterwards, with its fringe resting on thick-rimmed glasses. No, surely not?

"Hi fellas, I'm George Bezack"

His voice was soft and reasonably slow with a touch of Southern drawl. As he continued with this introduction our collective chins bounced off the floor with disappointment.

"How's the training going, you getting the hang of it yet?"

Despite the alarming first impression, by the end of his initial lesson, it was evident that George knew his subject inside and out. He was matter-of-fact with explanations and had real-world examples for all our questions. We spent the second week partly in the classroom and part at the sub, with George walking us through each system and how it was to be used and integrated operationally. At the end of the week we just about had all the ambiguity of week-one removed, and so with heads full of a whole new subject, it was time to put theory into practice.

The PC-1804 was loaded onto a flatbed Council truck, and we headed in convoy to Geelong, on Port Philip Bay west of Melbourne, to commence initial sea trials. The first of these were to be 'tethered' dives. This involved descending and ascending while still attached to a Council crane that was sitting on a Geelong wharf.

With the sub lowered into the water and weight off the crane's sling, the only part visible was the small conning tower and about 2cm of upper hull. We were motored over by rubber-duck in groups of three and cautiously positioned feet on the top rung of the conning tower ladder to descend into the pilot's compartment. I was last one in and saw Boney and Goose sitting on the floor of the main compartment in dim light with George as I eased down from the ladder.

"Ok Mick, you want to close up the hatch."

Standing erect, my head was level with the side-plate windows, and my shoulders were inside the conning tower. Reaching up, I pulled the heavy hatch-cover down and locked it in place with the twist of a wheel. Pausing briefly, I looked through the little windows as the rubber-duck driven by Nords backed away, getting my last glimpse of the surface for the next sixty minutes.

The pilot's compartment was small. If I were to kneel-up more than halfway, my head would touch the upper bulkhead. So for comfort, we pretty much bum-shuffled around on the rubber matting covering the deck.

At the front of the compartment was the large round window filling the space from top to bottom. Through this, I could see the dark green of Geelong harbour, before vision faded at about six feet. The ambient light this provided made for an eerie cocoon-like world inside the sub.

George spoke again when I sat down.

"Ok, let's get life support bumped up for the extra occupant."

Boney rotated a small control wheel on the O2 flow meter and a gentle hiss of gas that I'd heard upon entry increased slightly in volume. George tapped the carbon dioxide (CO_2) meter next.

"See this red line" we all nodded "if the needle ever gets near this make sure we get the scrubber running. Ok, systems checks."

George turned to a bank of circuit breakers and amp meters on the right side bulkhead. There were two rows of each, one for the 24-volt system that powered the main thrusters, and a 12-volt system for all the accessories. George ran a function/leak test on each circuit by pushing a button for each and then watching a corresponding status light and needle; he then turned to face us.

"Ok then, electrical is good. Let's check the trim now."

We had already placed lead ballast in a purpose built flat cage on the upper hull behind the conning tower, the aim being to have the PC-1804 trimmed level against our combined mass in the forward compartment. Despite this coarse correction we were slightly nose down as indicated by the bubble in one of two spirit level-type gauges mounted on the bulkhead. Moving to the left of the compartment George adjusted a series of valves, speaking as he went.

"Ok, first we identify the external seacock. We make sure this is closed to the sea. Then we select the forward trim tank and open the connecting valve; when this is done…"

Around ten valves were connecting three trim tanks to a pump and each other. After each valve was checked and positioned as required, George turned on the pump. The wine of an electric motor and the dull rapid thump of the pump filled the compartment for about eight minutes before the 'trim bubble' centred. George continued.

"Good, the VHF radio now please Goose."

Goose adjusted the volume and called the control station, a rented caravan sitting on the pier.

"Surface, surface, this is eighteen-oh-four, on VHF, over."

A clear radio response filled the compartment.

"Eighteen-oh-four, this is surface, standing by for your underwater telephone check."

George nodded to Goose who selected a different microphone. The outgoing message was much the same, but the reply was a distorted echo not unlike the RN's underwater telephone called 'Gertrude' which was used to communicate between frigates and submarines.

During my sonar days, we had transmitted the code 'November Echo Four' repeatedly on Gertrude when we were undertaking live depth charge trials. This international code was to warn any Soviet submarines to keep clear.

"Ok, Goose let them know we will be diving shortly."

Goose passed the message and shut down the VHF radio. It was time to dive.

Pointing to two main ballast tank vent valves on the upper bulkhead just forward of the conning tower entrance, George turned to me.

"Ok Mick, take us down."

Despite the training we'd received, and my years of diving, this was an anxious moment sitting inside the 13t coffin. Reaching up to the thumb-sized valves positioned about 1-foot apart, I quickly glanced at a BIBS (Built-in-Breathing-System) regulator to ensure I could grab the mouthpiece if flooding occurred. The other concern at the time was that the boys were observing me, because if I buggered up this relatively simple task there would be much piss taking afterwards.

Kneeling slightly with my arms positioned as though I was halfway through pushing a weight bar above my head, I cracked both vent valves a quarter turn and waited. My eyes were glued to a dinner plate sized depth gauge on the right bulkhead currently reading zero-feet, but there was no movement.

I could hear bubbling above and behind me and knew this was the ballast tanks releasing air, but still, there was no movement on the gauge. I paused, George was waiting patiently, not speaking, just a hint of a smile; should I crack them some more? A few seconds later the gauge moved, slowly at first, but then the speed increased as the PC-1804 inched away from the surface, but there was no sensation of movement inside.

I closed the valves and quickly moved my hands two centimetres outboard to take hold of two adjacent and slightly smaller 'blow' valves that would put air back into the ballast tanks. As the gauge continued down, I prepared to control the descent by expelling water with short bursts of air.

The depth gauge graduations continued to 1000-feet, but the first 100-feet was the most significant part of the scale for ease of reading at critical depths close to the surface. The needle was passing 4-feet and picking up speed, but I waited, knowing the harbour bottom was around 30-feet below us.

At 10-feet we began to move quicker, and I cracked both blow valves briefly and watched for a change in decent speed… nothing happened! Urgently, I opened both valves entirely to the sound of high-pressure air rushing into the ballast tanks. The green world outside the window in my periphery was getting darker, but thankfully the needle was finally slowing. As we reached 18-feet, I closed the blow valves and moved my hands to the vents, as the needle steadied and then crept upwards. Dumping the ballast again with a quick crack of the vent valves, I watched carefully once more and was happy to see the needle start to travel slowly downwards.

George flicked on the compartment lighting, and a subtle glow shone on the gauge. We were passing 22-feet, and the speed was beginning to increase again, but another quick crack and the descent rate was controlled once more.

As we passed 27-feet, I could see the bottom. Forgetting the gauge, I watched the closure rate with the seabed and cracked the blow valves just before we bumped gently onto the harbour bottom.

"Good Mick," George began "Ok everyone, now that we're on the bottom we run a complete systems check. Off you go."

Goose ran the electrical tests, and Boney checked the CO_2 level. The trim was fine and the atmosphere perfect. After around three minutes we were good to go.

"Ok, before surfacing on operations what we have to do is 'blow a bubble' to let the ship know where we are. We don't need to here, but why don't you have a practice, Mick."

We had briefed the procedure in the classroom. Goose called the surface to advise them of our 'bubble', and then I opened the vent valves fully and did the same with the blow valves, closing both after three seconds. There was a cacophony of bubbles above our heads.

"Eighteen-oh-four, eighteen-oh-four, this is the surface, we see your bubble. You are clear to surface; I say again, you are clear to surface."

Goose responded to the echo-like transmission, and George gave me the go-ahead to commence our ascent.

I gave the blow valves sufficient cracks until we bumped off the bottom and then with the PC-1804 more or less neutrally buoyant I bum shuffled forward to the window. Sitting sideways looking out into the dark green world, I picked up the thruster control box – it was about the size of a small toaster. On its flat surface were an amp meter and three toggle switches indicating FWD/AFT, LEFT/RIGHT and UP/DWN.

Watching out of the window I selected UP, and the sub immediately tilted up from the front-left corner as the sound of a high-pitch propeller and wine from its motor filled the compartment. The vertical thruster mounted on the crash-frame just outside the window was working as advertised. Flicking the switch back to the neutral position the sub levelled off, but was now a few feet off the bottom. The depth gauge remained stationary, so I flicked to UP once more and continued to do so until I lost sight of the bottom.

As we passed 20-feet, I left the thruster control and positioned by the vent valves. Monitoring the depth gauge in this position, before long the world outside the window became a lighter green and we broke the surface with the subs conning tower only just bobbing into view. I blew the ballast tanks entirely to raise the conning tower and looked to George.

"Good Mick, Goose you're next."

For the first four days, this is what we did, up and down, up and down. At the start and end of each day we conducted the pre and post dive checks, replacing gas cylinders, cycling valves etc. and during dives, George introduced us to emergency procedures. There were electrical failures, CO_2 build up due to scrubber failure, and emergency ascents. This was where we had to operate a manual hydraulic hand pump that pulled out pins holding the PC-1804's two very heavy cylindrical battery pods, which ran almost the length of the sub. When fully functioned, both pods would fall away making us very buoyant for a rapid rise to the surface. We considered this hand pump our 'ejection seat' handle, but like any pilot, we hoped never to use it. Although this was basic training, we were having a ball.

On the Friday of Geelong week-one George briefed the day's activities.

"Ok guys, time to let you off the leash. Today we will be inspecting the wharf pylons. You will have to conduct lateral sweeps up and down the pier at mid-water level, with the window about two feet from the pylons."

George's glasses rose slightly as a slight smile appeared on his face upon seeing our looks of apprehension.

"Piece of cake guys, I know you can do this."

Although I was confident that I'd be up to the challenge, there was obviously some concern remaining about the possibility of our window striking the solid ironbark pylons. Although George had reinforced to us several times that the window was rated higher than the rest of the hull, self-preservation ensured that I didn't believe him. And yes, the crash-frame was there too, but this did not protect us from protruding steel structures I had regularly found when diving on pylons. What could possibly go wrong?

My turn to be tested came on the second dive.

At a depth of 10-feet, I had the slightly shadowy vision of a pylon in sight and instinct told me I was too close.

"Mick you're about five feet away. Take us in closer; I want you two feet from it."

Selecting the FWD/AFT toggle to FWD, I pinched a dimmer light control below the amp meter on the control box and rotated it clockwise. The amp meter increased as the wine of the main thruster at the stern of the sub reverberated around the compartment. My eyes were locked with the pylon… movement… wait… a bit more… stop!

I wound the dimmer back to its stop and selected AFT knowing the 13t mass wouldn't stop straight away. The pylon was taking on more definition… a bit more… and… now! I wound the dimmer fully on and then quickly back to off. With forward movement arrested, my pylon was filling the window in front of me. Bar the sound of oxygen hissing into the compartment the only other noise was my rapidly pounding heart, but this was the easy part.

"Ok Mick, that's probably a foot and a half. Don't go much closer than that and start your traverse to the right."

Don't go much closer! Did George think I planned to stop where I did? Shit! I was staring at a solid chunk of wood through the window of my 13t cocoon, sure that the slightest bump would cause violent flooding, followed by desperate grasping for BIBS as we were forcibly pushed into the diver lockout by inrushing water.

My palms were, naturally, quite moist as I first selected the main thruster fully right and then selected the FWD/AFT toggle to FWD. Then, flicking the LEFT/RIGHT toggle to RIGHT and then immediately back to neutral, my pulse rate remained high as the sub yawed through about ten degrees to the right. I quickly followed this with a quick burst of amps to the main thruster and the sub yawed back the other way. As we settled, I noticed we had moved about half a pylon width to the right and that we were still about the same distance from the pylons. Bloody hell, it works! I continued this process moving right and left, descending or ascending at George's request to investigate a bit of weed here, or notch there on the chosen pylon. After 20-minutes I was feeling reasonably comfortable, and I handed over to the next bloke.

"Guys it's time for you to go solo."

Georges brief on day three of the second week explained how he wanted us to complete a search pattern of the seabed. We would be solo (no George on board), but a buoy attached by a line to the lift point would mark the position of the sub. We were to use a simple process of holding a heading and timing each leg of the search with a stopwatch, turning ninety degrees to complete a square with George monitoring our performance from the surface.

Sitting inside the sub with Tiny at the controls, me on the radios, Jet monitoring the systems and Goose spare in the diver lockout, we were a bit like kids with a driving licence out for a spin unsupervised for the first time.

"Take her down number two."

We cracked up at Tiny's request for Jet to commence the descent as he maintained position at the window, but we were soon all business. Holding an 'altitude' of 2-feet from the bottom, we rotated through the positions, checking systems every 15-minutes and communicating with the surface to gauge our travel; this was awesome! When it was my turn in the diver lockout, I peered down into the trunking and through a small window in the hatch. I could see the barren seabed moving as we travelled forward at the PC-1804's cruise speed of just 1-Knot. The view I had reminded me of camera vision from the lunar module as Apollo 11's crew approached the lunar surface. Although our 'surface' was just a muddy bottom, the realisation that we were controlling a 13t craft 2-feet from it was quite surreal, and I was getting paid to do it too!

By the end of the second week, George and his colleagues were happy with our progress. We all received a Perry Submersible certificate and farewelled the yanks during a good night out. We would shortly be heading to Cairns in Far North Queensland where the Blue Pig was completing a refit to accommodate the PC-1804 and would be undertaking open sea trials.

Freddo had chartered a business jet to transport the sub team to Cairns. It was medium sized and complete with plush seats and gold trimming on the wooden panelling. Unfortunately, my recent qualification as a duo-com operator meant that I wouldn't be going with them as someone had to man the roster – bastards!

The evening after the boys left, I was sitting in the canteen eating dinner with Rookie-8 and a couple of on-shift PJs when Freddo and Waldo walked in. Freddo spotted me immediately, and a look of confusion appeared on his face.

"Why are you here?"

"We were short a duo-com driver on the shift, John, I drew the short straw."

Freddo turned to Waldo.

"Yes, John. Mick was required to fill the roster."

Poor Waldo was looking concerned.

"But Waldo, he's done all the training; he's one of our main divers, why didn't he go?"

Waldo obviously had no suitable answer for the Freddo-Factor in play and was desperately trying to think of appropriate words when Freddo continued.

"Who else is available, there must be someone?"

"There is Houghton in Townsville, but I thou-"

"Do it, and put Mick on the flight with me tomorrow."

Freddo was talking about the Council's' new acquisition, a Falcon jet. It was small, with just four passenger seats and these had already been allocated to other staff. Waldo pointed out the problem.

"The jet is pretty full already, John."

Two executives and another PJ, Steve Greenfield, plus some medical stores for the Townsville base probably had the jet at its weight limits. This was hardly a challenge for John Friedrich though.

"Well if Greenfield has to be a casualty, so be it."

'Greeny' was sitting opposite me having dinner. His face dropped while mine battled to control a laugh. Rookie-8 witnessing this exchange chose to study the contents of their plates without moving.

The next afternoon I was waiting at the Falcon with my bag packed, but so was Greeny.

"Mick you will have to sit on the toilet, bit of a crowd with all the gear I'm afraid."

Freddo was right. The small and very narrow cabin contained four seats facing each other in pairs; there wasn't a great deal of leg room between them either. Forward of these was a bulkhead and a much smaller spare seat that was actually the toilet facing sideways. Around this area were boxes of medical supplies and in front, the narrow cockpit door.

As we rolled down the West Sale runway with my unrestrained arse sitting on a dunny seat, I smiled at the thought of luxury travel and my first flight in a business jet.

Shortly after take-off, Freddo called my name.

"Behind those boxes, you will find a fridge. We'll have a whiskey each, and you and Greeny had better finish the rum before we reach Cairns, if you want to keep your jobs."

Greeny, who was sitting in a luxury seat nearest the dunny - the bastard - accepted the challenge with me and we settled into the flight.

The sky was darkening; we were halfway through the bottle of Bundaberg and about the same through the bottle of Chivas Regal, the mood in the cabin had become a tad jovial. Freddo looked up from a book he'd been reading and sniggered.

"Apparently this is what I'm supposed to be doing with the NSCA?"

He was showing the others the cover of Air America, a novel depicting covert flying operations during the Vietnam War. His face had a mischievous grin suggesting 'little do they know'; anyway, that's how I interpreted it with a belly full of Bundy.

"How's the rum going Mick?"

With less than half of the flight to go the correct answer to Freddo's question should have been 'not good', but I chose a more appropriate response with supporting action.

After supplying another round, Freddo and the executives were on about their fifth; I discreetly poured Bundy into the Chivas bottle and by the time our wheels touched the Cairns tarmac our employment was guaranteed.

As the door of the jet opened an empty Bundy bottle rolled down the steps clinking to the tarmac. Fortunately, it didn't break. Greeny and I followed this, a tad wobbly, and proceeded to the jet's wing for a 'Bundy-drain' in sight of the tower and a lone airport security officer waiting with a car to transport us off the hardstand area. The hardstand was obviously not a public toilet, but this bloke wasn't about to challenge the Executive Director of the NSCA who had just arrived in a private jet, with his private security. Greeny and I were dressed smartly and looked like a couple of bodyguards, drunken ones admittedly, but bodyguards nonetheless.

We took one cab, another squeeze, to a hotel where the sub-team were staying, and I was ejected as Freddo and his entourage headed off to a more upmarket establishment. The boys were in the middle of dinner and somewhat surprised to see me.

"What the fuck are you doing here?"

I retold the story and settled into more drinks. They had put a training plan together, but there was to be a delay; a couple of days, three at the most, as the Blue Pig needed one or two tweaks to its new Dynamic Positioning System.

Next day Freddo came to a prompt decision.

"Steve, take the team out to the reef and get some dive currency. Charter a boat that can accommodate the gear you need."

And that's precisely what we did. Now, as this might appear one of many expenses that contributed to the demise of the NSCA, can I please reinforce that it was both cost saving and productivity rolled into one. You see, had we stayed in Cairns, at a hotel, running up food and room charges, the bill for the lot of us would have been higher than a couple of nights boat charter. Additionally, all we would have achieved was drunkenness.

Heading out on our Council funded dive holiday then, we were all pretty damn happy, because apart from the AGA gear we had several cartons of grog and the boat crew of three had stocked up on steaks. One of the boat crew, a Japanese girl of around 23, looked all right in a bikini too, which made for a pleasant distraction to the testosterone-filled world we operated in – I'm sure she didn't mind the ultra-fit bodies of Jabbers in speedos and boardies either.

I had never dived on the Great Barrier Reef before, and three hours after leaving Cairns we dropped anchor right in the middle of it. Did I mention that I was getting paid to do this?

We planned to do a deep work-up to 50m if we could find suitable anchorages but started with a perfect spot where we lowered the shot to 30m. Swimming free on AGA, the brief was to descend to the shot, put a back-splice into a rope's end and then ascend with a couple of precautionary stops, where we would put an eye-splice in the other end of the rope. One deep dive each day was to be followed by a less than 10m navigation exercise around the reef – read have a play around the coral with all the fish.

The reef was what I had expected, brilliant visibility and better colours than the Maldives where Mandy and I had spent our honeymoon. There were not as many fish though, but it didn't matter, I was diving on the Great Barrier Reef.

On the first of these shallow dives, Goose and I were buddies, and we played follow the leader swimming in and out of little coral caves and simple swim-throughs, seeing how tighter space we could fit through. On some occasions, this involved removing the AGA and pushing it in front of us as we felt coral brushing our backs. This was some of the most fun I'd had diving in a long while, but justifying our holiday, it was also valuable exposure to commercial work in and around wrecks or pipes, although I wouldn't recommend removing a set in such situations.

Goose and I repeated this type of dive the first night, with our torches providing plenty of visibility. Night diving on a reef is brilliant, the fish are out in force, and you find yourself floating through a surreal, alien world, which is so different from the daytime.

We were playing follow the leader again and had been in the water for around forty minutes when I followed Goose into a tight tunnel of coral. A bit over a body length into this I felt a breathing restriction. Goose's fins were against my mask as he inched his way forward, and for a just moment I thought of backing out, but overconfidence pushed me on. I was sure he would clear the tunnel any moment and so flicking on the AGA's reserve, ego was leading me into danger.

About 10-seconds later the tunnel opened out into a low cave (imagine being under a dining table) where Goose turned to face me. Using my hands with fingers pointed I asked him which way was out, but Goose just looked at me indifferently, shrugged his shoulders and pointed back the way we had come.

As my pulse rate increased, I noticed that sand was rising from the bottom of our small cave, reducing visibility. Turning quickly, but awkwardly in the confined space, I kicked up more sand. Briefly glancing at my gauges, I saw the contents needle over halfway into the red and that we were at 8m. I had just a couple of minutes before I was out of air!

Trying to remain calm I felt for the entry point that was no longer there. Searching with my hands in darkness was nothing new to me, but knowing that I was just several breaths away from a breathing restriction caused a bubble of panic to build inside me. I fought this with all my might, knowing that if I lost control, I would never get out, but I still couldn't find the exit. Shit! I was going to die on the Great Barrier Reef, not some shitty British dock, or from a soda-lime-cocktail, but the Great Barrier Reef, the place of my dreams.

In desperation, I turned to seek Goose's help, but he was nowhere to be seen. The bastard's gone without me! I quickly glanced at the gauge and saw the needle past the stop. No! Flicking my torch around the cave, it illuminated the tip of one of his fins about 2m away, and I bolted for it. My adrenalin filled body bumped and scraped past coral as I endeavoured to catch Goose's fin and then all of a sudden we were in the open ocean. Not stopping, I signalled Goose I was going up, not daring to look at my gauge.

We splashed to the surface 30m from the boat and removed our masks.

"Fucking hell Goose, that was close!"

"What?"

Hadn't he heard me? As I described the last few minutes, he just laughed, suggesting he had known the way out all along.

The next day we went back to the same spot with Nords. To get back inside where we had egressed previously required the boys to remove their AGA's, they beckoned me to follow, but there was no way I was going back in such a small space so soon.

We boarded the Pig on Monday and sailed out to an area of the reef where a floating hotel was moored. This tourist venture turned out to be a white elephant and was eventually towed away to an Asian destination, but for the next couple of weeks, it was to be our evening hangout. Steve assembled the team on the aft deck of the now 10m longer Blue Pig.

"This is a new launch and recovery system boys. It is bare bones for what we need it to do so let's keep this simple, if we fuck up, people will die."

There was no melodramatics to Steve's brief. Freddo was making do with a half-assed operation to justify to the board of directors that he needed to spend more money to by an appropriately sized ship with a suitable 'heave compensator' equipped crane. Therefore, if we could prove the concept with this fundamental arrangement we would get a bigger boat, equipped to launch and recover a more modern sub, in moderate sea states; but for now, we had to make do. Consequently, we took each part of the launch sequence very seriously.

Thankfully, on the day of the first launch, we had perfect conditions, just light airs and a barely noticeable swell on the deep blue ocean. Jet and the two Bass Strait divers were the first crew, and after all the pre-dives were completed we got underway. There was palpable tension in the air.

A rail system had been fitted to the deck of the Pig; this allowed the PC-1804, sitting on a trolley connected to the rail system, to be rolled back to a covered area just short of the accommodation. Below this area of the deck was a hatch system, which when completed, would allow the diver lockout trunking to mate with a decompression chamber on the deck below. This was an engineering challenge yet to be solved, but for our current training, it wasn't needed.

The sub was pulled aft on its trolley by a winch wire towards an adjustable 'A' frame operated by two very large lift-rams. As Zaggy managed this winch, ears and eyes were focused on both him and Steve as the PC-1804 inched towards the stern.

Once in position, a large lift-cable (as thick as your wrist) was lowered about 6-inches so that a shackle of equal diameter could be connected to the lift point. The trolley wire was then disconnected, resecured to the rear of the trolley and a towline attached to the forward crash frame. When all was ready, the lift-cable was taken up, pulling the PC-1804 about two inches off the deck and into a cradle at the top of the 'A' frame. The lift-rams were then extended to take the PC-1804 in a low arc under the helideck and out over the ocean.

In this position, still clear of the water, the window and the crash frame was only 3-feet from the Pig's stern ramp.

The PC-1804 was held in this position as a rubber-duck crew with Jet and the Bass Strait boys on board moved around to its stern. Here they attached a 30m line connected to a large sea anchor (an underwater parachute), and the Pig was moved ahead with just enough speed to maintain steerage. With the sea anchor's line now fully extended, tension was applied to the back of the PC-1804, and the main lift wire was lowered.

The moment the PC-1804 hit the water the sea anchor pulled it away as the towline was paid out. Continuing this process until the lift-cable was fully extended, the PC-1804 floated with the conning tower visible 10-feet behind the stern ramp. The rubber-duck then moved back in, the lift-cable was disconnected, and then the towline continued to be paid out. This continued until the PC-1804 was about 30m astern where the Pig was stopped, the sea anchor recovered and the crew climbed aboard.

Communication was established and the towline disconnected. The PC-1804 then left surface on the Great Barrier Reef for the first time.

This first dive was to be relatively simple, 20m straight down, systems checks and straight back to the surface. Despite the simplicity, we had the ROV and dive gear on standby to attach a lift line if we were to experience a worst-case outcome.

Not that long after descending, Jet's echo-like voice floated across the deck from the underwater telephone announcing their arrival on the bottom. Regarding subsea exploration, it was a minor event, but for the NSCA's sub-team it was like we had just landed on the moon. We had indeed come a long way in a very short time and were naturally proud of our progress, but this pride was tempered with the acknowledgement of our novice status. Therefore, just like moon missions, we too knew that real success required the safe return of our crew.

The bubble arrived on the surface about 10-seconds after the crew's call, and when the PC-1804 bobbed into view, the rubber-duck moved in. The towline was connected, and the crew recovered, smiling like successful astronauts. We then reversed the launch process to recover the sub. It worked as advertised.

The following days consisted of 8-hours a day (our battery duration) in the water, rotating 3-man crews every couple of hours.

On my third dive, I was at the controls following a course around a section of reef that required ascents and descents to clear coral. As part of this process, we also had to pull up to a large corral 'bommie' and conduct an inspection. The controls were becoming very familiar and we were operating them with relative ease, so much so that pulling up to within 2-foot of a specific structure was no longer a significant challenge.

Coming around a section of the reef at a depth of 28m I spied a turtle 20-feet ahead and below us; it was time to break the monotony.

"Goose, target sighted eleven o'clock low. I'm going down."

Opening both vent valves fully, I selected the thruster down too. The PC-1804 responded like a sluggish whale after a hard night, but the chase was on. Gauging the closure to the seabed carefully, I stopped thrusting, closed the vent valves and was ready with the blow valves… not yet… now! Opening them fully I selected the thruster up; I could feel the descent slowing and watched the seabed as it closed, keeping one eye on the turtle – it was 10-feet ahead same level. Closing the blow valves as our descent was almost controlled I wound the dimmer switch to full amperage and we were soon racing along at a power bleeding 1.5 knots, yeeeeharrrrrrrr!

I hadn't checked the descent sufficiently though, and with the turtle 5-feet ahead of us, the battery pods kissed the sandy bottom. Although the contact slowed us down, I'd selected thruster up for a second and we were soon back in the game. The turtle was onto us though, commencing an almost vertical climb.

Not so fast turtle-boy! With both blow valves fully open and thrusting up we chased him up the reef wall to our left. As he reached the top of the reef at a depth of 19m, he levelled off. Quickly closing the blow valves and opening the vents, I selected thrust down and checked our ascent at 16m, but turtle boy was now a good 20-feet ahead of us.

"I think that will do for now Mick. How about we get back on course?"

Tiny was always a voice of reason, but it was time to pass the controls to Goose anyway.

The first week's weather had remained the same. Although launch and recovery were never routine, we were very confident in what we were doing. On the second day of week two though, the weather changed. It wasn't bad, just a constant breeze. The wind had produced an increase in swell to about 1m though, and this was going to test our ability to manage the PC-1804 under the 'A' frame. With the increased swell, it was also decided that the crew would board on the deck to prevent waves potentially breaking over an open hatch.

We got underway, and things were proceeding as per usual. The sea anchor was attached, the Pig was underway, and the lift-cable was lowered. When suddenly, with the PC-1804 less than 2m clear of the stern ramp, the sea anchor failed!

Newton's third law was proved immediately. The instant the drag force of the sea anchor was gone; the PC-1804 began to swing back towards the stern ramp, its pace and trajectory instantly confirming to all that it was going to hit! Steve executed emergency procedures.

"Increase your speed, increase your speed!"

Even if the bridge crew had responded immediately on the first of Steve's radio calls, it wouldn't have made any difference. The PC-1804 was cocked off slightly and impacted the starboard side of the 'A' frame. A light on the crash frame disintegrated, and the frame bent slightly, as the horrible sound of steel-on-steel collision filled the stern area. Bouncing off the 'A' frame, the PC-1804 continued towards the stern ramp and the propellers below it. Fortunately, though, Zaggy was winching in full speed on the lift-cable and arrested further forward motion, but not before I saw the wide eyes of Greg in the window of the PC-1804 just inches from disaster. The PC-1804, still swinging horribly on its cable, was then unceremoniously returned to the 'A' frame with a loud clunking of more steel-on-steel before the team paused briefly to assess the situation.

The failed sea anchor was creating a minor rooster tail 30m behind the PC-1804, the Blue Pig was motoring along at about 5 knots, and the PC-1804 (and crew) was relatively secure under the 'A' frame. Damage to the PC-1804 was minor: a slightly bent crash frame, one destroyed light and potential damage to the manipulator arm control. The 'A' frame appeared undamaged apart from the loss of paint and, importantly, none of the deck crew had been injured; so less than a minute after being lifted the PC-1804 was returned to its trolley on the deck. The Blue Pig's forward motion was halted, and everyone breathed again. The crew advised they were thrown about somewhat but were not hurt. The most frightening part of the event for them was seeing the, "bloody screws getting very big in the window". They were happy to go again after repairs had been made, but Steve called a halt for the day. We were going to wait for better weather.

The system worked, but would hardly be a reliable tool for rescuing RAN submariners. The Bass Strait boys discussed options for heave compensators, but this required headroom that we didn't have with the helideck still in place. The purpose of such equipment, as its name suggests, is to keep the 'load' stationary regardless of the vessels movement and therefore permit launch and recovery in bigger sea states. Freddo would never remove the helideck though, so we were left with proving concept as much as we could in order to get the bigger and better-equipped ship.

The weather had improved the next day, and so we continued with practice to prepare for 'dry transfer' with a Collins Class submarine, which Freddo had apparently scheduled for mid-1989.

A dry transfer required the PC-1804 to be docked (or mated) with the Collins Class escape hatch. For us to do this, a 'skirt' would have to be fitted to our diver lockout trunking.

The skirt was a bell-shaped structure open at the bottom with a thick rubber 'O' ring embedded at its base. With the PC-1804 in position over the subs escape hatch we would then thrust down to maintain contact while pumping water from the skirt. Once a lower pressure was achieved inside the skirt, the 'O' ring was compressed, and the PC-1804 achieved a 'soft-seal' with the subs escape hatch. Then, continuing to pump all the water out of the skirt, the effect of greater ambient pressure on the 'O' ring formed a 'hard-seal'. This hard-seal was considered a weld and would permit both craft to open their respective hatches to transfer personnel in a 'dry' state.

The concept of dry-transfer had been around for decades and can be seen, albeit under Hollywood conditions, in the movie The Hunt for Red October.

Our skirt was currently being manufactured, but we had doubts about its effectiveness in the real-world. Standing at about a meter in height for example, how would we complete launch and recovery with the current system? That was an engineering problem for someone else to fix though; we just had to be able to position the PC-1804 over the Collins Class hatch.

On my second go at this, I had Boney in the lockout watching the target through the window in the trunking hatch.

"Forward two feet Mick, and you're two feet above the target."

I wound on a fraction more amps until the PC-1804 crept forward; I couldn't see the target and so was relying on Boney's conn.

"One foot... six inches."

I wound the dimmer off and selected reverse.

"Three inches."

I wound the dimmer until I head sufficient RPM from the main thruster and then wound it off again.

"Over the top now... and we're steady, two feet above."

Thrusting down with a quick on/off of the control, I listened to Boney closely.

"One foot… six inches… three inches and… contact. Mick, I have the starfish dead centre in the window."

Positioning over a slow-moving sea creature on a flat sandy bottom without any current required a degree of crew coordination, but it was hardly a test to verify real-world capability. If, for example, our Collins Class sub was not lying flat on the seabed, or there was a current of more than half a knot, it was unlikely we would achieve our goal. You see, despite considering options to pre-trim for a nose up attitude to account for the angle of an escape hatch, if we exceeded 3-degrees air would escape from the open bottom of the ballast tanks making precise maneuvering unachievable. The PC-1804 was an old model and not the best choice for Freddo's intended purpose. However, we'd done all we could with the systems available to us and had proved most of the concept. It was now down to Freddo to conn the board out of more funds.

We took the Blue Pig south to Townsville for a demonstration of its capability to the scientists of the Australian Institute of Marine Science (AIMS). These people were taken on jollies over the reef for around three hours. They also saw the ROV working and were pretty impressed with our capability, but a question at the end of their visit summed up the confusion over the NSCA.

"Which part of the government are you funded by?"

Who knew? Maybe we were government funded and who's to say it was the Australian government? Got to love a conspiracy theory though, don't you?

Despite our ongoing issues with the suitability of the Blue Pig and the PC-1804, word was spreading through different agencies and services about the NSCA's enhanced subsea capability. This was to prove very beneficial to Freddo when an oil and gas transport helicopter ditched off the far north of Western Australia, and a recovery mission was being organised.

Top: Goose, with AGA removed on 10m 'training' dive, negotiates a swim through

Bottom Left: PC-1804 launch and recovery, 'A' frame cradle above with lift wire attached Bottom right: Nords attaching the sea anchor and Goose ready to attach the lift line

CHAPTER 14

NSCA Pararescue (Flamingo Bay)

JET CALLED ME AT HOME in the early evening. We were catching a commercial flight in the morning from Melbourne to Darwin via Alice Springs. The ROV, now all packaged up in its own NSCA shipping container (one of the full ones), had already left. A Council mechanic called 'Pig-man' and his mate were going to drive nonstop to Darwin and they should be there within 48hrs, "Piece of piss".

In Darwin, we were to load the ROV and its supporting gear onto a ship called the Flamingo Bay, on which we would sail a day and a half to where an oil and gas transport helicopter had ditched into the sea, and subsequently sunk to the bottom.

This job had been put together quickly, and cheaply. Bell Helicopters was apparently paying the bill, and they had contracted a diving company from Darwin, a private vessel owner and us, to recover the downed Bell 214-ST transport helicopter. This large workhorse of the oil industry had ditched near to Troughton Island, an oil and gas staging point for the Timor Sea. All passengers and crew had successfully escaped from the upturned hull, but the machine had sunk in an estimated 70m of water, and Bell Helicopters needed to know why (quickly) to prevent grounding the 214-STs globally.

Sitting in the full economy cabin of a Boeing 767 somewhere between Melbourne and Alice Springs, Jet cast a look around the many passengers.

"Hey Mick, imagine jumping to one of these?"

Every emergency service has a worst-case scenario. Pararescue's was a ditched airliner far from home. In Australia, this meant either the Great Australian Bight (flights to and from Perth) or the Tasman Sea (flights to and from New Zealand). Although highly unlikely ever to occur, this is what we trained for. If the worst-case was realised PJs, each equipped with 80kg of medical and survival equipment, would jump in pairs from Council Dorniers' to coordinate the rescue of passengers either by helicopter, or more likely, a vessel of opportunity. To aid this process, the Dornier crews would drop additional life rafts and survival equipment and, to expedite bringing life rafts together on the open sea a new Council concept, jet skis.

To practice for this eventuality, each PJ completed a minimum of seven water jumps in addition to the twenty land jumps during rookie training. If the PJ rookie couldn't demonstrate the ability to land within 10m of the designated target they wouldn't pass the program. The water part included jumps to life rafts, medical exercises, recovery of survivors and, on the last jump; the PJ would follow a jet ski into the water for some outstanding fun.

Water jump currency was also undertaken at least three times per year and at least once with PJs from other bases during a scheduled training-week. Simply put, we were very good at long-range open sea rescue; so much so that the head of United States Air Force (USAF) Pararescue (Lieutenant Colonel Donald A Towner) even advised John Friedrich in writing that 'the NSCA had no peers'. Nevertheless, looking around the cabin of the 767 I didn't doubt we would be worked to the max if we ever had to put training into practice.

Walking into the Darwin airport arrivals hall in the late eighties was a bit of a culture shock for a pommy boy who had never visited the Territory before. There was no air-conditioning to combat the heat and humidity, just a ceiling full of humming fans and hard men beneath them wearing singlets, with either a beer in hand or one close by – not quite, but you get the idea. After all, "this was the Territory mate", where "blokes had goatee beards, drank piss, rode bulls and fucked sheilas".

Collecting our hire car, we headed off to the CBD and a hotel on the Esplanade. This was a street on high ground with brilliant views that overlooked a lush green park and just beyond it, the Arafura Sea. We dumped our bags and headed down to the pier, but there was no sign of the Flamingo Bay. However, this was a hurried job, and we were advised she was expected, soon. With not much else to do we walked to Mitchell Street, one street behind our hotel and went for an early dinner on Freddo's dollar.

The next morning a truck carrying a green container with the letters NSCA ROV stencilled on its side was angle-parked 50m from our hotel. Pig-man had made perfect time, apparently stopping for a couple of hours sleep south of the city because he didn't want to enter Darwin in the early morning darkness.

We were opening up the container doors when two blokes, probably in their forties, one with a beard and plaster cast on his forearm, one clean-shaven; both wearing shorts, polo shirts and running shoes (had to be yanks) walked up behind us.

"Morning guys," the bearded-broken-arm one began, "I'm Jack Mitchell from Bell Helicopters, and this is Joe Walsh."

We shook hands and introductions were made. Jack was the designer of the 214-ST, and Joe was a senior test pilot with Bell. They told us it was suspected that a device called a 'Drag-Brace' had failed in flight. This had to be verified, as it was a critical component holding both of the 214-ST's huge rotor blades in position as they rotated. If it had failed, Jack would have to determine why, but as other 214-ST's had ditched and confidence with the machine was dwindling in the oil and gas industry, it would likely result in a global grounding. So simply put, they needed a video of the machine's rotor system ASAP to support this critical decision. Moreover, the video was required before any recovery could be undertaken to prevent 'contamination of evidence', and that's where Freddo came in after a request from the Department of Aviation.

The Flamingo Bay had entered Darwin's Stokes Hill Wharf and was secured by 7 am the next day. At 36m, it was an old 1956 Belgian coastal patrol vessel designed for the harsh conditions of the North Sea. Painted white, with a small bridge and accommodation superstructure, there was less room on the after-deck than a Mine Hunter had, but there was enough space for the ROV gear.

The skipper and owner, a reasonably loud American, had done a fantastic job fitting her out. She was designed for paying customers whether they were scientific, tourist or salvage crews. The relative luxury inside included some large windows in the main salon to ensure scenic views, wooden veneer panelling, very efficient air-conditioning and a well-appointed galley. Below the salon via a wooden staircase were 11 double berths, small, but compared to a Mine Hunter absolute luxury. On the bow, a walk on 'bowsprit' had been fitted, which included flood lighting for observation of the sea below as the Flamingo Bay cruised through tropical waters at night. With a cruise speed of 10-12 knots, she was relatively slow but had a range of 5000 miles, which was more than enough to get us to Troughton Island and back.

Pig-man had the ROV container positioned close by, and we commenced the unload/load of ROV equipment under the guidance of the skipper.

"Just hook it on, and I'll lift it using a line on the nigger-head there."

Even in the late eighties use of discriminatory racial language was a no-no, but the skipper must have missed the brief. Nonetheless, the

Flamingo Bay's old style derrick crane with a pulley system rigged from the top of a single boom that ran back to a deck capstan that, if you really used your imagination looked like an African male, was used to lift all of our equipment on board. The most significant items, the ROV and its sizeable cylindrical tub containing 300m of umbilical, were left on deck. The other things: Simrad tracking system, control system and a range of monitors and cabling were all unpacked and manhandled below to a small office where we set up the control station.

The divers lugged aboard umbilicals, KMB-10's, a bundle of plasticised fabric that I guessed was a lift-bag, large air cylinders, a divers cage and around twenty 44-gallon drums that were secured at the bow – more lifting equipment I imagined.

In between loading the diver's and our gear we 'stored ship' with large quantities of foodstuffs and drinks (soft and alcoholic). It took a chunk of the morning to complete, but just after midday, we set up the ROV to run some function tests.

Mostly, I was Jet's labour during this part of the operation. We ran cables from the control station up passageways and out onto the deck and when everything was connected Jet fired up the system. It didn't work. Not deterred, Jet set about routine troubleshooting that continued into detailed fault finding. Eventually, he found a failed circuit that was likely damaged by vibration experienced on the drive north. Worse though, he confirmed that the spares we needed were in the shed at West Sale base. It was around 2 pm.

Jack Mitchell was expecting to sail that afternoon and was noticeably concerned at the delay this would cause us. He was obviously unaware of Freddo's way of getting things done.

A phone call was made, the required parts were located, packaged up, and put on the Council's Falcon jet at West Sale for a direct flight north. After landing in Darwin, the pilots grabbed a cab, came straight to the pier and by 7:30 pm the same day the ROV was serviceable, and we were leaving the harbour.

Seeing the shocked expressions of a couple of very capable Americans as they witnessed the Council machine in full swing was rewarding, but as we worked for Freddo, his very proactive approach was nothing unusual, "It's just what we do mate."

On the passage to Troughton Island, we got to know the Flamingo Bay's crew and the rest of the team a bit better.

The divers were from a local Darwin operation. One supervisor, a short and nuggetty bloke, plus three divers including a former Welsh sheep shearer were typical of a dive team you would find anywhere. With some irony though, the Welshman had left sheep shearing because he was fed up with all the drinking – welcome to the Territory mate!

The crew consisted of the skipper and his wife who had their accommodation behind the bridge; plus one engineer, one deckhand, a cook and a nurse. The nurse was also qualified in hyperbaric medicine and would attend to bent divers in a 4-man decompression chamber if required, which was positioned behind the skipper's quarters. A beautiful woman in her early thirties, one of the younger deckhands was smitten with her. This didn't go unnoticed by the divers who regularly took the piss out of the poor bloke.

The cook was a large and bubbly Darwin girl who made sensational food every day. A senior member of the team was the Department of Aviation investigator. He was a pleasant enough man, but apparently there with a fair amount of responsibility.

Finally there was Joe Walsh, he remained quiet and serious; not saying much at all unless it was to deliver regular advice.

"One moment, I will check with Mr Mitchell."

He and Jack were apparently under a lot of pressure too.

As we approached Troughton Island, the skipper adjusted course for the crash datum using an early model Global Positing System (GPS). Taken for granted these days, the Flamingo Bay's GPS required a 'satellite window' for it to function because at the time the Americans were still launching satellites to complete the global network. What this meant in the late eighties was that a small satellite window, with minimum satellites, was available several times in each 24hr period. Fortunately for us, there were sufficient satellites available when we approached the area.

The Flamingo Bay's anchor was dropped, and the divers boarded a 'tinny' with a hydrophone and headset to commence a series of runs up and down the area to find an Emergency Location Transmitter (ELT) that was hopefully still pinging away in the 214-ST's tail boom. The ELT had a lifespan of 72hrs, but this time had expired several hours before our arrival, and so fingers were crossed as the little boat went back and forth in search of the helicopter.

While the divers were searching, Jet and I lowered our hydrophone over the stern and secured it in place. The hydrophone was part of the Simrad tracking system and would be used to indicate the centre of our electronic search grid. When we had completed the necessary checks, we saw that the divers were returning to the ship. All smiles, they had located the ELT and had left a buoy in the area to mark the chopper's rough position.

With the divers back on board, the skipper then maneuvered the Flamingo Bay over the area and dropped two additional (smaller) anchors to establish a 'three-point mooring system'. This held the ship in approximate position over the point where the divers had dropped the float. This position, produced by gauging the ELT's signal strength each time the tinny passed by, was just an estimation. In reality, the 214-ST could be over 100m from the marked spot. Nevertheless, it was time to put the ROV in the water.

The final pre-dive preparations involved securing a transponder, the size of a bottle of wine, to the Flamingo Bay's anchor cable and another to the ROV's crash frame. Completed, Jet went to the control station, and I supervised the deck operations. We communicated via radio.

"Put her in the water when ready Mick."

With the divers assisting, the ROV's crash frame was positioned on two carpet-covered rails used to launch and recover the tinny. These were just the right width, and so we were able to slide the ROV down into the deep blue waters of the Timor Sea with ease.

Not wanting to foul the umbilical, Jet thrust ahead to clear the stern by about 20m before descending. A few minutes later he called up.

"Approaching the bottom Mick, come and have a look."

The divers were obviously used to umbilical management, so I left them to direct the red cable as I went below.

With the Simrad system active, one of the monitors showed a red grid on a black background. The grid consisted of four squares scaled to 50m by 50m, forming one large square (100m by 100m), and each of the 50-50 squares had within it a further grid pattern of 10m by 10m squares. A small red ship-shape at the centre of this display was our hydrophone, and a short distance from the hydrophone was a green number '1' indicating the transponder on the anchor cable. These two figures indicated the bow and stern of the Flamingo Bay and behind the ship was a green number, '2' indicating the ROV.

On a separate monitor was a dark blue screen with a data bar at its bottom. This bar contained a compass heading and a depth gauge, currently indicating 58m and descending. The room was darkened with only the glow from the monitors providing illumination, but I could see Jack, Joe and the skipper watching intently. Jet, not turning, provided commentary.

"Ok guys, we are on the bottom now at sixty-two meters. If you look at the Simrad display, you can see that the ROV is in the top left grid, about 15m from the anchor cable."

All eyes were glued to the monitors and heads were nodding, acknowledging the accuracy of Jet's brief. He continued.

"Ok, when I switch from camera to sonar."

In the place of the dark blue, almost black ocean, there was now a solid black screen containing five red circles, each of greater diameter expanding from the centre. Close to the centre of these 'range-rings' was a red and blue image that depicted the Flamingo Bay's anchor cable.

"Ok, with the clarity of the cable there, I think we can all agree that a helicopter will stick out like dogs bollocks," More nods, "What I plan to do is position in the centre of each fifty-meter grid, conduct a sonar search and investigate any targets."

The first grid revealed nothing and Jet, good man that he was, handed control to me for the next search. Flicking to the camera, we called the divers and advised them we were moving.

Using two toggle controls the size of your thumb, I moved the ROV off the bottom and then moving forward I followed the desired compass heading while scanning to the Simrad display to gauge progress. Arriving in the centre of the second grid, I thrust down until we contacted the bottom; a small amount of sand floated up into the camera vision, but it soon settled. I flicked the monitor to sonar.

Despite my knowledge and confidence in operating the ROV, the sight of a red and blue helicopter, admittedly a distorted sonar version of one, just 20m ahead of the ROV was quite incredible. Apparently, everyone else in the room thought so too as a loud "Yes!" echoed around the space.

Creeping forward with small toggle movements, I closed the gap to the target. At about 10m I noted the heading and switched back to the camera, and with lights on we had about 6 to 8-feet visibility. This was sufficient for what we needed to do, but I eased forward cautiously just the same, as the ROV's compass indicator was very sensitive making it hard to judge accurate heading. I stopped again at about 5m and checked the sonar image; we were still on track. Flicking back to the camera I moved closer, and a large, solid object began to appear. The room erupted again, but this time a more controlled exhalation. We were next to the 214-ST and were acutely aware of the fouling risk for our umbilical.

The area we approached first was the right-hand side of the tail-boom. I checked the video was recording and then rotated the ROV right to look along the 214-ST's 49-foot long body. There were seat cushions, still attached, floating from an open door and other bits of debris on the seabed. Peering into the cabin we couldn't see much in the shadows, but my mind quickly imagined the moment of impact and the hurried egress – not nice. Despite the crash and plummet to the seabed, the 214-ST looked reasonably intact, but what got all our attention was one of the large blades moving out from our vision to the right.

We called the divers and advised we were backing up and then slowly backtracked, keeping the blade in view and the umbilical clear.

Arriving at its tip that was resting on the sandy bottom, I prepared to 'fly' up it to the rotor head. The Drag-Brace was located there, next to the root of the blade connected to the trailing edge.

Manipulating vertical thrust as needed, I thrust forward slowly up and along the 25-foot blade. Although I couldn't see it, I was acutely aware of my red snake-like umbilical trailing behind the ROV. Even though it floated, and therefore should be clear, if it were to foul on any part of the helicopter, freeing it would be an arduous and lengthy process due to the depth of our operation.

The rotor head was coming into view, and the site of this additional 'ROV fouling machinery' caused me to pause a little longer than Jack Mitchell desired.

"I really need to see that Drag-Brace, Mick."

I turned to Jet, who was equally concerned about the umbilical, and we exchange a brief 'fuck it' expression. What could possibly go wrong?

The camera wasn't adjustable. What this meant was, as I moved to a range close enough to view the Drag-Brace, the fixed camera angle caused it to disappear from view. The only option I had was to nudge the crash frame up to the rotor head and thrust forward, using this as an anchor to allow me to (gently) thrust up at the same time to drive the camera angle downwards. If the crash frame were to jump forward though, we would either smash the camera, or cause the umbilical to snag, or both. Any of these outcomes would result in a bad hair day for Jet and me.

However, after maintaining the desired thrust for about 10-seconds though, the plan worked, and the Drag-Brace came into view.

And, importantly, we kept good vision of the device that, even to my untrained eye, appeared to be damaged. Jack's expression was not good, but satisfied, we cautiously backed away, and I handed over to Jet who completed the inspection of the other side following the same process.

Jack looked like he had the weight of the world on his shoulders when we finished; nonetheless, we gave him a copy of the tape for further review. Our part in the operation was over, but the divers still had to recover the 214-ST to provide a closer examination of the Drag-Brace.

At the time of this operation, to dive greater than 50m required divers to hold a level-4 certification under the relatively new Australian commercial qualification system. Additionally, they would need a dive-bell and the necessary support equipment, none of which were available on the Flamingo Bay. Although this presented a significant glitch in the salvage plans, the dive supervisor had a solution.

Using a long pole (broom handles tied together), his divers would pass a line around the rotor head and then pull it back up to their cage that remained at 50m. From here they would pull a larger lift-line around the rotor head using the first line, and then commence securing the lift gear (bag or 44-gallon drums, yet to be confirmed). As this plan sounded a little haphazard, Jet suggested we pass the line using the ROV's manipulator arm. We had done this type of operation, maneuvering ropes around obstacles, previously in training exercises and it worked relatively well. After he finished explaining the process, the divers looked happy, but I wasn't surprised, as the pole option seemed a bit optimistic.

The ROV was lowered into the water again with the line attached and managed from the tinny, keeping it clear of the umbilical, and we commenced our descent.

Using a device called a 'happy-hooker' connected to the manipulator arm we intended to push up against the root of a rotor blade and in one motion release the line and pass it around the root. The design of the happy-hooker retained the line allowing us to simply back away, recovering the line to the surface, with the ROV's camera providing confirmation that the line was positioned correctly. Although the risk of fouling remained, both Jet and I were happy we could control the ROV appropriately after the first dive. We pushed on towards the bottom.

About halfway down though, the camera monitor mysteriously went blank. Sonar and tracking were out too. We commenced recovery straight away, but to make matters worse, without the ability to gauge the ROV's progress the umbilical became fouled on the main anchor cable and took around an hour to untangle. Once back on the deck, Jet unscrewed the umbilical connection to check for circuit continuity and was greeted with dripping water and fizzing circuit boards. There would be no more ROV operations for the rest of the trip. It was back to the pole option.

The Flamingo Bay's anchors were adjusted to position the stern and divers cage, connected to the derrick, directly over the 214-ST. The divers had two umbilicals connected into a small plastic panel that was actually a Pelican-Case plumbed to accommodate surface supply diving operations. There was only one reducer in the centre of this panel though, meaning that both diver and standby were supplied from the same system? This meant if there were a failure to the diver's supply, there would also be a failure to the standbys - not good if you expected the standby to come to your rescue!

In the one-man cage, they also secured a large air cylinder with a reducer and single whip hose to be used as an additional reserve system. The sheep shearer told me the whip hose would be pushed up inside the neoprene hood of the KMB10 to supply air directly to the oral-nasal in the event of an emergency. This was needed because the tiny bailout cylinders they had would supply little air at a depth of

50m. I had never seen this type of set up before and questioned the supervisor.

"No harm in a bit of extra safety, mate."

On closer inspection of his panel, I had to agree. He had the back exposed, and I noticed that the single reducer was plumbed with what appeared to be cheap plastic tubing. Were these even rated for the pressure required at 50m? The Council's panel, like the RN's, was made of alloy and steel and had a similar pressure rated plumbing. Such a panel was deemed critical to safe diving operations and treated as such. The Pelican-Case set up, however, looked like something that might be used to support fun dives in a resort swimming pool.

As they prepared for the first dive with the pole I seriously doubted how they would make this work, and was beginning to suspect that it was just a smoke screen to make us believe they were sticking within regulations. The pole, though, turned out to be the least of their worries.

10-minutes into the first dive the panel exploded into a rush of high-pressure air as a connection failed. As the supervisor went to work shutting valves and grabbing at hoses, the standby diver, without any air, remained on the surface awaiting directions. Then the comms-box sparked up. It was the Welsh sheep shearer.

"Gas failure, gas failure... I'm ok, on reserve."

The diver's calm words relaxed the supervisor and everyone else on deck. He must have been a pretty cool customer to use their improvised reserve system at 50m, or perhaps he was just used to it? Anyway, repairs were made, the job continued, and after half an hour the diver was on his way up to his first decompression stop with the line successfully attached.

Watching proceedings with the rest of the crew, I looked over at the decompression table the supervisor was running; it was for 70m?

"Hey mate, why seventy-meters for a fifty-meter dip?"

He looked at me suspiciously, sizing me up.

"The extra stops are for added safety mate, if this turns out to be a long job it will keep the boys out of danger."

I left my casual inquiry at that but was sure now that the pole had just been a charade and that the diver had descended the extra 10-12-m to secure the line, hence the 70m table. Either way, he arrived on the surface in a healthy state and preparations got underway to connect the 44-gallon drums to the line, as the Flamingo Bay's derrick wasn't rated to lift the 7 tonne 214-ST.

What the divers planned to do was interesting. The initial line was already secured to a buoy floating astern of the Flamingo Bay. So, first, they would lower each drum (that had a lift-eye welded to it) individually to a depth of 40m, attach it to the line and fill it with air. They calculated that two groups of 10 drums each would be required for this initial lift of the 'staged lift', which would permit the divers to work at a shallower depth and bring the 214-ST up to a depth of approximately 30m.

Once this first part of the operation was completed, the diver's lift bag, which turned out to be homemade, would be attached to the rotor head and inflated to bring the 214-ST up the final 30m to the surface. Then, apparently, when on the surface the 214-ST was going to be secured to the stern and then brought aboard the aft deck using a heavy line relayed through pulleys from one of the anchor winches. The fact the 214-ST was at least twice the size of the aft deck and that even a basic understanding of rigging suggested a lift to the deck wouldn't work, didn't appear to worry either the skipper or the dive supervisor. Anyway, the divers got on with their lengthy task, and we worked on a suntan.

Early in the afternoon as the divers toiled away a pod of about 20 dolphins began circling the Flamingo Bay. They were playing about, leaping out of the water and doing 'tricks' like you see at Sea World as though they were interested in, or perhaps just showing off to, the strange steel thing floating in their ocean.

This was an opportunity not to be missed. About six of us grabbed masks and snorkels and hopped in with them. There we were, in the middle of the Timor Sea swimming with wild dolphins, it was brilliant! They would swim right up alongside us with their eyes checking us out as that dolphin smile encouraged one of our own. It probably sounds a bit hippie, but being so close to those eyes and watching their movement, their mouth opening, it felt like they were trying to communicate. Yep, that does sound hippie. Anyway, we continued swimming with our new friends for quite some time as I ticked a long-held item off my bucket list.

Eventually, the other crew headed back on board and it was just me, alone in the Timor Sea with 20 dolphins, this was surreal. Dolphins were swimming by, deep blue void all around, and dolphins brushing up alongside me, when one of the dolphins started swimming strangely. Not up and down tail movements, but side to side. Shit! It was a shark, and a big one too, 3m was my alarmed guess! It was bigger than me anyway. My inner voice immediately began re-runs of old TV show narrative.

'Don't worry; if a shark comes the dolphins' will chase it away. They will lead you to safety.'

But it was just the shark and I now; there were no dolphins with it. Turning quickly, adrenaline buzzing through my senses, I realised there were, in fact, no dolphins anywhere in sight. They'd just left me. Those bloody stories were bullshit!

'Ok, keep calm, start swimming back to the boat, slowly'.

I lifted my head and my heart sank further, the boat was about 200m away; I would never make it! Being a trained professional though, and someone formally qualified in underwater warfare, I acted in a way that would have got my peers attention.

"Sharrrrrrk!! Sharrrrrrk!!! Sharrrrrrk!!!!"

A few heads casually turned in my direction and waved in a relaxed, 'yeah, we know the dolphins are cool' way. The noise of generators must have been muffling my desperate pleas for help?

'Deal with it dickhead.'

I put my head back in the water and checked on the shark. It was about 6m away, its tail moving slowly, eye watching me as it circled my position, but the circles were getting smaller.

'Keep calm idiot, just keep swimming, and don't splash.'

As I performed the most even and no-splash-making breaststroke possible, the shark changed its course. Instead of circling, it now swam parallel to me. It was only 4m away, eye locked with mine, tail barely moving. The friendship and love I had seen in the dolphins' eyes just moments before was nothing like the death radiating towards me from the ugly black ball now only 3m away. Fucking dolphins!

As I swam on, my inner monologue continued with that night's news report.

'Diver is eaten by a shark in the Timor Sea' and 'man missing believed taken by a shark' and 'it was thought that dolphins tried to save the man…'

Yeah, sure they did. Fucking dolphins!

Suddenly the shark was gone; it had just drifted away from me until it disappeared from view. I was only 100m from the safety of the Flamingo Bay, but this was the worst part of all.

'They strike from below, often charging up at their unsuspecting victim at great speed.'

I kept swimming slowly, preparing to brace for impact, my arms and legs buzzing with adrenaline. Finally, about 20m from Flamingo Bay, all composure was lost and I bolted for the ladder like Ian Thorpe, my frantic arm and leg actions not stopping until I was on deck.

"Why didn't you bring the tinny, a shark has been circling me for the last ten minutes!"

Although still a buzz of adrenaline I managed to keep my voice under reasonable control so as not to destroy the myth of PJ superheroes. They were completely unaware though, believing, as I'd suspected, that I had just been calling about the dolphins.

Contemplating my fate had the shark attacked me I couldn't find any positives, but with hindsight, the shark probably just wasn't interested. Moreover, had a marine biologist been in the water they would have likely told of a 'wonderful encounter'. Perhaps? I bet they couldn't explain why that chicken shit pack of dolphins had pissed off though!

About three hours later the divers had attached and filled all the 44-gallon drums with air and these were on the surface marking the 214-ST's position below, and the homemade lift-bag (that had no relief valve) was being connected. Without a relief valve, I wondered how it would cope with the rapidly expanding air as it ascended from 30m. I asked the dive supervisor.

"Mate, it has a large throat. Any excess gas will just vent past that, not a problem."

He appeared very confident and a little annoyed with my question, so I left him to it.

The entire crew were watching the surface about 20m from the starboard side where the drums were positioned, cameras ready, waiting for the moment of triumph. A diver was standing by to attach the lift/security line and then the voice of the diver filling the lift bag crackled through the comms box.

"On its way, I'm moving clear."

We waited, fingers on camera buttons, any moment now…

Do you remember those old WW2 movies where the ship drops depth charges on the submarine? Well, picture the moment when the charge goes off, and crews watch the effect on the surface. A large area of blue ocean suddenly turns white, and from the centre of this, a massive mound of water erupts upwards from the expanding pressure of the explosion.

In our case, we just got the huge mound of white water erupting upwards as the lift bag failed. For a moment, the two sets of 44-gallon drums remained on the surface, but as the 214-ST mass accelerated downwards past 30m, they disappeared, a couple breaking free to return to the surface as the 214-ST crashed onto the sea floor for the second time.

Thankfully the diver was clear and recovered safely, but Mr Mitchell was not looking particularly happy.

"That will do thank you. Skipper, we can head back to Darwin when you're ready."

The Flamingo Bay would not be coming back. A far more costly operation was to be mounted using an oil and gas barge with a heavy-lift crane, but at least we had captured critical video and Freddo was very happy with that.

The divers were a bit down after the event, but the alcohol we'd loaded in Darwin that had remained unopened was now easing their misery. By late in the evening a party was in full swing. The cook had made up cardboard helicopter badges which everyone was wearing, with the words 'No Helicopter, No Worries' at their centre. Some of the divers were trying to crack onto the nurse, but the star of the party turned out to be Joe Walsh. Now very relaxed with beers in his system, he was performing like a professional party animal and with barriers down he revealed some of his past.

It turns out he was a former Top Gun pilot who'd flown Phantom Jets off carriers during the Vietnam War. He'd had to eject once while attempting to land too.

"Yeah, the arrestor hook hadn't dropped down far enough, and the damn throttle wouldn't open fully after landing. I punched out going over the side. Turns out one of our flight mechanics had messed with the controls, believing that if enough jets crashed he would get to go home. Anyway, let's have another beer."

News Headline:

Efforts by the Department of Aviation to examine the oil and gas transport helicopter that crashed off Troughton Island near the northern tip of West Australia last Monday, received a setback today when lifting equipment used to bring the Bell 214-ST helicopter to the surface suffered an unexpected failure. Arrangements for a second salvage attempt are currently underway.

Pig-Man's truck on the Darwin Wharf loading the Flamingo Bay

Top: Jet (left) and author undertakinfg ROV preps,
divers checking lift lines

What can possibly go wrong

Top: The homemade lift-bag fails in dramatic fashion – Bottom: Party on the bowsprit

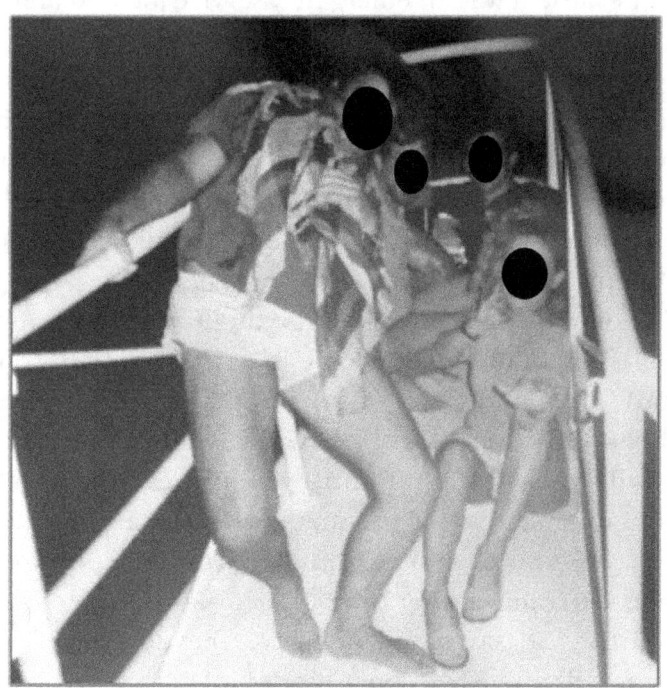

CHAPTER 15

Melbourne Fire Brigade (Unknown Chemicals)

AFTER THE DEMISE OF THE NSCA in 1989, I was fortunately offered a job with the Melbourne Metropolitan Fire Brigade, MFB for short. Fortunate, because it was an emergency service job and an immediate paycheck for my young family, which was about to include our second child. Unfortunate, because we would have to sell our first house in the country town of Maffra and move back to the city. An equally sad factor had nothing to do with geographic relocation though; this was simpler, at the age of 30 I was going to have to start at the bottom of another organisational structure and, once again, complete a recruit course. Oh, this was going to be so much fun!

On day one, assembled in a large auditorium were two recruit classes consisting of about 20 people in each, plus the MFB training college staff. Keen and eager to get started, we were addressed by a senior officer whose weight and girth equalled his high rank.

"This will be the hardest training you have ever undertaken..."

This opening statement was made with the arrogance of someone who believed his own press and the rest of his speech continued in the same vein, amounting to not much more than cliché-ridden-diatribe. Suffice to say it did not have the desired effect on the eleven former PJs and NSCA operations blokes that had taken up the MFB's offer.

At the risk of sounding arrogant, please consider the world we had recently come from; high-tempo, complex operations, where intense training, physical fitness and innovative thinking was considered the norm. Commencing training with the MFB then, was like someone had pulled on the handbrake and insisted that a Luddite mentality was now praiseworthy. Unwisely, though, one of our numbers didn't keep these feelings to himself and made an infamous statement to one of the training college staff (right Greeny?).

"Mate, it's like stepping out of a Porsche into a beat up old 'V-dub'"

This naturally went down well, and we were to receive extra attention because of it.

"Where are all those 'Nescafe' boys then?"

The senior course instructor had assembled both courses on the training college fire ground and was about to make his point. He scanned the recruits gathered in front of him, sneering every time he sighted one of us.

"So, you reckon you're better than the rest of us do you?"

Fun times were coming our way.

Early in the course, we commenced hose drills. This was running out hose this way and that, connecting to hydrants and pumps, replacing damaged lengths of hose and running hose 'aloft' (up a ladder). Each part of a drill was worked in sequence until we were doing it by numbers, as per the MFB procedure, and responding to changes determined by the instructor, for example:

"Add a length... that hose is burst, replace a length... there's fire on the first floor, run a hose aloft and add two lengths..."

This was good training to organise teamwork, but not truly reflective of operational procedures when 'on shift.' Additionally, the way the instructors delivered the training was not what we were used to.

With a couple of exceptions, the training college staff appeared to favour intimidation, belittling, and arguably, bullying as training techniques. Maso shared an example of this when he and another recruit were tasked to secure the top of a ladder to a balcony:

"The young bloke with me had tied the clove hitch incorrectly. The instructor inspected the knot, assumed I had tied it, and then laid into me verbally. Seriously, this prick just yelled abuse, telling me I was hopeless and any other derogatory comment he could think of. I just kept a neutral expression, not really giving a shit and it made him angrier. He was nothing but a fool though, who hadn't even grasped the basic concept of training. He was more interested in telling people how good he was. Remember the dick who kept on going on about his martial arts prowess? Well, it was that tosser. The poor bloke with me was trembling in his boots and learned very little, apart from never to question the instructor. That instructor didn't change throughout the course, and the MFB system didn't appear robust enough to identify the weakness. I seriously hope the modern MFB has identified that it takes more than years of service to make a capable instructor."

At the time, Maso held a physical education and teaching degree and was an experienced rock climber who relied on knots to prevent unwanted trips to the ground. As a Nescafe boy, he had also undertaken a week of knot tying at the commencement of PJ training. This was under the guidance of a former Victorian rigging inspector, who had also served on Atlantic convoys during WW2. The knot tying component of PJ training had concluded with the construction of a rope traverse over a river at the height of 100-feet. During this drill, recruits were required to demonstrate their knot tying ability by splicing two eyes into a length of rope and then attaching their handiwork to the traverse line for the jaunt across the void. Simply put, Maso knew how to tie a clove hitch and could have taught the instructor a thing or two.

Later in the course, we were introduced to high-expansion foam. This was produced using a knee-high fan that was powered by a fire hose; the result being something like dishwashing bubbles that could fill a large area very quickly. I had used this before at the Port

Emergency Service (PES) before joining the NSCA. It was used to rapidly fill a ship's hold to remove the bulk of the oxygen and therefore extinguish any fire; at the MFB we were using it as part of a Breathing Apparatus (BA) drill in a 3-story 'firehouse'.

The same instructor was explaining the drill as we stood on the flat roof of the building looking down into a central void now filled with foam. A ladder was protruding from this, and I sensed another 'let's make the Nescafe boys look stupid' moment coming. Turning to one of the Council blokes I quickly asked for his BA tally – this was a small metal tag retained by a BA 'entry-controller' for recording your name and cylinder pressure. Ours were blank due to the relative simplicity of the drill. The instructor was coming to the end of his brief.

"...And so it is important you remember the 'BA shuffle' as you proceed due to the lack of visibility. Right, Macfarlane you're first."

I moved up to the ladder. The instructor smiled, unclipped my BA tally, and then turned to face the other students.

"This shouldn't be too much of an effort for a Nescafe boy now, should it?"

A few chuckles broke out amongst the students. He turned back to look me in the eye; satisfied he had me, and then turned back to face the students as he casually tossed the tally into the foam. No one heard it hit the ground three floors below; smiling smugly he continued.

"Off you go then, I want the tally back before you run out of air."

I descended the ladder to the bottom, didn't move, waiting for about 30-seconds and then ascended it again. When I showed him the (other) tally, he didn't have much to say, and the drill continued.

In training at the PES, we were made to walk into 'high-ex' with just our helmets covering our faces. This required very gentle inhalation to prevent foam getting into the helmet and taught us that despite manufacturer's claims, there was breathable oxygen in high expansion foam. Oh, and we also learned several of the standard tricks instructors played on students too.

Despite the occasional abuse from staff, MFB recruit training wasn't so bad. There were some excellent blokes, who liked a beer, and a couple of them would have probably cut the mustard at the NSCA. And even on the occasions we were to receive punishment for some misdemeanour or other, well, let's just say it was different to what we had been used to:

"Right, no morning tea for the lot of you!"

During the four years I spent at the MFB before finally getting a job back in aviation rescue, I worked with some pretty sharp operators at some different fire stations. But this was still the MFB I had described earlier, and I was to bump into Larry-the-Luddite or his brother regularly.

One afternoon after lunch we were sitting in the mess watching TV, and a union organiser was having a bit of a rant.

"Fuck em! They don't appreciate what we do each fucking shift and that's got to stop. Let's face it, boys, we are lucky to go home alive each day!"

I considered his words as I licked my ice cream on the comfy couch. We had indeed had a challenging day to that point where a response to a false alarm in the city had caused us to risk back strain as we hurriedly got off the couch, and some hydrant inspecting (this was re-painting markers) had resulted in white paint nearly splashing onto my clothes. Furthermore, before lunch, we had worked up a significant sweat playing cricket in the yard where one of the boys copped a pull-shot to the aggots. I guess from his perspective the union guy was right. Nevertheless, 'lucky to go home alive' seemed a tad melodramatic.

On the occasions where challenge had presented itself following a 'turn-out' though, the MFB's tried and tested procedures kept 'fireys' pretty much out of harm's way. I mean, from my first night 'on shift' it was reinforced to me that a fiery running into a building to rescue a baby was nothing but Hollywood hype. Although this type of advice was typically delivered in parlance derived from much real-world experience, 'only a dickhead charges into a building mate.' That's not to say fireys wouldn't enter a burning building to search for 'confirmed' missing or trapped persons. This occurred at least two times on my shift during the short time I spent with the MFB. The difference being it was done with control. For example, there would be a team of two wearing Breathing Apparatus (BA), they had a charged hose-line, and a backup crew similarly prepared to rescue them if needed. But this type of job was very infrequent, and I soon learned that the bigger the fire you were confronted with, a simple rule was applied: stand further back and increase the pump pressure.

Supporting the robust safety incorporated into everything we did was the need to complete specialist training before you were permitted to undertake extra hazardous response work. One such course that I applied for but was never accepted on was the Breathing Apparatus program.

Although every recruit learns how to use BA, on this program, you used variations of it like oxygen-rebreathers, special gas suits, etc. and when qualified you could be rostered on the 'BA Bus,' a unique vehicle that only turned out to the big jobs. This was cool, not just because of the big job interest, but because you got to spend 99% of your night shifts tucked up in bed due to the infrequency of such big jobs.

I had the opportunity to pursue my BA ambition one night when I spent a shift at a different station to fill in for someone chucking a 'sickie'. The senior station officer had organised a drill on the relatively new positive-pressure BA set the MFB had introduced, and this bloke was BA qualified and had taught the program at the college. If I made a good impression, who knows, that might open the necessary doors to get on the course?

The senior station officer was in the process of describing how air was transferred from the cylinder to the wearer's mask.

"Ok, so we have a 300-bar cylinder with a first-stage-reducer connected to it. This device takes the 300-bar and lowers it to an intermediate-pressure inside the housing. From here a further reduction takes place where a line-pressure delivers air up the hose at a breathable level to the second-stage demand valve connected to the mask."

He scanned around the dozen or so fireys trying to keep their eyes open. BA was, after all, something we used at least once a shift cycle. My enthusiasm to get on the BA course must have caught his attention.

"Mick, what is the intermediate-pressure?"

Fucked if I know big fella. The first response I thought of would not have won me any brownie points, so I changed tack.

"Well, as it is the job of a maintenance technician to service the reducer I never really focused on this pressure, but the line-pressure is -"

He cut me off.

"A professional firefighter should know every aspect of his job and the equipment he may have to deploy, Mick. That is why all firefighters are taught the relevant criteria in training. Now, what is the intermediate-pressure?"

We had been taught about intermediate-pressure, but like any other bit of useless information, my brain had discarded it ages ago. I had never found a use for such data during my diving life, which utilised far more complicated equipment, but old-mate senior station officer was staring at me, and an awkward silence was developing. Time to execute plan 'B.'

"Well, that is right. I have been taught that, like everyone else…" I looked around the silent room at the other blokes in an effort to share the love, "…but as a 'bum-on-a-seat,' isn't my job about completing safety checks and then donning the BA when needed?"

He paused, just a second, cogs quickly realigning.

"No! Your job is to know everything about it, as you were taught in training."

Well then, no BA course anytime soon for me. The drill completed just before seven, and we headed off for tea. On the walk to the mess, one of the other blokes offered some advice.

"Mate, he's a fucking wanker! He does this every drill. You know, he reads up on some worthless piece of brigade shit and then drivels more shit to try and impress the boys. If you ask him what fucking intermediate-pressure is next week I bet the cunt wouldn't know."

I wouldn't have to wait so long.

We turned out to a second-alarm sometime during the night. It was a small factory, not quite fully involved yet, but there was smoke billowing from areas of the roof and flame was licking around roller doors.

We were given the rear sector to manage and directed to protect exposures. This meant we should not let the fire spread to any adjacent properties. Once parked up around the back it was apparent the nearest exposure, another building across some waste ground, was not under threat. The senior station officer made a simple decision for us to support containment of the fire and relayed this to the district officer running the fire ground.

We had two lines aimed up at the back wall, directing our water streams into a small opening where flames could be seen. While we were doing this, the senior station officer disappeared to conduct a check of the sector.

A few minutes later he came over to me on the first line as I was adjusting my branch with the intention of aiming a better spray-pattern into the small opening. Pointing towards a fire escape, he directed me to secure the branch, leave it on the ground and go with him.

The fire escape was a small balcony that may have provided us with better access to get water on the fire, but to get to a window where we could do this would require walking through some thick black smoke.

"Mask-up and check if we can get a line up to the window."

He was pointing assertively to the stairs leading up to the balcony.

"I can't do that." I shook my head purposely.

"What?" There was disbelief in his eyes. "Why not!?"

"I can't remember what the intermediate-pressure is inside the first-stage reducer." Anger filled his eyes. I pushed further, "Can you remind me what it is please?"

More cogs realigned, but much quicker this time.

"Shut up! Just get fucking masked-up and check that balcony out!"

We held eye contact for just a second, but the point was made. As I moved through the smoke to check out the balcony window I was grinning like a child behind the oral-nasal of the BA mask.

Fortunately, a new MFB endeavour was to fall in my lap to relieve the BA frustration and it was one that would utilise some of the NSCA experience.

The High Angle Rescue Techniques (HART) program came about after a Rookie-8 PJ, now fire fighter, Bill Rouse, had a chanced discussion with the MFB District Officer in charge of brigade research and development. Bill, a former Australian Commando, had completed a Mountain Leader course with the British Royal Marines and was passionate about ropes and rescue; the two of them hit it off and soon after Bill was given a budget. In the months that followed I would help out after my shift had finished, or would work between shifts when Bill needed a hand. Bill taught me more about rope rescue than I had learnt at the NSCA, and soon, with two Station Officers supporting, we ran the first MFB HART program. This program had required training in lift shafts, outside of buildings, trees etc., and had culminated with a week at Mount Arapiles in central Victoria where high traverses, lead climbing and vertical rescue techniques were honed.

After this had been completed the Brigade asked if we could do 'something' for the MFB's centenary celebrations. Bill came up with a simple plan, "How about a team rappel off the top of the Rialto Tower?" The Rialto building was, at that time, the tallest building in Melbourne. However it was still a fraction short to break the current Guinness Book of Records height for 'Abseiling' down a building, a feat that would shine a spotlight on the MFB. This didn't stop Bill. "Ok, we'll build three levels of scaffolding on top and break the record!". So that's what we did. On the 20th of February 1991, Bill, the two Station Officers (Trevor and Alun) plus I stepped off the scaffold for the 251.5m descent, each carrying 400m of rope in huge bags. Unfortunately the bags had only been delivered the night before, so despite endless practice with smaller 200m bags this added an unnecessary 'unknown' to the task that was to be broadcast live on breakfast television. What could possibly go wrong?

The descent went well for about 12m, it was only then that we we realised the narrow neck of the bags was causing the rope to twist and jam preventing further travel. Not good. Suffice to say, our planned 5-8 minute descent became an ardours 30+ minutes as we locked off, pulled out slack, freed the jam, descended until the next jam and then repeated the process again, and again. At times the wind picked us up and blew us 20-30 feet from, and around, the building; this unique experience allowed us to test the strength of the Rialto windows as we came smashing back against them. Halfway down my focus on untwisting rope was distracted momentarily as some people in an office on the 32nd floor were waving energetically – it was Mandy, with Jessie and Lachie happy to see Daddy at work. After just a brief wave hello, we continued on. The wind had picked up even more and began blowing us further around the corner of the building, but this was why we had 400m of rope, "We could do a complete lap if it gets bad" Bill had told the MFB during preparation.

As we approached the last four to six stories the wind took us towards a low rooftop and I saw a cameraman filming. Remembering Nords advice about colour and movement I waved at the guy only realising it was Sparksy (the Sky God's cameraman) at the last instant. In a surreal moment we shook hands, had an inane conversation, before gravity pulled me away.

Despite the glitches, the rappel was a great success for the MFB. We were invited into the chief's office for tea and presented with a Guinness World Record certificate for the highest single pitch, team rappel.

Within months of this display, the HART team were called upon to rescue two window cleaners whose cage had dropped to an alarming 40-degree angle around 20 floors from the ground. For this operation, Bill was lowered by other HART operators including Phil Jones (another Rookie-8 PJ) and Station Officer (now MFB Commander) Marc O'Connor, who managed a complex rigging system from the rooftop. Both cleaners were recovered safely, resulting in Bill's concept becoming a proven tool for the MFB to draw upon in future operations.

Before all this, I had been undertaking basic HART training at the college. A BA course was running at the same time, but I was kind of over the BA ambition now – well, not quite really.

The BA course was coming to the business end of the program, and they were undertaking rescues in confined spaces. This consisted of crawling through narrow spaces with limited visibility where your BA scraped the roof, all the while testing your tolerance for claustrophobia. Adding to the joy of this type of task was the effort required to drag the training dummies (heavy, but lighter than a real person) out to safety.

Standing on top of the seven-story training tower in 33-degree heat assembling an anchor system as part of a rope traverse, the HART crew's attention turned from ropes, pullies, karabiners, and rigging plates, to an ambulance approaching the college entrance. Its warning lights were still flashing, but the siren was silenced as they entered the gate. What was wrong?

From our high position, we watched as it descended a ramp to the lower-yard, past the base of the tower and over to where the BA compound was. As it pulled to a halt, the BA crew exited their building with someone on a stretcher. It wasn't a dummy.

"I bet it's fucking Mary! Told ya they shouldn't let sheilas on the course!"

Mary, not her real name, was one of the first women accepted into the MFB - can you imagine the reaction when that happened? No? Overweight men who could barely do one push up, nor could run out of sight would, in between mouthfuls of fried chicken or meat pies denigrate everything female to have this decision changed.

"Sheilas aren't suitable for this type of work you blokes. I mean, they couldn't handle the pressure, or even keep up with men. We'd be carrying them the whole bloody way!"

Despite this regular yet unproven misogynistic form of attack, the MFB board had finally succumbed to the modern world, and after almost a hundred years of existence, women were permitted entry.

Mary was one of about six women at the time I joined, and even if the old school-misogynists wouldn't acknowledge it, she, like the others, had to possess physical capability over a typical male recruit just to get in the front door. Mary was, in fact, a competitive triathlete, whom I always found to be just as professional and capable as any of the male fire fighters I respected. Moreover, for the misogynists' reading this, she never played the 'female card.' Just the opposite actually, anytime I heard her questioned about the 'purpose of women in the brigade' she would often just smile.

"I'm here to do the job mate, not change it."

Typically, she would then quickly and skilfully change the subject so as not to upset the moron asking the question.

Back to the BA course then: it turns out it wasn't, "fucking Mary," but she was very much involved in the incident. While in a tunnel and working in groups of two to locate the dummies, the bloke with Mary began to struggle. After all, it was bloody hot inside the confined space, and even the fittest blokes were questioning the instructors about whether the training should continue. When her partner suddenly collapsed Mary,' for a sheila', did a pretty good job. She raised the alarm, cleared the airway, confirmed he was breathing and then dragged the bigger bloke out to a point where other men could assist. Despite this result, which perhaps the MFB could have used to reinforce the capability of women in the brigade, little was reported internally about the event.

Anyway, hopefully, you have got the idea that in the early nineties getting onto the BA course was deemed special within the MFB. What's more, if you passed and were afforded the right to wear a small red 'BA' sticker on your helmet, not too many of them on each shift, well, you were the man! - Or in Mary's case, the wo-man.

So this brings me to early April 1993 and my last nightshift at Richmond fire station. Like any other night, I had arrived about five-thirty, thirty minutes before the shift change at 6 pm. I did this to ensure the bloke I was relieving could get an early-knock knowing the same favour would be returned the next morning.

After the regular back and forth about how the day had been; any good jobs, what's that tosser been up to, get a root last night, etc. we would say goodbyes, and I would place my turn-out equipment on the 'gear' I was 'catching.' On this night the gear was 'Pumper 10B'. That is a typical frontline fire truck, albeit an older MK2 model. After placing the equipment in the rear cabin, I was just a bum-on-a-seat this shift, I opened a side locker and checked my BA: full, high and low-pressure tests all good, straps adjusted ready for immediate use. I then headed up to the mess and put my dinner in the fridge, chicken pasta to be reheated later on.

At the shift muster, a reasonably casual affair for the moderately sized station, our senior station officer confirmed names against gear and advised what drill we would be doing that evening before tea. Tonight it was to be a lecture on open water pump operation where we might have to connect all the pump's 'suction hose' to get water from a river or lake - in recruit training we were taught that the MFB didn't 'suck', the MFB 'induced a vacuum', funny how every pump had 'suction hose' though.

Richmond, or 'number 10' station, had a couple of pumps and a truck that could load a selection of shipping containers each filled with differing 'specialist gear' depending on the job it was responding to.

Martin 'Marty' Kingston was driving 10B, Phil Small was our station officer and in the back with me was an old hand called Bill. We hung around after the muster was over, talked a bit more shit and then headed off to the mess for a brew before the drill was due to start at 6:30. The alert tones sounded before I had taken three steps towards the mess.

When these relatively soft, so as not to wake people too harshly, tones silenced after about 10 seconds, the MFB control room operator's voice came over the public address.

"Pumper 3A, Pumper 10B, District Officer 1, Telleboom 1, Pumper 35; Second-Alarm, Non-Structure fire with unknown chemicals, Footscray..."

The unknown chemical bit was all I focused on. I hated chemicals, especially un-fucking-known-ones! When union-boy had his rant about being lucky to go home alive this was perhaps the real message he should have utilised to seek extra pay over. Although I was sure we would go home alive, the constant exposure to chemicals was a persistent issue for fireys and one that may have prevented them 'retiring alive' as some hidden disease slowly ate away at their cells.

Marty was a good driver. He had 10B moving purposely through peak-hour traffic, crossing onto the wrong side of the road as needed and making maximum use of space afforded by Melbourne's tram tracks. We had a brilliant run through the city and as we turned onto Footscray Road heading for the docks we saw Pumper 3A merging from the north.

"Fucking losers!" we commented in unison.

3A was from Carlton and much closer than us to the site of the fire, they must have had shittier traffic to deal with, but they were still losers.

At the time of this job Footscray Road was the main artery exiting the city to the west. Traffic was heavy, and Marty was weaving his way towards the wharf where the non-structure fire had been reported. Non-structure could mean a range of things, but it was not a house, factory or other building. We would find out what it was soon enough.

It was a relatively warm early autumn evening, and we had the windows down to take advantage of the air flowing into the cab. Then all of a sudden we saw the smoke. It was crossing Footscray Road, white in colour, and covering an area about 50m wide. We were almost on it, still around 300m from the wharf entrance when Phil, the seasoned professional that he was, called for immediate precautionary measures.

"Wind your windows up, boys!"

We didn't need to be told twice. I held my breath as Marty charged in and out the other side. Almost comically, we wound the windows down again straight away as though this had been a documented procedure. What elite, trained professionals the 10 boys were.

Turning into the gate and back up towards the smoke, we saw the fire for the first time. Standing alone about 200m from anything else on the deserted laydown area was just one 40-foot shipping container. However, it had smoke billowing angrily from both ends. Fuck, fuck, fuckity, fuck!

The image brought forth immediate memories of the PES where I had spent another four years responding to jobs in the Melbourne docks. One of our bread and butter tasks at the PES was un-stuffing containers after un-known-chemical leaks. We did this while wearing full gas suits and driving a forklift, often in 30+ temperatures. I don't know anyone at the PES who enjoyed this work, and there are now growing numbers of former PES blokes that had died, or were slowly and painfully expiring as some form of cancer ate away at their bodies.

Ten meters from the shipping container was Pumper 2A, the first responding truck. There should have been another truck with them, but I have no idea where this was. The 2A blokes had lines operating and were cooling the container from upwind. All this was processed in a heartbeat, but I'm sure all our hearts skipped a beat when we noticed that the sides of the container were bulging and water hitting them was producing a fair amount of steam!

We pulled up close to the 2A pump, and Phil turned around.

"Right, I want two of you to go and block traffic on Footscray Road."

He was all business, and so Marty and I were quick to offer our services. Bill and Phil hopped out, and I jumped in the front with Marty. We drove back towards the city as fast as the old pumper would allow, following the wharf boundary fence looking for another gate. We were both pissing ourselves laughing, knowing we had dodged a bullet.

The first gate we came to was locked, but it didn't matter as every fire truck has a 'universal key.' With the bolt cutters performing as advertised, we pulled out onto Footscray Road with lights and siren cranked up.

Traffic immediately, albeit a little bit screechy, pulled to a halt, and we got out to advise drivers of the situation.

"Sorry mate, big fire down the road, you'll have to do a U-turn."

Most drivers acknowledged this with a touch of frustration knowing their trip home was going to be a pain in the arse, but they weren't stupid and quickly followed our directives. However, there is always one smartarse.

"Listen you blokes, I can see the smoke, and I live just down the road there. For fuck's sake, it's not that bad."

Although we had some sort of authority in this situation, we weren't going to convince dickhead by preaching legal stuff to him. We cut to the chase.

"Suit yourself mate. The smoke is coming from a shipping container full of unknown chemicals that's bulging like an egg. It's probably going to explode and the cops are currently evacuating half of Footscray..."

As the sound of his screeching U-turn filled our ears, we both laughed at the driver's change of heart. However, the irony of our tall-tale was that the police were, in fact, evacuating part of Footscray and the MFB were now responding with a third alarm due to the escalation potential of the unknown chemicals. But at least we were safe on traffic duty as other BRTs (big red trucks) charged towards the danger.

Shortly afterwards, a police sedan pulled up in front of us. One cop got out and provided information that we could have done without.

"Thanks, boys, I've got this now, you can head down to the forward control point."

I think we almost asked if he was sure he didn't need a hand with the traffic, but the result of his arrival was our much slower transit back to where we had dropped off Phil and Bill.

The 'FCP' was now a hive of big red trucks, and we pulled up at the back of them all – furthest from the blast zone, with lots of protection in front of us.

There were about four pumpers and a teleboom directly involved, and these had water arcing towards the container; the rest, with us, were lined up about 200m from the container in a 'staging area' – standing by until someone thought what to do with us.

In amongst this group of 'BRTs' were the BA Bus and a gaggle of elite blokes with their BA stickers easy to see on the side of their helmets. No easy night shift for you blokes tonight hey? I chuckled at the prospect of them having to un-stuff this mess once the fire was extinguished.

The MFB's Mobile Control Bus was at a safe distance too, and senior officers were busy trying to work out why all the 'wet stuff' wasn't putting out the 'red stuff.' At some point, a call was made to the specialist advice number on the HAZCHEM label attached to the container. This was barely readable now, but at least the first on scene had taken down the details.

The sudden call of, "Water off!" that followed the phone call quickly saw ground-monitor streams fall away and then stop as pump operators wound back throttles and closed valves. We found out later that the specialist had somewhat alarmingly told them under no circumstances to put water on the fire.

No flies on the MFB command! What to do then?

While the Mobile Control Bus gang continued to make calls seeking a solution, we simply milled about, keeping well away, talking shit – hey, we were fireys. But when a district officer (DO) came out of the bus with a thermal imaging camera, looking for a volunteer, it was surprising how quickly people vanished.

Unfortunately, I hadn't hidden very well. When I poked my head around from behind one of the pumps I alarmingly made eye contact with the DO standing only a meter from me. He had a senior station officer with him and was looking very serious.

"Right, I want you to get a gas suit on and take a thermal reading of the container. We need to know where the hotspot is."

You want me to do what now??? I looked over my shoulder towards the BA Bus, but it was like it had been abandoned years before, not a soul in sight. The DO noticed where I was looking.

"Good thinking. You can get a suit from there, and I'll get someone to go with you."

He headed off in search of another volunteer while the senior station officer and I went over to the bus. Seriously, the DO had to search in amongst six big red trucks for a fiery!

He returned with a kid, probably 20-ish, who was fresh out of the training college. Where the fuck was the elite BA team? Resigned to my fate, I pulled on a BA and slid my feet into the boots of the one-piece plastic gas suit. My companion was doing the same as we worked through the dressing procedure. We were about to go on air before being zipped in behind the sizeable clear visor when the DO came back with a final bit of advice.

"Ok, listen up. We think it might be about to explode, so move in quickly and give it a good scan."

Really! That's how you motivate your men? What a fucking tosser! To add to the joy of the situation a fiery that I'd known at my first station, now a station officer, appeared just after the DO turned his head to walk back towards the Mobile Control Bus. With BA sticker shining brightly in the blue and red flicker of flashing lights, this tosser, looked at me and then to the young bloke with me and smiled superiorly.

"Your first command, hey?"

Wanker!

With suits zipped up, we commenced the 200m slow-ish walk towards the container, during which time I gained a vague understanding of what it must be like to walk the green mile. I mean seriously, what command training anywhere on the planet would produce a commander that made such a decision? Who knows, maybe the MFB had a monopoly on this?

MFB Command training 101: if you are out of ideas merely sacrifice men on a futile errand to save face, works every time chaps.

Not only was this moron risking one man's life, he thought it best not to let him die alone? To be objective though, just for a second, lack of command situational awareness was possibly one factor supporting my predicament. So to be fair, if the collective management contained within the Mobile Control Bus had not seen the bulging container, with its sides almost glowing, just 200m away, use of thermal imagery might have seemed like a useful option? So what did they hope to achieve with the thermal camera? Ah, that's it. Not a fucking thing!

The camera was a relatively new acquisition for the MFB and to the best of my knowledge it had never been used in anger before. The DO, or one of the other tossers in that Mobile Control Bus, was probably going to claim it as a first:

'Yes, using the available resources I had on that evening, I determined that the best course of action was to, blah, blah, blah - be a dickhead!'

We got to within 60m of the container, and I pointed the camera, the size of a loaf of bread, in the direction of the smoke and heat. There was just a blurry image, and so I guessed I had to get closer, but how would I know, as I'd never been trained to use this tool. I don't think anyone on my shift had either, apart from the DO and his mates, but I didn't see any of them putting on a gas suit.

Despite a strong feeling that I may need to relieve myself very shortly, my mate and I headed closer towards the container to achieve the task we'd been given. At a range of around 20m the radiant heat was becoming overpowering though, so we stopped and pointed the camera one more time. It appeared to be working now as I saw a vague outline of the 40-foot frame, but everything else was merely glowing white. No shit!

We turned around and walked back at a much quicker pace towards the BA Bus. There were now several helpers to get us out of the plastic suits, but no proper decontamination apparently, just a quick hose down as we walked closer to the assembled mob.

When I came off air the DO was there, smiling, looking like a pompous commander from a low budget war movie.

"Where's the hot spot?" he asked enthusiastically.

"It's all white Sir, end to end."

"Right... ok then..."

The DO headed back to the Mobile Control Bus to discuss his findings with the rest of them. I returned to 10B and hid until about 1 am when another pump crew finally relieved us. I never found out what the unknown-chemicals were, or how the situation was resolved and quite frankly didn't care. I was about to leave Melbourne to start a new job in WA.

News Headline:

In what had been described as a unique and challenging emergency that saw part of Footscray evacuated, senior MFB officers had to call upon specialist teams to combat a fire in a shipping container where chemicals of an unknown type or quantity were stored.

MFB Graduation Display 1989 – Ironically, the two jabbers in the 'plane' are terrorists in a modern world who attack a building

Firey's putting the wet-stuff on the red-stuff

What can possibly go wrong

MFB Graduation Day – Once Were PJ's

HART tower 'ablaze' with flares

Left to Right - Bill, Trevor, Alun and Mick. A link-rope between us ensure safety if someone loses control.

CHAPTER 16

Helicopter Rescue (Double Stretcher)

I HAD A PLANE TICKET for Perth and was pretty excited about the change in career, or perhaps re-alignment to my chosen profession after a deviation to the MFB. Despite the excitement, I was a tad anxious at four years absence and what I may have forgotten or, what may have changed. I wanted to do well.

This new opportunity had come out of the blue one day when an old Jabber mate called me.

"Mick, ya dumb bastard! How the fuck are ya?"

I recognised the dulcet tones of Steve 'Sharky' Ward immediately. He had been stationed at the Royal Australian Air Force (RAAF) base north of Sydney, RAAF Williamtown, during the NSCA days. The 'Willy' boys had undertaken one of the rare operational jumps after a military aircraft crash. Jumping in, they had arrived at the crash site well before any other agency, but unfortunately, all personnel on the aircraft had been killed on impact. Medical equipment packs remaining closed then, they coordinated operations until police arrived and were to receive a nice pat on the back for their efforts from RAAF commanders nonetheless.

Sharky was now the Chief Crewman with Lloyd Helicopters, the company that had picked up many of the NSCA contracts. 'Lloyds' had just been awarded another one at RAAF Pearce, north of Perth and Sharky continued his introduction without preamble.

"There's a down the wire job going at Pearce mate; you want to put ya hat in the ring and move west?"

I answered yes immediately, which was unfortunate. I was in the kitchen of our Melbourne home, and Mandy was two feet away. As she tuned into the conversation, a frown growing, I knew this was going to get complicated. Mandy had a part-time job in her preferred career, Jess was in the first year of primary school, Lachlan was in kindergarten, and we had close family support. Moving west would have its challenges.

A week after the call I headed off to Adelaide, where Lloyds had their headquarters, to attend an interview. Before this was undertaken though, just one other successful applicant and I were taken to a sports facility to complete a fitness test.

I had remained reasonably active while at the MFB but did not possess the same fitness as required to be a PJ. Fortunately, though, Lloyd's 'Rescue Crewmen' were not required to be as fit.

After a 3-kilometre run in under 16-minutes, 40-push-ups, 50-sit-ups and 10-chin-ups, where my fellow applicant had struggled, we commenced a 1-kilometre swim that was to be completed in less than 20-minutes. I touched the wall dead on 16-minutes and got a reassuring wink from Sharky who was supervising. At around the 22-minute mark, my competition glided into the wall.

"I know that wasn't the best time, Mr Ward, but just so as you know I am willing to work on this once I am in the position."

Sharky's face remained impassive when he responded.

"Righto mate. Get changed, and we'll head back to the office."

If Sharky had anything to do with it, this bloke wouldn't get the job, because a high-level of fitness, as every Jabber knew, was baseline criteria for efficient SAR operations for those persons leaving the aircraft. So, if I didn't stuff up the interview, I was in with a pretty good chance of getting the Pearce slot.

Walking into the interview room, I saw a panel of three people behind a desk and a vacant chair, positioned in front of them, for me to sit in. Sharky was there and a pilot I knew from the NSCA, Pete, but I didn't know the other bloke. Even sitting down I could see he was tall, smartly dressed and looked reasonably confident about himself.

I was asked to sit down and introductions began.

"And this is Simon Trapp; he's our company safety officer."

Standing, I took Simon's hand; shook once with eye contact and the interview began. Simon was apparently the bad-cop judging by his opening question. Either that or he was just a tosser.

"So Mick, why on earth do you want to leave the MFB and join Lloyds? As far as I can see you have a pretty cushy shift system and the pay is better than you will get as a Rescue Crewman?"

He was right on both points. I answered honestly.

"Since the demise of the NSCA, I have been looking at every opportunity to get back into aviation rescue. It is a profession that I am passionate about, and I want to spend my working life getting more and more involved in."

He wasn't impressed.

"Yes, but surely," he checked his notes, "with a young family income is more important than following a dream?"

He was correct, of course. The time before travelling to Adelaide had been spent crunching numbers with Mandy and her dad trying to work out how we could afford to live on the reduced salary. Simply, we couldn't. So if Mandy failed to get a job we were buggered. I lied.

"On paper, yes, but I have discussed this with my wife and family, and we are satisfied we can make it work."

There were one or two more challenging questions from Mr Trapp, but mostly the interview was positive.

We had to complete a psychological assessment next. You know, a range of endless mind-numbingly boring questions. For example:

Q23: If you were standing next to a cliff, might you consider jumping?

After experiencing the thrill of acceleration leaping from the Swan Airship one fine Council day, my answer was yes, provided there was enough time to deploy the canopy. But they wanted to know if we would do it without a parachute? Although I doubt I ever would, I occasionally imagined what it would be like if I stepped off from height without a parachute, or if a chute failed. Would I scream like a baby, or do something cool like 'track' directly into the roof of an office containing someone I didn't like maybe? The question only allowed for a one-word answer though, so I circled 'NO' and continued this same process until the end.

Picking up my bits and pieces about to leave after all the testing was over, Sharky came through a door and beckoned me to follow - I was in. A short tour of 'head-office' followed where I was introduced to some people including, Guy Lloyd, the founder of the company who was, sadly, to die of a brain tumour a couple of years later.

Before continuing this chapter it is important that I introduce you to Phil and Lars, because the training, accountability and friendship we shared over the years were a significant factor in our crew's success during the thirteen years I served at RAAF Pearce. Indeed it was a lesson from Phil that was to save my life several years later - see the final chapter.

Walking through the gate and into Perth domestic arrivals area in mid-April 1993, I was met by Phil, another ex-NSCA Jabber.

Phil had served at the Wollongong NSCA base and had received additional training as both an aircrewman, and dog handler. The former of these qualifications saw him tasked with a job requiring a high stretcher winch one Christmas morning to recover a boy scout who had been injured. Due to the complexities of this task, a 'stretcher spin' developed requiring Phil to take decisive action.

Stretcher spins are very dangerous, and in a worst-case scenario they could end catastrophically should the wire entangle in the rotors. Equally, for the casualty and stretcher attendant, they were no joy.

Phil had two realistic options: conn the helicopter towards the trees he was winching between to make the stretcher connect with them to stop the spin – not good for casualty or attendant. Or, he could attempt to grab the stretcher himself – very risky to his own flesh and bones. He chose the latter, and fortunately both casualty and attendant were recovered, but not before Phil's outstretched arm was caught in the stretcher's webbing to be broken badly as the spinning forces were transferred to his radius and ulna bones. How he got the stretcher back on board with 'useless arm dangling' was a source of PJ legend for some time afterwards. Moreover, Phil rightly received the Royal Humane Society's Bronze Medal for bravery for his efforts.

The other qualification saw him, and three other PJ's (Jacques, Bear and Jimmy-two-heads) attend the Victorian police dog-handler program where they undertook the same 'tracking' training as the cops. In addition to this, there were some unique NSCA boxes to tick too.

Canine underwater search and rescue is not what you might imagine; there are no doggie scuba sets for example. However, when a body is left unattended, it begins a process of decomposition, and this process naturally releases gasses and subsequent odours. Such smell can easily locate a body on land, but it is not as easy if the body is underwater, as humans do not have suitable sensory organs - but dogs do. We tested this process under the supervision of a canine specialist from the USA.

With one Jabber breathing from his LAR-5 at the bottom of a lake (no giveaway bubbles), Jacques, Jimmy, plus Jimmy's dog (Gus) boarded a small boat to commence a creeping-line-ahead search pattern. Apparently, a dog could detect the smell from even a living body underwater; a dead one would be easy. We were about to test this theory.

We all knew roughly where the Jabber was as the boat went back and forth, but Gus didn't. When we approached the approximate position, however, to our complete amazement, Gus started barking. The engine was revved four times, and the Jabber surfaced two meters in front of us. Score one to John Friedrich and his passion for enhancing SAR capability. Although this method would likely only help in body recovery, at least a grieving family would stand a better chance of having their loved ones remains returned.

The other Council box to be ticked involved winching and parachuting with a dog attached to the Jabber's chest in a suitable harness. The intent of this was to get PJs to remote or isolated areas to search for missing and injured persons when other means were not available: think tsunami or earthquake. Phil had told me that dogs only 'jumped' once a year because they saw no reason to expose them to danger unnecessarily. Instead, Jabber's used a doggie-dummy to maintain their far more regular skill currency. I gained an understanding of Phil's concern for the dogs during a West Sale open day in 1988 not long after the dogs had been made operational.

Five of us PJs were going to perform a carousel, a kind of follow the leader jump with smoke trailing from a device at your ankle as we all descended toward the target area in front of the crowd. Before we were to do our bit though, Jimmy-two-heads was going to leap out with Gus.

We taxied past the crowd with Jimmy and Gus in the open door knowing the commentary coming over the PA was our PR man selling Pararescue to the masses. Guessing that he was up to the 'look and the brave doggie' bit as we approached centre-crowd, we noticed that Gus was about ready to shit himself. You see, Gus had done this before, and he knew exactly what was coming! Consequently, he had dug his claws firmly into the floor of the aircraft and was intending to stay there judging by his expression. Sticking to the script though, Jimmy prised a foot free so that Gus could wave to the crowd.

Fifteen minutes later and three thousand feet higher as Jimmy positioned in the doorway, Gus's tail was still between his legs but now suspended from the harness and about to leave the aircraft. The Jumpmaster gave him the nod and Jimmy, supporting Gus's body and legs with his folded arms, pivoted from his left foot into space in a maneuver designed to enhance efficient canopy deployment. The last thing I saw of Gus was his fear stricken face emitting a silent bark as his head grazed the rear side of the door as they fell away. Gus was uninjured, but you can probably see why Phil had the doggie-dummies made up.

Within a month or so of arriving at RAAF Pearce, I was back in the groove of aviation rescue. Phil and I were doing runs and swims together, and despite just having one helicopter to play with, it was a bit like the good old days.

There was a mixture of experience in our brand new team too. One of the pilots, Luke, was a former South African Special Forces (SF) captain who had paid for his flying training after leaving the military. Another pilot, Nathaniel Fauntleroy, had worked his way up through General Aviation (GA) flying tourists, plus some corporate flying for a building magnate, and had finally scored his first SAR job. Other aircrewmen were Terry and George, both former Navy Chiefs who had been there and done that in Wessex and Sea King machines wherever the navy had sent them. A late addition to this team turned up one morning, and we were keen to see what sort of bloke he was.

Lars, at around the six foot five mark, reflected his resume at first glance, but importantly, as I got to know him over the years, his documented potential was often demonstrated. Although Phil and I had some pretty good jobs together, when Lars and I were rostered some awesome challenges just seemed to fall into our laps. As a result of this 'luck', we had to literally place our lives in each other's hands more than once over the years.

Lars had been a Dutch Marine posted to 'Whiskey Company', the Dutch SF unit. Additionally, he had undertaken postings on 'Lynx'

SAR helicopters as a Rescue Crewman. These postings had given him insight into the dark and shitty conditions that an angry North Sea could produce without warning. One story he retold summed up the type of challenges.

After being winched aboard a small fishing boat and subjected to the violent movement of an angry sea, Lars had to hacksaw through a steel wire that had penetrated a fisherman's leg to ready him for the winch. The fisherman lived, kept his leg too, and as these tasks mounted Lars got a solid understanding of what real-world SAR was all about.

Not surprisingly he had one or two good suggestions to aid our preparedness, but typical of Lloyds at the time his ideas usually fell on deaf ears, because after all, 'he was just a Rescue Crewman'. Not deterred, we continued to practice 'hard', knowing that we were the only dedicated SAR aircraft for all of Western Australia at the time.

The aircraft we used was a Sikorsky S76. When first introduced into RAAF SAR service it was considered state-of-the-art because of an avionics package that permitted night over water rescue in relative safely. From a rear crew perspective, however, it was reasonably small and required specific and challenging drills just to bring a stretcher on board through the narrow doorway.

With this aircraft then, the RAAF contract required us to lift two pilots from the ocean in stretchers and two in strops. Furthermore, while undertaking such a task we had to be able to carry a RAAF doctor and medic, plus the crewie and rescue crewie. It was a theoretical squeeze. I say theoretical for two reasons: firstly, because the RAAF never asked us to demonstrate this capability in all the years I was at Pearce and secondly, the time it took for us to practice such a task off our own initiative meant it was unlikely to occur. This was not due to lack of motivation, but because we were only allocated so many (expensive) training hours a year and we had many other training 'boxes' to tick too.

Although we had a unique stretcher rack system that folded away when not in use to help with stretcher operations, even a single winch involved disciplined coordination between crewie and rescue crewie to 'dip' the stretcher just to get it from outside onto the rack. Once inside, the stretcher had to then be secured to the rack, and a brake released before the stretcher was finally moved across the floor and rotated to fit fore-and-aft on the left side of the cabin. This is what we spent most of our allotted training hours doing and re-doing until we were reasonably confident at it. The next step in a double winch required entering the boot through a small cabin hatchway, retrieving the second stretcher and starting the recovery process again.

The second stretcher would be positioned on the floor diagonally, under the first, just clear of the rack's base. This could be achieved with a degree of comfort when practising in the hangar, but doing it in the hover where any loose equipment may find its way out the door would require appropriate attention to detail. Furthermore, when training in the hangar we didn't have the doctor and medic to worry about, nor did they have to care for a genuine casualty lying in the first stretcher. We were confident we could make it work if a real task arose, but there would no doubt be issues to debrief afterwards.

Although rotary-wing aviators are acutely aware of this, it's important to reinforce that helicopters do not naturally hover. To keep a helicopter stationary at a set height requires a pilot to move three primary flight controls in an assertive yet precise manner to correct height, yaw and lateral movement relative to an aircraft's position next to a structure – tree, cliff or vessel. In such circumstances, precise movement is critical to prevent contact with the structure; add gusting wind, or moving objects (ships at sea) and both pilot (and aircraft) workload increases significantly.

On the 28th of September 2001, eight years after first meeting Lars, we were sitting in the crew room at Pearce before first light. We were no longer working for Lloyd Helicopters; this company had changed hands a couple of times and was now the Canadian Helicopter Corporation (CHC) Australia.

John 'Shipo' Shipton, an ex-RN pilot who had joined the team a couple of years previously, was giving an update on the job we had briefed the previous afternoon.

"Right, morning boys. I just got off the phone from AusSAR, and the job is still a goer."

Affirmative nods from everyone, we hadn't got out of bed early for nothing. John continued.

"The ship will be in a position approximately one hundred and thirty miles north-west by the time we rendezvous. One casualty, reportedly still the same as yesterday's brief with acute appendicitis."

John continued with a standard meteorological brief that included discussion on reserve fuel and instrument approaches, but as he was concluding he turned his head to look through the window to our parking area.

"The 'Doc' and JD are pulling up now, any questions? Alright, Mick, your winch brief when they're here?"

Two years after joining Lloyds' I was trained as a crewman. I had undertaken my first operational winch on a Saturday evening about a month later. With no formal standby arrangement in place, our after hours service was voluntary only, but I don't remember a time when we knocked back a job; although sometimes, perhaps we should have. Lars, Luke and Nathaniel were around at my place for beers when the call came in, so we promptly put beers down and said goodbye to the girls. Phil arrived just as we were heading out the door and assured us, with a grin, that he would look after the girls for us, as he twisted the top off a beer.

There had been an engine room fire aboard a vessel now about 16 miles past Rottnest Island. It was drifting without power, and two seamen had been badly burnt. The light was fading by the time we got on the scene, but we recovered the casualties and transferred them to advanced care before complete darkness. With the exception of Lars, we all lost our new-role-virginity on that job, and I still look back at all the mistakes I made and cringe. Fortunately, though, we got away with it and continued to learn.

My brief consisted of standard winch emergencies and likely sequence of events for the RAAF medical officer (the Doc) and JD (The RAAF medic). Lars suggested one or two points, and then I turned back to John who scanned the faces before him.

"Any questions? Right, let's go."

We had fuelled to the brim the night before. In theory, our maximum range was 150 miles out with time on the scene to meet RAAF contract requirements, but everyone except the RAAF seemed to know this was bullshit. At 150 miles we would be doing no more than a quick snatch and grab before returning to the beach.

The ship we were about to depart for was a mid-sized fishing vessel, allegedly with its rigging sufficiently clear for us to winch, allegedly advised to have the casualty ready at the winch point, allegedly aware of winch operations and so, allegedly, ready to turn into the wind before our arrival. Because so much unverifiable criteria existed on a SAR task a smart crew always built in a decent 'fudge factor' when planning such missions. Insisting that the ship, then fishing well off the continental shelf, should close to at least 130 miles was one of our key criteria for accepting the task. This would give us a very comfortable 30 minutes on scene and time for the Doc and JD to do any required stabilisation while Lars prepared the stretcher for winching. Routine operation basically, what could possibly go wrong?

About 30 minutes after leaving Pearce we entered a storm front that John had briefed us about. Despite the prior knowledge, the fact that the ordinarily steady S-76 was bouncing a bit in the turbulence added to the subtle task pressure we always experienced on the way out.

With Australia well behind us, I was running over options and emergencies in my head when the aircraft phone rang. Selecting the comms-switch to the phone position, I pushed the green receive button.

"Chopper 5, Mick speaking."

We all heard the familiar voice of the RAAF Pearce Search and Rescue Officer (SARO) in our headsets.

"Oh, hi Mick. John, I guess you're listening?"

"I'm here, Samuel." John was smiling; the SARO, although a nice bloke, wasn't always the sharpest tool in the shed.

"Of course, John I've just had a call from 2XD Radio in Sydney, they would like to do an interview about the rescue you are on the way to undertake. The RAAF are happy for you to do this, but it's up to you?"

John selected intercom for a moment.

"Anyone got a problem with that, keep the client happy if nothing else?"

He got no negative responses and a couple of sniggers from the RAAF members on board. He selected back to the telephone.

"Not a problem at this end mate."

"Thanks, John, I will give him your number."

The phone rang about five minutes later when we were in the thick of the storm. What followed was a standard interview, but John's voice vibrated slightly with the aircraft's shuddering adding to 2XD's dramatic broadcast, 'live with the captain of the rescue helicopter on the west coast, flying through the teeth of a storm, about to undertake a daring rescue.'

Twenty minutes later we were through the worst of the storm, but 2XD didn't need to know that. Anyway, the sea was still sufficiently angry to produce a large swell with lots of whitecaps. As we continued, John and Nugget, the co-pilot (a Northern Territory boy and ex-stockman) were adjusting the radar to locate the ship.

"That's gotta be him, John. Further out though, what do you reckon?

"Yep, that's him all right. Fuck! That puts him at, err, one hundred-and-forty-two-miles according to the GPS. Nugget, take us down to two thousand, and I'll give them a call."

Leaving our cruise height of five thousand feet, Nugget commenced a slow descent. We had about fifteen minutes to go.

"Sensei Dragon, Sensei Dragon, this is Chopper Five, Chopper Five on marine channel sixteen."

There was no response. Sensei Dragon should have been able to hear us at the range and height we were at, but many things could have prevented an immediate response. John tried again.

"Sensei Dragon, Sensei Dragon, this is Rescue Helicopter Chopper Five on sixteen; change your course to the east. I say again, change course to the east."

A short moment later a slightly broken voice with a heavy Japanese accent responded.

"Ye… Ch…Fie. Two cas… eady for…inch rescue…"

"Did he say two casualties?" John asked nobody in particular.

A moment later the phone rang. It was the AusSAR officer coordinating the medevac – this relatively new addition to the aircraft was proving a big bonus.

"Yes John, their shipping agent advises they have just had a man fall and hit his head. He is semi-conscious, and the captain is very concerned about him. Our medical advice is that he will need to be medevac'd and additionally, the first casualty is deteriorating. Are you able to winch two?"

Good question. John said he would let him know and asked the AusSAR officer to direct the master of the ship to turn east to close the distance. Then after cancelling the call, he twisted in his seat to face the rear cabin.

"Mick, Lars, we'll have less time on scene, what do you think?"

Lars and I made brief eye contact, and then I responded on our behalf.

"Possibly, we'll brief in the back for a double stretcher, but if it all gets too hard (low fuel), we will just take the one."

John selected his comms-selector to 'front' so that we wouldn't interrupt his notification, while we came up with a plot in the back.

"Ok," I began, "Lars down first with one stretcher and the oxy-viva. Then you Doc, with the Thomas Pack (the RAAF medical pack), and last down will be you JD with the second stretcher."

I got definite nods from all and continued.

"You determine who comes up first Doc, but remember fuel is going to be the issue here. We're heavy, and the seventy-six will be working hard. If we're lucky, John will give us fifteen minutes. So Doc, JD, if we can do a load-and-go with the casualties that would be best, but it's your call."

More positive nods, they knew the only other option was a long boat ride if we had to return to refuel, and that this may also be detrimental to the casualties. I handed over to Lars.

"When you get on the deck hang onto your gear, don't let go of it! The ship will be pitching and rolling quite a bit in this sea. I will help you on board, but disconnect quickly and keep alert ok?"

The Doc had done a number of 'aid to the community' tasks with us previously and was looking confident. JD was on her first winch job but keeping it together well. We repositioned equipment ready for the winch.

Our first look at the ship came from around a thousand feet at one mile to run. It was about a hundred and fifty feet in length, a total rust bucket, with a superstructure forward and an open deck aft. This deck was covered in winch unfriendly rigging, and a hive of activity confirmed the worse, they were still fishing and heading down swell too. This meant that a course change was unlikely, especially with the limited time we had.

As we closed on the ship, John cleared me to open the back right door, and we completed just one circuit quickly assessing the obstacles. John made a swift decision.

"Starboard side just forward of the bridge, unless anyone can see a better spot?"

At the position he identified was a small area of clear deck just ahead of the bridge superstructure. In front of this was a short mast containing wires leading to the rails and the usual anchor handling gear on deck, behind these obstacles was the bridge and the mass of rigging to handle the fishing gear. The ship would be 'the wrong way around' too, but the spot John had identified looked to be the best of a bad situation. As I spoke, I continued to monitor the movement of the ship.

"Yep, that's ok, even with the bigger swells the roll is acceptable, and I will keep Lars clear of the deck if a big one goes under as we move in..." I was a little concerned about the boat's vertical movement, or 'heave', but the key for me was John's comfort to maintain a precise hover "...are you happy to winch facing the stern?"

"I'll manage mate."

"Ok," I continued, "Winch checks please."

As we powered up the two-hundred-and-fifty-thousand dollar winch above the right cabin door, John flew an abbreviated circuit to position us for the winch. During the circuit I secured Lars, the first stretcher and oxy-viva to the winch hook. We had done this sort of winch many times, but even with Lars sitting against the left door with his gear on outstretched legs, and the Doc and JD lifting their feet clear, it was always a squeeze.

Lars was still on comms as John rolled out on final approach and gave me the conn.

"Ok boys, twelve minutes to bingo, your conn Mick."

Lars and I acknowledged the return-to-base-time with a thumb up, and then I put my head back out into the airflow.

"Roger, twelve minutes. Target is in the one o'clock with seventy to run, reduce speed and increase rate of descent. Lars and equipment secure, this will be a single-plus-stretcher and oxy-viva down to start with."

John wouldn't acknowledge my conn verbally; he would just fly as directed. Looking ahead I saw the closure rate reduce and the S-76's height above the bridge decrease. As we approached closer our rotor blades, a blurred 'disc' above me, were about 50 feet adjacent to and 60 feet above the starboard bridge wing. I was aiming to pull up with the S-76 about 40 feet above and 40 feet to the side of the winch point. This was to ensure John had a good visual reference to judge movement and obstacles by, as well as to allow me to lower Lars over water.

"Height and speed good with twenty-five to run, and twenty, reduce speed further with fifteen... ten... five... standby, and steady."

John commenced a hover in the desired position. I had a quick glance for previously unsighted obstacles, checked the disc in relation to the ship and then got on with it. 11 minutes and 45 seconds to bingo.

"Height and position good, clear to winch?"

"Clear."

This curt approval was from John, but only after receiving a thumbs up from Nugget who was monitoring instruments. Lars removed the wander-lead and unplugged his helmet.

"Moving Lars outside, height and position still good."

Lars shuffled along the floor as I winched in the slack. We both quickly re-checked the connections with his legs dangling over the edge, and I sent him on his way down. There was white water passing beneath us, a combination of breaking swell and water moving past the bow, but my focus was scanning between Lars, the winch point and both the main and tail rotor discs.

"Lars's twenty feet below, main and tail are clear, maintain this height and move right thirty."

The aircraft moved as I winched out and Lars transited over the water towards the winch spot at a reasonable speed. I held him at 5-10 feet above the boat's guardrail when this was at the top of its heave upwards.

"With fifteen to run, height and speed are good, Lars's ten feet above, winching out, five feet above, Lars's passing over the rail now, standby... and steady."

Lars was about 3 feet off the deck when the boat surged backwards as a large wave slowed its progress. His feet were immediately smashed into the rapidly heaving deck.

"Move forward, three!"

I winched out at the same time as giving the conn, knowing the deck would drop away just as quickly as it had risen. But John had moved us forward promptly resulting in Lars receiving no more than a bump as he crumpled to the deck. He disconnected quickly and held the winch hook and wire clear of the rail.

"Empty hook, clear of the deck and winching-in full speed; clear back and left to the datum, my eyes are inside, your reference."

"My reference" John acknowledged - 11 minutes and 5 seconds to bingo.

The datum was a position safely clear of the ship where the pilot could maintain position ready to move back in when directed.

The Doc had his pack ready and both it, and he were in the door in quick time. As he approached the winch spot, Lars guided the Doc's feet, and he was safely on board with the hook disconnected a moment later - 10 minutes 25 seconds to bingo.

During our preparations, I had opened the boot hatch and positioned the stretcher so that it was ready to be pulled out. As the Doc was on his way down, JD had just about pulled it entirely from the boot, as per our brief, and was presenting me her karabiner and the stretcher 'D' ring by the time my eyes were back inside.

"Ok, JD has the stretcher, clear for the final winch down?"

"Clear."

I assisted her with the bulky Ferno stretcher as she moved across the cab, and completed the pre-descent checks as she adjusted one of her leg restraints. Lars was there ready to assist, and she arrived relatively smoothly, after just one brief separation of her feet from his fingers as the boat dropped away. By the time I had the winch hook stowed, Lars was already assembling the first stretcher that was folded in half for the winch, and both the Doc and JD were inside the superstructure in search of our patients - 9 minutes and 30 seconds to bingo.

To assemble the stretcher rack, I had closed the door, and John and Nugget had departed the datum to commence a fuel-efficient orbit of the ship. As I worked away assembling the notoriously-finger-pinching-scissor-framed-apparatus, the boys checked on Lars's progress.

"Rescue Crewman Primary, this is Chopper Five, how's it going, Lars?"

A curt, Dutch-accented, response filled my earphones.

"First one will be ready for the winch shortly. The other is being moved from the sick bay just now!"

Lars, whose nickname was 'Sledgehammer', had obviously put a rocket up the Japanese seamen for not having their casualties ready, as requested.

"Roger, Lars." There was a hint of humour in John's routine acknowledgement, despite the time clock winding down to bingo. He checked on me next.

"Mick, you about ready?"

I had the stretcher rack scissor-frame assembled and had just one of its four rail attachments yet to line up. These were a pain in the arse and seemed to delight in ruining the crewie's day.

"One pin to go. Once Lars calls ready, run into the datum, and I'll take it from there."

The next voice in my headphones was Lars, and as John rolled out on final shortly afterward, I had the stretcher rack positioned on its floor rails in the open door ready to receive the first stretcher. John gave me the conn - 6 minutes and 25 seconds to bingo.

"Roger, same position as before, the Doc and Lars are standing by. Move forward and right fifteen, height is good, maintain. This will be a stretcher with an attendant, and eight to run, good line."

As my vision increased, I could see that Lars was still connecting up the last casualty restraint buckle. This completed, I saw him run a finger to each of the four buckles and check the lifting bridle too. He was working hard and fast.

"With three, standby... and steady."

Every time a helicopter launches into the air, or approaches to land or hovers during a winch, pilots will monitor the engine and gearbox performance carefully to ensure no damage is sustained. With the notoriously gutless performance of the S-76, this meant that turbine speed, identified as an 'N1' percentage for each engine, could reach its safe limitation quickly. Although manufacturers permitted short excursions into emergency power, it was never something a crew would include in a flight plan, and so as power crept up the non-flying pilot would regularly report N1 figures. On a typical day with minimum fuel and a minimum crew, N1 during a winch was typically in the 90's. And on hot days it crept towards the upper limit of 100%.

During the first lot of winches on this task, I had heard Nugget's routine reports that included N1's peaking at the 98.8% mark. I knew this was due to the high fuel load we were carrying, plus the rapid power adjustments John was using to maintain position, but as we were about to bring on two extra for the return trip, I wondered just how much fuel (weight) we would have burnt off.

"Lars is connecting the Doc and stretcher; go up two and back two, position good... thumbs up from Lars and the Doc, winching in the slack, clear to winch?"

"Clear" John acknowledged.

"Ninety-nine point one" Nugget cautioned.

Due to the tight space, I rolled the control wheel of the pendant slowly, aiming to time the lift with the next heave. Lars had the tag-line ready to prevent a stretcher spin but would assist the Doc and stretcher over the rail first.

The moment to winch-in came.

"Standby the weight… and clear of the deck." I informed.

As the wire pulled tight Nugget relayed the new data.

"Ninety-nine point five".

If the weight were too much, John would order me to abort and put them back on the deck.

"Continue."

"Roger, clear of the rail and winching in. Move back and left to the datum, Lars has positive control of the tag-line."

The Doc's waist was level with the outside of the stretcher as he hung suspended from the winch hook. The patient was, thankfully, a reasonably small man and as they closed on the belly of the S-76, I could see his face was either screwed up in pain, or he was just shitting himself. That was the Doc's job to manage though.

As they approached the cabin, I repositioned the stretcher to run parallel to the door and continued winching in slowly until the winch hook was almost at the stop. Then, with the stretcher and Doc now hanging at mid-door level, I made eye contact with the Doc and nodded. I pushed the head-end down to the point it could be rotated inwards, an alarming 35-40 degrees, as the Doc assisted as best he could. Quickly rotating about the hook, the stretcher and patient's head were now inside. I then winched out to lower the stretcher onto the rack beneath it.

"Height and position good, my eyes are inside, your reference."

"My reference."

"Ninety-nine point seven."

With our routine calls out of the way, I continued with the task.

I lifted the two rack clips into position on the sides of the stretcher and then pushed them downwards, locking the stretcher in place.

The Doc, still half in and half out indicated with a head nod that he was ready to assist.

I released the rack's wheel break with my foot and pushed the stretcher forward while winching out some slack wire and the patient was slowly traversed and rotated across the cabin, followed by the Doc who was still connected to the winch hook. Once in position against the left door, I reapplied the rack-lock to stop further travel.

The Doc, kneeling on the rear bench seat to keep clear of me, had grabbed the spare wander lead and secured it to his harness 'D' ring. With a thumb up, he then disconnected himself from the hook and commenced securing seat belts to the stretcher as per his training. I took the hook and moved back to the door, leaving the doc to his work - 4 minutes and 55 seconds to bingo.

Lars and JD were hurriedly securing the second stretcher straps as we approached overhead the winch spot. I held us with the hook in space just above the guardrail and 2m clear of the side. Lars cocked his head sideways and saw the hook. He had the Thomas Pack and oxy-viva with him, and I could almost hear his thought process; 'fuck, should have sent the oxy-viva with the Doc, what can go with this stretcher?' he elected to keep things simple.

Seeing his extended thumb, I conned us in, and he connected the stretcher only – 4 minutes 20 seconds to bingo.

Lars was ready to assist the stretcher over the rail as before but had decided that it would be quicker (and easier) for me to bring this second one in without an attendant. I took in the slack and was cleared to winch.

"One hundreds'."

It was not always easy to discern emotion behind the Northern Territory drawl of the former stockman, but I think a hint of concern was there in Nuggets report as the engines strained. However that was for he and John to deal with, while I focused on the second stretcher just coming level with the door. There would be no rack this time, and as I handed position responsibility to John, I checked to see if the Doc was clear. He was, squashed in the back left of the cabin next to the foot end of the stretcher.

Undertaking the same dip procedure, I pulled the foot end in first but needed help to get it in all the way.

"Pilot's controls, winch out."

John moved his left thumb onto the winch control on the collective lever and pushed it forward.

"Winching out."

As the stretcher descended to floor level, I pulled with two hands on the foot end bringing it further inside. When it contacted the floor I directed John to stop winching and then, moving like a two-legged spider; I tiptoed towards the head end avoiding the Doc and second casualty. The head end, alarmingly for the patient, was still outside the cabin. It was a very tight squeeze, but in the position I needed, I angled the foot end forward and with the aid of the Doc slid the stretcher home. The Doc started securing restraints straight away.

Of the four seats available on the rear bench-seat, there were just two left, and I was in one of those. Fortunately, there was a fifth seat behind John that was used when operating the infrared system. Just Jack and JD to go then – 2 minutes and 48 seconds to bingo.

With my eyes back outside, I could see that John had closed on the datum position to within half a disc, he was apparently keen to get going. Lars and JD were ready, Lars with the Thomas Pack on his back and oxy-viva in hand, both with karabiners held up.

"Whenever you're ready Mick."

Despite John's courteous manner, lurking underneath was the frustration of someone not entirely in control of the winch operation.

"Roger, move right only five, the hook is approaching the rail and Lars is reaching for it."

"One hundreds."

"Standby and steady, good height and position, Lars is connecting up now."

"One hundreds."

"Winching in the slack, clear to winch?"

"Clear."

"One hundreds."

"Standby, taking the weight... now."

"One oh ones ... one oh one point three. That's one oh one point seven... point eight."

As the engines above and behind me protested in a high whine, I was quietly amazed at Nuggets calm, almost routine reports as Lars, JD and their gear rose off the deck.

The numbers were travelling in one direction though and didn't sound like they were going to stop anytime soon, and so I expected an abort call any moment.

"Continue. Tell me when they're clear of the rail please, Mick."

As Lars and JD transitioned away from the rail, John moved the S-76 forward at fast walking pace maintaining the same height. Lars, 40 feet below, looked up with a 'what the' expression as they flew past seamen working the fishing gear on the aft deck. However, he probably had a good idea what was happening, and I was trying not to laugh.

John had utilised 30 seconds of emergency power to complete the winch but hadn't wanted to push the engines too much and risk an engine failure that would have resulted in an immediate ditching. His transition forward had eased the engine load as airflow over the disc and into the engine intakes increased. Although this action increased the risk for Lars and JD, it ultimately reduced the risk for the lot of us.

As we climbed away from Sensei Dragon heading for Murdoch hospital, south of Perth, the Doc and JD, stepping like spiders in the limited space, got to work.

Both our patients were classified Priority One. Keeping things simple, 'P1' meant that they had to be in hospital urgently for potentially lifesaving surgery. The acute appendicitis patient was in a great deal of pain, but this was both good and bad. Apparently, if the appendix ruptures pain is reduced significantly, but then the individual is exposed to the significant risk of septicaemia, as well as shock from potential blood loss. There was little the Doc and JD could do apart from providing some pain relief and prepare for the worst. To do this, large-bore bilateral intravenous lines were established, and close observations of vital signs were maintained.

The other patient was responding to voice commands appropriately, but he had a large lump on his head and an increased blood pressure. The Doc was concerned about the possibility of intracranial bleeding, but at this stage, his pupils were equal and reactive to light – a good thing.

We were flying at a lower altitude on the return journey to mitigate the risk of exacerbating trauma, but the storm front we had flown through on the way out was now centred over Perth, which was going to mean an additional challenge, but at least the high wind was now assisting our trip home. Unfortunately, though, the dark-grey-rain-filled-clouds of the storm, now surrounding the aircraft windows, were causing John and Nugget extra drama as they worked out the best way to get to the hospital.

Due to the seriousness of the situation we completed an automatic 'let-down' off the coast until we were visual with the ocean and suburbs just south of Perth. From there, we stayed low level, transiting to Murdoch Hospital down the freeway at a height not above 300 feet, about 50 feet below the base of angry storm clouds covering the city. It was pouring with rain and wind gusts made for an interesting approach to Murdoch's pad (an open car park) between light poles.

We landed with wipers working full speed and could see a bunch of hospital staff looking like drowned rats waiting to assist. Behind this lot were a couple of media crews; 2XD had apparently spread the word to their west coast counterparts. John shut down quickly, engaging the rotor brake and moments later eager hands were assisting us to unload the patients.

The Doc was handing over to the senior physician as we walked up a long path towards A&E when, to our side, I saw a media guy with a sound boom walking sideways next to his cameraman. This bloke took a step back onto what looked like another path covered in rainwater when all of a sudden the path swallowed him up. Seriously, he just disappeared! A moment later, however, it was apparent to all that he had stepped into an ornamental lake as his saucer eyes and soggy sound boom reappeared. Like a casualty of war though, he was left to his mate as the medical convoy pushed on towards its objective.

Considering the challenges of that job, a saturated sound boom operator as the only additional casualty was a good outcome. The engines sustained no damage, and both patients lived, naturally both good results; but selfishly, we were delighted to hear that the appendicitis guy had made it to theatre 'just in time'. The selfish part was reassurance that our, 'bending' of some rules had been worth it.

News Headline:

Rescue crews working in horrendous conditions evacuated two crewmen from a Japanese fishing boat that was over 140 nautical miles from land in the middle of yesterday's storm. Described as being in critical condition by medical staff from Murdoch Hospital when they arrived yesterday, both crewmen are now said to be stable and likely to make a full recovery.

Top: Stretcher dip for entry into the S76 cabin.

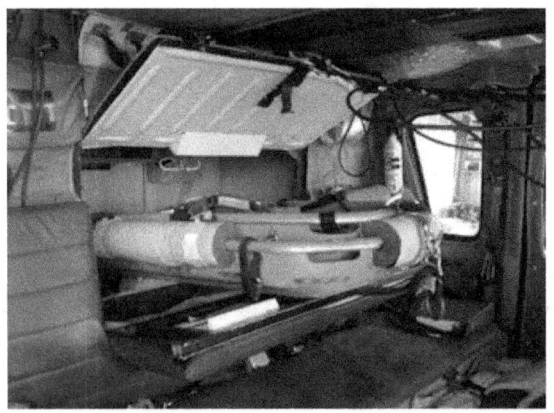 

Bottom: Second stretcher in the boot-hatch, main stretcher secured to rack.

What can possibly go wrong

Top: Aircrewman and pilot practicing communication skills in the Exmouth ranges

Bottom: Double stretcher positioning

CHAPTER 17

Helicopter Rescue (Xanana Gusmao's Been Shot)

THE SMALL BRASILIA TWIN-ENGINE TURBOPROP was approaching the high mountains of East Timor from the southeast a little over an hour after leaving Darwin. Unfortunately, these mountains were covered in cloud, so I hoped the pilots had improved their capability to fly in IMC (Instrument Meteorological Conditions) after hearing a frightening story told by one of the UN drivers.

"Mate, they were reading the approach-plate the wrong way and were about to descend, turning back towards the mountains! I was in the jump-seat as I knew these blokes and saw what they were doing and so quickly suggested they reverse their turn…"

The story from Roscoe, one of the CHC Australia captains serving on the United Nations Aero Medical Evacuation (AME) contract was fresh in my mind as our descent commenced in thick cloud. I was towards the back of the full cabin in an aisle seat and therefore could only see grey outside the small airliner's window as our slightly turbulent descent commenced. Looking ahead up the narrow aisle towards the cockpit door I guessed the pilots had the same view out of their window too and I realised my palms were moistening. Well, I figured, if they did fly us into a mountain at least they would die first.

Comoro airport on the outskirts of Dili was pretty basic. Located on the coast to the west of the town centre, dense vegetation surrounded it on the ocean side that contained a scattering of small, bare-bones dwellings. On the town side were the prominent and steeply rising brown mountains and the flat green belt of East Timorese 'suburbia'. Closer to the airport I could see a basic car park, an adjacent road leading to a large roundabout and a mixture of burnt-out and what appeared to be run-down buildings. However, despite the mainly overcast sky, the ocean to the north was deep blue and Atauro Island off the coast looked beautiful.

As the Brasilia decelerated down the runway we passed several white UN fixed-wing and rotary-wing aircraft, including a gigantic Russian MI-26 helicopter. It was twice the length of the Brasilia and was used for heavy-lift tasking all over the country. In amongst the UN aircraft were some green military helicopters and a collection of commercial aircraft; the majority of these craft appeared to be supported by makeshift hangars and donger-type accommodation.

The UN had been in East Timor since June 1999 as the United Nations Assistance Mission East Timor (UNAMET) after the populace had pushed for independence from Indonesia. This first mission was 'blue hats only' as a cautious lead up towards a transition process where the Indonesian military would withdraw from the country. The tension at the time was acute due to uncertainty over who controlled the military and therefore what the military may do.

The Indonesian military, the TNI, had been maintaining control of the country by force up to this point. An example of the force they were willing to use in order to hold onto power was first revealed to the world in October 1975 when five Australian journalists were executed in the remote town of Balibo. Indonesia denied the atrocity, and as a result, numerous Australian governments entered into a period of political tiptoeing with our nearest and most powerful neighbour. Tension flared again in November 1991 following an incident at the

Santa Cruz Cemetery that became known as the 'Dili Massacre'. Although Australia's foreign minister at the time, Gareth Evans, tried to downplay it, independent reports confirmed that the TNI and their militia forces slaughtered 271 people.

Finally, after much condemnation from around the world, the Indonesians agreed to uphold the request for independence and the UN stepped up its work under the United Nations Transition Administration East Timor (UNTAET). Under the leadership of Sergio Vieira de Mello, a very well respected UN operator, real progress was made, and in late September through October 1999, the International Force East Timor (INTERFET) lead by Australian Major General Peter Cosgrove entered the country to uphold the peace as the TNI withdrew.

As part of the UN establishing its presence and capability early on, helicopter AME contracts and general cargo, or 'hash-and-trash' contracts were awarded before INTERFET arrived. In the months that followed, the Australians operating the white painted CHC aircraft came to realise the brutality of the TNI and, despite what the worlds media were implying, a realisation of the fact that the Indonesians were not going to leave with smiles and handshakes.

At one stage during this *peaceful* process, the TNI apparently took a fuel truck down the main drag of Dili and pumped jet fuel into the houses of known or suspected FRETILIN (resistance fighters) sympathises, torching them as they moved on. The sound of machine guns during the day and night was commonplace and bodies were regularly seen in the streets.

This was a time of immense uncertainty for the unarmed civilian crews based at the smaller heliport closer to the centre of Dili, but not much was mentioned of this to the outside world as the TNI had scared off many journalists. At one point, after the TNI had been firing their weapons outside the CHC crew's hangar in an effort to frighten them (they had), there was a vote where all pilots, engineers and support staff determined whether they would stay or go. Amazingly, they voted to stay. The rationale being they did not want to let down UN personnel they were supporting at remote mountain sites.

Unlike the Australian Defence Force (ADF), these aircrews were receiving no hazardous duty pay, just a routine allowance for being away from home. With this in mind then it is perhaps worth discussing a couple of incidents that the civilian pilots and their crews undertook in unarmed and unarmoured helicopters before the ADF arrived.

Rob and Chris were flying a routine re-supply mission when they noticed a load of civilians evacuating their village from an approaching militia force. This was one of the TNI sponsored groups responsible for the mass slaughter. The pilots, 500-feet above, could see that the militia would soon catch the villagers and therefore, upon their own initiative, they decided to act. Knowing they were breaking rules that could see their pilot licences withdrawn, they flew low over the approaching militia and then tracked away from the villagers to commence a low hover over some jungle. The militia, not the sharpest tools in the shed, took the bait believing that the small Bell 212 helicopter was about to evacuate a village load of people. And so with the militia's change of course, the boys maintained their ploy long enough for the villagers to escape.

Another example was more or less sanctioned by the UN air operations commander.

Captain Harold Pammer and other Australians flying two Super Puma helicopters were tasked to the village of Liquica, west of Dili, to evacuate the entire community. A large militia force had been reported approaching and UN commanders were sure another massacre was about to occur.

Harold and his colleagues had landed on the Liquica soccer pitch and were in the process of carefully loading men, women and children into their 18-seat aircraft. It was estimated there were around 60-80 people in all and, believing they had several hours; Harold and the other crews were working on completing the task in two trips, when suddenly, a commander orbiting above them in a smaller helicopter relayed an urgent instruction.

"Militia are only minutes away, leave now! I say again, leave now!"

Harold looked at the tree line about 200m away and saw armed men coming out of the scrub. His crewman had seen this too, as did the other crew. Moving quickly they dispensed with polite boarding instructions and pushed villagers onto both aircraft as pilots brought idling rotors to flying speed. Picture a Tokyo platform guard pushing people onto a train - that was the crewmen as they pushed all the villages onto the aircraft.

The militia was discharging their homemade weapons by the time the crewmen had squeezed on board via the pilots' doors, and both pilots made use of emergency power to get into the air with a short run along the soccer pitch.

Throughout this ordeal, the UN commander above was reinforcing his directive for them to leave, but the dumb-arse Australians ignored him. Harold and his colleagues received a UN citation for their efforts that day, but no one heard about it in Australia, or anywhere else in the world for that matter.

The day I arrived in Dili one overcast afternoon, the 6th of June 2002, the dust of the transition had settled. The ADF was well established and were supported by other military forces including, Kiwis, Portuguese, Jordanians and Fijians - much to the relief of the UN AME crews. Although the TNI was no longer in the country, security briefs regularly provided updates of incursions along the border with West

Timor. So, although I was technically 'deployed overseas' my job was to be reasonably tame, with just routine AME and occasional resupply missions to the more remote military bases. What could possibly go wrong?

Fred Trafford, a former ADF, 5 Aviation Regiment aircrewman who'd served on Blackhawks, had been a CHC crewie for several years. He met me at Comoro after I came through the very antiquated customs process and we drove away from the airport in a beat-up white sedan with a red cross on each door and a red light on the roof. This was the AME crew vehicle and was equipped with a siren too, all improvised by the CHC boys over the years to expedite transfer from the CHC 'house' to the heliport. The traffic they had to maneuver past during an AME response consisted of slow-moving beat up busses and cars, motorbikes, pigs, dogs and the occasional buffalo, all of whom didn't pay much attention to either siren or light on the kilometre drive to the heliport.

The main drag looked more run down than it had from the air and I was to see numerous examples of the TNI's handiwork as we past charred skeletons that used to be two-story houses next to plush homes with tiled verandas.

About five minutes after leaving the airport, we'd had a good run, and about halfway to the centre of town, Fred sounded the car's horn. Fifty meters ahead and on the right side of the road a large blue steel gate slowly opened, sliding into an eight-foot-high wall surrounding our compound. The wall next to the gate had CHC hand painted in a kind of child-like scrawl, but apart from that, it looked no different to some other compounded buildings along the main drag.

Fred waved to the security guard, a young local bloke that didn't inspire any confidence, and we drove up to the house positioned towards the back of the somewhat untidy yard, 60m from the gate. The house was a white single-story building that reminded me of an old colonial mansion, albeit a smaller version. White pillars were supporting the black tile roof over a white drive-through carport and a wide, white porcelain-tiled veranda, but in front of the house were some modern additions. There was a beach volleyball court with lights for night games and an above ground pool equipped with decking and pool bar.

Fred saw my smile.

"You reckon you can cope for the two-week swing Mick?"

Behind the house were a series of dongers, an ablution block and a similar arrangement was set up behind the pool. New arrivals slept in the dongers, but everyone used the facilities in the house. These included a TV room; games room with car racing and shoot-kill-maim entertainment, a basic gym and just to be sure, another bar too. This one had an old wooden canoe above it and was, appropriately, called the Canoe Bar. Meals were served in a large dining room to accommodate the 20-ish CHC staff that was there during any given two-week swing supporting the UN contract and an oil and gas contract operating more Super Pumas from Comoro. Marie, a Darwin girl who could hold her own with the boys, ran the kitchen. She had a couple of locals employed as kitchen hands and prepared excellent food all the time I was there.

After dropping off my bags, I asked Fred if I had to throw any money in a kitty for the upkeep of all the gear. He smiled and advised that the social club took care of that. The social club turned out to be a beat up old road roller that came with the house. The boys gave it a bit of a service, replaced one or two parts and then hired it out to the UN for the ongoing road repairs around the country. Suffice to say; the social club had paid for most of the additions to the house including a large generator and three other staff cars. Fred's earlier question had obliviously been rhetorical.

We drove to the heliport to check out CHC's set up and slowed as a couple of pigs and one buffalo crossed in front of us. I made some joke about traffic and Fred gave some critical advice.

"If you ever hit a civilian don't stop. This is the advice from the UN. Notify them straight away when you are clear of the area, but don't stop. If you do, the locals will blame you and will likely beat you pretty bad. Worse than a civilian though, don't ever hit one of their pigs or buffalos!"

Dili was a different place all right, but I knew immediately that I was going to enjoy touring there.

We entered the heliport past a security gate manned by the Portuguese. The soldier who checked our credentials looked very casual. I have never been a soldier, but his weapon was slung nonchalantly, and he had an arrogance about him that didn't encourage respect.

Driving up to a large hangar I saw one of the white Super Pumas being worked on by our engineers and some locals. Out by the short runway were two, Bell 212's and another Super Puma, and on the far side of the runway were three Russian MI-8 helicopters. We pulled up at the duty 212 aircraft, and Fred gave me the tour. It was a standard AME setup; when tasked we would be taking a RAAF doctor and nurse who were now part of the United Nations Mission of Support East Timor (UNMISET) established after the long awaited independence ceremony back in May.

Typically, I would have flown into the country in the afternoon after the duty (only) crewie had flown out in the morning. I would read his handover notes at the house and then commence my swing, but as this was my first trip, Fred had stayed back a day to give me the full tour. This was concluded with a trip to see Jesus, a large Rio-type statue to the east of Dili's large bay on a prominent headland.

Halfway back to the house Fred's phone rang. It was the UN Air Operations officer.

"We have a job, Mick, bus rollover near Gleno."

I assumed this meant I would hold the fort at the heliport as Fred took the job so that space would be available for casualties in the machine. To my delight, however, Fred wanted me to come along too. I was getting a pretty good handover.

15 minutes later we were in the air climbing over the initial mountain range. Behind this the mountains climbed even higher, the highest

in the country is around 10,000 feet. In the back was an experienced RAAF doctor about to complete his second 3-month tour and a nurse with similar exposure to the country.

Roscoe was flying, and after around a 15-minute flight from Dili, we were descending between some lush green hills, covered in high trees with occasional cleared areas containing a few huts and pens holding pigs and buffalo. Ahead I could see a large village in amongst more lush green landscape. It had a soccer field that we were approaching – there were soccer pitches in just about every significant village, and they served as very suitable helipads.

As we closed on the landing area, I realised that hundreds, if not thousands of people were surrounding the pitch, and around the permitter of the field were about twenty soldiers with rifles pointing towards the crowd.

"Hey Fred," I asked on intercom while pointing to the soldiers, "I thought you said the unrest had died down?"

"Just routine security Mick, probably good with it being market day."

The crowds were there for the weekly market where villagers had travelled from the surrounding area along narrow and unstable roads – the cause of our bus rollover. This slightly alarming sight for the new-boy was in fact just an average market day in Gleno – but why the need for soldiers?

After landing, the soldiers separated the crowd, and an ambulance was driven onto the pitch; by 'ambulance' I mean a Toyota Troup Carrier with a red cross on the door. There were no casualties inside and not a lot of medical equipment either, this vehicle was to transport us to the Gleno hospital. We loaded on two stretchers and the Doc's gear and headed into the multitude of people at a snail's pace. After five minutes the driver gave up, we were going nowhere.

"It looks like we are going to have to walk." Suggested the Doc.

Collecting a stretcher each, Fred and I followed the Doc, nurse and Roscoe through the throng of East Timorese on a shopping spree.

The driver was going to attempt to find another way, and so we headed off alone, leaving the co-pilot with the aircraft.

As we bumped and squeezed past hot sweaty bodies (my flight suit was dripping), I suddenly realised there were no soldiers with us, and this caused a degree of concern. I was to find out later that their primary function was to prevent damage to the helicopter – another newboy anxiety relieved.

Leaving the central market area, we moved up a narrow street with overhanging frangipani and other lush greenery (plants aren't my thing) to where a basic white painted stone building stood out from the rest. It had no glass in the windows, and a crowd of people were sitting on the steps leading up to its main entrance. Standing there was a woman who could have been in her late forties to mid-fifties; she was the sole Australian nurse in town and appeared to have her hand's full judging by her opening remarks to the Doc.

"The bus rollover you were advised of was actually a tip-truck. It had fifty people on board when it rolled down the mountainside. I have about thirty in here, three of which are critical."

As we walked through the un-air conditioned fly buzzing passageway, I saw that people with broken arms and legs, and lacerations lined the corridor. Some were moaning some were just sitting patiently. The nurse continued her brief.

"Most of them have just headed back up the mountain, some of these will likely give up too, but the most critical ones are in here."

We turned into a room containing a couple of hospital beds. The first casualty the Doc went to had a tension pneumothorax, flail ribs and head trauma, the second had a compound femur and pelvic fracture. Both casualties were poorly perfused, displaying classic shock symptoms and were barely responding to commands. The nurse had done all she could without adequate medical supplies, and alarmingly this included no oxygen.

Many of the casualties would be disfigured for life and others would just die. During subsequent tours, I was to occasionally see people with deformed limbs who I assumed did not get fractures set correctly. These sights became pretty commonplace and were in part due to the standard of care afforded by the TNI and now, the East Timorese government battling to return to a stable democracy; this level of care never really improved during my tours in 2002.

We took the first two casualties and transferred them to the UN hospital in Dili where they had a reasonable chance of full recovery. During my last swing in 2002 locals were no longer getting this service; instead, they were taken to the local Dili hospital where the chance of success was not as high.

I drove Fred to the airport the next day; waved him goodbye and my first swing in the country officially began.

A typical day at the house commenced with a communal breakfast where Marie would always provide a broad range of tropical fruit and the usual western dishes. As people munched away or sipped a coffee the differing flight schedules for the day were discussed.

The oil and gas crews started early on their 'crew-change' flights, and the UN Puma crews were pretty much out all day on hash and trash operations around the country. On these tasks, they would have the rear cabin stripped of seats and replaced with stores covered with a cargo net, and beneath the same Puma attached to a length of wire was a similar 'underslung' load. Local blokes had been trained to assist with this type of operation, and they did a pretty good job too.

Unless a training flight was scheduled, the AME crew had a more sedate day. After checking the aircraft, it was hurry up and wait, which typically consisted of overdue paperwork, email correspondence and the occasional UN meeting. The first one of these I went to, a security briefing, was not what I had expected.

The senior RAAF officer was running things, and the assembled flight crews listened in reasonably politely. When he stated that the threat level was low, however, there were many whispered conversations from people who disagreed. UN police (international officers in blue berets from around the world) who we met in remote sites would disagree too. These blokes often reported rising tensions and that *it* would erupt sooner or later. As the RAAF officer was concluding, he asked if there were any other questions. A Canadian who flew a fixed-wing spoke first.

"Yes, ok, what's happening about Comoro's air traffic control," There were several grunts of acknowledgement, "Because they generally give you incorrect information and when we challenge it they just go bloody quiet!"

This was an apparently long-standing issue, and many other voices joined in. The RAAF officer did his best to reinforce UN policy of training locals so that true independence could be achieved, but for the men and women who flew close to high terrain that was often covered by cloud the official agenda of the UN wasn't cutting it. Voices became raised, and the meeting was getting a tad out of control when the RAAF officer spoke in his command voice.

"Ok! I know, it's not good enough." Voices were lowered, and he continued. "But hey, that's why you're here. Apparently you people have the necessary experience to manage a less than perfect situation. So, if you're not happy with it, leave."

There was silence for a few moments, and then the meeting erupted again, but he had made a good point. East Timor was not Sydney, London, Vancouver or New York; it was a third world country slowly emerging from decades of brutal rule and people operating there were expected to put on their 'big boy pants' and deal with it.

Evenings at the house consisted of movies, action games, swimming in the pool, or simply, drinks at the bar. Such activities supporting a complete wind down at the end of a long day; unless you were the only crewie on permanent standby and therefore not permitted to drink! When I tell of such hardship to blokes I now work with who'd spent many a mozzie infested night on patrol along the border, as you may have guessed, there is little sympathy.

On Wednesday and Saturday nights things were a little different from the routine relaxation at the end of the working day though. You see these were 'UN nights' where just about anybody stationed in Dili who had time off came to the house. There were volleyball competitions, drinking, swimming, and more drinking and; you probably get the picture, a gigantic party was entered into twice a week. During one of these parties an AME pilot, who will remain nameless, was about to demonstrate his famous party piece – stopping a ceiling fan with his head.

"It's just a matter of understanding aerodynamics you blokes."

Despite the Jack Daniels slur from the AME driver (and former United States Navy test pilot), the crowd were intrigued. Crouching on a chair our hero slowly extended his legs and the crowd's roar dropped to a whisper. Now usually, this worked a treat, and more Jack Daniels was consumed as the crowd cheered, but tonight wasn't as successful, probably due to too much Jack Daniels beforehand. A significant gash later, this was to be the last performance of the now infamous fan trick.

This didn't slow the tempo of Wednesdays and Saturdays, where even some people still on duty managed to find a way to attend a CHC house party. An ADF Blackhawk crew came up with a pretty good plan.

Flying in from Wallaby Base on the other side of the country, they just happened to break down at Comoro one Wednesday afternoon and were unable to repair their aircraft. They advised their superiors that they would see if CHC engineers could assist and headed off to the house, killing time. Around 6 pm the flight crew further advised their Wallaby masters that, 'unfortunately CHC couldn't assist', and were subsequently informed that the necessary spares would have to be flown to Comoro in the morning due to a hectic night flying schedule – that they already knew about. Oh well, party time!

I had never worked with Russians before. As a kid in the navy they were the enemy of NATO and our days and nights were spent preparing to fight them, so I wasn't sure what to expect. What brilliant blokes they turned out to be, their equipment, however? While Russian machinery was mainly sturdy and very reliable, it was not what we were used to, and this was to prove a challenge for some of the RAAF.

When our AME aircraft was down for maintenance the RAAF medical team were assigned to one of the Russian MI-8's, and I was to piss myself laughing when a medic relayed a winch brief she had received from a Russian flight mechanic.

Walking around to the ramp of the MI-8 they saw a pot-bellied mechanic sitting on a deck chair inside the helicopter smoking a cigarette. They advised him who they were and the purpose of their visit and the mechanic slowly rose from his relaxed position.

The medic noticed there were no seats in the back.

"Where do we sit?"

The mechanic turned his head slowly, pointing to the floor with his chin whilst exhaling smoke.

"You can sit anyvere."

The rest of the brief tempo remained much the same and was coming to an end when they realised there was no rescue winch on the helicopter. Not fazed at all, the mechanic escorted them, at a very casual stroll, to the Russians' hangar. Here he opened a locker to reveal a winch mounted on a bracket. It was dust covered, broken strands could be seen on the winch wire, and the RAAF crew were understandably alarmed.

"Is that, err, serviceable?"

The mechanic shrugged his shoulders, took a long drag on his cigarette and exhaled slowly while speaking.

"I myself vos not going to use it, but you can if you vont to."

My first official job during that initial swing was to evacuate a villager who had sustained spinal injuries. The fact a severe kicking from other villagers caused these injuries and that these people were still at the site of the attack meant that UN police would be meeting us on a ridgeline above the village to escort us to the hut in question.

The ridge we landed on was small, but clear of large trees and so the 212 fit reasonably well, despite the end of the tail boom being positioned over ground that descended rapidly to a valley far below. On the downslope of the ridge, I noticed a narrow path leading into head-high coarse grass as we commenced the gear unload. Up this path came two UN police officers with backpacks; they looked buggered. One from New York, the other Melbourne, it turned out they had walked from a neighbouring village for about five hours, starting before first light on a journey much shorter to our own, which had us taken less than fifteen minutes.

We picked up all the gear and began the slow plod through the long grass to the village. The cops advised it was about 150m away, but less than half this was covered when I realised I had left the Kendrick Extrication Device (KED) back in the machine. The KED was designed for extracting spinal cases from wrecked motor vehicles and would be very useful as our casualty was positioned somewhere inside a pole-style hut, 3m off the ground. Feeling like a bit of dick, I handed the stretcher to the medic and jogged back up the ridge.

After retrieving the KED, I was halfway back, walking quickly when I came to a small clearing. Standing in it, blocking my path, were five young blokes of around the 18-20 age group. Wearing jeans, some were bare-chested others had ratty old t-shirts, but they all held machetes and were swinging them loosely at hip level.

Hmm, I never got this brief in the handover…

I had a brief recollection of a police citation on my elder brother's wall describing how "…Constable Alex Macfarlane…" had used words to defuse a tense situation where a samurai wielding man had severed another's hand". Unfortunately, Indonesian/Portuguese plus a range of dialects were not my strong point.

There was no sign of the cops, and I felt my pulse increase as I got to within four meters of them, as my mind ran away with imagined 'news reports'.

'Police found blood trails believed to be an indication that air-crewman Macfarlane met a grizzly death...'

Fortunately, I remembered my old Melbourne Port Emergency Service (PES) trainer, Alf, and some advice he had passed on.

Alf had been tasked to assist our first aid officers to a ship where the captain had been assaulted. When he arrived, he found several rather large islander crewmembers blocking the gangway; these were the blokes who had attacked the captain.

"Mate, I just trusted the authority of my uniform and pushed through them. It worked; I guess the western authority figure carried more weight than their islander captains."

With Alf's words in my head, I reflected on my flight suit. It had three red bars on each shoulder, an Australian flag below the red bars and my crewie's half-wing on the left chest; hopefully, these were enough to impress the men before me. Despite Alf's words, I still had the KED in front ready to be used as a shield and pushed on with a purpose in my eyes to hide the actual fear bubbling inside me. To my relief though, all they did was stare with vague expressions as I edged past.

The casualty was located in the furthest corner of the hut from its vertical ladder. He definitely needed the KED too, as reduced sensation in his legs confirmed possible spinal injuries. In addition to this, he had more obvious injuries consisting of an open head wound and bruising around his back. I drew on more PES training combined with PJ/MFB skills to rig a line and lower the bloke to the medic. She eased the KED-restrained-casualty feet first into our standard stretcher as I slowly inched the rope from above. Together, we had him secured and ready to transport in short order. There was a slow plod back uphill to the 212, but apart from that the rest of the job was routine.

When discussing the machete event though, back at the house, I found myself on the wrong end of some severe piss taking.

"Fuck me, Mick, you were lucky to get home alive…." and "Hey, dickhead, it's called a 'Dili-Leatherman'; every local carries one around here if you hadn't noticed?"

A number of swings later I was to find out that some of the locals carried more than a Dili-Leatherman.

As part of our handover, Fred had given me instruction on Night Vision Goggle (NVG) use. In Australia, we were not permitted to use them as our company believed they were too dangerous. Instead, we used the Nightsun searchlight that, as far as anyone who had used NVG before would advise, was an old, somewhat obsolete tool. Simply put, with NVG night turned to day, albeit a hazy green day that became blurry in the rain and gave the impression you were further from the ground than you actually were. Although this depth perception issue did, in fact, provide a safety fudge factor as new pilots and crewman made cautious approaches to the ground.

One of our check and training captains, Croaly, was forever pushing NVG limits for the AME operation. Officially, we were to use them for just transit along designated low-level night routes between 'A' and 'B', but Croaly was very aware that this limited our capability to undertake night rescues in confined areas. He intended to build us up to the point where we could perform any SAR/medivac task the UN offered us, but unfortunately, some conservative management back in Australia kept pulling the handbrake on Croaly's plans. What this meant in an operational sense was that AME crews had to reject tasks and people suffered as a consequence.

Ironically, just about all AME helicopters in Australia today operate with NVG and people who have never used a Nightsun before wonder how its operation was ever condoned previously.

I was at the house when Roscoe yelled across to me after putting down a phone. It was a job to Baucau, a moderate hop east of Dili along the coast to pick up a 'superficial gunshot casualty'.

A new RAAF doctor met us at the heliport, this would be his first job, and he was accompanied by an old-hand nursing officer I knew from RAAF Pearce. She wasn't at all fazed by the task, bored almost, but hey, as first jobs go the Doc was being broken in gently.

Baucau had a relatively grand soccer pitch with some tiered seating and a wall around its perimeter. On final approach, I saw a couple of medical vehicles (more Troup carriers) near an opening in the wall to the pitch, and we landed about 30m from them. As per usual the Doc and nurse headed over, and I picked up the stretcher to follow along a minute or so behind. By the time I got there, I could see this was not a routine job; our superficial wound turned out to be a bullet entry point in the centre of the forehead without an exit wound. The Doc's assessment confirmed that the casualty was still responding to pain, although inappropriately. The inappropriate response to painful stimuli indicating significant brain trauma – Derrrr, he was shot in the head?

The poor Doc was under the pump as he tried to intubate the casualty; he was struggling to insert the tube, but no matter how he adjusted the metal Laryngoscope designed to aid this process he couldn't do it. Offering a solution, the nurse had suggested paralysing their patient and was preparing the required drugs as the Doc battled on.

With not much to do as my stretcher was assembled waiting for its casualty, I just watched the Doc and nurse do their thing when suddenly a whole load of Timorese-Ninja-Turtles streamed into the ground and began taking up positions around its perimeter. The Ninja's, special response police, had been given their derogatory name due to the significant amount of black body armour they wore, which included a big helmet with grilled visor.

Their presence was a bit over the top, I thought naively, when Roscoe jogged over from the 212 and filled me in.

"Didn't you hear the gunshots and ricochets?" I hadn't; ignorance was bliss. Roscoe continued "There's a gunfight going on down in the town between some former FRETILIN blokes and the cops, it started with this bloke being shot apparently. Air ops are sending the QRF."

The Quick Reaction Force was made up of whichever battalion had the duty, and today it was the Fijians. The no longer routine task the Doc and nurse were undertaking had just stepped up another notch, but the Doc was still having troubles with the airway. He needed to have this established before we became airborne if the casualty was to have any chance of survival, because definitive in-flight treatment was much harder.

As he battled away the first of two MI-8s commenced an approach to the centre of the field, but as their downwash was going to create havoc for the Doc, Roscoe got on the radio and directed them to the other end of the pitch. Moments later, seeing a gaggle of gigantic Fijian warriors spilling out of the back of the machines was a relief, and then watching them deploy through the grounds entrance towards the unseen danger was even better. Either way, the Doc finally got his tube in, and we loaded the casualty onto the 212 without me ever hearing a single shot.

As we were strapping in, the local medical team asked if we could take a friend of the casualty to Dili with us. We had a spare seat and so not giving it much more thought, we took him too. This poor bloke just sat there watching his mate, not moving, just lying there, alive, but hardly stable and in a very critical condition. I found myself feeling sorry for him.

Arriving back at the heliport there was no waiting ambulance, as per usual operations. We had to call one and when this turned up no one seemed to give two shits about the casualty or the events of the day. Had we missed something? The casualty was transferred to the Dili hospital, and I never heard how he fared, but interestingly we were to find out that his mate was perhaps not such a good mate after all.

It turned out that he was, in fact, the bloke who had shot him. We had carried this gunman, unrestrained, without so much as a rudimentary frisking for weapons, in the back of our helicopter. What elite professionals we were!

The reason for the gunfight was interesting. After decades of fighting the TNI, when peace finally came many of the FRETILIN blokes assumed they would be looked after and assigned functional roles in the newly independent government - police positions and the like. It didn't work out like that though. Worse, some of the people who had apparently sucked up to the TNI were now in police uniform, and so the FRETILIN blokes figured they could change that.

As the UN police had warned us, there was an underlying tension and trouble was brewing.

One morning we had an early mission to take five Portuguese soldiers to a patrol area. This was a remote mountainside where we merely landed, offloaded them and then headed off back to the heliport, but as I had passed them their packs I was surprised at how light they were. My only relative experience was carrying a 'land equipment pack' as a PJ, but as my pack had been far heavier I wondered what they hoped to achieve with what amounted to just a bushwalking daypack and a weapon each.

Later that morning we were tasked to recover an AUSBAT (Australian Battalion) soldier who had been bitten by a snake. When his mates passed me this bloke's pack, I had to strain with all my might to pull it up to the cabin as it contained enough ammunition for a sustained fire-fight and plenty of water. The ADF obviously did things differently to their Portuguese counterparts.

Standing by the 212 at the heliport later in the afternoon I was doing a routine check of SAR gear and looking forward to a swim back at the pool. It was an unusually hot day, and I had just noticed a large column of smoke to the east. Smoke in Dili was a daily occurrence as the locals were always burning something or other, but the column I was watching seemed bigger. As I began a scan around the horizon, I noticed another similar smoke column, when the duty phone in my pocket rang.

"This is UN Air Operations; we believe that Xanana Gusmao's been shot. We are sending a military intelligence officer to you, and we want you to get airborne to provide a SITREP on potential rioting in progress."

Fucking hell! Xanana Gusmao was the very popular President of East Timor; if he'd been shot, it would be the trigger for pent-up frustrations to be released. After acknowledging the call, I quickly did a three-sixty scan of the horizon. There were around half a dozen large smoke columns, and they were getting bigger. I called the duty crew and then started pulling tie-downs and bungs from the machine, but one-handed, I had another call to make.

"Hey babe, if you see a shit fight on the news tonight don't worry we have a perfect getaway vehicle."

Mandy interrupted me.

"What do you mean? There's nothing on the news."

I realised I was being a dick.

"Oh, ok, probably nothing, but there is a bit of a riot building here that's all. It may look worse than it is on the news. I didn't want you to worry."

We said goodbyes and a couple of minutes later the boys pulled up. There was a quick discussion on 'plan B' if things got out of control, and I suddenly realised my passport and wallet were locked in my room. Worst case, we would collect up all the CHC staff we could and head out of town, or over to Wallaby Base if needed, but hopefully, that wouldn't be required. All the same, it was nice to have a plan 'B' ahead of time.

As the boys were completing their pre-start checks, a UN 4WD carrying one Australian soldier arrived. He gave us a quick brief on the situation: although there had been a report of Xanana Gusmao being shot, it had not been confirmed. There was significant rioting, and a large shop owned by a government minister was one of the first to be torched, crowds were building, their intent unknown, but it was suspected government property/personnel were their targets.

We were airborne shortly after with a directive to orbit the town and provide situation reports (SITREP's) to both UN Air Operations and military intelligence via our passenger's radio.

Andy, the base manager, was captain and Dave was co-pilot. Andy got Dave to fly while he worked the radios, as these were reasonably busy from the get-go.

The smoke was coming from several buildings that the mob had set light to. Estimated to be 500 strong from the initial reports that were supplied to us, the mob was probably closer to 200, or at least the group we were orbiting above was about that number. Buildings were well alight and revealed the path the mob had taken; they were now heading up the main drag, past our house, to a police station around 300m on the airport side of the compound. Inside this building were around a dozen non-FRETILIN police officers barricading themselves in, and glancing up and down the main drag, I saw that this usually bustling road was empty.

Andy and the army passenger were busy communicating the situation, but looking up and down the road, it was blatantly obvious there was no cavalry on the way. Then suddenly, a fire erupted in the middle of the crowd that had been growing in size around the police station. Someone had set fire to a motorbike's fuel tank and the mob, even more excited, pulled back from the flames chanting and waving.

Debris was being thrown at the windows, and they were trying to break in the door, but still, nobody was coming down the street to assist.

I had the horrible realisation that I was probably going to watch people be dragged out of the building below us and killed on the street when, reinforcing my fears, another motorbike was set on fire.

Then hope appeared, but not much, as a lone UN 4WD approached from the airport side of the road.

"That's our guys' in the Land Cruiser." The army officer advised on the intercom.

Was this a joke? One 4WD to counter a mob of 200 angry people possibly intent on murder. I hoped additional forces were responding.

The 4WD slowed down to fast walking pace as it got to within 30m of the mob, slowing further it approached to about 10m, at which point the mob suddenly acknowledged them. Instantly the rioters engulfed the 4WD!

I looked at the army intelligence bloke who was anxiously issuing instructions on the radio. From my vantage point at the open door, I could see that back on the ground there appeared no easy escape for the occupants of the 4WD.

Don't get out of that vehicle! Don't get out of that fucking vehicle!! Despite my silent pleas, doors opened, and I watched four men exit with hands up, gesturing, 'hey, calm down', but the mob didn't appear interested. Just when I thought these men had no hope a very calm Australian voice came through my headset from the ground.

"We are confident we won't be engaged."

Who the fuck was this, and what on earth made him feel so confident about his situation, had he not read the reports from Baucau? Around a minute later the same voice came back at a significantly higher pitch.

"Shots fired, shots fired!"

Below us, I saw one of the 4WD occupants moving for cover behind a wall; I could no longer see the others. Turning, I saw Andy very busy on the radio, and the army officer was likewise. The main drag was still empty both ways.

"Dave, what do you reckon, how about a quick-stop on top of the crowd, it may give those blokes a chance?"

CHC's management would not have condoned the maneuver I had suggested to Dave. It required him to approach the mob fast at a low level and then pitch up aggressively to bring the machine to a rapid halt. Such a maneuver would be very loud and produce significant downwash onto those below. The intent was obviously to provide distraction and a chance for those four men to escape, but it would also expose our aircraft to the range of whatever weapons they possessed, not to mention the risk of clipping unseen wires.

Dave had pretty much the same view of the intersection as I had through the large 212 pilot-door window. With just a couple of seconds thought he began a descending turn that would have us running in about 20 feet above rooftop height. As we approached the intersection, I called 'on top' and felt the 'G' forces as he pitched up. With movement arrested, I looked below and saw the wild, angry eyes of men waving machetes, but only for a moment, as Dave pushed the nose over to clear the area quickly.

We climbed back to 500 feet and looked back to the intersection. I couldn't see any of the 4WD occupants and feared the worst, but then all of a sudden the mob scattered up alleyways like cockroaches caught in a light. In their wake, there was just burning motorbikes and rubbish.

Looking up the road, I saw the reason for the hurried exit; the Ninja Turtles were on the way. They were hanging on the side of their truck, weapons on hips like something out of a John Wayne movie, but they had served their purpose.

Andy advised we had to depart immediately due to low fuel and so I never saw what happened when they reached the police station.

Minutes later, after landing and shut down we had a 'fucking hell' moment – you know, did that really happen? The UN 4WD entered the heliport shortly afterwards, and the army officer headed over to talk to his colleagues who were, fortunately, all there, very wide-eyed, but thankfully uninjured. Another plus was a perimeter of Fijian QRF now deploying to protect the heliport, but there was no sign of the Portuguese gate security. Either way, it looked like plan 'B' could be put on hold.

I had a chat with the occupants of the UN 4WD: three RAN officers and one Portuguese army officer. They had that 'just survived a near-death experience' hype about them, but seemed like a good bunch of blokes. When I asked one of the RAN guys whether the quick-stop had helped, he smiled.

"Actually, I think it just pissed them off more."

There's just no pleasing some people.

News Headline:

Good luck finding one?

Jesus, looking towards Dili during the dry season

What can possibly go wrong

High orbit over the police station, with the heliport at top right.

Rioters pull back as fire erupts in front of the police station.

On approach to Gleno, even on 'clear' days cloud could quickly develop.

The main drag Dili, 2002, with school kids on left. The CHC house is on the right with the blue gate and elite security guard

What can possibly go wrong

Un Night at the CHC House – RAAF Nurse wearing the 'ARSE' Shirt Aeromedical Rescue and Specialist Evacuation

CHAPTER 18

Helicopter Rescue (Walpole)

AT THE TIME OF 'THE Walpole Job', (9th April 2005) the majority of Australian SAR crews did not utilise Night Vision Goggles (NVG). Instead, a Nightsun searchlight was typically used to 'let down' to unlit areas. From a pilot's perspective the 30 million candlepower Nightsun produces just a pencil beam of light that only becomes effective at the bottom (dangerous part) of any descent. The benefit of this light has been akin to driving down a winding country road with just a torch out of the driver's window to guide the way.

Additionally, pilots find it virtually impossible to hover over-water at night (especially without visible horizon), let alone a reference point to judge movement by. In this situation, a pilot's response to position corrections from a crewman will be inaccurate at best, catastrophic at worst. So to prevent disaster during night over water rescues, helicopters can be equipped with a special avionics package called Autohover.

The type of Autohover installed on the aircraft utilised for the Walpole SAR relied on several sensors to judge movement by: Doppler radar, GPS and radio altimeter being the key components. These three, plus other sensors, are interfaced through a couple of computers which in-turn send information to a four-axis autopilot which allows the helicopter to either remain stationary or be moved by pilot or crewman using a 'witches-hat' control not dissimilar to that of an XBOX or Play Station.

Although Autohover allows night over water rescues to be completed, they will take much longer than a daylight task due to the delay caused by sensors passing information to autopilots and then autopilots passing information to control surfaces. If you add wave action and poor visibility (driving rain) to this equation, a live night Autohover winch becomes a far from routine exercise, even in training.

It is because of this added risk SAR crews in Australia rarely conduct live over water winch training at night. Instead, they typically use a grappling hook on the end of their winch wire to recover wooden targets. The effectiveness of this training to prepare SAR crewmen and rescue-crewmen (swimmers) for the unpredictability of real-world operations is a point often debated in crew rooms.

Matt put down the phone after a phone call from the ambulance control centre and gave us the latest on the skydiver at York, who was looking doubtful. They were probably going to transport him by road; his injuries just weren't that bad apparently, but these sorts of decisions were never made quickly.

"You told them it would be nice to do it before last light, Matt?" I prompted with a hint of sarcasm.

Matt Falconer, the duty St John Paramedic was relatively new to helicopters. Although a very competent medic, it didn't hurt to remind him that reality is often entirely different to the movies when it came to operations.

"Yeah Mick, but I'm afraid it's standard ops tonight." His raised eyebrows and shrug of the shoulders told the usual story of indecision.

Well at least we would get to eat tea now, remembering my half defrosted meal in the microwave, making up for the loss of what would have been the first job for the 24hr shift. I began to move toward the kitchen, but before I had gone more than a couple of paces Andy walked into the room moving with purpose. Andy, the duty captain,

(I first met in East Timor) had been on the phone for a while to whom I had believed to be his wife, but as his expression was all business heading straight for the large wall map, tea was again put on hold.

"We're on standby for a job. Two adults and two kids on a boat near to Walpole, engine is u/s, but they have an anchor out..." Andy began.

I thought of the drive to work. It had been pissing down as rain squalls crossed the city.

"...Volunteer rescue squad launched a boat, but it's run aground..." Andy half smiled; some volunteers were very good, some weren't; but all, just like the rest of us, occasionally ran out of luck. "...They're readying another boat to rescue the first lot and maybe have a go for the others if conditions improve."

It had stopped raining outside, but threatening clouds pretty much confirmed the MET report of continued squally rain all night; if we got the order to launch this would be an interesting job.

Andy ran his hand down to the bottom of the map to a point near the most south-westerly tip of Western Australia. The next landfall south from this was Antarctica, and between this barren place and the town of Walpole was some frigid and often angry ocean.

"Any coordinates mate?" I quizzed.

Usually AusSAR would provide reasonably accurate latitude and longitude details following one or more satellite pass, and this information was extremely helpful when planning a long-range task.

"The call came from the cops; they're still running things at the moment and have requested assistance from St Johns." Again, Andy raised an eyebrow.

Normally this type of request would mean that the police helicopter was either unserviceable or on another task, but not tonight, tonight it simply meant that 'Polair' would be of little use in a rescue attempt. It was close to a two hour's flight to Walpole, and it would be dark in less than half an hour. The police obviously knew this and were well aware that their BK117 was not the machine of choice for a night over water task. Despite this acceptance, they always seemed to wait until the last moment before calling in an 'outside' agency, and once again we were being called when things had become 'ugly'.

"Well we're lucky the seventy-six is here, I guess?"

My question generated many others that would need to be answered, but they could wait for now.

Chris Hutton was Andy's co-pilot for the shift, and he too was standing with us in front of the large wall map. He was generally based at RAAF Pearce, north of Perth, but had been rostered to the Ambulance base as the different aircraft type required two pilots as opposed to just Andy and me for the Bell 412. This machine, which normally fulfilled the ambulance contract, was down for routine maintenance.

"Chris, can you start to put a plan together please," Andy asked over his shoulder, "We have the range for this, but before we commit to the task I want to make sure it looks good on paper?" Chris nodded. "You'll need to re-check the NOTAM's to see if Albany's ILS is serviceable, and also see if you can find out about fuel at Walpole… and Augusta too?" Andy called out as an afterthought to Chris as he left the room.

This job was well outside the contracted range of Rescue 65's operations, and often details regarding available fuel in remote areas were sketchy at best. In the past, jobs close to the South Australian border and the far north of the state had made for interesting planning exercises.

With Chris in search of the appropriate charts and phone lists, Andy turned to me.

"There is one other problem here," a smile, "I haven't done Autohover training for over four years." His smile suggested he didn't want to die tonight trying to become current either, "Are any of the RAAF Pearce captains available do you think?"

It was around 7 pm on a Saturday evening. Of the two captains the company had on the Pearce roster, it was possible, although unlikely that either would be alcohol-free.

"Try Shipo first mate". I suggested.

John Shipton was the RAAF Pearce base-manager, but this was not why I had suggested him. As a former Royal Navy helicopter pilot and current company check and training captain, who operated with the adage 'train hard fight easy', Shipo was the sort of driver I would like to have running things on a dark-shitty-night. And if we launched on this task, I suspected that's what we would be travelling into as we headed south.

A couple of minutes later Andy put down the phone in his office.

"Shipo's on his second bottle with the wine club," We both smiled at the regular event at the Shipton household, knowing the sore heads it had produced in the past, "but fortunately Trevor is free and will be on his way here shortly, should be forty minutes or so."

Trevor Henderson wasn't a Shipo. He was, however, a competent and enthusiastic captain who'd had real-world experience during a number of day SAR tasks since his arrival at RAAF Pearce. Prior to SAR duties, his primary role was as an offshore driver who'd ferried workers to oil rigs, but in addition to this, he had served with the UN in East Timor conducting a variety of medical, and re-supply missions to UN forces. Despite this valuable experience, if we launched tonight, this would be his first ever night rescue and an Autohover one to boot. 'Hendo' would undoubtedly be under the pump, and this pressure would be compounded due to the fact Chris, his co-pilot, despite having undertaken intensive training would be on his first ever rescue mission.

"Ok mate, good." I responded to Andy, "I'll give Matt a brief on Autohover-ops and get the seventy-six prepped. This is happening then?"

Andy began dialling,

"I'd say so. I'll let the police know we have a crew for Autohover ops and then it's up to them."

Matt and I headed off to the hangar in fading light. The building was about two hundred meters away - the geographic pain-in-the-arse indicating the early stages of the current contract. The long-term plan was for a new complex with crew-room and accommodation adjacent to a purpose-built facility, but for now, we made our way to the Jandakot Helicopters hangar we shared with the local flying school.

"So Matt, when was your last boat winch?"

Matt and I had done a few ambulance-type jobs together, and I had been impressed by his calm demeanour as he dealt with the multiple traumas of road accidents.

"A few months ago with George, we did some wet stuff too, doubles and hypo's. So what's the deal with night winching over water, is the Autohover any good?"

That was a leading question if I'd ever heard one! George, who I'd first met at RAAF Pearce, had conducted Matt's initial training and only had positive things to say about his ability and potential. At about my height but slimmer, Matt had the build of the classic 'rescue hero', although it was his attitude and not his physique that impressed me most. He was always positive, wanting to learn,

"Depends on the conditions and any glitch's that decide to make themselves known, but it works some of the time mate."

Unfortunately, my remark wasn't flippant.

"Ok…"

Matt smiled, but he was far from happy. I continued.

"The Autohover is basically controlled by a couple of computers mate…" Matt raised an eyebrow, but said nothing, "…These magical boxes receive information from a variety of sensors which allow them to determine where the machine is in space, and whether it's moving or not. The main sensor that allows the whole system to work is the Doppler radar; there are actually four of these. They point down from under the belly at forty-five-degree angles to the ten, two, four and eight o'clock positions. The Doppler sends out an elliptical torch-beam-like signal to the ocean surface and interprets this based on the time it takes to return and does this several times a second…" Matt was all concentration, but I was wondering how much of this meant anything to him in real-world-hanging-on-a-wire-below-the-aircraft terms. "...With this information processed the computers then tell the four-axis autopilots to follow the commands of the pilots or the crewman. Any command information is entered by the pilots via a flight-director, or, directly by me using a witches-hat control on the winch pendant to either keep the machine steady or to make it move. Make sense so far mate?"

"Basically," Matt indicated reasonably confidently, "So apart from millions of dollars worth of avionics doing a wonderful job, I am just swinging on a wire as normal, although in the darkness?"

Even though Matt's voice was firm, his humour was masking a respectable dose of apprehension.

"If the system works well mate, basically, yes; although you will have some illumination from the down-light, but wait, there's more. Unfortunately, there are some ways the system can, and regularly does, try to ruin your night." I had his full attention. "Un-commanded movement happens fairly regularly, every fourth training flight I'd say. What this means in simplistic terms is that the computers get confused and do something not requested, and for you, on the wire, this can be a pain in the arse and potentially very dangerous. When and if this happens we, that's the pilots and me, obviously try to correct the problem, but we also try to avoid and anticipate any movement before it happens with the checks we do before putting you out the door. On a big swell though mate, the aircraft may decide to do its own thing."

"Swell?" Matt asked.

"Yeah, basically the seventy-six will ride up and down with the swell; it even surfs on bigger waves. When this happens the pilots monitor the controls even closer than normal and will have the system set for 'high-sea-state' in preparation for the conditions; but, and this is a reasonably big but, sometimes the machine will launch off the top of a swell and keep going up. When this occurs, it isn't so bad for the crew..."

Matt's smile masked the drama he knew this would expose him to, but he kept listening intently.

"...But they have to watch closely when the system tries to reset itself. You see the height correction that the computers *will* automatically attempt after they work out the problem with the climb can potentially over-torque the engines, and if we're heavy - that's lots of fuel on board; this is a genuine possibility. So, in this circumstance, climbing off a swell, the pilots may have to 'fly-away' to prevent an over-torque from happening as the aircraft resets itself."

Matt asked his next question with some apprehension,

"So, what do you do when this happens and I'm on the wire?"

"Depends on the speed of the climb; if it takes off quickly and I think it isn't going to stop, or the pilots are slow to respond, I will immediately winch in. Now, this may leave you exposed on the wire as they fly-away mate, and I can't pretend that this isn't dangerous – but it is better than the worst case option where I've determined that the only thing I can do, for your safety, is to cut the wire. If that happens ... well, you are probably on your own until first light, or if you're lucky, until a boat to finds you."

Matt was doing an excellent job of looking professional. When discussing this type of stuff on training flights with the crew at Pearce the worst case scenario element was always briefed, but that's what it was, worst case, and highly unlikely on a training flight. Tonight though, preparing to launch for what a RAAF SAR crew consider their most demanding discipline, well, it focused your mind.

I had only completed one other real-world Autohover job, and that resulted in the rescue-crewman (Lars) being awarded the Royal Humane Society's silver medal for bravery for his efforts (and the danger) he had been exposed to. And of the half-dozen or so rare 'live' night training sorties I had completed before that task, none had really prepared me for the unforeseen challenges of a dark night when I had a good mate a hundred feet below the aircraft swinging on a wire. Apart from the height, this was because every crewman knows that the wire would love nothing more than to wrap around limbs and then chop them off the moment a big wave washed over their rescue crewman. Night Autohover work was and still is, far from routine.

"Vertical travel is one form of un-commanded movement anyway," I continued "The seventy-six can also move laterally which will result in pretty much the same actions by the crew, or, it could descend. If that happens, we can only hope the pilots have their shit in one neat pile and pick it up quickly; otherwise, we will be joining you in the ocean quick-smart."

"So then," Matt cleared his throat, "Basically, we don't want un-commanded movement tonight."

Matt would be ok. Well, at least he would be no worse off than other RAAF SAR rescue-crewmen on their first night wet winch, and there were still a few of these blokes in the company who had yet to complete a night wet winch despite being deemed 'qualified'. Basically, Matt met an unwritten rule my PES instructor, Alf, first reinforced to Slopstick, Chris, Dave and me, as we neared the end of ESM training and had asked about our final test.

"Boys," Alf began stern faced, "It's simple, I need to know that I could trust you going to my family's aid tonight."

The boot of the S76 is large, about a third the size of the rear cabin and contains a mountain of additional rescue equipment including a second stretcher, passenger lifejackets, thermic recovery capsules (TRCs) and other RAAF related items. Before undertaking any AusSAR, or other tasks, it was my job as crewman to determine what, if any of this gear, could be left behind to reduce weight and therefore maximise aircraft performance.

Matt and I were at the pad outside the Hangar. The S76 had its four rotor blade tie-downs and engine bungs removed, and was essentially ready for flight. Standing next to the machine at the right-hand-side boot door with Matt, I opened this and locked it in position.

"Let's just get it all out mate," I suggested, "then put back only what we need."

After five minutes the boot contained only a toolbox, hand fuel pump, passenger (PAX) lifejackets, the 'Heave In' (HI) line and two TRCs. The rear cabin was as we had found it, and we moved off to the Hangar carrying the discarded gear in the second stretcher.

Placing the stretcher at the foot of a storage rack, I motioned to a large fiberglass box that was big enough to contain an anorexic bar fridge.

"Have you been shown how the Air-Droppable liferaft works Matt?"

Matt helped me pull the container down from the lower shelf.

"No mate."

"Well..." We opened the catches and lifted the 50 odd pounds of the plastic-canvas covered raft from the container, "...Essentially it's a liferaft like most others. It will support four people with a squash, more if you have to; but only if you really have to. The beauty is, Matt that by using the HI-line..." I pulled a rope-bag from the container, "...I can drop this weighted supply-bag to the vessel in need."

The supply-bag was the same size as the HI-line rope-bag and contained a radio, safety lanyards, lead-shot-satchels and a simple plastic-coated set of instructions – this system was introduced after the significant challenges both aircrews and yachtsmen were confronted with during the disastrous 1998 Sydney to Hobart yacht race. Matt gave a cursory glance at the items.

"How's the raft inflated?"

"Well, I position the raft back from the door with the HI-line connected to the tag marked 'A'..." I pointed to one of two tags protruding from the raft "...And then the line is connected to the supply-bag. When this is ready, I connect the other tag marked 'B' to a floor anchor point. Once the survivors have the supply bag, which I obviously lower to them, I dispatch the raft, which in turn pulls on the tag 'B' line secured to the anchor point. The raft pulling on this line does two things: firstly it activates the inflation cylinder, and secondly, it breaks the weak-link from the raft to the anchor point. All I have to do then is recover the few meters of the remaining line from tag 'B' as the raft inflates on the way down, pretty simple really. If the raft were to fail to inflate on the way down the survivors can pull it alongside and then have a go using the other lanyard."

I could see Matt was picturing the liferaft operation from his position in the water and that he appeared reasonably comfortable with how it was to work.

"Ok Mick, what's the plan for tonight then?" He inquired

"Depends on what we find. I reckon there is still a chance the second boat will get them, but we won't know about that for a while yet, probably not until we are well on the way down south. The main factor tonight will be fuel. Travelling straight from here we should have some time on site before having to depart for Albany, or possibly Walpole if there's drum-fuel there, or even Augusta maybe? We will have to see what the boys find in their planning first."

Matt nodded acknowledgment.

"Anyway, we'll work on a simple job and have options for if and when things get worse," Matt nodded again, "Ok then, the main thing is that once we have a survivor on the wire, we don't want to lose him. These people are probably bloody cold by now and might not cope well with a high winch, especially the kids. So it's up to you to make sure we have all bases covered Matt."

"No worries" Matt asserted confidently, "I guess that means double lifts using the hypo strop for all of them?"

"Correct. But I also want you to put one of our PAX jackets on each survivor first, in addition to securing a cyalume to their arm with gaffer tape. If, and I stress if, they fall from the strop we want to be able to find them quickly."

Matt nodded positively. He knew full well that a hypothermic patient may well 'collapse' after rescue, that's why we used the hypo strop. Secured under the knees in addition to the normal chest fitted collar, it brought them up in a reclined sitting position to aid a survivor's blood staying in the brain, and therefore keeping the person conscious.

On my last Autohover job, Lars had to hold the survivor in the strop during the 100ft winch (choking the collar with his hands and gripping with his legs) because the old style hypo strop had become fouled in a light orange line, preventing its use. The bloke in the strop pretty much gave up trying to live the moment Lars arrived alongside him in the 4m breaking seas. He had been there for over five hours and the psychological battle not to give up had taken all his effort. We guessed that he had seen Lars as some kind of Superman there to save him and his exhausted body just went limp the moment he arrived. The resulting drama required me dropping Lars back into the water with the survivor so he could refit the strop, and this gave fate another chance for the winch-wire to wrap around both of them. We got away with it though, and Lars certainly earned his medal as he battled away with the ever-present danger of snaking winch-wire as waves crashed on top of him.

I continued with the brief, "We'll load up the PAX-lifejacket-bag with four jackets, a bunch of cyalumes and some gaffer tape, plus a spare beacon and strobe – just in case. You will take this down with a hypo-combo strop, and I will put you in the water close to the boat, about five or six feet away if possible. Once there you will board, brief and then prep the survivors. "

"Do I stay connected to the wire?" Matt asked.

It was a fair question.

"In the perfect world Matt, I would say yes. But tonight, because of the possible conditions and the risk of fouling the wire, let's plan that you disconnect once on board. We will move back and keep you in the searchlight beam, and then while you are preparing the survivors

I will set up the HI-line to assist with the recovery. You will have to brief the two adults on how this works for when you come up with the kids, but it isn't rocket science mate, and once they see how you pull the hook in I'm sure they will get the hang of it."

"So, it's the kids first then?"

"Yes, Matt." I confirmed.

"Should I secure them in the chest strap too?"

This was another relevant question demonstrating his understanding of the risk, but also his inexperience. Inside the chest-collar was an additional restraint for small people/children. It was time-consuming to fit and not strictly required for a safe winch because it could potentially hold up proceedings during a critical operation, such as water rescue in big waves.

"Your call on that one, Matt; if for a moment you think the kids are too small or are approaching panic, yes, definitely use it. If they are bigger kids, however, or reasonably calm, it would speed things up if you didn't."

I could have directed Matt either way, but the call had to be his - he nodded again, apparently confident with the plan so far.

"Right then" I continued, "if things go as planned we will recover all four in this manner, just drop the HI-line as you leave the boat for the last time."

"No worries. What's plan 'B'?" Matt was smiling now, but he was still cautious.

"It's more of a plan 'A' mark-one, two, three, and so on. If we have a drama getting you on board the first time, fuel is going to become a very real issue. Therefore, if once you are on board and the drivers decide that they can't complete the task due to fuel, I will dispatch the raft for safety before we depart. I might also do this if the conditions are such that winching from the boat would prove too dangerous. But if we were to bug out for fuel though, you should enter the raft in preparation for winching when you hear us return. Now, I know you will have comms via the rescue crewman radio if we do leave, but it's nice to have a plan if it were to die a watery death, yeah?"

Matt agreed. If the radio should fail, despite being waterproof, it was nice to have an option. As we continued through several more scenarios, my confidence in Matt grew. He was asking the right questions when appropriate and listening intently while I gave instructions, but there was something I needed to go over in more detail.

"Emergencies requiring a cable-cut: whether it is because of uncommanded movement or mechanical failure this is the worst case scenario for you Matt, because should a cable-cut be required, you will most certainly be on your own until morning. No other aircraft can come and get you on this side of the country, and boats will have a serious time just getting out of the river at Walpole, as we already know. We used to carry a one-man liferaft for cable-cut eventualities, it was connected to the back of your harness - but we don't anymore."

"Why not?" Matt frowned.

"Good question. Not that this will help if things go bad tonight, but we've been waiting for nearly two years now for a replacement to the old rafts after the company removed them from service. They were too old apparently and may have failed, but nobody thought to ask the opinion of people that depend on them."

"Sounds like your management works to the same book as St John's, Mick." Matt shrugged.

What else could he say, 'that he didn't want to play anymore?' I had to advise him of the one-man raft issue though – bloody desk bound bean counters!

"Probably right mate, let's go and see how the planning's going shall we."

After placing a canvas bag containing marine-marker flares on board the S76 I glanced at my watch before leaving the Hangar, thirty minutes had passed since we left the office - Hendo probably would have warmed the motor of his car on the way down and was no doubt in the office already. As we walked up the path leading away from the Hangar I looked up to the dark sky as a few drops of rain hit my face – there was not one star in view, and the wind was whistling through the trees along the road.

Planning was still in progress; or rather Hendo was undertaking last minute checks of Chris's plan. Our brief exchange contained the satisfied grin of a SAR crew with a decent job before them.

"Hey mate, how was the drive in?"

"The car didn't quite overheat, but I got here. How's the machine looking?" Hendo inquired.

"Twelve hundred pounds of fuel, the tanker's been ordered and should be here soon. We were planning on full fuel, but wanted to make sure you were happy with that?"

There was the option of going to Bunbury (about half way) and topping up there to give us more endurance to complete the task – but this would delay our arrival.

"Na, full to the brim thanks, mate."

"Ok. We have the Air-Droppable raft on board, plus pyros and we've dumped the second stretcher plus some other gear." As I spoke, I could see Hendo mentally checking off items.

"The fuel pump?" he quizzed.

"In the boot, and the test gear is in the toolkit. How's it going here?"

"Just about done, Chris's still trying to find out about fuel at the Walpole strip but no one's answering the phone; Andy's expecting a call from the cops any moment."

"So, you reckon its Albany for fuel first then?" I asked.

"Maybe, I'll try the coppers on the way down and see if they know anything; that's if Chris has no luck here of course."

The aircraft mobile phone rang, and Andy answered it.

"Yes, full both sides thanks mate… Ok, cheers. That was the refueller; he's there now and will top it up." Andy advised Hendo.

The base manager's phone rang the moment he had spoken, and so Andy swapped handpieces.

"Andy Symonds. Yes… probably fifteen minutes at the most," Andy looked to Hendo and gave him a thumbs up, "Ok, thanks for the update, I'll call you when they're airborne. Trevor, that was the police communications commander; the police would like your assistance if it's not too much bother."

We all chuckled at Andy's tongue-in-cheek formality.

"Ok." Hendo picked up his 'nav' bag and a folder containing the weather forecast, maintenance release, and other documents. "We'd best be on our way then."

"I'll keep trying the Walpole numbers, and if I get anything I'll call you on-route," Andy advised more seriously. Then, "Good luck boys, I guess we'll see you for breakfast."

Once Hendo and Chris had both engines running I ran a check on the winch as they programmed the nav computers. It had been checked and found serviceable at the start of the shift, but if this additional check found a fault, we could get the duty engineer in to fix it before departing. A fault was unlikely, but the check also served to reassure the rescue-crewman who would be trusting his life to the apparatus secured above the right cabin door in the near future – I was always glad to see the crewman take this seriously the times I had gone 'down the wire'.

I also powered up the FLIR ball mounted next to the nose wheel; the picture was clear, although the usual black and white shades that the thermal imagery produced. This was a new FLIR system the company had recently purchased. There had been some regular faults with it along the lines of teething problems at this stage, but these could be rectified relatively quickly with a purpose fitted 'reset' function. There were no problems during my test, and as the pilots finished their pre-flight checks, Chris made a traffic call.

"All stations Jandakot, Chopper Six, a Sikorsky S-Seventy-Six is becoming airborne from in front of the tower and will be departing on runway heading climbing to two thousand before turning to the south on climb to three-thousand-five hundred, all stations Jandakot, Chopper Six."

"Lifting mate," Hendo advised, "Your trims."

"Roger, my trims." Chris responded promptly; it was just before 8 pm.

"All clear right, no traffic on final," I confirmed routinely.

"Thanks, Mick." Hendo acknowledged. He then pulled up on the collective control to bring the S76 into a low hover. "In the green, all stable. Moving right and rotating."

With rotor blades biting into the cold night air, the machine dipped at the nose and accelerated forward parallel to the duty runway.

"Roger…airspeed's alive… thirty-five…forty-five," Chris advised.

"Committed mate."

Following Hendo's call advising that he had single engine performance, Chris selected the undercarriage up, and the S76 climbed quickly away from the field.

"Turning left," Hendo cautioned as we passed two thousand feet.

"Clear," Matt advised from the rear left seat.

Looking back through the left window I occasionally caught a glimpse of lights at Jandakot airport through the cloud, but then they were gone altogether.

"Compass check, passing two-zero-zero." Hendo verified.

Chris looked at his instruments.

"One-nine-nine my side and the standby is indicating… one-nine-eight, all aids tracking."

"Good," Hendo acknowledged, "rolling out on one-eight-five, passing three-thousand for three-five."

"Check, five-hundred to run," Chris confirmed.

As the boys continued with the departure and climb to cruise height, I looked out of the window. We were flying in and out of a layer of patchy cloud, below us was blackness and looking up I couldn't see any stars. The weather on the south coast was forecast worse than the city, and thinking of the low hills around Walpole and Albany a slight moisture developed on the inside of my gloves as I came to terms with the reality that this wouldn't be a simple job. My mind continued to wander until the sound of the aircraft phone ringing brought me back to the immediate.

"Get that please Mick," Hendo prompted.

The phone was on the side of the centre pillar and a pain for the drivers to reach. I moved forward and pressed the receive key, and then rotating my radio-switch to '5' I spoke through my helmet microphone,

"Chopper-Six, Mick speaking."

"Hi Mick, Andy here, I have the Walpole police number for you."

"Go ahead, mate."

"Zero, four, zero, seven, two..."

As Andy read the number I copied it to my knee-board.

"Roger, that's zero, four...?"

"Correct. That's the mobile of the sergeant running things at Walpole. He's informed me that the second boat would not be going to attempt a rescue. Apparently, they had a hard enough time with the first lot, so it's over to you now boys."

"No worries Andy," Hendo piped in, "Mate, the way the wind is at the moment I may consider going directly to Walpole, we should have around twenty minutes on site, I'll keep you posted as things develop."

"Ok Trev, good luck boys."

As we continued south, Hendo and Chris kept updating estimates for either a direct track to Walpole or for a divert to Albany to take on fuel. The knowledge that we were now the only option until daylight made Walpole the preferred choice, but Hendo wouldn't do that if getting to Albany after the job meant eating into his reserves. This thinking may have appeared harsh because of the genuine danger the people on the boat were facing, but an extra forty minutes or so to take on fuel was something we could accept assuming poor conditions over the vessel. This extra fuel would give us the flexibility to consider differing recovery options if things were to go bad – but even so, it was a hard decision to make with lives in imminent danger.

During the track south Matt and I pretty much just twiddled our thumbs and considered the challenges that were not too distant. We had discussed the options for the recovery, and all were happy with the plan I'd come up with – the many variables were a regular part of rescue operations, and although you very rarely reached the worst case option, it was nice to know where your cut off point was. This 'cut off' was the point where you took your bat and ball and went home early without finishing the game.

At about forty minutes out from Walpole, Hendo had me dial the police number, and we all waited as the ringtone filled our headsets.

"Sergeant Smithwick." An obvious police voice reported.

"G'day mate, Trevor Henderson aboard Chopper-Six, the rescue helicopter on route to Walpole."

"Ahh, g'day Trev, Steve Smithwick, how far away are you?"

The sergeant responded with a more friendly voice; there was a hint of relief there too.

"We should be overhead Walpole in forty-two minutes, Steve. I have two questions for you?"

"Go ahead, Trev." Smithwick advised.

"The Walpole airstrip" Hendo began, "is there any drum-fuel there? And also, do you have a Lat and Long for the vessel?" At this point, we only had a rough position to go on.

"Ten drums Trev, we checked them tonight, and they've all got over seven months left, they're normally used for the fire bombers you see. Standby for the position please, I'll check."

"Hey Hendo," I interjected on the intercom, "you might want to check that's Jet A1 mate and not avgas for the fixed-wing bombers?"

"Ok mate" Hendo acknowledged, "Steve, is that turbine fuel you have, it should be marked Jet A1?"

"That's affirmative. It is confirmed turbine fuel, the CALM guys checked it out earlier this evening."

The Conservation and Land Management people had been down most of the summer in support of the bushfire season and they were mostly pretty sharp operators.

"Thanks, Steve, that's good news, we'll be proceeding directly to the point near Chatham Island to start with. If you can get us an updated position on the vessel that would be great, but either way we will be coming back to the Walpole strip for fuel. Can you have someone there with their vehicle lights on for us please?"

"Understood, I'll be there with my car, and it'll have the beacons flashing. I'll get back to you soon about the position. Oh, and just to let you know, it's raining pretty heavy here at the moment."

"Thanks, Steve." Hendo acknowledged before addressing us, "Everyone happy if we get straight into it, the ten drums should give us plenty of 'fat' for the task and Walpole is only ten minutes at the most from the reported position?"

Hendo's assessment was spot on. The fact that fuel was available at Walpole was immense relief in the planning stakes: he received only positive responses.

"Mick, should I get my wetsuit on now?"

Matt's voice had a trace of concern. The uncertainty of your first operational night winch generally produced a few butterflies. Although there was still plenty of time until overhead the target, getting dressed early would give him something to occupy his mind.

"Yeah, ok mate. No rush, and keep your helmet on so you can listen in on things in case we have a change of plan."

As Matt changed into his wetsuit, I ran over the automatic 'letdown' procedure in my head. This additional feature of the avionics package allowed for 'fully coupled' and therefore safe descent through the cloud to a given target. Hendo would probably opt for an 'Approach 1' (descent to 200ft and 60kts) once we were clear of high ground near the coast. He would have to descend to two-thousand feet first for the program to be accepted, but as the highest point of land on the coast was less than seven-hundred feet that shouldn't be a problem.

We had been advised that the police had people on the point of land closest to the boat and we'd been given their exact position. The boat was a mile or so offshore from the police, and although the stricken vessel didn't have a homing beacon the occupants apparently had a strobe light, and this should be relatively easy to see despite the shitty weather. There was constant rain outside now, and the aircraft strobe lights reflected on this making the outside world appear like a surreal, almost alien domain.

"Got the coast on Radar, and I'm getting the occasional patch of light through the cloud from what I guess is Walpole in the eleven o'clock," Hendo advised. "Ok Chris, set two-fifty feet per minute, let's descend to fifteen hundred."

"Two-fifty set, leaving three-thousand-five-hundred, for fifteen-hundred," Chris reported after adjusting the vertical speed control.

"Understood mate" Hendo acknowledged, "How's it going with you, Mick?"

The cloud directly ahead of us was broken, so I quickly scanned the FLIR image before speaking.

"Matt's just putting his fins on, and then we will be ready. Although I'll wait until we have the boat sighted for winch checks mate, and you're clear ahead on FLIR as best as I can see. This rain isn't helping much, but I do have the coast in sight."

I signalled for Matt to move over to the right door in preparation for the winch. He unbuckled his seatbelt and shuffled across to the right bench seat and then re-secured himself. Kneeling before him with the roof mounted 'wander-lead' attached to my harness, I checked off Matt's harness and made sure the cyalumes on his helmet and wrists were firmly secured. Matt also had the bag containing the PAX jackets and spare gear looped under his arm – we both checked the contents of this and then gave each other a positive thumbs up. For his first night winch, Matt was looking remarkably relaxed.

"I've got a strobe-light left of the nose lads." Hendo informed, "It's pretty close to shore, maybe less than a mile. I'll take us over the top for a descent to seaward. Standby Approach One."

"Ready Approach One," Chris advised.

"Position is marked… and Approach One engaged," Reported Hendo.

"Aircraft is decelerating and descending, leaving fifteen-hundred for two-hundred."

Chris was monitoring the aircraft instruments and would now pay particular attention to the automatic program in progress.

Hendo's task was to steer us to a position downwind of the vessel by rotating the 'bug' on the console. He could actually do this without seeing the vessel as the GPS display now had a small green star marking its position. Had we been clear of land a Mark On Target (MOT) program would have conducted the full letdown automatically, but with rising terrain close to the target the two-stage Approach program was the safest option.

"Turning us to the right, Mick have you got that large island on FLIR, it's about two miles west on radar?"

"Yes Hendo and the coast's easy to see too, both well clear, but I haven't seen the boat yet."

"Roger", Hendo acknowledged, "it should be coming through the three o'clock according to the FMS. I'm going to roll out about a mile downwind from it."

"Are you ready for some winch checks?" I prompted.

"Go ahead," Hendo confirmed.

"Hoist power?"

"On, with a green light."

"Green light in the back also; cable-cut circuit breaker?"

"In," Hendo reported. The explosive chisel that could sever the winch wire was now armed.

"Identify cable-cut?" I requested.

"Identified in the front."

"Identified in the rear", I touched the guarded switch above the rear-right quarter window. "Clear to unlock?"

"Yes Mick, unlock only." Hendo authorised.

"Standby master-caution, unlocking right door only," I advised, before moving the slide-lock forward. On top of both pilots instrument consoles a purposely attention-grabbing light illuminated.

"Master-caution!" Chris assertively, yet routinely, informed Hendo.

"Roger, door-lock only." Hendo verified after checking the caution-warning panel between them. Satisfied the light was indeed in response to my notification, he pushed the master-caution to cancel the light.

The boys had the gear down now, it was part of their descent checks, and this enabled them to turn the landing light on. Out of my window, all I could see was white light and a wall of water passing by at ninety degrees. But this too was normal in rain, the angle caused by our speed – still 60kts at this stage, but slowing.

"Passing fifty knots," Chris advised.

"Clear door," Hendo advised me, satisfied the speed was safe to push the plug door out into the airflow.

"One in a seatbelt, one on wander-lead, and the cabin is secure; opening right."

I pulled the handle down and pushed the door outwards and then, sliding it backwards onto two locating lugs I quickly became saturated, it was literally bucketing down!

"Still clear ahead on radar, how's the FLIR Mick?" Hendo requested

"Clear mate." The rain affected the picture, but I could still make out a blurred horizon.

"Roger", Hendo continued, "have you got a flare ready Mick? We'll run over the top first."

There were two Mk58 marine markers in a bag at arm's reach; as I spoke I pulled one of the fire-extinguisher-sized flares out, "Roger mate. Clear to arm?"

"Clear to arm, with point-two to run." Hendo advised.

Point-two or about two hundred meters meant that I had just a few seconds until we were overhead. I quickly pulled the pear-shaped foil cover from the top of the flare exposing the saltwater activation system to the sea, and stuck the sticky cover to the side of the pyrotechnic.

"Flares armed mate; ready with a Mk58 on your command."

"Roger" Hendo called, and then counted down as the image of a helicopter on his display approached the small green star "... Steady, steady... drop."

"Smokes away," I watched the flare tumble into the ocean and waited for it to ignite – this normally took just a couple of seconds... Damn! "It's a dud Hendo, you want to position for another?"

"Na, we'll get on with it..." Hendo answered abruptly, the failure causing slight frustration.

Although the flare primarily served as a secondary position indicator when sophisticated avionics were available, the site of a smoke trail confirming wind direction and the old school security of a visual datum point was always preferred.

"...I have the position marked and have a reasonable idea of the wind."

Hendo's joke was an indication of the swell and rain he could see. He conducted one brief orbit back to a downwind position from the boat, and then prepared to descend to hover-height.

"Standby Approach Two, Chris."

"Ready Approach Two." Chris acknowledged, eyes scanning the primary flight instrumentation.

"Approach Two's engaged." As Hendo pushed the button, the computers sent messages to the autopilots.

"Roger, leaving two hundred for seventy-five feet. My decision-height set for sixty-five."

Closely monitoring the approach, Chris put his height alarm ten feet below the height we were descending to, should this alarm sound it would be a good warning that something may have gone wrong with the system.

"Roger," Hendo acknowledged, "mine's set at fifty-five."

If Hendo's sounded it would be a fair indication the system was having a bad hair day and therefore probably time to run away home.

"Passing one-hundred for seventy-five feet, speed's coming back and the nose is pitching up,"

As Chris continued to monitor the Approach program, I searched outside for the boat, but all I could make out was an inky black ocean through the rain. The speed was less than 15kts at this point yet the rain was still almost at right angles with water entering the cabin.

"The rains pretty heavy mate, it's soaking the cabin."

My call wasn't a whinge, but just advice to the drivers about the visibility I had. Rain on their windows was just more rain; they had instruments to monitor and wouldn't be spending much time with their eyes 'outside'.

"Roger Mick, the boat's in the one-thirty at about point-two. Are you visual?" Hendo challenged.

I could make out a faint strobe but not the boat.

"Yes mate, looks like a three-meter swell too with occasional bigger ones coming through, and the wind is on the nose. There's a big one coming under us now. I'm bringing in the hook."

The S76 was already established in the hover as the swell went underneath. We rose slightly as it passed, but the system held together and we settled back at hover-height without any drama. I gave the winch hook to Matt, and he began connecting it to the Capewell winch-release-system already attached to his harness.

"Thanks, Mick," Hendo acknowledged, "It handled that well, are you ready for hover-trim?"

"Ready," Chris advised

"Ready" I responded in turn. "Target sighted in the one o'clock at approximately two-hundred."

"You have hover-trim control."

Hendo's comment confirmed I now had control authority to move the S76 in any direction up to a speed of five knots. I had the winch pendant in my left hand, and using my thumb I pushed forward on the small 'witches hat' control.

"Trimming forward, call the numbers, looking for five."

"Roger Mick, nothing as yet."

Hendo was monitoring a device called the AL-300 that indicated the speed inputs that I requested of the computer with my witches hat control.

"Ok, well we're moving," I confirmed "possibly three knots or so. Trimming right also."

The lack of indication was an occasional glitch, but nothing new. The AL-300 was generally slow to respond to inputs from the 'back', although no one from engineering seemed to know why, and the lack of speed indication just added to frustration on training flights – whatever, we had coped with the problem in the past, we could deal with it now.

"Closing nicely now, I'm guessing five forward and one right."

"Roger Mick, still nothing on the AL-300," Hendo informed routinely.

"About eighty to run" I continued "reducing the right trim to zero… and the line's good now with the target on the nose,"

I could just make out the shape of a boat, its white hull was reflecting in the searchlight Chris had positioned down to the forward and right.

"Forty to run, reducing speed," I could see the boat more clearly now, although it was still somewhat of a shadowy blur through the rain and limited illumination the winch down-light provided. But something else was wrong! We weren't slowing, despite my inputs.

"Hey Hendo," I started, a hint of frustration in my voice, "problem with my trim control mate, it won't slow down. Passing over the top now; come on you fuck! Nah, it ain't going to stop mate. Zeroing my trim!"

I pushed down on the witches' hat to cancel all inputs, but we kept moving, "Mine's not working mate, try yours."

The boat was slowly fading from view as the S76 continued at a fast walking pace in the opposite direction.

"Roger, trimming back," Hendo confirmed. The forward movement continued.

"I've still got five knots forward on the Doppler bars Trev," Chris advised.

"Still moving outside too," I informed Hendo, confirming what Chris's display was presenting.

"Zeroing pilot's trim." Hendo explained, with a noticeable edge to his voice now.

Hendo's attempt to arrest the movement also failed - things had just become a tad more 'ugly'. Although this was somewhere we had been before in training, it would have been nice not to have to deal with it at the time. However, the fact that two kids were on the boat somewhere behind us, with the added fact that their boat was dragging its anchor towards some pretty treacherous rocks, motivated us to work with the problem a while longer as opposed to just aborting the task then and there.

Despite the edge to his voice, Hendo was pretty calm at this point as he continued with the troubleshooting procedures.

"Resetting autopilot number-one."

"Roger." Chris acknowledged.

"And resetting number-two..." A pause from Hendo, "...Ok, I'm trimming back on pilots controls."

"We're slowing mate, that seems to have fixed it?" I offered.

"Appears to have. Can you conn me back, Mick?" Hendo requested.

I still had a distant strobe through the rain, which had eased thankfully.

"Yes mate, continue this line and speed with about one-hundred to run."

As we moved back I moved my eyes 'inside' and re-checked Matt's equipment. The hook's connected with the strop, Capewell's connected with release secure, leg and waist straps secure, hook-knife fitted, lifejacket on, helmet on, strap connected and the gear bag has one strap passed through a karabiner, good. I looked back outside.

"With about forty to run Hendo, reduce your trim to one-back."

"Roger, one-back indicated. Do you want hover-trim now Mick?"

"Thanks, mate. I have hover-trim control."

"You have control," Hendo confirmed.

The boat was about fifteen meters away, and we were closing on a perfect line. Although I could see movement in the dimly lit shadow of the open deck at this range, it was still hard to determine how many people were there. The boat was a seven-meter half-cabin cruiser, and there was room to get Matt on the deck, but as the boat was pitching quite a bit on the swell, I decided to stick with the original plan of putting him in the water.

"Reducing to zero, with eight to run..." I watched our speed against the ocean below. Nothing changed. "Fuck! It's not stopping Hendo, I'm trimming forward...Fuck it! Nah, try yours, my fucking zero's failed again too!"

"Mine too, damn it! Resetting the autopilots," Hendo repeated the procedure, his voice becoming urgent, but fortunately, the S76 came to a hover with the boat 5m behind us. "Ok, that's got it" Hendo advised with obvious relief, "It might be the swell lads; a big one went under when the trim shit itself. Let's just watch it a second or two and see what happens."

Another large swell passed underneath, and the S76 began to surf with it. Watching as the swell had passed the boat I noticed that the relatively small craft pitched violently on the anchor line – it wasn't a pretty sight, and my stomach tightened.

"Chris, I'm going to wind us up to one-hundred-and-ten for a better Doppler spread," Hendo advised.

"Understood, hopefully that will help?" Chris acknowledged optimistically. His eyes were still glued to the displays that showed us very close to the ocean.

"Are you happy with that too, Mick?" Hendo asked.

The extra height would reduce my vision further, making the winch more difficult, but if the increased height made the boys happy, I was all for it.

"Fine with me mate."

"Right then, that's one-ten set..." another large swell passed underneath, "...and she seems to be coping a bit better now. Mick, you ready for hover-trim control again?"

"Yes mate."

"You have control."

With Hendo's confirmation I re-commenced the task.

"I have hover-trim control, trimming back and looking for one."

The rain was picking up again. It appeared as though another squall line was about to pass the area, but at least the system was working correctly now.

"Clear to winch?" I asked Hendo.

"Clear."

I cracked the cyalumes on Matt's helmet, and he did the same to the ones on his wrists. I then gave him one more quick check over, ensuring that the hypo-combo strop was rigged correctly and that he was still happy to go. The thumbs up was the same as before, and I pointed to his seatbelt, he released this in preparation to move out, but then quickly adjusted his fin straps – the unnecessary action no doubt breaking the tension he must have been feeling.

"Matt is checked off, and I'm putting him outside."

I rolled the thumb-wheel on the pendant backwards, and the foot or so of slack wire pulled tight as the winch wound in. Matt lifted from his seat slowly, and I hung onto his harness as he swung outside the machine suspended from the hook. Receiving another thumbs up from Matt, I rolled the thumb-wheel forward.

"Winching out, the target's five behind in the four o'clock, zeroing my trim."

It worked as advertised. Matt rotated slowly as he descended into the gloomy world below the aircraft. The two cyalumes on his helmet were glowing like a beacon indicating his position in space, and as he tried to counter the force of the rotor-down-wash, I saw the wrist cyalumes moving with his arm action. The boat was still in a reasonable position, and as Matt closed with the ocean, I moved him closer to it.

"Twenty feet off the water now, trimming back and right with small movements."

By just flicking the witches-hat I could edge the S76 closer to the target without risking sudden and potentially dangerous movement for Matt who was very close to the solid structure of the boat.

"He's close enough; I'm putting him in the water... big swell coming under."

Despite the heavy rain that was passing the door again, I could see Matt swimming the short distance to the boat's stern, the fast-moving wrist cyalumes reflecting his effort. But just as he was about to climb up at the transom, the aircraft began to move forward and left. I winched out immediately, hoping to allow him to board as we rode the surf, but we kept moving, and the speed increased.

"It's moving forward and left Hendo!" My concern was obvious to all, "Zeroing my trims... fuck! Not stopping, try yours!"

The speed was increasing at an alarming rate now, but I continued winching out hoping Hendo could fix the problem again - Matt and the boat were approaching twenty feet behind us in the four o'clock position.

"Mine's not responding either Mick!" Hendo advised promptly.

"Winching in!" I informed, trying to sound calm but failing; both our voices were more than a little strained now. However, as Hendo continued to troubleshoot, the urgency in my voice became obvious, "We're dragging Matt!"

I could see Matt bouncing along the surface; at times he was crashing into waves and going underwater. I was winching in at full speed of 250ft per minute, and this combined with what appeared to be 15 to 20kts of aircraft movement was making for a wild ride.

Resetting the autopilots did nothing this time, and I could hear Hendo selecting the opposite Flight-Director out of desperation. As he did this Matt launched from the ocean as the winch finally pulled him clear of the water, but this just caused another drama. He swung forward with the momentum and continued into what was developing into a massive arc. I quickly winched out again and advised Hendo what was happening.

"Big swing Hendo, I'm putting him back in the water to dampen it." Matt smashed back into the ocean.

"Ok mate," Hendo began, "Chris's Flight-Director is doing the job, and I'm slowing her down now."

I noticed the reduction in speed in my periphery, but my focus was still on Matt. I had pulled him from the water again, and thankfully he hadn't become entangled in the wire and was now approaching halfway to the cabin - that drag and unceremonious return to the ocean could have injured him quite severely. I stopped the wire momentarily as Matt approached the door, a routine control check, and then brought him on board. He climbed in himself and appeared to be uninjured – thank fuck for that! How was he mentally?

Hendo reported that the system was now functioning correctly again and that this appeared to have something to do with the fact that it had stopped raining. He was happy to continue if I was, but indicated that we would have to depart for fuel in the next ten to fifteen minutes. We were now several steps down in our preferred method of recovery.

We possibly should have called a halt at this point, leaving the kids until morning, or at least until we had taken on more fuel; but ironically, it was the uncertainty with the system that prompted me to continue. I believed then, and still do today, that it was possible to work around the faults we were experiencing, and because of this belief, I determined that we could remove the kids and adults from the genuine danger they were in. But, and this was key to my thinking, if we were to achieve this goal safely, Matt would have to board the boat at some time to prepare the kids appropriately for the high winch to maximise the chance of a safe recovery. Furthermore, the longer we gave him to do this could only help to ensure he got things right. Therefore, by putting him on the boat before we went for fuel, although risky for Matt, would ultimately help achieve success, and equally important it would save valuable time should the uncertainty over the boat's anchor become a reality. However, despite briefing this eventuality at Jandakot, Matt would now have to agree to risk his life again after what he had just been through.

I acknowledged Hendo and then moved over to talk to Matt. His eyes were wide as saucers, not surprisingly, but he appeared alert enough to make a decision. I pulled back his helmet and moved my mouth close to his ear.

"Matt, we've had a problem with the Autohover," My voice was raised sufficiently so that he could hear above the turbine wine, "but it appears to be fixed now. I will only have two more attempts to get you there, but after that, I will abort. Are you happy to give it another go?"

Matt paused for only a second, then yelled 'yes' as he nodded his head and gave a thumbs up.

"Ok mate," I continued, "I'll be dropping the raft to you, and we will be going for fuel after that," he nodded, "we'll take the kids first, Ok?"

I observed his eyes to gauge how he really felt, but there was no need. His positive reaction once again confirmed my assessment of Matt as a rescue crewman – he was undoubtedly a gutsy operator.

I moved us into position and commenced the winch. Matt arrived in the water in much the same position and began swimming to the stern. As he climbed aboard my thumb was poised on the witches-hat ready to zero the trim if any movement should develop, but it didn't, and Matt disconnected the hook as briefed.

"I have an empty hook," I informed Hendo, "winching-in full speed. Pilot's trims, back one and left one."

"Back one and left one set," Hendo responded; his voice calm again, but with just a hint of fatigue about it.

"Ok boys, once I have the hook secure I'll set up for the raft. How much time do I have?"

"We have to bug out in ten minutes, Mick," Hendo confirmed, not needing to reinforce that I don't delay.

"Ok, this should only take five."

With the hook housed, I released the restraint on the Air-Droppable raft and moved it to the door. Quickly setting up the tags and the bags, I monitored our movement relative to the boat.

"Ok I'm ready." I had the rope and gear bags between my knees, "Pilot's trim, forward one, and right one."

Hendo acknowledged his inputs and the machine moved toward the boat on what appeared to be a perfect line.

"Clear to lower the gear-bag?' I requested.

"Clear."

The light yellow line ran through my gloved fingers as the gear-bag closed on the ocean. I stopped it about twenty feet from the waves and gauged our travel… it was pretty good.

"Closing nicely with another five to run," I prepared to lower the bag to the deck, "Another three, two…"

The boat rose on a swell and was about to move behind us as it slid off the other side. Shit! We wouldn't have time to reposition if I missed. I let the bag drop into free-fall and immediately noticed the heat through my gloves. Then gripping the line tightly to reduce its speed to prevent it impacting someone on the boat, I felt immediate pain on one of my fingers as the rope burnt through the leather. But thankfully, I saw Matt's cyalume-marked wrists catch the bag and pull it on board.

"…The bag's on board, zero your trims Hendo…" I continued.

As the trims were zeroed, the nose pitched up slightly, as was normal, and we moved back from the boat a couple of meters before establishing in the hover.

"…And pilots trim, back one…"

I requested this movement to move us clear before dropping the raft. As we moved further away from the boat, I re-checked the rigging of the raft.

"...Clear to dispatch the raft?"

"Clear."

With a firm shove, the raft dropped away, the line to the anchor point snapping tight a second after it was gone.

"Raft's away, recovering the lanyard." I saw the raft hit the water with a large splash; it was already half inflated. "It's inflating Hendo, closing up the right door, you're clear to rotate."

"Thanks, mate. We're clear ahead on radar, confirm FLIR?"

"Clear ahead."

A quick glance at the screen was all I needed to confirm open ocean.

"Roger, engage Climb," Hendo commanded.

"Climb engaged... speed increasing and on climb to two-hundred." Chris reported.

"Engage Go-Around, and continue the climb to fifteen-hundred please Chris."

"Go-Around engaged," Chris acknowledged, "leaving two-hundred for fifteen."

"Roger mate." Hendo rotated his comms selector switch. "Matt, Matt, Matt, this is Chopper-Six on rescue-crewman primary, how do you read?"

Silence followed the call. Hendo tried another couple of times, even trying the alternate frequency, but there was no response. The radio had been tested and worked fine prior to departure. Hendo tried a few more times without success. It clearly was going to be one of those nights!

We turned for the coast once at a safe height and tracked towards the GPS position of the airfield. At about four miles out both the pilots spotted the lights of Walpole Township and a minute or so after that they picked up the police vehicle beacons flashing at the dirt airstrip – this was just a couple of tiny flashing lights, with no visible horizon once we passed Walpole. Essentially, we were flying on towards blackness.

"We'll descend on this heading. There's a bit of a crosswind, but we can accept that to keep lined up with the strip." Hendo advised, "Firing up the Nightsun lads, Mick have you got the strip on FLIR?"

The picture was hazy, but the heat from the police vehicle and a couple of other cars were clear to see on the side of what had to be a dirt runway.

"Yes mate, high ground to the left, but the approach is clear. There is some more high stuff out to the right and in the distance too, but it's well clear of the strip – looks like some more shit weather coming in too as the high ground to the left is partially obscured."

"Thanks, mate." Hendo acknowledged, "Chris, are you happy to continue the approach? There is some weather coming in according to the radar, which looks like the stuff Mick is seeing, but we should beat it."

"Yes, Trev," Chris confirmed.

"I'm standing by right door Hendo."

"Roger Mick. Back to fifty please, Chris."

The speed came back smoothly, and I was cleared to open the door. The ground was just becoming visible in the winch down-light as we passed through nine-hundred feet – shades of grey, no discernible features. Kneeling in the doorway and alternating my focus between the FLIR screen and ground every few seconds, I also occasionally scanned forward to check what was revealed by the Nightsun's beam – essentially a thin tube of light angled down at forty degrees.

The Nightsun beam allowed the pilots to search ahead for obstacles on our descent path, but at this stage, Chris was still descending on instruments as Hendo swept the beam from left to right. Chris would only 'look up' into the tube of light as we descended below five-hundred feet, because above this height, despite its thirty-million-candle-power intensity, the Nightsun didn't provide sufficient illumination for a pilot to achieve adequate depth perception. Although this type of approach was standard for SAR crews in Australia, it required great confidence from a pilot to continue a descent as the ground approached due to the limited visual references. Basically, it could be bloody frightening – occasionally causing a pilot to initiate a 'go-around' in training.

My right wrist was resting casually on my knee with my hand in the airflow as we continued down (a procedure taught not by the company, but by Phil) and I was reassured to feel the constant air pressure on my palm. I was very relaxed indeed - the hard part was over as I saw things. Yeah, the Autohover had behaved like shit, but the boys looked to have sorted that out. The rain appeared to be the main problem for the system, but hey, why would you want to be out on a rainy night? State-of-the-art helicopter my arse! Anyway, we could work around that. By the time we got back to the boat, Matt would have the kids ready, and all we'd have to do was HI-line them off as we had briefed – piece of piss.

"Err, Trev; with this crosswind, I'm losing sight of the lights on the runway, can you take over?" Chris requested routinely.

"Yes mate, taking over."

"Handing over," Chris confirmed.

A few moments later my hand slumped forward as the air pressure dropped. Quickly shifting my eyes outside to the winch down-light, I confirmed that the speed was indeed washing off; this was not good.

To conduct a safe Nightsun approach pilots' will set up on a long approach path and descend gently, maintaining a set speed. Should the speed reduce below about 25kts and/or the rate of descent becomes too high there is a danger of, in simple terms, catching up to the aircraft's own downwash. If this happens, the aircraft can enter a state known as 'Vortex-Ring'. Although pilots will often debate the technical cause and effect of this state, often resulting in a lengthy discussion over just the correct terminology, the effect on the aircraft remains the same. Vortex-Ring causes an aircraft to accelerate down - not just drop a few feet, but to increase its rate of descent rapidly. Furthermore, when in this state should the pilot apply more power to arrest the descent, this will only cause the aircraft to accelerate downwards even more. Therefore, if you wished to come home alive, monitoring the speed and rate of descent during Nightsun approaches was critical!

"Check speed."

This was my immediate call on noticing the speed reduction, but before I had finished the last syllable we'd stopped moving forward, and the nose began to pitch up.

"Nose forward, Nose forward!"

I yelled urgently, but it was too late. I felt something like a left-right yawing shudder through my feet and knees, and off we went. The rate of descent was incredible!

"We're going down!"

From the time of my first check-call to screaming we're going down there was no more than a three-second interval. As we raced towards the earth my eyes fixed with a spot on the ground and I watched in horror as it rushed up to meet us. This was probably going to hurt, my inner voice informed me. But just as my muscles began tensing, the S76 suddenly pitched forward to about twenty degrees nose down causing a further increased rate of descent. One of the boys had shoved the cyclic forward to get us moving out of the Vortex-Ring state, and thankfully, his actions and those of previous test pilots were right. Accelerating forward allowed lift to be restored to the rotor blades and we recovered to safe flight, but not before losing about five-to-six-hundred feet in the process. This had put us just a second or two from impact.

Fucking hell! Fucking hell! My mouth was dry and my body a buzz of adrenaline. For a second or two I just stared out of the door at the ground that was now reassuringly stationary just two-to-three-hundred feet below, although thankfully moving 'backwards' as we flew on towards the Walpole strip.

"You still got the airstrip boys?"

My voice was weak, the words sounded hollow almost, it was as though someone else was speaking.

"Yeah Mick, half a mile to run on the nose,"

Hendo's voice wasn't much better, and Chris was quiet.

"Ok then, I can see it now; that's a good line and good speed, with four hundred to run."

My mouth was incredibly dry, and there was a dull ache in my stomach, my arms felt heavy, and I needed time out of the machine desperately. The boys can't have been much better.

We crossed the fence shortly after, landing about 30m from a shed that probably housed the fuel. The vehicles were another 30m or so past the shed, and I could see people standing alongside them.

"Shutting down."

Hendo's words came out almost like a sigh of relief, and as the blades slowly wound down, we sat in zombie-like silence for a few minutes. Then as the blades finally came to a halt a wind gust blew a few drops of rain in the open right door and onto my face, it was as though the chill of the drops on my cheeks was encouraging me to move – they didn't succeed.

Eventually, there was movement by the cars, and seeing people coming our way I was about to advise the boys when Hendo spoke up.

"Here come the cops' lads."

He had tried to sound purposeful, but there was little enthusiasm to his voice. Even so, we climbed from the machine putting on our collective best attempt at a brave face.

"How'd you go fellas?"

I couldn't see the speaker's face that clearly in the dim torchlight, but he sounded like the bloke on the phone and spoke with reasonable authority, so I guessed he was Sergeant Smithwick.

"Not bad." I began, "Our paramedic's on the boat now, we dispatched a raft to them and came back to get some fuel; that first winch was a bit tricky. Are the drums in that shed mate?"

Thankfully I had worked some saliva back into my mouth and my voice was back to normal - although this was far from how I felt.

"Yeah, you blokes want a hand?"

"Never knock back assistance mate, by the way, the name's Mick." I held out my hand, which he took.

"Steve Smithwick, I spoke to one of your pilots on the way down."

"That was me, Steve," Hendo appeared alongside me, "Trevor Henderson, how's it all going for you blokes?"

"Had better nights Trev," his humour masked a long day, "We got the boats back though, and that's one thing." Then looking towards the S76, he asked a question that we didn't want to hear, "How long before you go back out?"

Thankfully Hendo took that one.

"We'll get some fuel on board first and then come up with a plan, probably twenty minutes?"

Smithwick appeared happy with that and took the time to introduce us to the other people with him. There were some of the marine rescue blokes and a few CALM people.

"And this is Clive, he's the skipper of the rescue boat."

Clive looked like the 'old man of the sea'. He had a big bushy white beard, and even in the poor light, I could see the weathered face of a man who'd not spent his life behind a desk.

"Shocking conditions out there tonight, that anchor of theirs will have a hard time holding their boat. Good job you blokes are here" Clive remarked with confidence.

That's just what I didn't need to hear. My confidence of just minutes before was shattered, and already I was thinking that this job could wait until till first light – despite that being around eight hours away. Anchor dragging hey? Shit, they were a mile offshore; surely it would take ages for them to reach the rocks?

We moved off to get the drums. The rain had started to fall steadily again, and there were no stars visible through the low cloud layer that had blown quickly across the airstrip. No… I didn't want to get back in that helicopter, not just then.

"Is it in date Mick?" Hendo asked when the others were out of earshot.

"Yeah, they all are. How many do you want?"

"One each side should do it." Hendo's voice was about as enthusiastic as I felt.

We rolled the drums over to the machine with a minimal exchange of words; we both wanted to say more, but with the others close by this was proving reasonably awkward. Finally though, Chris, Hendo and I had a moment alone as the others went off to check on something or other. Hendo extended his hand, and I took it.

"Thanks for saving my life, Mick; I just lost awareness for a moment…"

His voice trailed off. Admitting that had taken a lot of courage, and although Hendo's apology was genuine, he was apparently after some reassurance.

"We're still alive mate, no worries… And hey, we could probably wait to first light, you know…" I suddenly felt guilty about what I had begun to suggest. Matt was still out there, and despite the raft, he and the survivors were still in serious trouble, "…but I'll give it a go if you two want to?"

We moved to the other side of the helicopter to pump the last drum and taking advantage of the relative seclusion the three of us had a private chat in whispered tones. Although the system had worked as advertised on the last winch, we were all still pretty shaken up by the departure from normal flight; but in theory, at least, we all agreed that the machine was still serviceable.

'Departure from normal flight', what a bullshit statement! That's what an investigation would call it though. Formal language helps so much when disciplinary action is required, and the company just loved to scalp first and ask questions later. But formal language couldn't disguise the real fear this 'departure' had inflicted, or the very real danger the kids were in. Moreover, perhaps, the sudden descent had made me fear for my life more than I had in a very long time, but was this incident more frightening than others? Possibly, it was certainly more immediate and of sufficient severity to instil doubt into me about going out again; but the anxiety I was experiencing wasn't just because we may have to get airborne again. No. We could easily justify staying put if we wanted too, that would be easy. The anxiety was also because of an old motto that I'd always believed in.

As a Para-Jumper, a 'PJ', with the NSCA, we had trained and operated with a code that had been laid down those who had come before us: "These things I do, so that others may live." This is the oath of allegiance all United States Air Force PJs swear before graduating from their training program. The NSCA PJs had this motto too. It was effortless to quote, and a nice throwaway line; but now, with the lives of two children, two adults and our paramedic at stake did I really believe in it... could I cut it?

A company 'professional' would have aborted the task much earlier, and certainly wouldn't risk the aircraft or the lives of his crew by pursuing a bad situation – that's what an investigation would be sure to find. And the company would respect such a man and possibly see him as someone to promote in the future, but how could such a man live with himself if people died as a result of his inaction when there was a course of action available – albeit risky? It wasn't as though a road ambulance could reach these people. No, the reality was, that if we waited until morning, these people might well perish.

As we wound the last few litres of fuel from the drum we had about convinced each other to call it off until morning, but then Steve Smithwick came running over.

"They're taking to the raft!" There was real urgency in his voice.

"What? I mean, how do you know?" Hendo asked for all of us.

"Our people on the beach can see them evacuating now; they've just called in."

We didn't say anything to each other, but when Hendo spoke, we were with him. "We're fuelled up Steve, we've just got to stow this pump. Probably be airborne in five minutes or so."

Smithwick was happy with that, but he had a suggestion also.

"Would you like us to take some fuel to the town oval for you? Much better lighting there and we have access to the clubrooms."

"That would be a big help, Steve." Hendo confirmed, "I'll call you on your mobile to let you know when we are on the way back."

As we climbed aboard the S76, the rain was easing again, and in the direction of the ocean, we could see some stars. Maybe fate was turning in our favour.

"If we're all happy lads I'd like to track out low level, four-hundred AGL using the Nightsun. It will avoid us having to do a letdown again. The boat is no more than eight minutes from here, what do you think?" Hendo requested.

We both agreed. Although the system checks had passed without fault, we were all probably still a bit wary of another failure. So after completing pre-take-off checks, Chris picked us up into a hover and Hendo selected the Nightsun to 'on'. Scanning the beam ahead, Hendo found a suitable departure path, which I confirmed with the FLIR. It was time to go.

"Ok, your trims Trev, lifting."

Chris commenced a towering departure, and at 100ft he nosed forward and we accelerated away. I had a good FLIR picture, and the terrain was well clear ahead. Hendo was aware of my view on the screen, but as he and Chris didn't have a FLIR display up front, he kept sweeping the Nightsun through an arc to ensure a clear path ahead. So far, so good, I thought.

Suddenly, the Nightsun failed as we passed 300ft!

"Fuck!" Hendo's voice was combined fear and anger, "Chris, best rate-of-climb this heading."

Losing the Nightsun that close to the ground without a visible horizon was like the lights of a car failing on a windy road.

"Climbing!" Chris acknowledged, and my bum squashed into the seat as we headed up like a homesick angel.

Shit! What can bloody well go wrong next? Although my stomach had tightened slightly, I was happy with the action the boys had taken. We were now well clear of any high terrain or remote power line that might have been ahead of us and hard to see on FLIR, but we were also back in the cloud and had the prospect of another automatic let-down, and just for fun, the stars we had seen were no longer visible.

The NSCA's psychologist, Gavin, first described critical incident stress to me in these simple terms.

"Mick, imagine an empty bottle" he'd said during my PJ training course. "During the day certain stressful events occur such as a crying baby, a fight with your wife, aggressive driving, etcetera, and all these events begin to fill up the bottle with stress. On your average day most people will half fill the bottle; but at the end of the day, after a beer or two and a good night of sleep the bottle empties and you start the next day stress-free."

"Well," he continued, "If you had a bad day at work where the bottle was nearly filled, and then, when you got home the beer was warm, and your wife was screwing your best mate..." Gavin always had a good sense of humour "...the next day the bottle would be still close to full, meaning that your stress levels were higher at the start of the day and therefore, so was your tolerance of certain situations. Now, you have to be very aware of this in Pararescue, because during your career you will be exposed to many stressful situations that will leave warning signs, and it's up to you to recognise these, because if they are left unchecked, and your bottle remains full? Well, it might just overflow..."

As we forged on into the gloomy night sky, I was acutely aware that my 'bottle' had overflowed after the fall out of the sky, and that by the time we had relaunched it was probably at least two-thirds full.

What can possibly go wrong

But now, with this piece-of-crap-aircraft beginning to shit itself again, I had no doubt it was back close to the brim.

I reached for my water bottle and took a long swallow. My mouth was as dry as sand, and I bet the boys were much the same.

"Any of you two want some water?"

"Yeah cheers, Mick." Chris got in first. Hendo took a large swig too, and their somewhat tense voices relaxed a notch as we cruised at a safe height.

"Got a strobe down here Trev, it's away from the boat," Chris advised a couple of minutes later. There was a break in the cloud, and he had picked up the raft.

"Visual mate," Hendo advised, "turning left onto one-five-zero. I'm going to take us over the top, remark the position, and then conduct an Approach 1."

"On heading one-five-zero, and ready for Approach 1." Chris acknowledged Hendo's course change.

"Roger... Approach 1 engaged...Fuck!" The edge was creeping back into Hendo's voice. "...It didn't work! I'm recycling the autopilots... re-engaging Approach 1... shit! Ok, trying the MOT...Come on you bitch! I'm trying the MOT again."

Hendo continued recycling and pushing buttons, but nothing would engage. The fact rain was pissing past the windows again kind of told the story, what a heap of shit this aircraft was! Yeah, if you got into strife on a beautiful clear night, it was a bloody star, but woe-betide you on a night like this.

I dialled the number Hendo requested, as he selected his comms switch to phone and waited to give the bad news. The number rang twice and then we heard a familiar voice.

"Steve Smithwick speaking."

"Steve, it's Trevor here mate, our Autohover has failed. We're going to have to abort this task until first light."

There were several seconds of silence where I could almost see the look of disappointment on Smithwick's face, poor bastard.

"Ok Trev, nothing you can do then?" He asked hopefully.

"Not without the Autohover mate. We're going to head for Albany for an instrument approach; I'll give you a call once we land."

I cancelled the call and moved back to my seat. I had only caught a brief glimpse of the strobe, but knowing there were a couple of kids attached to it, plus Matt and two other blokes, well, it played on my mind.

"Ok Chris, come left mate to zero-eight-five."

"Hey boys," I interrupted, "How much time have we got before we're bingo for the Albany ILS?"

"Err..." Hendo was reading my mind, "With this tailwind, probably forty to forty-five minutes, why?"

"How about we orbit for a while and see if the system won't reset again?"

There was a moment's silence up front before Hendo spoke.

"Chris?"

"Yeah, a few minutes can't do any harm."

"Ok then. Set eighty knots, right-hand orbits with no more than five degrees angle of bank."

After two orbits of troubleshooting, Hendo swapped to Flight-Director number-two and tried the MOT for about the fourth time... it engaged. He quickly disengaged the program, and we continued the current orbit.

"It's working again lads, what do you think?"

It had stopped raining too, and this must have encouraged us all to try one more attempt. So, once again, Hendo positioned us over the top of the raft and Approach 1 was engaged.

"Leaving eighteen-hundred for two-hundred, airspeed is reducing." Chris advised cautiously. The aircraft descended as it should, and as we passed 500ft Hendo figured we were far enough to sea.

"Ok, I make that four miles, turning right, back towards the raft. Mick, have you got the island on FLIR?"

"Just sweeping right now mate… Fuck!" The FLIR ball mounted beneath the nose of the aircraft locked in the one-o'clock position, "…FLIR lock Hendo, I will have to rest the system!"

"Damn it! I'm turning us back to the left Chris. Mick, how long?"

"Probably a minute or so, this has happened before mate. The new FLIR's proving to be a bit of a fucking lemon, but I can fix it."

With the FLIR running again we turned back for another go with light rain falling, but none of us mentioned this, probably because we didn't want to tempt fate. The boys had completed their checks, and we agreed on a hover height of 110ft again, and after the winch checks were completed we were ready.

"Ready Approach 2."

"Ready," Chris confirmed as we closed on the strobe visible in the distance.

"Approach 2 engaged." The S76 banked to the left away from the intended heading, "Fuck, Fuck, I pressed the fucking MOT; disengaging, shit!" The aircraft immediately rolled level as Hendo cancelled the command.

"Hey Hendo, that's good mate, it shows the system is working. Do you still have the boat?"

I hoped my voice sounded calm because I didn't feel it, poor Hendo was loaded up to the max.

"Err, yeah. Sorry lads, my fault… target's back on the nose; I'm now re-engaging Approach 2."

On the FLIR screen, I saw a black dot shoot up from the water trailing a light-black tail.

"Flare on the nose, and there's another. I have the boat too now and can see the raft. How's the fuel looking Hendo?"

"Err, about 30 minutes Mick."

"Passing fifty knots," Chris reported.

"Clear doors Mick."

"Standby master-caution, opening right."

"Approaching one-ten, the nose is pitching, and power's coming in." Chris's voice sounded a little tense, but he was doing the task by the book.

"Confirm the wind for me, Mick?"

"On the nose mate," The wave action was the same.

"Ready for hover-trim control?" Hendo sounded calm now, but I doubt he really felt it.

"Ready," Chris advised.

"Ready also, target sighted on the nose at seventy." I could just make out the raft each time it rose up from behind a swell.

"You have hover-trim control, Mick."

"My control, Hendo I have the HI-line attached to the hook, clear to lower the shot-bag?"

"Clear Mick."

"Lowering away, and can you give me four forward on pilots trims?"

I requested the pilot's trims because I no longer trusted mine, guessing that water had entered the device and that maybe this had caused some of our problems.

"Four set."

I watched the flicker of the cyalume attached to the shot-bag as it danced in the rotor-wash on the way to the ocean, and as our speed picked up to the desired rate, I determined that our course was as requested too. Scanning from the shot-bag to a collection of cyalumes on the raft as we got closer, I noticed that we had moved slightly off course.

"Pilots trim, one right."

"One right selected."

The correction quickly had us going back on a line over the raft. And as we closed to within thirty feet I had Hendo reduce the forward speed to two. The line was still good, but watching the wave action, I noticed that as the raft rose with each passing swell, it threatened to slide down the face away from us as the boat had before. If this happened it would require quick last minute adjustments – I kept it going as we were, with fingers mentally crossed.

"With five to run, this line and speed are still good. Coming over the top now…" The moment I saw the shot-bag cyalume line up with the two cyalumes on Matt's helmet I dropped three meters of slack that I had gathered in my spare hand, "Zero your trim."

"Trims zeroed." Hendo confirmed.

"Roger, they have the HI-line, and I'm paying out the remaining rope. The raft is in the one-o'clock now, at five; we are maintaining a good hover."

I didn't say it, but my internal thoughts were repeating 'hey it's working, it's working'. I tried to ignore this though, not wishing to tempt fate.

"Clear to winch?"

"Clear," Hendo confirmed.

As the hook approached the raft I could see the two cyalumes on Matt's helmet moving back and forward in time with his arm movements, there appeared to be a collection of other cyalumes in the black shadow of the raft too, so I guessed that Matt had the survivors prepped as briefed.

"Matt has the hook now, position it still good."

The raft was in the two o'clock, and I winched out about twenty foot of extra wire into the ocean to prevent fouling it on someone. The wire would sink allowing a buffer between raft and aircraft movement. I could see Matt working pretty hard, and then one of his wrist cyalumes began a slow circling motion: the winch-in signal.

"I've got a signal to winch from Matt. Pilot's trims, forward one and right one… winching in."

As the S76 moved back towards the raft, I winched in at a moderate pace watching the direction of the wire intently. If I noticed anything remotely like fouling, I would winch out immediately, giving Matt the opportunity to free the wire. As we arrived over the top, the wire began to tighten; it looked to be clear in the dim light.

"Zero your trim and standby to take the weight." I cautioned.

As the last bit of slack was taken up the first survivor burst from the raft as it dropped into a trough between swells. Shit! Why wasn't

Matt with this kid? As I watched, the cyalume attached to a dark form swung toward our six o'clock as the machine pitched slightly to the rear. Hendo cleared me to continue.

"Clear of the raft, slight swing fore and aft dampening that now."

By pushing and pulling on the wire against the direction of swing I was able to correct the minor problem quickly, and once the survivor was relatively stationary, I continued to winch in.

Closing on the door, I saw that the first one was an adult. This made me mentally question Matt's actions again, but only briefly and I informed Hendo that the survivor was approaching the door.

"Yeah he's an adult all right; Matt must have a reason though? I'm reaching for the survivors strop now, and bringing him on board."

The bloke was relatively dry but looked quite cold. I pushed him to the far side of the cab and got him onto the bench seat. After helping him with his seatbelt, I removed the combination strop from his legs and shoulders - one down, three to go.

When I looked for the HI-line attached to the hook, it was gone. Damn! I was sure it was there when the bloke came up. The pissy little new snap-hook that had replaced the older and more reliable metal ring must have failed. I looked around the door rail but there was nothing fouled there so it must be back in the ocean. Oh well, at least it was clear. Best get on with it – without a HI-line the task would take a while longer due to repositioning between winches.

"The HI-line's disconnected mate, it must have rolled-out as he came aboard. I still have the raft visual though. It's in the two o'clock at ten, clear to winch?"

I had Hendo trim us over the top again and watched as Matt took the hook for the second survivor. There was a blur of cyalume action on the raft, and it appeared as though Matt had some sort of drama, but after less than a minute of tense trim inputs, I saw what I thought was an OK signal.

"Signal from Matt, and winching in, standby to -"

The machine rolled dramatically to the right, probably six degrees - much more than the standard gravity shift associated with a live winch. I rolled the pendant thumb-wheel forward, quickly dumping some wire and the machine steadied.

"What was that Mick!?" Hendo asked urgently.

"Don't know mate. I got a signal from Matt, and he's still signalling to winch, I'll try again."

The same thing happened again and I winched out to steady the aircraft once more.

"Hendo, I can see Matt and I can see what looks like the remaining survivors, Matt's cyalume is rotating slowly in the agreed ok signal – I'm going to try again, standby the weight."

"Standing by." Hendo acknowledged.

The S76 began to roll again, but then Matt and another survivor burst from the raft to swing in an arc under the belly. Why was he coming up with kids still on the raft?

My mind was a frantic patchwork of information: earlier briefings, a ticking clock to bingo fuel, rain starting to fall, company procedures being breached, but my focus kept coming back to the two kids in the raft.

"This one's a double Hendo, Matt's coming up with what looks like another adult?"

"What about the kids?" Hendo's voice shared my alarm, but there must have been a reason for Matt's action.

"I'll confirm that when he's on board mate."

The swing took a bit more effort to dampen than the first one, but as I pulled another middle-aged man and Matt on board I could see a look of relief on Matt's face.

"Matt," I shouted in his ear, "No more down there?"

He chopped his hand across his throat and mouthed that this was it. A measured relief flowed through my body, but as we were still over water, I kept it in check.

"That's it Hendo, Matt confirms the raft is now empty. I'm housing the hook and closing the door."

I slammed the door shut and slid the lock forward. We had no idea where the information about kids on the boat had come from, but we could sort that out later. After climbing to a safe height, Hendo turned for Albany and the instrument approach, but then he had a thought.

"I'll just give the Nightsun another try, you never know?"

On the fourth try, the 30,000,000 candle powered searchlight flickered into life, and we all agreed that the five minutes or so to Walpole for a brew would be better than the thirty or so to Albany.

The towns' lights were quite visible as we cleared the inlet, and some floodlights around the oval made for a pretty routine Nightsun approach and landing. Bloody hell, we'd done it! We were probably going to get our arses kicked for the next month or so for taking 'unnecessary' risks, but shit! We had done it. It was the most challenging rescue I had ever been involved with – ever. The fact that the ongoing Autohover problems had contributed to most of the hardship hadn't quite registered as my restrained elation bubbled away!

The two blokes were local fishermen whose grateful handshakes crushed our tired hands. Steve Smithwick proved to be a much-relieved individual during our welcome brew and homemade scones that we savoured in the clubrooms next to the oval - some of the wives of the rescue crowd had made fresh ones – gotta love country hospitality.

Matt had a shower and changed back into his flight suit looking none the worse for wear. He had shown incredible courage to get back in the water after being dragged the first time, but the poor bastard probably didn't realise that every winch job from this point on would be a bit of an anticlimax. Such is life.

We chatted for about forty minutes or so, and then after a top-up of the tanks we said goodbyes and strapped in for the almost two-hour trip home.

I was kneeling at the right door as Hendo commenced the towering departure. As he called 'committed' at one hundred feet and was just nosing forward, I pulled the door forward to close it... but something was blocking it!

"Steady Hendo! The door won't close..."

We were at a critical point of flight, if something went wrong Hendo would either have to descend back to the oval or fly into the dark with the door open, perhaps having to make another Nightsun approach. He stayed where he was.

"What is it, Mick?!" Tension filled his voice.

"Standby..."

The upper door-rail has a small stopper on one of two 'slides' incorporated in the door system and this stopper occasionally becomes loose, but not tonight, Tonight it had failed completely, and the slide had shifted forward blocking the door!

"...The stopper's gone mate; I'll see if can't push the slide back."

I reached out and up and pushed the slide home. Then carefully, I pulled the door closed, and we were on our way. Just what else could possibly go wrong?

"Airspeed's alive..." Just as Chris was calling the numbers for the departure, the Nightsun failed again.

"Fuck! Fucking heap of shite, ok there's forty-five; on climb and looking for seventy-five knots."

Poor Hendo was having a worse night than me. Despite getting our attention, the Nightsun was to prove the last failure of the night. The SAR modes were checked on route, and all functioned as they should - go figure.

We landed as the first hint of dawn filtered into the morning sky and shortly after commenced the hardly joyful but quite essential task of cleaning and preparing the aircraft for immediate service.

News Headline:

Sergeant Smithwick of the Denmark police confirmed that the rescue helicopter crew recovered two local fishermen last night who had been stranded in their small boat a mile offshore near to Chatham Island, west of the Walpole Inlet. Sergeant Smithwick also praised the helicopter crew for continuing 'when their Autohover system failed', which made the task of rescue even harder in the trying conditions – Thanks mate, that's the quote that ensured we got our arses kicked.

Author sitting in the S76 FLIR seat waiting for air traffic control clearance for a SAR training sortie about month before the Walpole Job; FLIR screen at centre, above the red medical pack.

EPILOGUE

Chinese whispers were put down to the cause of the mishap over numbers on the boat. Having gotten into difficulty in the morning, the two fishermen we rescued had waved to people on the cliffs assuming that they were there to help, but they were probably just bushwalkers who waved back to the people enjoying a day of fishing. After a couple of hours when nothing had eventuated, the fishermen began mayday calls. Amazingly, these were first picked up on the other side of the country before being relayed through a number of people to eventually reach the WA police, by which time the many passed messages had seen two kids added to the equation. Communication problems will still be a point of SAR debriefs a hundred years from now.

Hendo accepted responsibility for the un-commanded descent, saying that he had forgotten to request a monitored approach from Chris. He further pointed out that he believed a gusting wind had contributed to the late decision to push the nose forward. When I first called check-speed both pilots had seen 35 to 40 knots on the airspeed indicator and assumed that I had overreacted; a gusting wind could well have indicated the higher speed at the critical moment, and it fit with the conditions of the night.

Matt advised that the HI line had become fouled and that he had disconnected it on the raft (I must have imagined seeing it during the first winch). And during the second winch, Matt informed us that the wire had passed under the raft as it moved on the swell. As I was winching in the second time, Matt was in the process of trying to free it - his desperate arm movements being mistaken by me for a winch in signal. As the wire had pulled tight the added weight of the raft, plus the water and people it contained, caused the large angle of bank we experienced. Fortunately, though, Matt had moved with purpose and was able to free it before the last winch.

The day after the job Hendo advised head office of the problems we encountered, including the un-commanded descent, but we were to receive no immediate feedback. The same day, in much nicer weather, the police went out to recover the fishermen's boat, but there was no trace of it or the raft.

Hendo, Chris and I went off on a RAAF deployment to the North West Cape of WA a couple of weeks later. While there we conducted all the regular flight duties and even a stretcher winch during a civil medivac from a bulk carrier where a seaman had received burns following an engine room fire, but late in the second week of the deployment *it* began.

We were each formally requested to submit reports on the job and advised not to talk to each other about the documents we were preparing - talk about closing the door after the horse had bolted. Anyway, we produced three reports that described events from our perspectives and put them into the system. On return to RAAF Pearce, after a six-hour flight that included two refuelling stops, a company investigator met the crew, and the grilling began.

Despite the reasonably relevant fact of longstanding problems with the aircraft's avionics supporting some of our decision-making, the fact that the police were unable to find the boat the next day, and confirmation by other sources that reports of children on the boat were not made up (as suspected by the company investigator), our fate was as predicted and arse kicking's were the go for some time afterwards.

Frustrated with the increasing amount of derogatory secondhand evaluations of our performance, perhaps resulting from lack of formal company feedback/reporting, we found labels like 'loose-cannons' being attached to us (and to the RAAF Pearce base). Simply, this was a very hard time as we were challenged by peers and ignored by senior management. Eventually, Chris resigned, believing that his career prospects were better elsewhere he went to work for a rival helicopter company. Disgusted at his treatment, Hendo too put in a letter of resignation, but withdrew it at the request of the company. After a couple of letters further explaining my actions going nowhere, it was with many mixed feelings eight months after Walpole that I too resigned.

I now teach oil and gas workers how to respond to offshore emergencies. Training includes escape from helicopters that have ditched into the sea, ocean survival and firefighting, but my bread and butter work is emergency management. Training, and then putting oil facility commanders through their paces during emergency exercises is very rewarding, but I often find their knowledge of real-world helicopter Medevac and SAR less than desirable.

Part of my new role required academic qualifications, and so I completed a direct-entry Masters of Emergency Management degree with a thesis examining capability shortfalls of oil and gas helicopter SAR in the north-west of Australia. Many of the thesis's findings, that I received a distinction for, are now incorporated into our training.

I have found a renewed purpose in life and thoroughly enjoy the unique challenges my work provides. But yes, I do miss operational SAR's, and often glance upwards from my position of safety on the couch with a beer in hand when I hear a machine tracking overhead for the coast on a shitty night. Wondering if it's just another training flight, or if the boys have a decent job before them.

One final SAR close out: although USAF Pararescue Lieutenant Colonel Donald A Towner and a Command Master Sergeant, called Milstein, visited West Sale to observe our operations, I often wondered if Freddo had fabricated their letter of praise, *"you are at the forefront of open sea rescue...you have no peers..."*

Well, around the time of the double stretcher job, the United States Delta Force arrived at RAAF Pearce to undertake training with the Australian Special Air Service Regiment. Arriving with a C-5 Galaxy, two C-141 Starlifters, two C-130 Shadows and two Blackhawk helicopters in tow, the Delta Force deployment made an impressive entrance to the base. With an assortment of support staff, including a detachment of USAF PJ's, the funding and capability of this 'small' force would have taken a chunk out of the annual ADF budget.

The PJ's were assigned to Pearce SAR Flight and we undertook routine training with them. What followed was an awesome couple of weeks were we practiced and partied together. We introduced them to 'Tree Rescue' techniques the NSCA had developed after Phil had improvised a process to recover a fighter pilot who had ejected into trees, and showed them how we recovered pilots from the water using stretchers. On a SAR exercise we tested their capability with simulated live casualties too. I was umpiring this on the ground, and was pleased to see how quickly (and effortlessly) they worked to stabilise casualties and how rapidly they had adapted to the use of our Tree-Rescue techniques.

Towards the end of the visit, I gave them a copy of Rookie-6 PJ Troy Thornton's book *Pararescue* (co-authored by Richard McRoberts). Sitting in the crew room reading the book, their sergeant suddenly sat up:

"Shit! *The* Donald A Towner, and that old guy Milstein, he was in Vietnam too; when they came back from Australia I was sent to do an AFF course, we had never done that before. Was that *you* guys?"

I probably should have responded with 'it just what we do mate', but I said, "Yes, that was us, but a long time ago."

Approaching retirement now, our kids have moved out but are never too far from our thoughts. Apart from family, I have two passions in my life: mountain biking and sailing. The former keeps the waist from getting too big and provides sufficient challenge when riding with blokes nearly half my age on single-track courses in the hills to the east of Perth. Additionally, competing in four of the annual Cape-to-Cape races from Augusta to Dunsborough in the state's southwest has also helped with the fitness, and produces more than enough adrenaline for my tired aging body to deal with. As for sailing, Mandy and I have a dream of sailing around the world when we retire. To support this dream we have sailed with friends and done some bare-boating around the Whitsunday Islands. More recently though, we purchased a ten-year-old Hunter-33 monohull yacht. We plan to use this for 2-3 years to practice, build skills and confidence, and if all goes well, we will then trade up to a bigger boat and head off into the sunset. What can possibly go wrong?

Oh and one final thing; I shouldn't forget Matt; frustrated with St John, he left the WA ambulance service not long after the Walpole job to further his career in the mining sector. But for his efforts on the night of the rescue, he was awarded the Royal Humane Society's Silver Medal for bravery. Well done mate, you can rescue my family anytime.

Post Script: before leaving RAAF Pearce SAR, I penned a poem to be read at our Christmas party. Its intent was to reinforce the respect I had for the men and women I'd worked with, who'd both understood, and had demonstrated SAR principles well in excess of documented procedure. Hopefully you will see the combination of reward, happiness and frustration that such principles produced in the (partially) tongue-in-cheek summary below. It should be read in a pirate voice.

Memories of Pearce

From far off southern Ireland and the town of Shannon,
stories are told of the Pearce Loose Cannon.
It defies all logic and ops manual compliance,
but when lives need saving the key word's reliance.
Hire cars and drinking, deployments and sport,
combined produce an exceptional sort.
A Loose Cannon man may have strange habits,
don't let him alone with sheep or rabbits.
But on a howling night when birds don't fly,
where ships baton down hatches and seadogs cry,
Should you find yourself in major strife,
taking on water, in fear for your life?
Just look to the sky for the heavenly light,
of the Pearce Loose Cannon's, sun of night.
Through a storm they've flown, with some trepidation,
to save your life and bugger the regulation.
Returning to base, another life saved,
the Pearce Loose Cannon has misbehaved.
A back full of knives and a personnel file notation,
the Pearce Loose Cannon knows no appreciation.
But the calibre and courage of the colleagues he's with
will ensure he'll do it again… "So that others may live"

— — —

Loose Cannon

*Is it a loose cannon that endangers a ship,
or the ship being sailed poorly that causes a canon to become loose?*

www.ingramcontent.com/pod-product-compliance
Lightning Source LLC
Chambersburg PA
CBHW071851290426
44110CB00013B/1101